G000141826

A HISTORY OF WOKING

A History of WOKING

Alan Crosby

Phillimore

1982

Published by
PHILLIMORE & CO. LTD.
Shopwyke Hall, Chichester, Sussex

ISBN 0 85033 456 X

Typeset in the United Kingdom by
Fidelity Processes - Selsey, Sussex

Printed in Great Britain by
THE BOWERING PRESS LTD.
Plymouth, Devon

In Memory of my father,

George Hugh Sinclair Crosby

Acknowledgements

During the researching and writing of this book I have had the assistance of many individuals and organisations. To all of them I give my grateful thanks. Special reference must be made to the staffs of the following, who have been most helpful and patient with my many requests, and who provided space in which to work: the Surrey Record Office, the Guildford Muniment Room, Woking Borough Council, Woking Central Library, Guildford Library, Guildford Museum, the Public Record Office, Brookwood Cemetery Office, and the *Woking News and Mail.*

Amongst the individuals to whom thanks are due are: David Chapman, Howard Cook, John Wetton, Barry Lynch, Dawn Chinnery, Mrs. P. Fosberry and Mr. T. G. Fuller. My mother Elsie Crosby and my sister Alison gave up much time to type and check the first draft, and my wife Jacquie assiduously checked the final version, and showed a great tolerance of me during the time of its writing!

I am grateful to Mr. Arnold Ryde for permission to quote freely from the diaries and reminiscences of Edward Ryde; to the Earl of Onslow, for being able to make similar use of the material in the Onslow Collection held at the Guildford Muniment Room; and to Mrs. G. J. Jackman for permission to use the Jackman papers.

I wish to acknowledge the permission of the following to use copyright or personal material in their ownership:

The Master and Fellows of Trinity College, Cambridge, for passages from the diaries of A. J. Munby; the Author's Literary Estate and The Hogarth Press Ltd., for the extract from *Night and Day* by Virginia Woolf; William Heinemann Ltd. for the passages from *The War of the Worlds* by H. G. Wells; and the various extracts from *Buildings of England: Surrey* (Second Revised edition, 1970) are reprinted by permission of Penguin Books Ltd.

The photographs were provided by the following, and my thanks and acknowledgement are due to them for their permission to use this material:

Guildford Borough Council: Plates 1, 3, 9 and 13.
Woking Borough Council: Plates 2, 6, 11, 12, 24, 25, 27, 29 and 30.
Woking News and Mail: Plates 4, 5, 28 and 31.
John Wetton: Plates 7, 8, 20, 21, 22, 23, 26 and 32.
David Chapman: Plates 10, 14, 15, 16, 17, 18 and 19.

CONTENTS

List of Plates

(Between pages 48 and 49)

List of Text Figures

List of Abbreviations

B.C.	Borough Council
G.W.R.	Great Western Railway
G.M.R.	Guildford Muniment Room
H.D.	Highway District
L.B.	Local Board
L.G.B.	Local Government Board
L.C.C.	London County Council
L.S.W.R.	London and South Western Railway
M.H.L.G.	Ministry of Housing and Local Government
P.C.	Parish Council
P.R.O.	Public Record Office
R.D.C.	Rural District Council
R.S.A.	Rural Sanitary Authority
S.B.	School Board
S.D.D.	Special Drainage District
S.R.	Southern Railway
S.R.O.	Surrey Record Office
Sy.A.C.	*Surrey Archaeological Collections*
U.D.	Urban District
U.D.C.	Urban District Council
W.C.S.	Woking Co-operative Society

Introduction

THE LARGEST TOWN in Surrey is perhaps also the least known and the least appreciated. Woking, although it has a population of more than 82,000, is almost ignored by historians, and merits only a few lines in the published histories of the county. The writers of guidebooks and county portraits are just as dismissive, and usually very unflattering. National historians and geographers have ignored the town completely. To many people Woking is nothing more than a junction on the main railway line out of Waterloo, and to others it is a caricature, the archetypal suburban dormitory town, without a history and devoid of interest.

That is far from the truth, and the neglect and lack of appreciation are greatly to be regretted. Woking has a history which is complex and fascinating, presenting features which are not found in any other English town. It has a character and an appearance which is quite distinct, as a result of this unusual history. Unfortunately Woking and its people have always suffered, as they still do, from a severe inferiority complex. The town is overshadowed by its near, and far better known, southern neighbour, Guildford, and its own merits and fascination are all too often forgotten.

This book is an attempt to help to redress that imbalance. It explains the unique and bizarre process by which the town came into being, and traces the evolution and growth of Woking over the past century and a half. The story is a remarkable one, which stands comparison with that of any other town. By showing that the history of Woking is full of interest, I hope that I may help to increase the amount of attention which is paid to this aspect of the town. There is still no museum and no adequate local collection, and despite the best efforts of voluntary societies the history of the town is constantly facing the pressures of modern development and destruction. It is time that something positive was done to remedy this deficiency.

The book is devoted mainly to the period since 1800. Until that time the area was purely rural and agricultural; there were four small villages, Byfleet, Pyrford, Horsell and Knaphill, and one larger village, Woking, which had some of the attributes of a small town. Although the five communities could trace their origins as far back as the 7th century they had remained small and secluded. The brief period in the 15th and 16th centuries when there had been a royal mansion at Woking had failed to make a deep and lasting impression upon the area, and there had been few significant changes since 1620.

By 1800, though, the effects of the social and economic revolutions which were affecting the rest of the country began to be felt in the Woking area. The Basingstoke Canal was built through the heart of the district in the early 1790s. Enclosure of the commonlands and heaths was about to begin. This would greatly alter the appearance of the area, one-third of which was still occupied by heathland in 1800. In the Knaphill and Goldsworth district nursery gardens had been opened and were flourishing, providing for the first time a profitable trade involving close links with wider markets.

The early changes of the four decades to 1840 culminated in the opening, in 1838, of the new railway line from London, extended to Southampton by 1840. This was of crucial importance for the future of the area, for it placed Woking on a great national trunk route, and abruptly ended its old seclusion. But it should be noted that, although the railway allowed the town to develop, it was not directly responsible for the growth of Woking. For 20 years after its opening the railway station remained alone on the empty heath.

The true origins of the growth of the new town can be traced to two most unlikely causes: the refusal of the Church to allow burial anywhere but in consecrated churchyards, and the cholera epidemics which swept London in the 1830s and 1840s. These two combined to produce a gross and insanitary overcrowding of burial-grounds, and as a result the government was forced to ban future churchyard burials within the London area. As an alternative it was proposed that a huge national cemetery should be established, and Woking parish was chosen as the site of this extraordinary venture.

In 1852 the London Necropolis & National Mausoleum Company was empowered to acquire 2,600 acres in the parish, for the laying out of a cemetery. Woking thus became the child of a burial company, an origin unique in this country. The cemetery, opened in 1854, occupied only 400 acres, enough to make it the largest in Europe, but representing less than one-sixth of the original plan. After 1855 the Necropolis Company began to sell off its surplus land, and it was in the disposal of this land for speculative building that the new town was born.

New Woking expanded rapidly after 1870, outgrowing the neighbouring villages and eventually swallowing them whole. Despite its many and manifest deficiencies it flourished and sprawled. In 1907 it annexed Horsell and in 1933 Byfleet and Pyrford. By 1914 its population had grown so fast that it had overtaken Guildford in size, and was the largest town in West Surrey. Whilst it grew it attracted people from the entire social spectrum, from Irish and Scottish labourers and Devon farm-workers on the one hand, to leaders of politics, the arts and high society on the other. Accompanying them was a massive influx of criminals, the mentally ill and the delinquent, as institutions were opened in the town, making use of the freely available and cheap land. The town to which all these people came was a strange place, resembling in some aspects a Wild West frontier settlement, with mud streets, no sewerage or lighting, and with ugly makeshift architecture; yet only a mile or two away could be found large and expensive residences set in wooded grounds and housing the leaders of society.

The story is continued until the 1980s, covering the development of industry and the growth of commuting between the wars, and the radical changes which have, since 1945, transformed the character and appearance of a town which is still less than 150 years old. On 1 April 1974 Woking became a borough, having tried for over 40 years to attain such a status. It is with the Borough of Woking that this book deals.

Old Woking is, where appropriate, referred to as Woking village, whilst New Woking, a name which did not become widely used, refers to the area of the present town centre, around Woking station. Woking Urban District, which was formed in 1894, included Horsell after 1907 and Byfleet and Pyrford after 1933, and in 1974 became the borough without any change of area. The term 'Woking district' or 'area' is used to describe the four ancient parishes of Woking, Byfleet, Horsell and Pyrford before 1894, when they had no administrative connection.

List of Important Dates

1791		Basingstoke Canal opened to Horsell (to Pirbright 1792)
1808		Enclosure of manor of Sutton completed
1811		Enclosure of manor of Byfleet completed
1815		Enclosure of manor of Pyrford and Woodham completed
		Closure of Byfleet iron-mills
1830	(Nov.)	Civil unrest in Woking parish
1834		Guildford and Chertsey Poor Law Unions formed
1838	(May)	Railway opened to Woking Common
	(Sept.)	Railway extended to Winchfield
1845	(May)	Guildford branch railway opened
1847		First National School opened in district (at Pyrford)
1849		Necropolis proposed for Woking parish by Board of Health
1852	(June)	London Necropolis Company Act received Royal Assent
1854	(July)	Woking Commoners Act received Royal Assent
	(Nov.)	Brookwood Cemetery opened
1855		Necropolis Company began to sell land in Woking
1856		First building in future town centre (*Albion Hotel*)
1859	(Apr.)	Prisoners moved into Woking Convict Prison, Knaphill
	(Oct.)	First large auction of land in central Woking
1864	(Apr.)	Guildford and Chertsey Highway Districts formed
	(June)	Brookwood station opened
1865	(June)	Royal Dramatic College opened by Prince of Wales
1867	(June)	Brookwood Asylum opened
1869	(May)	Female Convict Prison opened
1872		Guildford and Chertsey Rural Sanitary Authorities formed
1874	(Apr.)	Woking School Board established
1877	(Dec.)	Royal Dramatic College closed
1879		Woking Crematorium built
1882		Public piped water supplies introduced
1883	(Mar.)	Worplesdon station opened
1885	(Mar.)	First cremation in Britain, at St Johns
		Oriental Institute opened
1887		Woking police-station opened
	(Dec.)	Byfleet and Woodham station opened
1889	(May)	Male convict prison closed
1889	(Nov.)	Mosque opened
1890	(Nov.)	Electricity supplies inaugurated
1892	(June)	Gas supplies inaugurated
1893	(Oct.)	Woking Local Board established

List of Important Dates – continued

1895	(Jan.)	Chertsey R.D.C., Woking U.D.C. and parish councils for Byfleet, Horsell and Pyrford all formed
		First street-lighting in Woking
	(Dec.)	Woking Fire Brigade established
		Female convict prison closed
1899		Victoria Hospital opened
	(July)	Oriental Institute closed
	(Dec.)	Woking sewerage system inaugurated
1902	(Aug.)	Street-lighting converted from electricity to gas
1906		Woking Park opened
1907	(Oct.)	Horsell amalgamated with Woking
1909	(Sept.)	Horsell sewerage system inaugurated
1912		Byfleet and Pyrford sewerage system inaugurated
1914		Woking County School for Boys opened
1920	(Aug.)	Woking's first council house completed
1925		Woking County School for Girls opened
	(Oct.)	Street-lighting begins in Byfleet and Pyrford
1929	(Mar.)	Woking Library opened
1931	(Oct.)	Conversion of street-lighting back to electricity
1933	(Apr.)	Chertsey R.D.C. abolished, and Byfleet and Pyrford joined with Woking Urban District

Chapter One

BACKGROUND

The Physical Setting

THE FOUR ANCIENT PARISHES which today comprise the Borough of Woking lie across the watershed between the basins of the River Wey and the Bourne. The latter, also known as Windle Brook and Hale Bourne, rises on Chobham Ridges and flows to the Thames at Chertsey. The Wey, which flows north-east to Weybridge and drains most of West Surrey, is joined near Old Woking by a sizeable tributary, which is usually called Hoe Stream in its lower reaches and Stanford Brook nearer to its source at Wanborough and Pirbright. It has also been known as Maybourne or Mayford Water. A small tributary of this stream rises on Bisley Common and flows through Brookwood and Crastock to the confluence at Kemishford. It has no name, although it is the 'brook' in the place-name Brookwood, but there is a possibility that it was once called Corsebrook. That name may have been derived from the Celtic word *cors*, meaning a marsh or bog; such an origin would certainly have been appropriate for its wet and marshy valley.[1]

The Rive Ditch rises near Horsell and Goldsworth, and flows eastwards to the Wey at Brooklands. Its course was affected by the building of the Basingstoke Canal, and today it is culverted or artificially straightened throughout its length, but until the last century it wound amongst the marshes and heathy moors which occupied most of its shallow valley. Before 1820, too, it fed a large peaty lake, Sheerwater, but this was drained and its memory survives only in a place-name. The word *rive* is Old English for a ditch, and the name of the stream is therefore a tautology.

These various streams have cut wide clay valleys in which they have deposited extensive sheets of gravel and alluvium. The ridges between the valleys, although low, give the area an undulating character. The most northerly extends from Horsell Church to Woodham and New Haw, via Kettlewell Hill. It is about 40 m. above sea-level at Horsell, falling to 30 m. on the Woking-Chertsey boundary at Woodham. The central ridge is a spur of the higher hill mass of Chobham Ridges, and stretches from Knaphill to West Byfleet, including Hook Hill, Monument Hill and Blackdown. It averages 45-55 m. above sea-level, and reaches a maximum elevation of 67 m. at Hook Hill, the highest point in the borough. The town centre lies on this ridge.

The ridge is broken in several places, with a gap at St Johns through which the canal passes, and also has several subsidiary spurs, such as that on which Pyrford Church stands. A third, but less continuous, ridge extends from Worplesdon to Sutton Place, and includes Burdenshott Hill and Pyle Hill. The ridges are composed of sandstones of the Bagshot, Bracklesham and Barton Beds, together with thin layers of clay and poor-quality ironstones.[2] They have been eroded by the rivers in places to create shallow flat tracts, which in the past have been poorly drained and peaty. Examples include Whitmoor Common (Sutton Green), the area now occupied by Goldsworth Park, and the Rive Ditch valley.

On the edges of these tracts, and along the perimeters of the river valleys, the sandstones form low but prominent 'bluffs', some of which are almost cliff-like. They are the most dramatic features of an otherwise unremarkable topography. The situation of Pyrford Church, at the summit of such a steep hill, is familiar, as is the slope westwards from there towards Hoe Place. Other examples include Anchor Hill at Knaphill (the name Knaphill itself means 'top' or 'summit'), St Johns Hill, and Constitution Hill in the centre of Woking.

The River Wey and the Hoe Stream also cut themselves terraces during earlier periods of erosive activity. Terraces are belts of flat land, covered with gravel and alluvium, and lying above the present level of the river. Two may be recognised in the Woking area. The upper terrace, at 15–18 m. above the river, forms the extensive tract of flat land between Pyrford Stone, Pyrford Woods and West Byfleet, and is also noted at Sutton Place and Pyle Hill. The lower terrace, 3–5 m. above the rivers, is better developed, and forms the land on which Byfleet village and Pyrford Green are built. Old Woking is likewise situated on this terrace, which extends along the Wey and Hoe valleys through Kingfield and Westfield to Sutton Green. The flatness of the terrace can be appreciated by looking eastwards from Warren Lane near Pyrford, and its height above the river is well seen at Hipley Bridge, Old Woking. The terraces are of great importance because they were attractive sites for early settlement, and several of the original villages of the area were built upon them.[3]

Prehistoric and Roman Settlement

It would seem that this part of the county was never thickly populated, and comparatively few archaeological sites of any importance have been excavated. There may be sites which are not yet known, and it is certain that the area would repay a more intensive investigation, but there is reason to suppose that the sandy ridges with their acid soils discouraged settlement just as they did in later centuries. The evidence of Bronze Age barrows on Horsell Common, near the Six Cross-roads, and of occupation sites of the Mesolithic and Neolithic periods at, for example, Parley Bridge, Old Woking and Byfleet, points to some settlement in the district, but our knowledge is scanty and a coherent picture is difficult to piece together.

Roman occupation is equally uncertain. Coins and pottery have been found at Coldharbour, and excavations have taken place at Old Woking, where there are Roman tiles in the fabric of the church, but these certainly do not provide a full picture. We can say with safety that there were poor peasant farmers living in the area in the Roman period, with some degree of cultural contact with the occupiers, for a farmstead of this type has been excavated at Woking Park Farm, Old Woking.[4] It also seems probable that the long-postulated Roman road from Farley Heath (near Shere) towards Maidenhead did pass through the borough. Its remains were found at Lightwater in 1972 during the construction of the M3, and a projection of its alignment points through Bisley and to Knaphill. It would perhaps then have crossed the Bridley area towards Merrow and Newlands Corner.

The Saxon Settlement

In recent years the conventional wisdom concerning the dating and sequence of the Saxon occupation has been rejected, and a new account offered. It was formerly accepted that place-names ending with *-ing*, such as Woking, represented the primary phase of colonisation, and thus dated from the earliest years of Saxon influence. Research has now shown that such sites are almost invariably remote from the pagan burial-grounds which certainly date from the initial period. Since the burial-grounds must surely be close to the sites of pagan Saxon settlement, it is argued, the *-ing* places cannot be of the first phase.[5]

They are now believed to date from the secondary phase of settlement, and are probably places founded or settled by colonisers spreading outwards from the earlier villages. In Surrey, it is said, the initial colonisation, immediately after the Saxon invasion, penetrated along the belt of land between the North Downs and the Wey valley marshes, towards Guildford. Woking and its sister parishes were perhaps founded, or occupied, by settlers coming from this earlier area, maybe in the mid-7th century.

We may also suppose that the Saxons did not come to an unpopulated district. The peasant farmers of Roman Britain doubtless survived in the Woking area after the Romans had left, continuing their traditional and relatively unromanized life-styles until the Saxons arrived. Their settlement was then taken over and renamed by the newcomers. Woking is held to mean 'the people of *Wocc*' (or *Wocca*) and is derived from a person of that name.[6] The obvious similarity between the names Woking, Wokingham and Wokefield suggests a direct relationship, with the people of Wocca being the founders of all three places, but although that is indeed a possibility it should be remembered that the name was unlikely to have been unique to one person, and that the distance of 15 miles between the places, across inhospitable moorland and forest, was quite an obstacle; there has been no administrative or social connection in recorded history between the Berkshire places and Woking.

The other place-names of the Woking area are almost without exception topographical (i.e. derived from natural features). Byfleet means 'by the stream', *fleot* being a common place-name element found, for example, at Fleet in Hampshire. The name is simply and accurately descriptive of the watery site.[7] Pyrford almost certain means 'pear tree ford', and again the first element is frequently noted locally. *Pyrige*, a pear tree, is found in the names Pirbright and Pyrcroft.[8] Horsell presents more of a problem, since the name is not recorded in documents until the 13th century. It probably derives from *horig scylf*, meaning a muddy slope or shelf on a hill, and presumably relating to the wet lands around the village site.[9]

Administrative and Ecclesiastical Arrangements

Our earliest reference to Woking appears in a letter from Pope Constantine, written in about 710. The monks of Medeshamstead (now Peterborough) had a small daughter-house at Woking, said to have been founded *c.* 675 by Brordar, a nobleman. The Pope was adjudicating in a dispute between Peterborough and the Bishop of Winchester over jurisdiction in Woking. Although the letter is known only from a 12th-century copy, there seems little reason to doubt its authenticity.[10]

The site of the monastery was probably that of the present St Peter's Church, the dedication of which is clearly derived from the religious house which preceded it. The river ran along one side, the Hoe Stream was a short distance to the north, and there were fordable points on both streams. Around this site the village of Woking developed. Guided by the long narrow strip of terrace between the two rivers it acquired a strongly linear plan, but the nucleus has been, for over 13 centuries, the area beside the ancient church.

Byfleet village also occupied a terrace site, within one of the great loops of the Wey. Close to this point, at the ford which has been succeeded by Plough Bridge, the slope of St. George's Hill came close to the river, and offered a dry route to the crossing point, in contrast to the extensive damp and flood-prone tracts to the north and south. The parish stretched right across the valley, from the heaths and moors near Sheerwater in the west to the summit of St George's Hill in the east: the centre of the parish being a broad belt of fertile and rich meadows and flatlands on both sides of the river.

Pyrford, as its name would suggest, lay at the point where the marshy Wey valley could be crossed, using a tongue of higher land projecting northwards from Ripley, with an intermediate 'island' at Newark: the priory was later built on this. The knoll on which the church stands commanded a wide view over the Wey valley and beyond, but the main centre of population was to the east, on the flat terrace around Pyrford Green. Horsell village was at the western end of the low Kettlewell ridge, and had damp lowlands on three sides. It was thus rather cut off and isolated. The parish occupied the southern side of the middle valley of the Bourne, and in the west included part of the wooded and hilly land which sloped up towards the Chobham Ridges.

The presence of the monastery gave Woking a greater importance, and although it was not one of the earliest settlements it became perhaps the most significant between Guildford and Weybridge. The church, or minster, was the mother-church of the chapelries (later full parishes) of Pyrford, Horsell and Pirbright, and had some authority over Send and Bisley.[11] There was a logical territorial unit focusing upon Woking, and extending across the middle Wey valley from the North Downs to the Chobham Ridges above the Blackwater valley, and in the 8th century that unit became formalised as the Hundred of Woking. The Hundred embraced Frimley and the Horsleys, but met at Harmesheath in Ockham parish, close to the edge of the area: possibly this was a reflection of the earlier settlement in the vicinity.

Chertsey Abbey, founded in about 660 by Frithwald, sub-king of Surrey, was amongst the richest religious houses in Southern England, and at an early date was endowed with extensive lands in North West Surrey: these included Bisley and Byfleet. The Hundred of Chertsey or Godley was created, based upon the lands of the Abbey, and so those parishes were included with it. Unaccountably, however, Pyrford and Horsell (which were closely associated with each other) were also included with Godley, even though their connections hitherto had been with Woking parish.[12] This anomaly was perpetuated for over 1,000 years, and was only ended by local government reforms in 1907 and 1933. It is fascinating to note that a protracted and important debate over sewerage and drainage, in the 1890s and 1900s, was caused in part by an administrative decision of the 8th century.

Woking was thus the centre for the middle Wey valley, although it remained a comparatively small village; for this reason it gave its name to the Hundred. The importance was retained for several centuries, but gradually the greater strength of the markets of Guildford and Chertsey eclipsed its potential for commercial significance, and the development of the great roads from London through Staines and Guildford left it stranded away from main arteries. At the taxation of Pope Nicholas in 1291 Woking church still had authority over Horsell, Pirbright and Pyrford, and the links with Horsell remained close, but by the 14th century the village was falling into obscurity and insignificance.

Of the four ancient parishes Woking (8,802 acres) was the largest. It comprises the western end of the sandstone ridge which forms the spine of the district, and included the lower part of the valley of the Hoe Stream and the left bank of the Wey from Burpham to Pyrford. The focus of the parish was in the south-east and the arc of fertile land along the two valleys contained most of the population. Behind the valleys was the expanse of heath and woodland occupying the sandy soils. The other three parishes, Horsell (2,920 acres), Pyrford (1,880 acres) and Byfleet (2,450 acres) show a similar pattern, with the 'active' part being near the river, and the empty wastes behind.

The wastes were carved up arbitrarily between the parishes, and the precise boundaries were not finally demarcated until the middle of the last century.[13] Natural features were used in the more populous parts, and, for example, the Wey was employed for this purpose along its entire course from Burpham to Wisley. Its course has changed subsequently in places, and the parish boundary there survives to mark the old line, as between Old Woking and Sutton, where it follows abandoned meanders of the river. The Bourne was the northern boundary of Horsell, and the Horsell–Woking and the Pyrford–Chertsey boundaries followed the marshy valley of the Rive Ditch, which was a marked physical barrier.

Elsewhere, though, the expanses of heathland gave less natural assistance, and when the lines were eventually fixed straight alignments were chosen across what had previously been a 'no-man's-land'. This accounts for the unusual straightness of many local boundaries. Examples might include that between Woking and Worplesdon across the former Whitmoor Common, and the borders between Woking, Horsell, Chertsey and Pyrford in the Woodham and Fox Hill area.

The Manors

The manorial system evolved parallel with that of the parishes, and was well established in the Woking area by the late 10th century. Manors, because they were bought, sold and confiscated, have a complex history, and since they did not necessarily coincide with parishes their geography is also confusing.

Woking. The largest of the local manors, Woking, eventually covered some 6,830 acres or about 70 per cent of the parish, but originally it was somewhat smaller. It was a royal possession before the Conquest, and as such was exempted from most taxes. In 1066 it passed automatically to King William I. It was formerly believed that there were two manors, one being the property of the Bishops of Exeter, but it is now known that this idea is based upon a mistake in the Domesday Book. The Bishop's manor was at East Horsley, in the hundred of Woking but not near Woking village; it was erroneously listed under the heading of Woking, not East Horsley.[14]

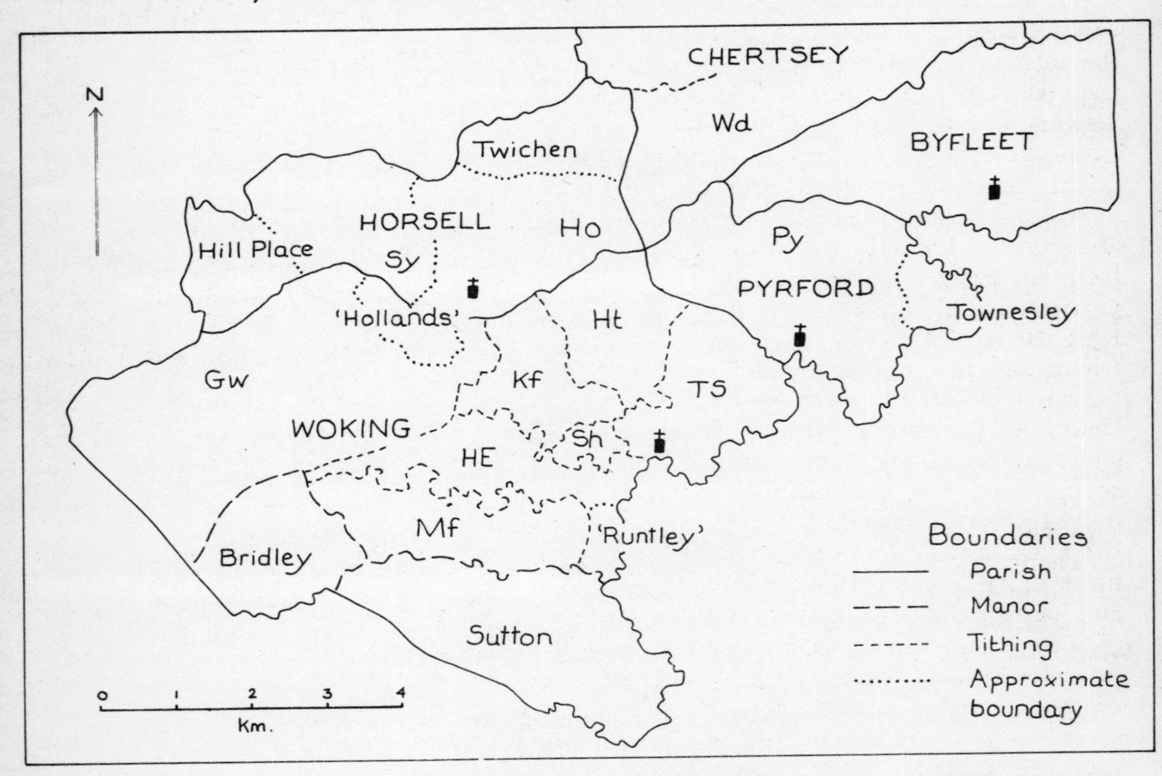

Fig. 1. Parishes, manors and tithings

Gw	Goldsworth	Ht	Heathside	Py	Pyrford	Ts	Town Street
HE	Hale End	Kf	Kingfield	Sh	Shackleford	Wd	Woodham
Ho	Horsell	Mf	Mayford	Sy	Sythwood or Sithwood		

In 1200 King John granted the manor of Woking to Alan Bassett, a close associate, and a member of a powerful noble family. The manor passed by marriage to Hugh le Despenser in 1260, and remained in his family until 1326, when his grandson, the favourite of King Edward II, was executed. Edward III granted it in turn to his uncle Edmund Holland, Earl of Kent, and despite fluctuating fortunes the Holland family held Woking until 1416. In that year Alice, Duchess of Kent, bequeathed the Lordship to her sister-in-law, Margaret Beaufort, Duchess of Somerset. She was the mother of Lady Margaret Beaufort, herself the mother of King Henry VII.

Lady Margaret Beaufort was given the manor in 1485, on the accession of her son, and lived in Woking for much of the remainder of her life. In 1509 she died, and left the manor to her grandson, Henry VIII, so that after 309 years Woking once more became a royal possession. It remained so throughout the 16th century, but in 1618 King James I, anxious to raise revenue and loyalty, sold the manor and lordship to a favourite, Sir Edward Zouch. The Zouch family became extinct in the male line in 1671, and the manor reverted to the Crown. In the usual tradition of royal favourites being granted the manor of Woking, it next passed to Barbara, Duchess of Cleveland, the mistress of Charles II, and after her death was held in trust. John Walter bought the rights in 1715, but his son resold them in 1752. The new Lord of the Manor of Woking was the Earl of Onslow, of a family which collected lordships and acquired extensive estates in Surrey. The family retained the lordship of Woking, and its subsequent manorial history has been uneventful.[15]

Woking manor house lay beyond the village on a low mound beside the Wey, just above flood level. It was moated, and was a substantial and well appointed building from the early medieval period. After 1485, when it became a royal residence, it was extensively rebuilt, to make it a house worthy of its illustrious occupants. In 1497 King Henry VII, who frequently visited the house, signed the Treaty of Woking, a friendship and non-aggression pact with Maximilian of Austria, perhaps the only occasion in history when Woking made an appearance upon the international stage! Henry VIII regarded Woking Palace as a favourite residence, and stayed there for some weeks almost every summer. He made major alterations and improvements, designed by the master builders Henry Smyth and William Virtue and completed in 1516.[16] It is said that Wolsey was staying with Henry at Woking when he received the news that he had been made a Cardinal. Legend also says that Queen Mary I was born at Woking, but that is quite incorrect. The Manor or Palace was built of red brick, and had the orchards, gardens and luxurious apartments that befitted its royal status.

Mary I and Elizabeth I viewed Woking with less favour, and only stayed there on infrequent visits. By the end of the 16th century it was falling into decay as a result of long years of neglect, and the sale of the manor of Woking to Sir Edward Zouch sealed its fate. He received licence from James I to demolish the old palace, and then used the materials for the construction of Hoe Place (not the present house), Woking Park Farm, and probably other buildings in the area. The deer park which had surrounded the palace, and which was at one time over five miles in circumference, was soon disparked and returned to farmland, and all that was left were the moats and a few crumbling ruins amidst the hummocky ground by the river. The destruction of the palace, although perhaps inevitable, was the greatest loss to the heritage of Woking.

The Zouch family also built the famous tower or beacon, its precise purpose unknown, which stood on the summit of the hill above Hoe Place: the hill became commonly known as Monument Hill. The tower, of red brick, octagonal and about 60 feet high, had a lantern on top: this provoked the suggestion that it was intended as a guide for travellers. It became ruinous in the early 19th century, and fell in a storm in 1868.

Sutton. The name Sutton means 'south hamlet', and refers to its position within the parish of Woking. Although it was probably always a separate manor, it never became a parish in its own right, although at one time it had links with Burpham, Merrow and Stoke next Guildford. In the 1070s the manor was given to Robert Malet, one of the closest companions of William I, and it was he who probably built the first manor house. Malet supported Robert, Duke of Normandy, in the dispute with King Henry I at the end of the 11th century, and so in 1102 the manor was confiscated, and became a royal possession, being owned successively by Henry I, Stephen, Henry II and Richard I. In 1200 John granted it to Alan Bassett, at the same time as he gave him Woking, and the two manors were thereafter held jointly and functioned as one unit.[17] Henry VIII broke the connection when, in 1521, he granted Sutton to a favoured courtier, Sir Richard Weston. The Weston family and their relations, the Webb Westons and the Salvins, held the lordship of the manor of Sutton for nearly 400 years, but in the early years of this century the line became extinct. After a period in the ownership of the Duke of Sutherland, who lived there in the 1930s–1950s, the manor was bought by John Paul Getty, the oil magnate, as his English headquarters.

The old Sutton manor house was described as ruinous as early as 1329[18] and had been demolished by the time the manor was separated from Woking in the 1520s. Sir Richard Weston therefore built himself a splendid new house, worthy of a rich and influential man. Sutton Place is on a low hill, east of the old manor site, and was started in 1525. It is incomparably the finest building in Woking, and one of the greatest in Surrey. It has been said that it is one of the two most important English houses of its time.[19] Ten years earlier the rebuilding of Woking Manor had been finished, on the traditional pattern with a moat, gatehouse and at least token fortifications. Sutton Place, by contrast, was the earliest of the great English country houses to have no pretence at a military role: it was a lavish house, not a castle or stronghold. Although only ten years and three miles separated the two buildings, they represented the last of the old and the first of the new styles, a world apart in conception.

Sutton Place is in red brick, the local material, with two storeys. It was originally a square around a courtyard, but the gatehouse and the north range were demolished in the 1780s. The house is ornamented with prefabricated Italian terracotta panels, one of the earliest examples of this Renaissance device in English architecture, and the symmetrical plan, around a central hall, was also a pioneering feature.[20]

As might have been expected, Sutton Place and its large estate dominated the manor of Sutton, which remained a semi-feudal community largely dependent on the manor until well into the 19th century. Although it was still within the parish of Woking the community was almost self-contained, with its own local services and with a sense of isolation and remoteness which still survives to a degree, even though it is midway between Woking and Guildford.

Bridley. In the extreme south-west of Woking parish was a third, and much smaller, manor, usually known as Bridley, sometimes as Crastock. Until the 12th century it was part of the manor of Pirbright, and was frequently included in that parish for other purposes. Fulk Bassett, Bishop of London and Lord of Woking (1242–49), bought the rights of Bridley, and thereby attached it unquestionably to Woking parish. He did not unite it manorially with Woking, and instead it became a tenanted manor under the overlordship of the former, but separately held and administered.

The tenancy was bought, sold and bequeathed, and through this process the links with Woking once more weakened, so that by the late 16th century Bridley was considered an independent manor, and held its own courts. No one family held the manor for any long period, and the history of its ownership is very complex. In the early 19th century it was enclosed privately by Sir Fletcher Norton, the Lord, with the co-operation of his major tenants, and it remained distinct from Woking until well into the present century.[21]

Other Woking manors. Mayford was considered separate from Woking and Sutton until the middle of the 13th century, but never became a manor in its own right. It was owned as a distinct entity by the King of England until the late 1240s, although it was always held by individuals on behalf of the king. In the 1240s Fulk Bassett bought the 'semi-manor' of Mayford from the trustees of Henry Kinton, as part of his policy of extending and consolidating the manor of Woking, into which it was thereafter absorbed.[22]

The Manor of Runtley, also known as the manor of Emlie or Emley, was a shadowy division, marked on maps of the 16th and 17th centuries as lying across the flat wet meadows between Sutton and Woking village. It was too small and insignificant to have a viable and separate existence, and clearly derived from a former property which, although not a true manor, preserved some vestige of independence. Locke suggested that it was part of the lands of the monks of Woking in the Saxon period, and was later held by the Rector of Woking as their successor. Alternatively it may have been associated with the priory of Newark, which had close links with the parish of Woking.[23] In the 17th century it was owned by the Emly family, hence its other name.

Rudehall or Hollands was an equally mysterious manor or sub-manor, in the tithing of Goldsworth, stretching across the site of what is now Goldsworth Park, between Wych Street and Littlewick. It is improbable that the name was derived from the Holland family, Earls of Kent, but it clearly has close connections with the tithing name Hale End and with the present place-name of Harelands, which is in the area of the former manor. The separate existence of Rudehall or Hollands had been ended by the 16th century, although it was never formally incorporated into the manor of Woking.[24]

The manor of Woking was divided for administrative purposes into seven tithings from at least the 14th century until the late 19th. Town Street was the area of Woking village; Shackleford covered the land around Gloster Road, Shackleford Road and Vicarage Road; Kenvil or Kingfield tithing extended as far north as the present town centre; Heath Side included Maybury, Heathside and the Walton Road district; Hale End stretched in a narrow belt from Blackhorse Road to the river at Woking village; Mayford embraced Smarts Heath, Mayford Green and parts of Westfield; and the very large tithing of Goldsworth included also Knaphill, Brookwood, Goldsworth Park and Hook Heath. For the purposes of parish administration, from the late 16th century onwards, two other tithings were recognised: Sutton and Crastock or Bridley, covering the area of the manors of those names.

Byfleet. The manor of Byfleet, which coincided with the parish, was held at the time of Domesday by Ulwin, a tenant of Chertsey Abbey. The manor had allegedly been granted to the abbey by Frithwald as part of his great endowment of 673, and even if the monks fabricated some of the evidence for the grant, as seems possible, there is no doubt that they had enjoyed possession for a considerable time. Byfleet was an unusual manor in that it included land in other parishes which, although legally distinct, was administered in conjunction with the main bulk of the lands. Thus it held property in the parish of Effingham, and had close ties with the manor of Bisley. Joint sessions of the manor court were held between Bisley and Byfleet as late as the 17th century.

For reasons which are obscure the manor of Byfleet passed, sometime between 1297 and 1315, into the hands of King Edward II, although the abbey retained a nominal interest. Since the king immediately made it over to his favourite, Piers Gaveston, it is likely that this was a deliberate confiscation to enrich the latter. On the accession of Edward III, after the fall of Gaveston, the manor was made part of the estates of the Duchy of Cornwall, and so passed from king to eldest son until 1533. In that year it was granted to Catherine of Aragon in compensation for her recent divorce from Henry VIII. She died in 1536, and in the next year the abbey of Chertsey, which still retained its nominal interest, was dissolved. Total royal control was therefore achieved for the first time.

Henry VIII then attached Byfleet manor to the estates of Hampton Court, and in that status it remained, although almost always leased to individuals, until 1650, when it was sold by the Commonwealth Government. Queen Henrietta Maria, widow of Charles I, was granted the manor and lordship on the Restoration in 1660, and once more the manor was leased, as a source of money for its royal owners. This time it was attached to the Oatlands estate at Weybridge, the site of a former royal palace, and in the 18th century the two estates were usually leased together.

In 1804 a private Act of Parliament allowed Frederick, Duke of York, the third son of George III, to acquire the manorial rights, lordship and lands of the manors of Byfleet, Weybridge and Walton Leigh. He died in 1820, and in 1829 the manor was sold to Lord King of Ockham, who was already the Lord of the Manor of Pyrford. On his death it passed to his relations, the Locke King family who held it until the middle of this century. They were prominent local benefactors and, perhaps alone amongst its many owners, actually took a real and lasting interest in the welfare and condition of their tenants and of the manor of Byfleet.[25]

Byfleet Manor, often known as Byfleet Park, was in the south of the parish, in the long loop of the Wey. The medieval house, of which very little is known, was pulled down in the 1540s by Sir Anthony Browne, the then lessee, and a new house was built in its stead, allegedly with materials from the recently dissolved Newark Priory. In 1615 Queen Anne, wife of James I, began extensive reconstruction work, completed in the 1620s by Sir Thomas Fullerton. In 1685-90 it was again rebuilt, because it was said to be too large. The only part of the Queen's house to survive is the magnificent pair of gateposts at the entrance to the manor, by the celebrated German architect Wendel Detterlein.

Further alterations to the house were made in the 1730s and in the late 19th century, although the basic Jacobean-type design remained unscathed. Finally, in 1904–5, the house was restored and an extra wing added, without harming the overall appearance of what Nairn described as one of the best houses of its date in the county.[26]

Pyrford and Horsell. These two manors have always been held jointly, with Horsell being regarded as the subordinate one of the partnership. That explains why it has never had a manor house of its own, alone amongst the four parishes. In 1042 the manor was owned by King Edward the Confessor, presumably including Horsell, although there are no documentary sources to prove that. From the mid-1050s it was leased to Earl (later King) Harold, and after the Conquest became one of the possessions of William I. In 1069 he granted it to the Abbey of Westminster in part, and the remainder was bequeathed to the abbey in his will. It remained a possession of Westminster until the final dissolution of the abbey in 1540. Despite this Pyrford, with Wisley and Horsell, retained a close link with the parish church of Woking, and later with the monks of Newark.

Apart from a brief period under Mary I, when the abbey was refounded, the joint manor was attached to the Crown until 1574, when Elizabeth I granted it to Edward Clinton, Earl of Lincoln. It then had a succession of different owners, ending with the Parkhurst family, who in 1677 sold it to the Earls of Onslow. In the middle of the 18th century the Onslows added the manor of Woodham, in Chertsey parish, to that of Pyrford and Horsell, constituting it a separate tithing.[27] At the enclosure of Pyrford and Woodham in 1805–15, the manor of Horsell was, for the first time in its history, treated separately and the connection was broken. Pyrford was enclosed, and the lordship of the manor was sold by the Earl of Onslow to Lord King of Ockham, whereas Horsell was not enclosed, and Lord Onslow and his heirs remained as the Lord of the Manor.

Other manors. The small manor of Toundesley or Townesley, recorded in 1297, was in the south-east corner of Pyrford parish, within a loop of the Wey, and extending almost as far as Pyrford Green. In 1366 it was acquired by Westminster Abbey and united with Pyrford and Horsell. The name of the manor survived, however, and today the Townsley Meadows, which were once the common meadows of Pyrford, recall the existence of a tiny manor which disappeared in the 14th century.[28]

The manor or sub-manor of Twichen in Horsell was first recorded in 956. It was in the north of the parish, between Dunford Bridge and Mimbridge, bordering on Horsell Common to the south and bounded by the Bourne on the north. This small area, only two farms in extent, was never able to develop a full manorial status, but was regarded as distinct until the 19th century, the name being used at least until 1874. It derived its name from the Old English *twicene*, meaning a meeting of the ways, referring to the junction of several tracks near Bonsey's Farm.[29]

Hill Place, at the extreme western end of Horsell parish, was recorded as a separate manorial unit in 1332, but like Twichen it never became a completely separate area. It comprised the hilly and wooded land between Bisley, Castle Green and Knaphill. There is still a farm, Hill Place, today: it is near Bisley Church, just across the border in Horsell parish.[30]

For manorial purposes the joint manors were divided into three tithings, Pyrford, Horsell and Sithwood, each with its own constable and ale-taster. Later the tithing of Woodham was added. Sithwood or Sythewood, which was the western part of Horsell, around Littlewick and Lower Knaphill, had fallen into disuse by the early 19th century, and the name was no longer current. It has now been revived for the part of the new Goldsworth Park development which lies in the area of the former tithing, an attractive piece of historical consciousness on the part of the decision makers.

Pyrford manor house originally stood on the edge of the River Wey east of the church, surrounded by a large moat fed by the river. It was demolished in the mid-16th century and replaced by a new building on a different site, higher up the slope. The new house, built by the Earl of Lincoln, was half-timbered, and was described by Defoe as one of the finest houses in Surrey. On his visit the writer was particularly attracted by the setting, which was 'exceeding pleasant, especially for the most beautiful intermixture of wood, and water in the park, and gardens, and grounds adjoining'.[31] Unfortunately this building, which would have been a notable addition to the architectural heritage of Woking, was itself demolished in the 1770s, and replaced by the present Pyrford Place.

Social and Economic Life

For most of its history the Woking area was almost entirely agricultural. Its only industries were those, such as brewing and tanning, that used local products and were for the local community alone. The Domesday Book notes the keeping of pigs in the woodland, although this evidence has been wrongly interpreted at times: the entry which refers to pigs in Woking numbering 133 in fact means that the woodland at Woking is worth 133 pigs.[32] Similarly at Byfleet it records fisheries worth 325 eels.[33] Mills are listed at Woking, Byfleet, Sutton and Pyrford, the last named having two. These were probably on the Wey, although it could be that one of the Pyrford mills was on a side-stream.[34]

The area was on the fringes of Windsor Great Forest, and periodically it was placed under Forest Law, which was much more harsh than that prevailing elsewhere. Henry II afforested Woking and Pyrford, including the wood of Brookwood, but this was not rigorously implemented. Richard I included all four parishes within the Surrey lands of the Forest, but in 1226 Henry III reversed the process, and disafforested not just the newly included area but also those lands in Pyrford and Horsell which had been listed as Forest in the Domesday Book.

In 1280 Edward I ordered a new extension of the Forest, and that remained nominally in force for over 350 years, until the reign of Charles I. There were frequent complaints about the damage done to crops by deer and other protected species, but the degree of control exercised by the Forest bailiffs was very variable, and in some reigns little attempt was made to enforce Forest Law. A Commission of 1642 accepted that it was unreasonable to apply Forest Law to North West Surrey, and therefore the area was effectively disafforested.[35]

Some indication of the relative wealth of the district may be obtained from the various taxation returns, which although not fully reliable do help to give a general impression. The Subsidy Roll of 1334 assessed Woking together with Horsell and Sutton, an indication of the close links between the three. They were jointly taxed at £10 13s. 7d. (£10.68), which may be compared with the figures of £3 11s. 1¼d. (£3.55½) for Byfleet and £2 12s. 0½d. (£2.60½) for Pyrford. At the same time Guildford was worth £15 2s. 9½d. and Godalming £16 9s. 10¾d. By 1636, when payments of Ship Money were exacted, Woking and Sutton were still assessed together, and were required to pay £56 10s. (£56.50). Horsell was told to provide £28, Byfleet £11 and Pyrford £14. Although there were clearly anomalies in this, for Horsell was almost certainly not worth more than twice as much as Byfleet, it does suggest that the relative prosperity of the area had grown, for Guildford was assessed at £58, Reigate at £60 and Walton-on-Thames at £38.[36]

The Wey Navigation

The River Wey has always been navigable for very small craft in its lower reaches, but was not suitable for commercial traffic on any scale. By the late 16th century it was felt that this fact represented a check to the potential growth and prosperity of Guildford, where the wool and cloth trade was in decline. A better access to London was needed, and the idea of improving the river arose. Vine quotes the earliest reference to artificial improvement of the Wey; in 1566 there was mention of 'a certen locke . . . between Woodham lande and Brooke lande upon the water of Weye'.[37]

Bills to make the Wey navigable were submitted to Parliament in 1621 and 1624, without success, and then the Civil War intervened. In 1651, though, the Commonwealth Parliament passed the Wey Navigation Act, which authorised the improvement of the river as far as Guildford. Its promoter was Sir Richard Weston of Sutton Place. The river skirted his lands, and he wished to introduce a measure of flood control, as well as to allow commercial traffic. He had seen canals used for navigation and drainage or flood prevention when on a visit to the Netherlands, and had been very impressed with the concept.

Work on the river began in August 1651 and was completed, at a cost of £15,000, in the summer of 1652. Unfortunately the cost was too great for Weston's finances, already weakened by his family's dubious commercial dealings, and he became bankrupt as a result.

His debts, and the uncertain political situation following the Restoration, combined with the poor quality of the original workmanship to produce rapid deterioration in the condition of the Navigation after 1660. By 1677 it was largely ruinous, and extensive and costly repairs were necessary before traffic could be resumed. Thereafter it had a long, profitable and uneventful existence, and is still heavily used by pleasure craft. The Navigation was the earliest English waterway to use pound locks, and was the first river navigation to employ lengthy artificial cuts or canals to bypass difficult or winding stretches of the natural channel.

In the Woking area the meandering Wey was shortened in several places, although of course the old channel remained. There was a new cut from Burpham to Trigg's Lock, and then from Walsham's Lock at Send a long channel, called the New Cut, went directly to Newark instead of the twisting natural course past Woking village. The loop at Newark was cut across the neck by a new channel, and at Pyrford Place the longest of all the new works left the river to bisect the parish of Byfleet and re-enter the Wey at New Haw, only a short distance above the Thames.

As it skirted only the southern part of the district the impact of the Wey Navigation was not felt in Horsell and the more remote western areas. Furthermore, industry was not yet at a stage where it could take great advantage of a waterway, and the main benefit was felt in the agricultural sector. In particular, the quick and cheap access to London benefited the local corn trade, and Woking Mills, which were close to the Wey Navigation, prospered as they supplied flour to the capital, using corn brought by water from Guildford Market.[38]

Prosperity and Stagnation

It is likely that Woking reached a peak of prosperity in the 16th century, and then experienced a long relative decline until revived once more in the mid-19th century. When the parish was the seat of royalty, and when the great houses at Woking, Byfleet, Pyrford and Sutton were in their heyday, there would have been a substantial demand for local goods, produce and services. Even though the court and the lords of the manor were only in residence for part of the year there were the considerable daily needs of the members of the households who stayed. In the late 15th and early 16th centuries the extensive building programmes and frequent visits by the royal family could not have failed to increase the wealth of the surrounding communities.

Once all the splendour had vanished the old agricultural economy and lifestyles were left to continue as they had in the past. The area faded into obscurity, and few outsiders came to see it. An extraordinary incident which is said to have taken place in 1769 will illustrate how little contemporaries knew of the area, and how much the district had become a backwater. Whether or not it is to be believed, it certainly shows that in the middle of the 18th century such a story would be given credence:

A NEST OF THIEVES

'There are not less than five hundred gypsies, vagrants and smugglers who have taken sanctuary in a wood between Guildford and Naphill. All the farmers and inhabitants thereabouts have suffered more or less from these rapacious vagabonds, who subsist chiefly by plundering people of their geese, fowls, ducks, or whatever may come their way. Fourteen pieces of cannon, mounted upon carriages, set out on Saturday, by order of Lord Albemarle who, together with the neighbouring gentlemen, are determined to dispossess, by force, this nest of thieves from preying upon the honest farmers.'[39]

Chapter Two

THE WOKING DISTRICT IN 1800

A DESCRIPTION of the area in the early years of the 19th century may serve as a prelude to a detailed account of the changes which had so profound an impact upon the four parishes in the hundred years which followed.

In 1800 the district was unremarkable. In common with most of Southern England it was largely agricultural, with few industries and little evidence of dramatic change in the preceding century. To the few observers who bothered to describe the area it seemed rather remote or secluded. Defoe, in 1724, had written in an often quoted phrase how, en route from Chertsey to Guildford, he 'went away south to Woking, a private country market town so out of all road, or thoroughfare as we call it, that 'tis very little heard of in England'.[1] Three-quarters of a century later the same character was still apparent, and writers suggested a sense of isolation, whilst the more romantic amongst them contrasted the faded air of Woking town with the thriving and vigorous community which they supposed had existed in the 16th century, when it was the seat of royalty. Thus Manning and Bray describe the town as 'small and inconsiderable',[2] and in 1840 Brayley remarked upon the 'many old houses erected in bygone ages'.[3]

The people of the West Surrey heathlands were, it would seem, regarded as rustic and boorish. Brayley repeats folk tales of neighbouring Pirbright to illustrate the 'ignorance which formerly characterised the inhabitants of this wild tract'.[4] Stevens records that as late as 1864 there was an incident of 'rough music' in Byfleet. This was said to be a once widespread practice, whereby the neighbours of an unpopular person would shout and jeer around his house at night.[5] There is no reason, though, to suppose that in reality the people were any different from those of other rural areas at a time when education was in its infancy, poverty was endemic and the horizons of most were limited to their parish and its immediate vicinity.

The physical remoteness, too, may be exaggerated, for the district was clearly more accessible than, for example, the mountain areas of the north and west. No turnpike road passed through Woking, but two great national routes, from London to the West Country and to Portsmouth, were only a few miles away. London itself was just 25 miles away, Guildford a mere six. Patterson's *Roads*, a volume of itineraries for travellers which appeared in 1822, gives a separate account of the 'London to Woking' route, and places Byfleet on the road from Windsor to Brighton, a journey doubtless suggested by the activities of the Prince Regent himself.[6] Both indicate that there were regular long-distance travellers to the area.

By the 1830s, too, there was a twice-weekly coach service from Woking to London, via Byfleet. *The Emerald* left the *White Hart* in Woking village at 6 a.m. on Monday and Friday, and travelled to *Blossom's Inn* near The Monument. Its route was through Byfleet village, Cobham and Esher, and it called at Piccadilly. The service was operated by Joseph Chitty, and was very expensive: 8s. 0d. (40p) inside and 5s. 0d. (25p) outside were the single fares, with a reduction of 1s. 0d. for Byfleet passengers.[7] The produce of local farms was also transported to market in Guildford and to London by road or water, and some 18th-century writers noted that the ponds on the heathlands of Woking were used for breeding fresh fish to supply the tables of the capital.

We may therefore regard the four parishes as having been secluded rather than physically remote. Possessing relatively little to interest the antiquarian writers who are the source of much contemporary description, they were given scant attention. They were simply 'typical' agricultural communities, comparatively untouched by the social and economic changes of the 18th century, on the fringe of, but by no means cut off from, the wider world.

The Waste

At the end of the 18th century several agriculturalists made critical analyses of conditions in West Surrey, concentrating their attention upon the waste, the accurately descriptive contemporary name for the areas which we now call heaths and commons. The Woking wastes were on the eastern fringe of a great expanse of such land extending from Bracknell to Petersfield, spreading into four counties and covering several hundred thousand acres.

The comments of the writers were unanimously hostile, for they did not enjoy the lonely beauty of these tracts, preferring instead a prosperous and well-ordered pastoral scene. Defoe set the tone in 1724, when he passed a famous and unflattering judgement:

> 'a vast tract of land which is not only poor, but even steril . . . horrid and frightful to look on . . . much of it is a sandy desert, and one may frequently be put in mind here of Arabia Deserta'.[8]

For a century and more after this few disagreed. Stevenson referred to 'wild and desolate heaths . . . dreary and irreclaimable',[9] and Brayley to 'black and barren heath lands'.[10] Today the heaths have been invaded by scrub, and latterly by full woodland, but at this time the grazing of cattle and cutting of vegetation suppressed the natural tendency to tree growth, resulting in a bare and bleak landscape that has now largely vanished. Only parts of Chobham Common serve to remind us of the appearance of much of the Woking area in the early 19th century.

The characteristic vegetation was a mixture of heather, furze (gorse) and bracken, with coarse moorland grasses and some birch and willow scrub. In places the peat-filled hollows contained bogs and marshes, where cotton grass was common. It is now extinct in the area, but its fluffy white heads were responsible for the place-name Whitemoor (now Whitmoor) at Sutton, amongst others. The infertility of the soil was determined by the sands and gravels of the Bracklesham, Barton and Bagshot Beds which, outcropping on the surface, almost exactly defined the limits of the waste.[11] The more fertile river alluvium and clays were cultivated at an early date, but the value of the sands was small. Until the later 19th century large-scale reclamation of the wastes was thus uneconomic.

The agricultural improvers bemoaned the poverty of the soils, using what seems to us to be wild exaggeration. Marshall felt that the soil was much inferior to that of the Scottish Highlands, whilst Brayley thought that the landscape resembled a 'desolate mountain moor in the Border Country'.[12] They were writing at the time of the wars with France, and urged that the wastes should be reclaimed by draining, fencing, ploughing and manuring, to create new agricultural land which would help to make the country self-sufficient in food. They were strongly biased in favour of this view, and were not prepared to discuss the possible value of the unimproved waste. There is much debate about this question, but it would appear that the peasant economy of West Surrey in the early 19th century was still heavily reliant upon the waste.

Technically the waste was the property of the lord of the manor, but freeholders and manorial tenants had various rights over it and its resources, and so it was known as 'commonland'. In the Woking area these rights included the grazing of livestock, the cutting of turf (peat) for fuel, and the removal of furze, brushwood, gravel and sand. All these were available for the commoners themselves, but were on no account to be used for profit, or for others, and fines were levied by the manor courts on those who did not comply with this restriction. In 1813, for example, Robert Donald of Goldsworth was fined at Woking because he had 'lately cut Turf, Sods and Mould from the waste of this Manor and carried the same off this Manor to the injury of the said Lord and tenants thereof'.[13]

In the absence of woodland, and with coal prohibitively expensive, the cutting of turves was of particular importance. In the 1880s, when Edward Ryde was recalling the Woking of 70 years before, he said that

> 'a very large number of turves were cut annually by the poor for fuel, turf being at that time almost the only fuel burnt by the cottagers. The custom used to be for the cottagers to cut their own turves with an instrument called a Turfing Iron, and for each farmer to send a wagon and horses to cart the turf for his own labourers'.[14]

The grazing of livestock was rather less vital because the riverside meadows were widely used. Sheep and pigs were put on the waste, since they could survive on the poorer vegetation, but at the start of the 19th century the improvers noted the inadequacy of the beasts belonging to the cottagers: 'we saw only a few starved animals unworthy of the name of sheep'.[15] Nevertheless, these two uses, and various minor ones, such as that recalled by the old name 'Candlerush Grove' for a part of the waste near the present Maybury railway arch, reflect the importance of the heaths.[16] George Bourne, writing of similar land near Farnham, considered that 'the Common [was] a supplement to the cottage gardens . . . furnishing a means of extending the scope of the little home industries . . . the village cows used to be turned out to graze on the heaths, and fir-timber fit for cottage joists could be cut on the common, as well as heath good enough for thatching and turf excellent for firing'.[17]

The Shape and Distribution of Waste

As the map (Fig. 2) shows, waste formed the spine of the Woking district, extending in a rough triangle from the Pirbright border in the west to the edge of Byfleet village the east, with outliers to the south in Westfield, Mayford and Sutton. It had changed its shape frequently, because since early times the piecemeal advances of agricultural colonisation had been reducing its extent. Although there was never a concerted attempt to reclaim the waste, new land had to be brought into use as the population grew, whilst landowners and farmers, great and small, attempted to expand their property by fencing in portions of heath. The process was discontinuous and fragmented, but since the 16th century the area of waste has been substantially reduced.

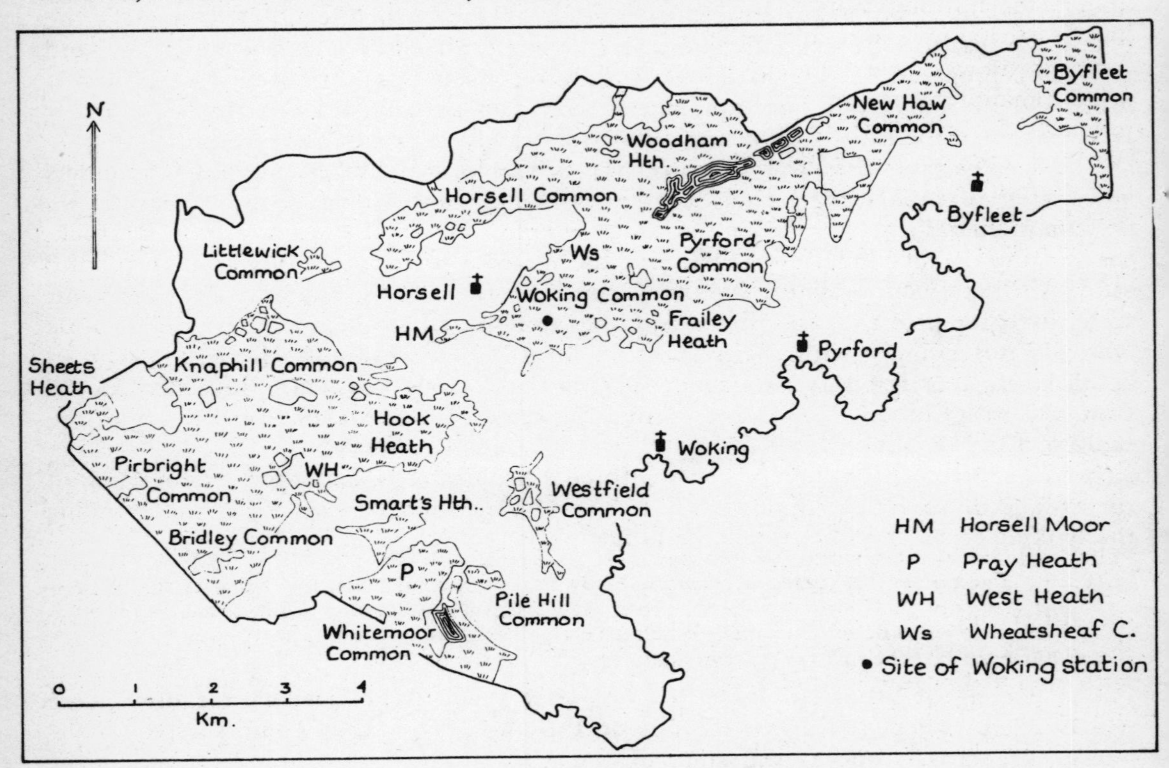

Fig. 2. The Waste of Woking in 1800

All those who wished to fence and cultivate land from the waste were required to obtain the approval of the Lord and commoners at the manor court. Permission was usually granted upon agreement to provide a lump sum payment or regular rent for the privilege. In January 1652, for example, the Manor Court of Bridley allowed John Palmer of Crastock to enclose waste on Bridley Common, at a rental of 4d. (1.6p) to be paid twice yearly, on Lady Day and at Michaelmas, together with 2s. 6d. (12½p) or 'one fatt capon' on Christmas Day.[18]

Such formal enclosures were commonplace, and a regular part of the business of the Manor. During the 18th century most of the major landowners made sizeable incursions into the waste, revealed on the map by the typical bites of 'Old Inclosure' in, for example, the West Byfleet–Pyrford area. In Sutton manor, Havering Farm had been carved out of the boggy heath around Whitmoor Pond, whilst on Pirbright Common the large enclosure known as Doctors Moor was associated with outward expansion from Pirbright itself, across the parish boundary.

The enclosures contrast with the illegal encroachments of those who, by neglect or deliberate decision, did not seek the approval of the manor court. Such authorised enclosures were numerous but often small, affecting only a few square yards of heath and being nothing more than the pushing of fences a few yards further. Others were more substantial, and involved sufficient land for a cottage and a garden or smallholding. It was clear that many such attempts were unsuccessful, for the proceedings of the manor courts are full of punitive measures against illegal encroachment. At the session of April 1802, for example, 23 cases were brought before the Manor Court of Woking, each involving between two acres and five square yards.[19] Fines were levied, or alternatively, the encroachment could be legalised by a payment similar to that in the conventional procedure.

At other times the court might order the destruction of the enclosure: thus in April 1825 the Woking court noted that

> 'several incroachments made in the previous year have all been thrown open, as then ordered, but that the same have been all again inclosed without Leave or Licence of the Lord or Tenants of the Manor — whereupon the Bailiff is commanded to throw the same open again'.[20]

Nevertheless some of the enclosures of this type escaped attention and survived, acquiring sufficient permanency to be accepted in time as legal. Their occupants thus became de facto commoners, and exercised all common rights, whilst in 1854 on the extinction of these rights they received compensation just as did the legal commoners. These illegal but permanent encroachments were known as 'squatter' dwellings, and in several places in the Woking area settlements grew up of the type that Bourne describes: 'hardly anywhere are there to be seen three cottages in a row, but . . . the little mean dwellings are scattered in disorder . . . wanting in restfulness to the eyes and much disfigured by shabby detail'.[21] Often these settlements would be on the farther edge of the waste, away from the focus of population and near the parish boundaries, where their haphazard plan of cottages, gardens, tracks and remnants of waste gave a chaotic and confused appearance of which traces may still be seen.

Excellent examples were those on the Woking–Horsell–Bisley boundary at Knaphill, a village composed almost entirely of this type of habitation, and at Frailey Heath on the Woking–Pyrford border. The latter was known as Bunker's Hill, and was notorious for the rough and poor people who lived there. In Horsell, Cheapside was a squatter settlement which formed a tattered fringe to the common, straggling along a track which is still unmade. Its name probably derives from Cheapside in London, and was attached humorously to the poor and makeshift cottages of the new community. A similar phenomenon was apparent in the Coldharbour Lane area of Pyrford. Elsewhere there were small cottages standing alone in the middle of the heath, surrounded by nothing more than a small plot or garden. These represented the first stage in the disintegration of the waste as it was eroded by colonisation, a process which in earlier times had produced the fragmented common at Westfield which we see today.

The proportion of land under waste is difficult to determine with accuracy, not least because areal measurement was so unreliable in the early 19th century. For example: the official estimate of the acreage of Woking parish was increased by almost 15 per cent between 1801 and 1851, although the boundaries did not change. The figures below are the most accurate which can be given.[22]

Table 1. Distribution of Waste in 1800

Manor	*Area*	*Under Waste*[a]	*Percentage under waste*
Bridley	650	325	50
Byfleet[b]	1,440	550	34
Horsell	2,920	900	30
Pyrford[b]	1,820	540	29
Sutton	1,440	350	24
Woking[c]	6,830	2,360	34
Woodham[d]	610	460	76
Present Borough	15,710	5,485	35

a. excluding village and roadside greens; b. excluding the part of ancient parish lost in 1933; c. including area acquired from Bisley in 1933; d. a tithing of Chertsey parish and manorially linked to Pyrford. N.B. All areas are in acres and approximate.

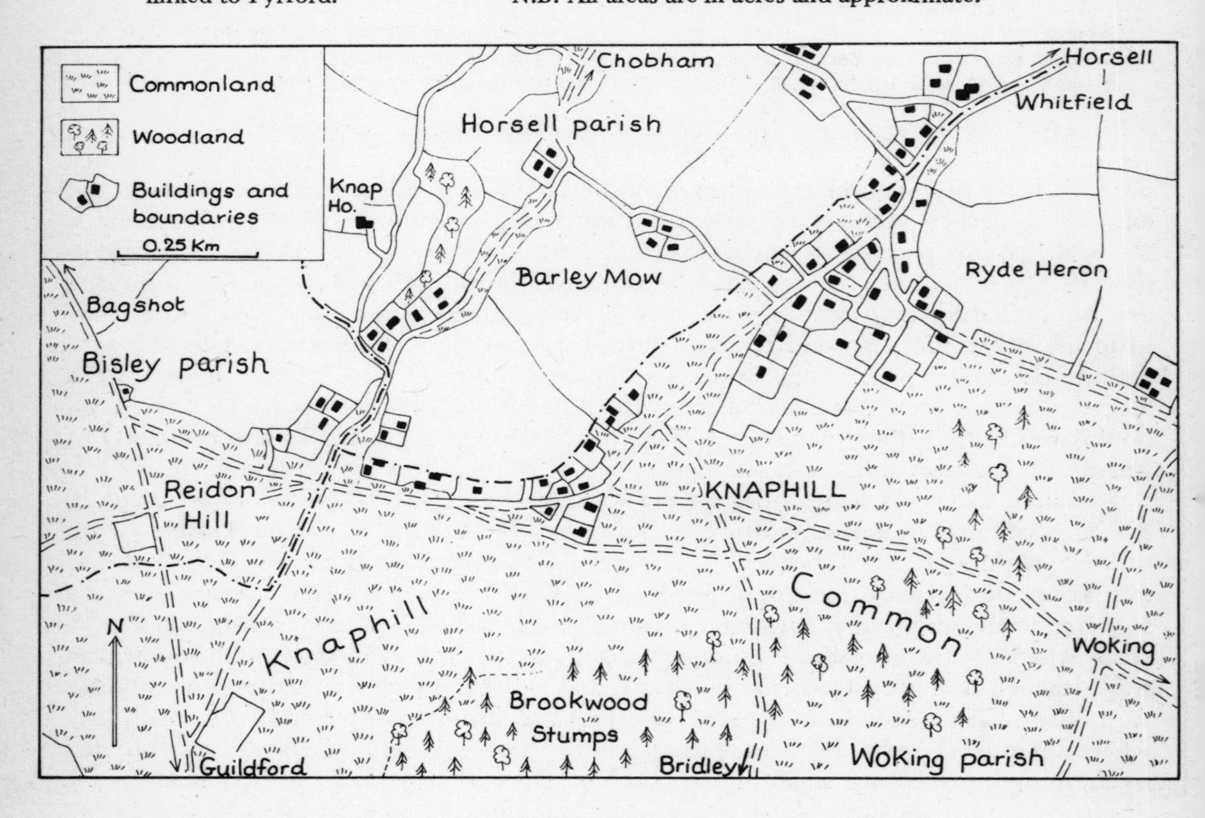

Fig. 3. Knaphill in the early 19th century.

With the exception of the special cases of Bridley and Woodham it is clear that over the whole area rather more than a third of the land was uncultivated, the proportion varying from 24 to 34 per cent. This may serve to correct the impression of almost complete desolation which is conveyed by contemporary writings. With about two-thirds of the area in productive use the importance of the waste must not be exaggerated. Nevertheless, in terms of its economic and landscape significance and its effect upon the future pattern of development in the area the waste is to be regarded as a dominant factor in the character of Woking in the early years of the 19th century.

The Open Fields, Meadows and Greens

Most parishes of North West Surrey had open common fields at some time, but piecemeal enclosure had reduced them to shrunken remnants by the end of the 18th century, when parliamentary enclosure first became significant in the county. Comparatively little is known about the open field system of the Woking area, and some of the published material seems to be in error. Contemporary agricultural writers suggested that there was usually a 'three-field rotation' of crops with one field left fallow each year, a system found in the upper Thames valley. Tate, however,

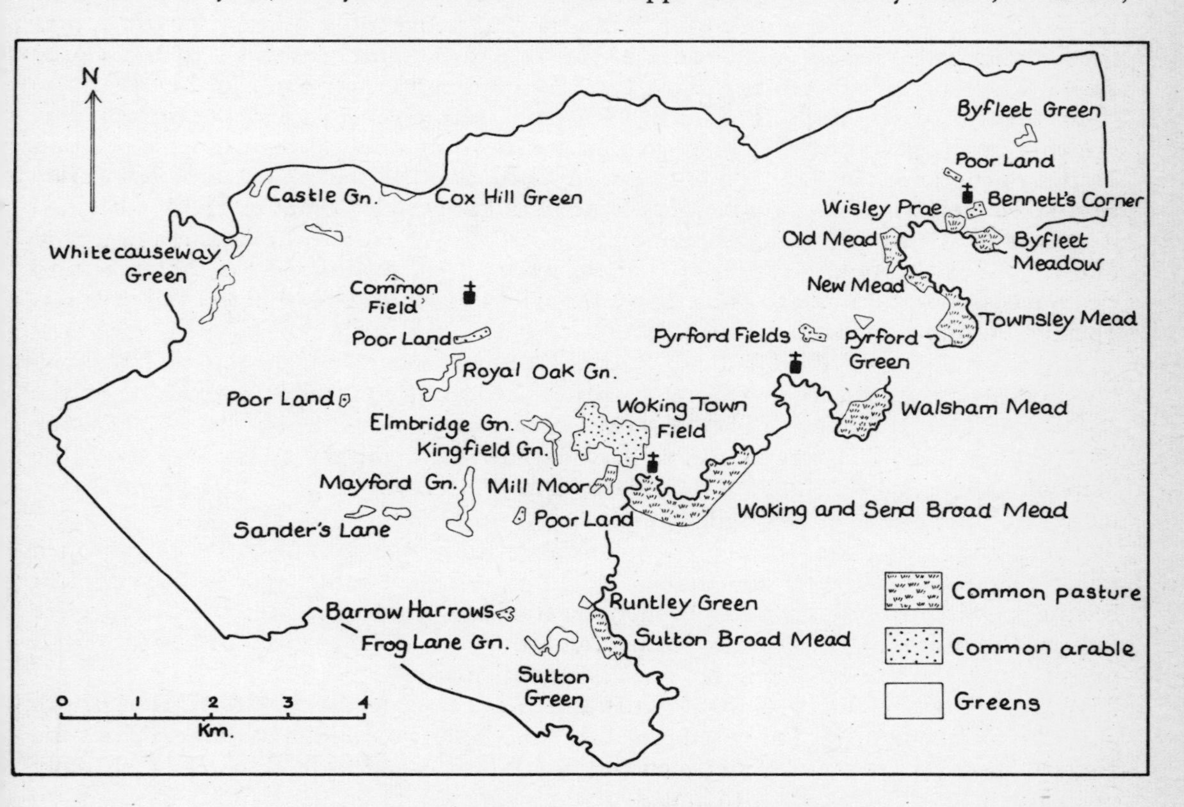

Fig. 4. Open fields, meadows and greens in 1800

considered that a two-field pattern was more likely, and that the fallow field was not needed because the waste provided adequate pasture in conjunction with the riverside meadows.[23] It is probable that formal rotation patterns never existed, and that there were many variations over time and between manors.

The location of the open fields is also subject to some conjecture (*see* Fig. 4). There were two major types, the arable and the common meadow. Gray states in *The English Field Systems* that Byfleet had lost its open arable fields and was thus completely enclosed, except for waste, by 1605, but this is not quite true.[24] In 1800 a fragment survived as the 11½-acre Bennetts Corner, lying south-east of the church and divided into a number of individual plots, some unenclosed. These represented the consolidated strips of the former open field, and elsewhere in the area of the village the sites of other open fields could be traced by the presence of long narrow plots, the relics of the old strip farming system. The area between the church and Eden Grove, and the land south of Winern Glebe towards the Wey was notable in this respect (*see* Fig. 8).[25]

In Pyrford parish the open fields had lain across the gentle slopes west of the Green and northwards from the church. In 1800 the field boundaries here revealed the same elongated plots which were the fossils of former strips. There were also two small fragments which were not yet enclosed, and were still common. They lay on either side of Sandy Lane north of Stone Farm, and although only 5½ acres each in area they retained the names of the once extensive parish common fields: Pyrford Upper Field, which extended west to Upshot Lane, and Pyrford Lower Field to the east.[26]

In the case of Horsell there was never any formal enclosure, and cartographic evidence is almost entirely lacking, so that we can only guess at the probable position of the open fields. In 1854 the area to the north-west of the village, between Parley Brook, Horsell Birch and Bullbeggars Lane, was known as 'Common Field', although it is doubtful whether it was commonly owned.[27] We may assume, therefore, that one of the open fields was in that area, whilst logic would suggest that a second extended across the ridge to the east of the village, around Grove Barrs: this area was open and unfenced until the 1900s.

The open fields of the Manor of Sutton had been separate from those of Woking, but had been reduced by piecemeal enclosure and by the extensive emparking of the 1520s, until in 1800 they covered only a tiny area of 3½ acres on the eastern slope of Pyle Hill. This field was known as Barrow Harrows,[28] and the evidence of the Tithe Map of 1848 suggests that Pile Hill Field and Whitemoor Field may have been the names of other parts of the original area.

The Manor of Woking presented a contrast with its neighbours, for here the open fields lasted much longer, and indeed were still distinguishable well into the present century. Quite why this was so is unclear, for the Onslow Lords of the Manor were favourably disposed towards enclosure, and this was a large and fairly prosperous parish where the new system might have been anticipated.

Woking Town Field covered the entire area between Kingfield Green, Hoe Bridge and the properties on the northern side of High Street, Old Woking. Until the construction of Rydens Way between the two World Wars this land remained virtually unenclosed and unfenced, with much of the character of an open field, although no longer farmed as such.

In 1841 the Tithe Map showed that 51½ acres in the tithings of Shackleford and Town End were still 'Common Fields'. The area was divided into 30 strips and plots of between ¼ and 4½ acres, with six different landowners and 13 occupiers. Of the former only one, Robert Hodd, was actually farming his land, the others renting their property to leaseholders. The map indicates that a process of consolidation of strips had been operating, for James Fladgate owned a block of eight adjacent parcels and Robert Hodd one of six, but these still preserved their long thin shape. In the vicinity of what are today Selwood Road and Shackleford Road the classic strip pattern was still clearly visible and functioning (*see* Fig. 5).[29]

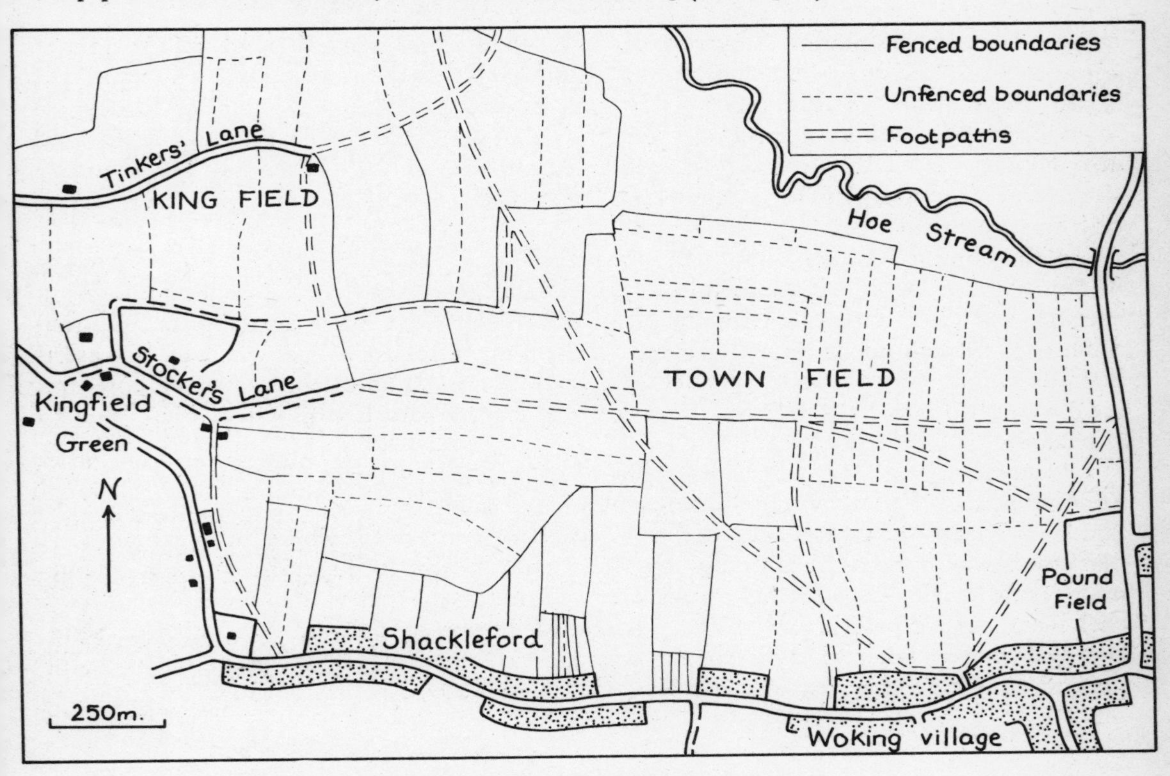

Fig. 5. Woking Town Fields in the early 19th century.

The other open fields of the parish had disappeared by 1800, but may be mentioned. There were two fields at Westfield, which preserves the ancient name of the second common field of the Manor of Woking. Lower West Field was between Hoe Stream and the site of Woking Football Ground, along Westfield Avenue, whilst Upper Westfield adjoined this and extended as far as the Common, covering the area of the present Westfield Schools. Thus the old Lower West Field was in a completely different place from the hamlet which today bears that name, on the road to Sutton Green.[30] In 1800 some long narrow fields beside Hoe Stream near Elmbridge marked the site of Lower West Field.

Kingfield was smaller than the other two, and disappeared earlier, so that in 1800 there was no definite trace of its strips. It extended from Elmbridge Green, where it adjoined the Lower West Field, eastwards across the site of Elmbridge estate, and north of Kingfield Green, towards Stockers Lane and the edge of Town Field. It is probable that at some stage 'King Field' extended farther to the east, but that it later became absorbed into Town Field. There was thus, at the time of its greatest extent, continuous open field from Westfield Common to Hoe Bridge, along the south bank of the Hoe. Although it is commonly supposed that Kingfield means that this field belonged to the king, the 16th-century spelling *Kynfeld* suggests a slightly different derivation, from the Old English *kyne* or *cyne* meaning, more generally, 'royal'.[31]

Elsewhere in the Manor, Mayford may have had a rudimentary open field system at some time, but all trace had vanished by 1800, whilst Bridley, which was small and had a tiny population was unlikely ever to have had such a feature. Goldsworth, beyond the hill to the north-west, probably had a small open field or meadow in the lowland area now occupied by Goldsworth Park, for field boundaries of the early 18th century show the characteristic long enclosures of a former strip system, but there is no documentary evidence.

All the common meadows were along the Wey valley, beside the river and its streams in damp areas unsuitable for arable farming. The meadows were apportioned between owners, usually in strips as with the open fields, but were made available to manorial tenants and freeholders for the grazing of livestock after they had had been harvested in midsummer. The Manors of Byfleet, Pyrford, Woking and Sutton possessed common meadow, although by 1800 the first and last named had lost much of theirs due to enclosure.

In the Manor of Pyrford each tenant was entitled to graze his livestock between 15 August and 12 January, the number permitted being one horse or gelding, two cows and five sheep for every acre of land owned or rented elsewhere in the manor. A herdsman was appointed annually by the Manor Court to supervise grazing arrangements, and to pay him for his duties a levy of 6d. (2½p) per animal was exacted from each user of the meadow.[26] Woking Broad Mead was actually in the parish of Send, and was shared between the two. It was a great expanse of 365 acres between the natural course of the Wey and the New Cut of the Wey Navigation. In 1794 about 50

Table 2. Common Meadows and Open Fields in 1800[33]

Manor	*Meadows (acres)*		*Open Fields (acres)*	
Byfleet	Byfleet Meadow	12½	Bennetts Corner	11½
	Wisley Prac	3½		
Pyrford	Old Mead	10¾	Upper Field	5½
	New Mead	13¾	Lower Field	5½
	Townsley Mead	57		
	Walsham Mead	56¾[a]		
Sutton	Sutton Broad Mead	30	Barrow Harrows	3
Woking	Mill Moor	15	Town Field	60
	Woking Broad Mead	365[b]		

a. Now in Ripley parish. b. In Send parish

people owned land in the meadow, and it had a rental value of £1 10s. (£1.50p) per acre. Hay was harvested in June, and then the Mead was closed until 18 September to allow the grass to regenerate. On that day it was opened to cattle and sheep, grazing being the right not just of the owners and tenants but also of all the parishioners of Woking and Send, and 'even of more distant places'. James and Malcolm regarded this as 'shameful practice' and urged that the area be enclosed, after which it would be worth at least £3 per acre in rent. Their advice was not heeded, and the empty flatness of Broad Mead remains little altered even today.[32]

There was also a number of 'greens' in the Woking area, although the classic English village green was not to be found. Rather, these were expanses of grass and rushes, usually with a pond or several 'splashes' (shallow pools) and edged by scattered cottages. The largest seems to have been Goldsworth Green, latterly called Royal Oak Green, some 11½ acres in 1800. It extended from Arthurs Bridge Road to Triggs Lane and St Johns Hill Rise, and is still visible between the Triangle and Goldsworth Road, although much eroded by house-building and road-widening.

More conventional triangular or quadrangular greens are found at Kingfield, Elmbridge and Mayford. The last was seriously damaged by the construction of a roundabout in recent years, whilst the little known Elmbridge Green is familiar to many as the area of grass and trees outside Woking Football Ground and Park. It was originally joined to Kingfield Green by a strip of roadside waste, and a similar elongation extended along Loop Road, which had four 'splashes'. The greens at Pyrford, Sutton and Byfleet were eliminated by the Enclosure Acts, which parcelled them out amongst various landowners. The first two are recalled by place-names still in use almost two centuries later, but of Byfleet Green there is now no trace. Sutton Green and Pyrford Green remained visible for many years after they ceased to be public land, and were used unofficially for grazing into the early years of this century.

Table 3. Greens and Roadside Wastes in 1800[33]

Greens (acres)		Major Roadside Wastes (acres)	
Kingfield Green	9	Whitecauseway Green	8
Elmbridge Green	3¾	Castle Green	6
Mayford Green	6	Cox Hill Green	6½
Goldsworth Green	11¼	Frog Lane Green	2
Sutton Green	9¾	Club Green	6[b]
Runtley Green	2½	Wych Lane	6¾
Pyrford Green	5¾	Saunders Lane	4¼
Byfleet Green	10½[a]	White Rose Lane	2¾
		Coldharbour Lane	3¼

a. Partly in Elmbridge district today. b. Now part of Littlewick Common

Other greens were simply stretches of waste, with grass and trees, along the roadsides. Examples were numerous, and there was no clear distinction between the terms 'green' and 'waste'. An excellent example which survives today is the extension of Mayford Green northwards to Barnsbury, on either side of the main Guildford road. The belt of wooded grassland along the Knaphill–Chobham road, from Barley Mow

Lane to Barrs Lane is likewise of this type. Many have been lost as a result of enclosure or, more frequently, road-widening, amongst these being Frog Lane Green (Sutton), Whitecauseway Green (Horsell) and the greens along Coldharbour Lane (Pyrford).

Agriculture

In 1800 agriculture was dominant in Woking; the only significant employer, the major source of income and the largest user of land. The evidence suggests that it was moderately prosperous, although not technologically advanced, but that poverty was endemic among the labouring population. In 1801 the clergy collected returns of the acreage devoted to specific crops, and this information provides a starting point in the investigation:

Table 4. Crop Returns 1801 [34]

Parish	*Wheat*	*Barley*	*Oats*	*Rye*	*Potatoes*	*Peas*	*Beans*	*Turnips*
Byfleet	141	131	84	25	17	26	18	80
Chertsey [a]	26	19	11	1	½	8	9	0
Pyrford	101	115	32	12	12	6	10	60
Woking	469	449	131	60	14	111	19	399

a. Including the tithing of Woodham. N.B. Returns for Horsell are missing.

At the time the leading crops in North and West Surrey were said to be wheat and barley, and the returns therefore suggest that the area was typical of the region, since these two crops occupied by far the largest proportion of land under arable use. However the returns must be treated with caution, for many farmers may have underestimated the areas cultivated, because they feared that the clergy would use the information to increase tithes. In addition, there was no attempt to include grassland, orchards, market-gardens and nurseries, and so we must use other sources to supplement this list.

James and Malcolm, writing in 1794, refer to the cultivation of root crops in the Woking area, where the deep sandy loams on the edges of the heaths were particularly suitable for this purpose. Potatoes, carrots and 'parsneps' were grown in considerable quantities for the London market and for seed, but not, it was claimed, for cattle feed.[35] The large area under turnips in the 1801 figures suggests, though, that there was some growing of root crops for fodder. It would certainly have been appropriate for the area, since Sir Richard Weston of Sutton Place was popularly credited with the introduction of turnips to England as a fodder crop in the 1630s, having seen them used as such in the Netherlands.

Carrots were clearly a leading local crop, for in 1800 another agricultural writer, Stevenson, noted that 'the culture of carrots is followed with . . . considerable spirit, skill and success, and to a considerable extent in the parishes of Chobham, Horsell, Pyrford . . . [and] Byfleet', and that in Pyrford and Woking the growers used formerly to select and transplant some of the most vigorous and healthy roots, but as the price of carrot seed is now very low, they are seldom at that trouble'.[36] The same writer devotes much attention to the rotation of crops, and it seems that the usual sequence was turnips, wheat, clover and peas, although as stated earlier there must be some doubt as to whether a strict pattern was followed. Edward Ryde noted that by the mid-19th century the increased use of fertilisers had made rotation unnecessary, and it is likely that in the earlier years of the century the system was already changing.

The general opinion was that the soils of the area were less than outstanding. Ryde considered that the riverside meadows were 'exceedingly low and damp, and where they are not very well looked after they soon become rushy and of very inferior quality'.[37] Stevenson found the sandy soils of the heaths 'barren, soft, deaf and duffy, mixed with a hungry poor gravel . . . very thin lying on small stone of a dead white colour'.[38] Nevertheless, when suitably dressed and manured the soils could be highly productive, ideal for nurseries and market-gardens. The digging of marl or loam for dressing sandy soils was a widespread practice, reflected in such place-names as Loampits Farm (Westfield) and Loampits (Pyrford Green). After the 1780s improvements in transport and in the science of agriculture encouraged a proliferation of nurseries in the Woking area (*see* Chapter 3).

Pasture was concentrated on the riverside flats, leaving the better drained lower slopes, with their more fertile soils, for arable use. Cattle were of some importance, but many of the peasants were only able to keep sheep and pigs, which were less demanding of good pasture and so could be grazed on the commons. As late as 1854 there were 6,900 sheep in the Manor of Woking, with 34 sheep owners,[39] and in earlier years there had been many more. Cottagers could often afford only a pig, and these animals formed the basis of the economy, as well as being a considerable public nuisance. In 1826 the Manor Court of Woking ordered that fines were to be imposed on those who 'Keep Hogs without Rings that are found in the Streets, Lanes and Commons of this Leet, twopence [.75p] per head for each Hog'.[40]

The proportion of land devoted to each use can be roughly estimated from the crop returns and from figures in tithe and enclosure documents, as well as from the few contemporary maps:

Table 5. Estimated Land Use by Parish in 1800

Parish	*Waste*	*Cereals*	*Other arable*	*Grass*	*Other*
Byfleet	36%	21%	16%	23%	4%
Horsell	30%	16%	11%	37%	6%
Pyrford	40%	14%	8%	35%	3%
Woking	34%	18%	10%	29%	9%

Industry

There were few industries of any significance in the four parishes at the end of the 18th century. This had always been so, for the absence of ores or building stones, of good transport facilities and of a large population had militated against industrialization.

With one exception those industries that were present served a purely local market and used local products. They were processing industries, typical of those in every rural community in pre-industrial England, and had existed for centuries. A few survive today, but most succumbed to mass production and specialization following the growth of the rail network.

Brewing is an example of such an industry. At one time there was a brewery in almost every village and in the Woking area, in 1800, they were found at Woking village, Byfleet, Horsell and Bridley, although others had operated elsewhere at other times. Today they are recalled by place and street names: Brewery Road and Old Malt Way (Horsell), Brewery Lane (Byfleet), and The Old Brew House (Old Woking). The hops were grown locally, as they still are at Farnham, and this is likewise remembered in names: Hopfield Avenue (Byfleet), near the Hopgarden Field of the 1840s; Hopfields (Horsell), and Hopkiln and Oast House Cottages at Bridley. The subsequent history of the breweries is recounted in Chapter Nine.

Mills were a similarly essential feature of village life, using wind or water power to grind local corn. 750 years after the Domesday Book had recorded five mills in the area there were still two, at Woking and Byfleet. That at Pyrford had been superseded by the famous and beautiful wooden mill at Newark, so tragically destroyed by fire in 1966. Woking Mill, on its ancient and extensive Saxon site south of Town Street, was one of the largest on the Wey. In the early 19th century it was a 'water corn-mill, the flour manufactured there being chiefly sent to London by road, the horses employed in drawing it there making the journey three times a week'.[41] There is no doubt that water transport was also used, since the Wey Navigation passed close by. The mill ground local corn, which was supplemented by supplies purchased at Guildford market, but in 1835, after a continuous history stretching back to before the Conquest, it ceased to grind corn and was converted to paper production.

Byfleet Mill was on a 14½-acre island between two arms of the Wey. In the mid-17th century it had been turned into a paper mill and was operated, with Downside Mill, Cobham, by the Company of White Paper Makers. A century later this enterprise was abandoned and the mill was then used for the smelting of iron. For about 60 years, until the end of the Napoleonic Wars, a small iron foundry flourished in the Weybridge–Byfleet–Cobham triangle, with a smelter at each of those places. The ore, an iron-bearing sandstone with approximately 23 per cent metal content, was dug in trenches on St George's Hill, Weybridge Heath and Wisley Common, and taken the short distance to the mills by pack-pony. This distant outpost of the Wealden iron industry was, in 1800, the only one in the Woking area not directly connected with agricultural products. Competition from the booming industrial areas of the North and Wales was strong, and in common with the remainder of the decayed Wealden sites the Byfleet iron mill closed in about 1815, and reverted to the grinding of corn.[42]

The remaining industries were on a small scale, little more than the efforts of individuals to provide for their own needs. Lime kilns, burning chalk brought by water from Hampshire or by road from the North Downs, and producing lime for dressing the acid peaty soils, were common in the area, and most farmers with more than a few acres had their own. As elsewhere, Limekiln was a widely used field name, a useful indicator of location since usually no trace remains today. Examples might include Kiln Field, between Oyster Lane and High Road, Byfleet, and Great Limekilns, at the junction of Smarts Heath Lane and Saunders Lane, Mayford.

Brick kilns were also common, and used small local deposits of clay and the sand which was so abundant in the area. The bricks produced were for domestic purposes or for use in the immediate vicinity, and were entirely hand-made. Sutton Place estate had its own kilns in the woodland overlooking the Wey, at the southern extremity of Woking parish. Rocque, in 1762, marks a brick kiln east of the Hermitage, in what later became St Johns.[43] When the Basingstoke Canal was built (*see* Chapter Three) it used locally produced bricks for bridges and lock chambers, and the kilns here were extended, as were those nearby at Harelands. The bridge over the canal at St Johns became known, as it still is, as Kiln Bridge.

In 1812 the Earl of Onslow, Lord of the Manor and owner of the land, leased 'all those edifices and Buildings with their Appurtenances called Brookwood Brickkilns and the adjacent New Coppice' to William Woods of Knaphill: the coppice presumably provided timber for firing the kilns.[44] It was the Brookwood and Hermitage kilns which were the precursors of the substantial brick industry in St Johns and Knaphill in the later 19th and early 20th centuries.

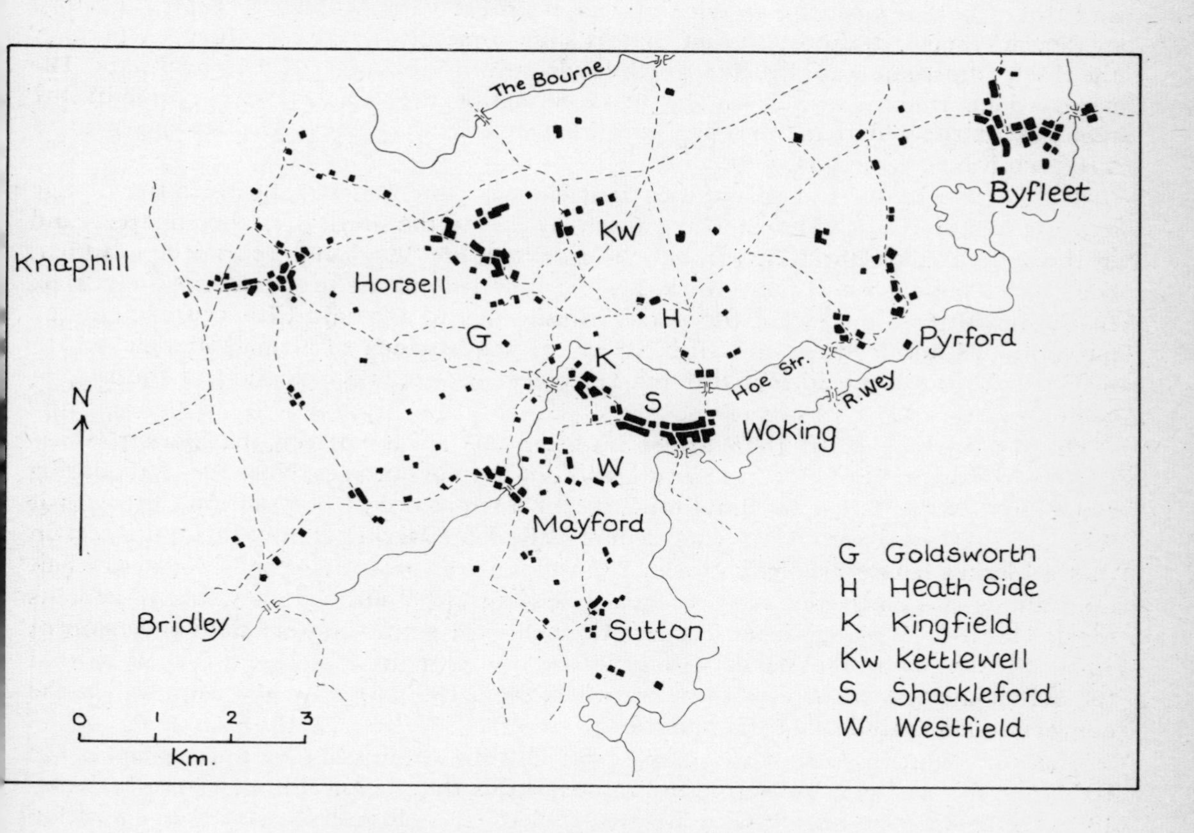

Fig. 6. Villages and Hamlets in the early 19th century.

The Villages and Hamlets

Woking, the largest of the settlements in the district was a failed market town, in size no more than a large village. It stretched along the southern edge of the terrace which separated the Wey from the Hoe Stream, on the peninsula between the two rivers. In 1800 it still had its Whit Tuesday Toy Fair, which it was said had been granted by Henry VI in 1442, but the weekly market which had been founded by Sir James Zouch in 1665 was by this time moribund.[45] The 1660s were unusually late for the granting of a market charter to such a small place, and the strong competition from nearby Guildford, a theme familiar in the history of Woking, prevented its growth. Indeed, there is reason to suppose that it was never a serious project, but was merely an attempt to increase the value and prestige of the Zouch estates.

The village was close to the River Wey, and to the east lay Woking Park Farm, occupying the angle between the main river and its tributary. The Farm included the materials taken from the demolished palace, and in the fields next to the river were the fragmentary ruins of this building, surrounded by a moat. The main road from Woking to Byfleet made a very sharp bend beside Woking Grange, at the east end of the village, and this, together with the absence of a direct route from Woking to Ripley, Pyrford or Newark make it almost certain that at some time in the 16th century, or perhaps the 15th, the road was diverted northwards, around the edge of the royal park. The narrow lane running east from the bend, alongside the Grange, thus represents the remnant of the old road, pointing towards Newark and Ripley. The Rocque map of 1762 reinforces this impression.

The nucleus of the old village was, as it is today, the half mile between the Grange and the Manor House. The ancient church lay just to the south of the main street, and in the short road, Church Street, which leads to it are 'Wey' and 'Lea' cottages which, containing some 15th-century work, are the oldest domestic properties in the village. In Church Street, too, were the parish almshouses of the mid-17th century. At the junction of Church Street and High Street the roads widen to a small triangle, which marks the site of the former tiny market place: its size is a reflection of the lack of trade (*see* Fig. 7).

On the north side of High Street tradition has always placed the Market House built by Zouch in 1665. Recent investigation of the old cottages, Nos. 193–197, during restoration work, failed to show evidence of 17th-century construction, although it was said that these were converted in the shell of the Market House. It is quite certain that a Market House *was* built, for in 1813 the building was described as 'out of repair . . . ruinous and dangerous to passengers [passers-by]'[46] and orders were given for its repair. In 1908 Woking Urban District Council gave permission for the conversion of what was said to be the Market House into a row of eight cottages.[47] It may be that the actual site was slightly to the east, where Nos. 199–203 stood, or simply that the conversion amounted to a total rebuilding.

The narrow main street also included the Old Brew House (1715), described as old fashioned for its time, by Nairn, and opposite this the Manor House, of the 16th and 17th centuries, in red brick with a Dutch gable.[48] It is close to the street, in a position which could not have been favoured in a wealthier or more sophisticated town. Locke suggests that it was built from the materials of the old riverside palace, but it predates the demolition of that building. Today its setting is marred by the busy road, waste ground and ugly modern development.

At the junction of the three roads, to Byfleet, Send and Guildford, was the *White Horse* inn, one of the oldest and most picturesque in the area. It was probably built in the 16th century, and survived, as one of the last half-timbered properties in the village, until the 1920s, when it was demolished for road-widening that has still not materialised. Its disappearance, and that of the small cottages which stood on the other two corners of the junction, tore the heart out of the old village, and destroyed the ancient character; a matter for profound regret.

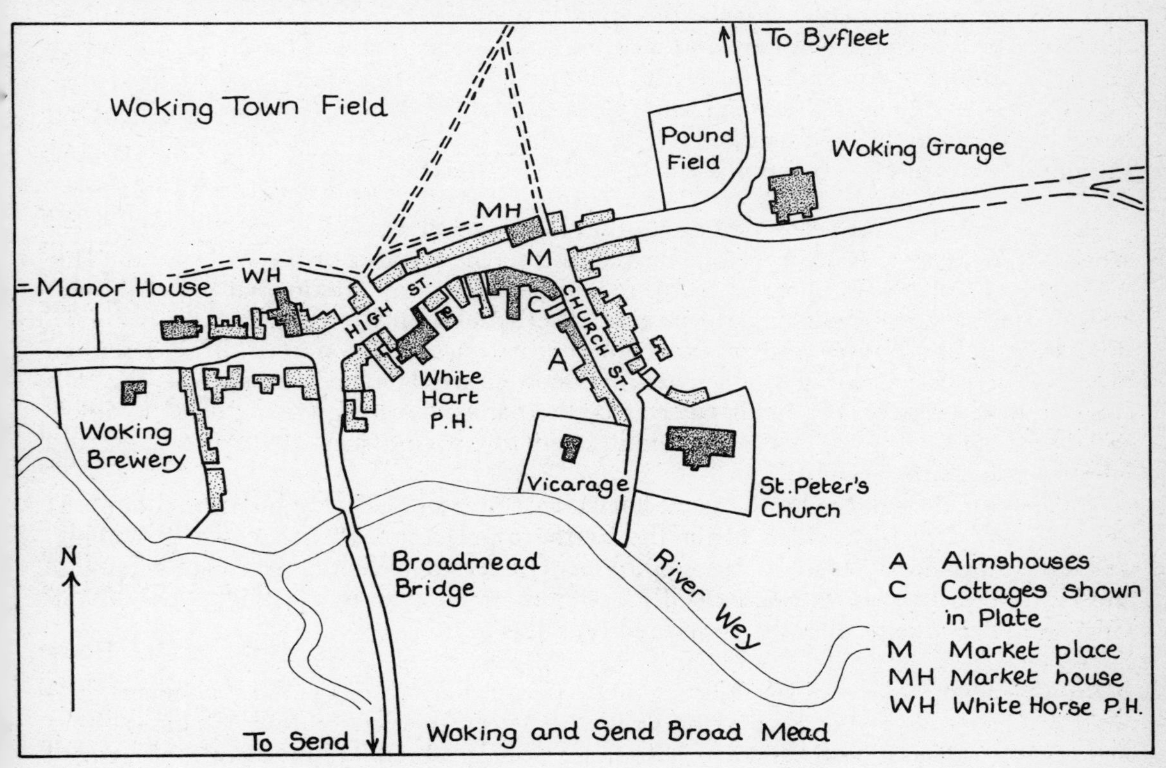

Fig. 7. Woking Village in the early 19th century.

Beyond the Manor House there was a discontinuous line of cottages and farmsteads, strung out along the road towards Kingfield. To the south were the flat floodlands of the Wey valley, to the north the open field of Woking stretching across to the Hoe Stream. The single street was then known as Town Street, although in the later years of the 19th century the present name, High Street, became usual. Originally there was a small but distinct settlement at Shackleford, consisting of a few cottages and farms on the main road, and some scattered dwellings in the fields towards Westfield and at Sundridge, on the edge of the open field. Several of the buildings of Shackleford remain, notably the half-timbered Old Cottage, beside Gloster Road, but their setting has been sadly altered since this was a rural hamlet. By the early 19th century Shackleford had coalesced physically with Woking village, although it remained a separate tithing.

Kingfield and Westfield were also distinct hamlets, grouped around the Green and the Common respectively. The tithing of Kingfield was poorer, in the early years of the century, than the rest of the parish, but it had several larger farms, including one, Howards Farm at Kingfield Green, which is almost unaltered today. At Westfield was the parish workhouse, built in the late 18th century when the workhouse system first became popular with parish authorities. It was close to the present *Cricketers Inn*, on the edge of the Common, and nearby were some strips of arable land which provided food for consumption by the inmates, and for the other poor of the parish of Woking. A similar area was set aside close to Arthurs Bridge, Goldsworth. The poor land at Westfield is now marked by the 'island' of housing in the middle of the Common between Moor Lane, Balfour Avenue and Westfield Way.

Sutton and Mayford resembled each other, being small clusters of cottages and farms around their greens. Both were on the flat and fertile terraces of the Wey and the Hoe Stream respectively, and because of their distance from Woking village and their manorial history they had a greater degree of self-containment. They had, for example, their own public houses and in the 19th century each had a smithy. Bray described Mayford in 1841 as 'a fine open space, surrounded by detached cottages . . . the hills clothed with verdure, the fields cultivated, the banks and hedgerows gay with violets and other spring flowers'[49] and he contrasted this idyllic scene with the black and inhospitable heaths around.

Sutton was dominated by the great mansion of Sutton Place, lying on the summit of the long wooded ridge which forms the southern projection of the parish of Woking. The estate provided most of the employment, exerted tremendous social, economic and cultural influence, and embraced most of the Manor, so that nearly all the inhabitants were dependent, directly, or indirectly, on its activities.

Bridley, in the extreme south-west of the parish, had no nucleated settlement, and apart from a row of cottages along Crastock Street there were few dwellings other than Bridley Manor and its farm labourers' homes. Much of the Manor of Bridley consisted of woodland and heath, and the only area of fertile land lay along the north bank of the Hoe Stream. Historically the Manor had had more in common with Pirbright and with Worplesdon than with Woking, and even in the early 19th century its orientation was in this direction.

Goldsworth and Knaphill were similarly remote from the rest of the parish, cut off by the hill ridge of Hook Heath, and by the empty commons across the northern slopes of the Hoe valley. Goldsworth consisted of a scattering of cottages on the better drained land south of the basin of Parley Brook, but it also had some small brick industries and the canal had recently been built through the area. Knaphill, at the farthest point of the parish, four miles from Woking village, was a quite separate and self-contained community, which had grown up as a result of squatter settlement carved out of the heath. It had an impressive site, looking out over the Horsell low-lands, and its confusion of smallholdings, rough cottages and tracks spilled down the slope of Anchor Hill and over the perimeter of Knaphill Common. There were several shops and trades in the village, which had come to act as a service centre for the north-west of the parish, for Bisley and for the western part of the parish of Horsell, a role that it has played ever since. In 1801 the parish had 1,340 inhabitants, of whom an estimated 750 lived in the village, Kingfield and Westfield.[50]

Horsell was a small and poor village in 1800, and the parish was the only one of the four never to have had a 'great house'. It had nothing of interest to attract the anti-quarian writers, and so there are no detailed contemporary descriptions. Manning and Bray dismiss the village as 'some few farms and scattered tenements [cottages]',[51] and many other writers ignore it completely. Horsell village, like Woking, was a single street of cottages, farms and workshops, extending across the western end of the low ridge which separated the Bourne valley from the shallow and marshy depression through which the Rive Ditch flowed. At the summit of the village street was the ancient church of St Mary the Virgin, and at the foot of the hill was the village brewery, beside Horsell Moor.

At the other end the village petered out into the untidy string of squatter dwellings which fronted the Common and Horsell Birch. The parish workhouse was at Grove Barrs or Grobarrs Farm, immediately to the east of the village behind the church. The parish also owned some cottages for the poor which were situated as far as possible from the village, at Dunford Bridge, on the border with Chertsey. In 1801 Horsell village probably had about 250 inhabitants, there being 493 in the parish as a whole.

Pyrford was a parish without a village. It had the smallest population of the four. 230 in 1801, and it would appear that there had never been a nucleated community. There were, instead, two smaller settlements, centred on the church and the green. This arrangement is not uncommon locally, and Send provides a close comparison. A group of farms, with their attendant cottages, grew up on the north and east sides of the prominent knoll on which the church stands. These farms form a little community which has remained unaltered in its essential appearance for over three centuries, and thus represents a unique survival within the Woking area, 'a genuine village, not even a preserved one'.[52]

Nearly a mile to the north-east were more cottages and smallholdings, along two sides of the triangular green. The village pound was to the north of this, bordering Lock Lane, and the tiny parish workhouse on the west side, behind the cottages that still survive here. More farms and labourers' dwellings lay in a straggling line along the road to Byfleet Corner. Pyrford Green, too, has shown a remarkable capacity to endure in the present century, and today has the largest concentration of listed buildings in the borough, with the exception of Old Woking village.[53]

Byfleet was the second of the four villages in size and importance, with about 350 inhabitants in 1801. It was situated on the lower terrace of the River Wey, just above the normal flood levels, but the whole area was damp and low-lying. The village itself was intersected by the ditches and drainage channels which criss-crossed the floodplain, and one flowed through the centre, close to the line of High Road. To the north, east and south were water-meadows and branches of the river. The church lay to the south, well beyond the edge of the village: the isolation of the church from the main settlement is frequently found in West Surrey, Bisley and Windlesham being other examples. East of the church was Byfleet Park, with the large Manor House close to the river.

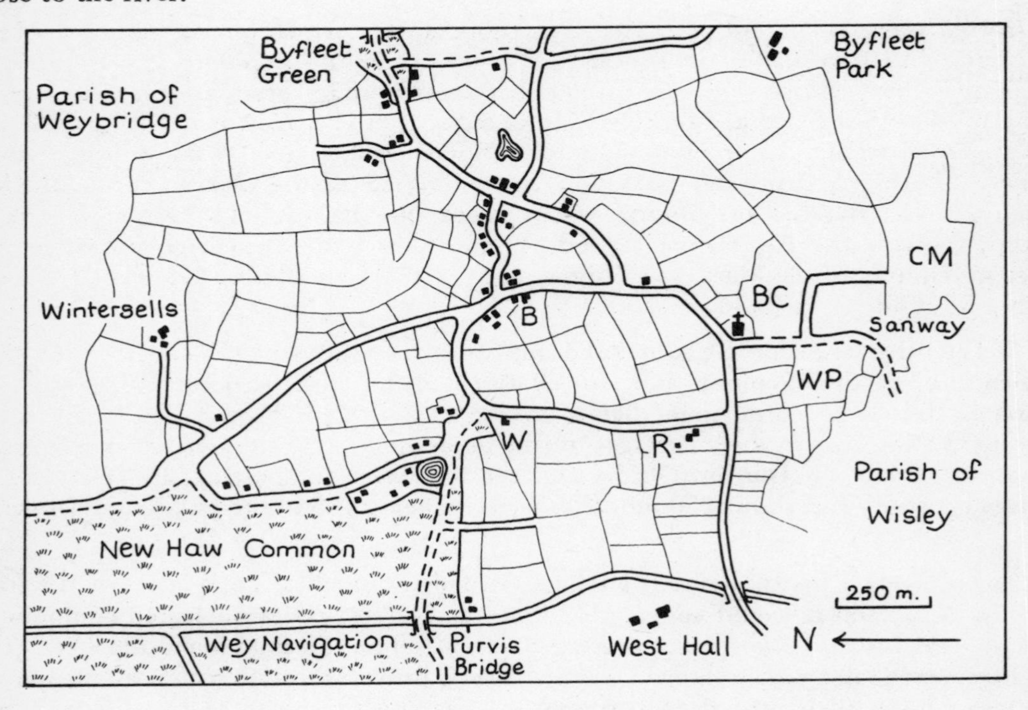

Fig. 8. Byfleet Village on the Eve of Enclosure.

B	Brewery	CM	Byfleet common meadow	W	Workhouse
BC	Bennett's Corner (open field)	R	Rectory	WP	Wisley Prae (meadow)

Byfleet Mill was north of the Park, on its large island, and below that was the ancient Plough Bridge, except for the bridge at Weybridge the last crossing point of the river before it reached the Thames. The village green lay around both ends of the bridge, for until 1933 the entire western slope of St George's Hill was in the parish of Byfleet. At the opposite end of the village was another green, an extension of New Haw Common, which was no more than an enlarged piece of roadside waste projecting from the Common along High Road and Rectory Lane. The village pond was in the angle formed by Chertsey Road and Parvis Road, occupying part of this second green (*see* Fig. 8).

The village itself comprised a discontinuous line of houses and cottages, with several farms, along the twisting main street, now High Road, and along the Chertsey Road and Rectory Lane. There were the usual local craft trades, including the village smithy in Rectory Lane, and the Byfleet brewery was at the junction of Oyster Land and High Road, beside the present *Plough Inn*. The parish workhouse was in Rectory Lane, which in the early 19th century was usually known as Workhouse Lane. The building survived until the late 1960s (Plate XVI) and the inmates worked on the cultivation of the workhouse allotment, which was in the area between Rectory Lane and Brewery Lane.

In 1800 the four parishes which today comprise the Borough of Woking had reached the end of their centuries of rural calm. Changes were taking place which, with quickening speed, were to transform their character and appearance. Within 40 years the railway was to end their seclusion for ever. Already the Basingstoke Canal had bisected the district, and the Parliamentary Bill for the enclosure of the Manor of Sutton was imminent. These fundamental changes are described in succeeding chapters.

Chapter Three

THE INITIAL CHANGES: 1800-1850

The Basingstoke Canal

IN THE LATE 1770s businessmen and landowners in North Hampshire promoted a canal from the small market-town of Basingstoke to the Thames, via the Wey Navigation at Byfleet.[1] The route lay through extensive heathlands and it was hoped that the waterway would stimulate agricultural development in these areas. There was little opposition to the plan, so the Bill had an easy passage through Parliament, receiving Royal Assent on 15 May 1778.

The end of the war with the United States was followed by a recession, and the proprietors found it impossible to raise the necessary capital. It was not until 1787 that serious efforts were made to begin work and only in October 1788 that John Pinkerton was awarded the contract for building the canal. He started immediately, the first soil being turned at Woodham, a mile from the junction with the Wey Navigation; but progress was slow, and the first section was not opened until the middle of 1791. 'The first tolls were collected on twenty-eight tons of merchandise carried from the Wey Navigation to Horsell.'[2] A year later the canal was navigable to Pirbright, and the final section, to Basingstoke, was opened on 4 September 1794.

From the Wey Navigation the Basingstoke Canal followed the damp valley of the Rive Ditch through Woodham, and then crossed Woking Common to Arthurs Bridge, where it entered the basin of Parley Brook. A natural gap between Hook Hill and Knap Hill at St Johns led into another marshy vale through Brookwood, when it rose to the great cutting at Deepcut. The canal climbed from 68 feet above sea-level at the junction to 158 feet at Brookwood, and accomplished this with 14 locks, six in Woodham, five at Goldsworth and St Johns and three at Brookwood.

It is usually supposed that the canal had no influence upon the area, but this is not so. Although it passed through uninhabited heathlands, and did not fulfil the aim of its promoters in reclaiming them for farming, there were some changes. The demand for bricks to build bridges and lock chambers stimulated local production, because it was uneconomic to transport this low value commodity over long distances. Vine states that Pinkerton advertised for sub-contractors to supply bricks, and that they were told that 'Mr. Wildgoose of Horsell would know the places where clay could be found'.[3] The kilns around St Johns, Knaphill and Goldsworth were expanded, and flourished; the last, at Knaphill, did not close until the Second World War.

The canal provided cheap bulk transport, encouraging a number of concerns to begin to import coal and chalk into the area, for domestic fuel and for agriculture. This reduced fuel prices, and turf began to decline as the major fuel for the poor.

The wharves where these commodities were unloaded, at Woodham, Wheatsheaf Bridge, Arthurs Bridge and Goldsworth, attracted limited development, but more significant was the impetus given to the growth of St Johns; for the wharf at Kiln Bridge, the *Rowbarge* public house, and the brick kilns were the beginnings of the district. There were only eight bridges between Byfleet and Brookwood, and only two in the area which was later to become the centre of Woking. The shape of the town which grew up along its banks was thus substantially affected by the presence of the canal.

It is well known that the canal was a financial disaster. Building costs were over 60 per cent higher than the original estimate, and from the start the company was burdened with debts. Attempts were made, between 1795 and 1815, to extend to the south coast, whilst in 1801 a branch to Bagshot was proposed, but these projects were abortive. The canal settled down to a quiet and highly unprofitable existence as an agricultural carrier. The maximum traffic was in the 1830s, when it was used to carry construction materials for the new railway, but as soon as this was opened the competition led to a rapid decline in canal business. In 1859 the arrears of interest on the original debt of £32,000 were said to amount to £105,000, and in 1866 the Basingstoke Canal Navigation Company was finally forced to go into liquidation.

During the next 44 years there were six owners, all of whom found the canal to be hopelessly uneconomic. The Woking, Aldershot & Basingstoke Canal Co. (1896) had some success, freighting timber to Spantons' and Brewsters' wharves at Woking and to Basingstoke, and profits were anticipated, when disaster struck in September 1899. The bed of the canal at Horsell Moor collapsed into a tunnel being driven beneath, as part of the Woking Council sewerage scheme (*see* Chapter 6). Traffic was suspended for six months, and this ended any hope of viability.

In 1910–13 there was a lengthy dispute between William Carter, the latest of the owners, and Woking Council over the liability for repairing and reconstructing six of the bridges, which were in a dangerous state. The Council obtained a private Act of Parliament authorising it to undertake the work and recover the costs from the owners.[4] This was challenged in the High Court, and the Council, although it did the work in 1923, never received any money, not least because nobody connected with the canal had any to give.

By 1914 the canal was semi-derelict, with long stretches silted and weed-choked, and bridges, buildings and locks decaying and crumbling. The last traffic above Horsell was in 1921, and thereafter the only cargoes were coal to Woking gasworks and timber from London Docks to local wharves. In 1936 the Woking District Gas Company ceased to manufacture its own gas, and the canal lost its last heavy traffic, the 14,000 tons of coal which had been delivered each year to the gasworks. Regular timber traffic ended in 1947, and on 15 March 1949 the final load was carried to Spantons' Yard beside Chertsey Road. After 157 years commercial business on the canal had come to an end, and it appeared as if the canal had died too.

Nurserying

Another change which had its origins in the 18th century was the expansion of the nursery and horticulture business in west Woking. The sandy soils are, when suitably dressed, exceptionally well suited to gardening. In the 1750s this became clear to nurserymen who were being displaced from East London by the outward growth of the city. Some moved to West Surrey to carry on their work, and at the same time local farming families realised that this represented a way of making use of the hitherto barren sandy soils. They began to diversify from agriculture into horticulture. A century later Woking had become one of the foremost centres of horticulture in Europe.

Goldsworth Nursery, perhaps the best known of all, was founded in 1760 by James Turner, on land near the foot of Goldsworth Hill, near Harelands.[5] Early in the next century it was bought by Robert Donald, a specialist in rare and unusual trees and shrubs. He was a friend of the highly influential landscape architect and designer John Claudius Loudon, and used his connections to build up a profitable business, supplying trees and shrubs for fashionable residences. He later developed a reputation as something of a landscape specialist himself, and was responsible for the splendid planting of Brookwood Cemetery.

From the early 1790s the Waterer family of Knaphill bought land around their existing farm to use as nurseries. In 1802, for example, 'Michael Waterer of Knaphill nurseryman, bought Ryde Heron for £132 5s. (£135.25)'.[6] This land is today remembered in a street-name. The family eventually acquired most of Lower Knaphill, around Whitfield and Barrs Lane. The Jackmans' nursery business was founded by William Jackman (1763–1840) and then taken over by his two sons, Henry (who left in 1832) and George.[7] The latter built up the extensive nursery gardens in Mayford and Goldsworth, and in 1863 produced his most famous creation, the superb purple *Clematis Jackmanii*, which became popular throughout the world.

Brayley gives a lyrical description of the nurseries of Woking, as they were about 1840. Of Waterers' at Knaphill he says that 'it comprises about [120] acres of ground which were enclosed from the bog and heath and progressively stocked with numerous exotics from America, which now flourish with even more than their native beauty and luxuriance. . . . In May and June one entire mass of blossoms which perfumes the air for miles around'. There were also nurseries in the vicinity of Horsell village, where Rosehill Avenue and Nursery Close are today. Brayley noted that the nursery of Henry Cobbett was famous for its roses, and that 'many persons visit them in the summer season, for the purpose of seeing the flowers in a high state of perfection'.[8] Market-gardening was rather less important, although there were some specialised growers. In July 1867, for example, Edward Ryde recorded in his diary that he and his wife had driven with a friend 'to the Strawberry Gardens beyond the Hermitage'.[9]

During the 1850s and 1860s there was a temporary decline in the nursery business, such that in 1870 the formerly flourishing Goldsworth Nursery had shrunk to only 24 acres, 'weedy . . . in bad repair . . . and of small importance'.[10] In 1877 Walter Slocock, a friend and protégé of Anthony Waterer, bought the nursery and began its revival. By the time of his death in 1929 there were 420 acres and 161 employees, and other nursery owners in the area had seen similar growth. They had made use of the canal to bring large quantities of manure from the stables of London.

Later in the 19th century the value of the land itself increased rapidly, as the town of Woking grew, and the district became a popular residential area. Between 1880 and

1939 large parts of the older nursery lands were sold for building, and the owners instead acquired new property in the damp lowlands around Littlewick and Knaphill for their nurseries. For example, in 1893 on the death of George Jackman, the extensive sites on both sides of St Johns Hill Road were sold by his family. The sale catalogue made use of the former role as a nursery: 'situated on high ground, commanding most beautiful Scenery, and adorned with fine specimen Conifers, Deciduous and other Flowering Trees, and Shrubs of Mature Growth'.[11]

By the end of the 19th century nurserying had become a vital part of the economy of Woking. In Mayford, St Johns and Knaphill extensive areas were occupied by plantations of shrubs and specimen trees, by rose gardens and greenhouses, and by colourful beds of herbaceous plants. The Woking nurseries had played a major part in introducing to English gardens such familiar and beautiful plants as the clematis, rhododendron, azalea and magnolia.

The Enclosures

The exhortations of the agricultural improvers in the 1790s had the desired effect, and the early years of the 19th century saw, in Surrey, a period of parliamentary enclosure. In the Woking area three Acts were passed for that purpose after 1800: they involved the manors of Byfleet and Weybridge (1800), Sutton next Wokeing (1803) and Pyrford and Chertsey (1805).[12] Parliamentary (as distinct from private) enclosure was authorised by Private Act following a petition from the owners of two-thirds or three-quarters of the enclosed land in a parish or manor. By it all common rights were abolished and the unenclosed lands were parcelled out amongst the holders of these and amongst landowners.

For the Byfleet enclosure there have survived the Minutes of the Commissioners appointed by the Act to plan and implement the scheme, and these may serve to illustrate the procedures involved.[13] The Commissioners, of whom there were three, first met on 27 June 1800 at the *Ship Inn*, Weybridge, and during the next six months heard the complaints of those who expected to suffer from enclosure, and the claims of those who wanted an allocation of land. They also went to the areas concerned and inspected the proposed new boundaries before giving their approval to the plan.

These tasks completed, on 7 December 1801 they 'directed that certain Parcels of the Commons & Waste Lands in the Parishes of Weybridge & Byfleet be sold by Auction for the purpose of defraying the expenses pursuant to the Act'. Three auctions raised £1,915 17s. 0d. (£1,915.85) from 92 acres, and this sum paid for the costs of surveying, the expenses of the Commissioners, and probably gave them some profit. There were 'professional' commissioners who undertook dozens of enclosures, and became rich on the proceeds: one of them, Thomas Hopcraft of Northamptonshire, was involved with the Sutton next Wokeing Act.

During 1802 the Commissioners finalised their allocations and directed that from 1 June the common rights in the two manors were extinguished, and legal title was vested in the new owners. Orders were made on 29 June 1802 'for removal of Trees, Manure and every sort of Rubbish lying and being on the lands allotted to the sev^{l} proprietors'. The remainder of their work was concerned with the implementation of the plan. The highway surveyors for the relevant parishes undertook to lay out new or improved roads and on 17 November 1802 orders were given for the stopping up of all footpaths across the former commons. In March 1803 the final announcement instructed the new owners to fence and enclose all their lands before 1 July.

Allocating the Land

The methods of allocation varied, but there were some general features. The lord of the manor usually received, as of right, one-sixteenth of the lands to be alloted, and as a landowner he would receive part of the general distribution. If, as was usual, he was wealthy he might also buy some or all of the lands sold to raise money. He would thus be a major beneficiary of enclosure, and was frequently the leading petitioner for the original Act. The tithes on the new lands were often commuted on enclosure, and to compensate for the loss of income the Church was usually awarded lands from the former waste to provide revenue. The parish was customarily given land for a gravel pit, to provide road-mending materials, and if there was sufficient concern the Commissioners might reserve some of the waste for the poor, to provide for their necessities, particularly fuel. In Pyrford, for example, the Common owes its survival to the reservation of 51 acres for 'Fuel Allotments for the Poor of Pýrford Parish', whilst at West Byfleet the land which is now the Camphill Road recreation ground was similarly protected (*see* Fig. 10).

The remaining land was then divided, roughly in proportion to the existing land holdings of each freeholder, with small plots being awarded to the holders of common rights. The table below shows the details of each Act. The wide disparity in costs is explained by the method of sale: in Byfleet there was an auction, in Sutton a private sale, and in Pyrford the land was so poor that it was sold at 'give-away' prices.

Table 6. The Three Enclosure Acts[14]

Allotted to:	*Byfleet (1800)*[a]	*Pyrford (1805)*[b]	*Sutton (1801)*
Parish sand and gravel pits	2	16	2
Parish poor lands	49	70	—
In lieu of tithes	114	151	51
Sale for expenses	92	423	93
General distribution	494	803	191
Total enclosed, to nearest acre	751	1,463	337
Amount raised by sale	£1,916	£2,510	£1,390
Average price per acre	£20 18s.	£5 18s.	£15 0s.

a. Excluding Weybridge, enclosed by same Act.
b. Including 256 acres in New Haw, not in Borough of Woking.

The differences in the distribution of the lands reflect important variations in the character of the manors. The contrast between Sutton and Byfleet is particularly marked. Sutton was a 'closed' manor, one in which the lord and his estate had a dominating influence, providing most of the employment and occupying much of the cultivable land, so that there was a semi-feudal society. In Sutton the Lord of the

Manor, John Webb Weston, was by far the greatest beneficiary of enclosure, as well as one of its instigators, and few others received any allocation of valuable lands. Many cottagers and tenants, who had formerly exercised rights over the common-lands, received little or no compensation, and much distress was caused. The following anonymous poem, written about, although almost certainly not by, a cottager of Sutton Green, eloquently expresses the grievances and bitterness of one who was dispossessed by enclosure. The poem reveals, in particular, a very strong antipathy towards John Webb Weston, the architect of the enclosure, and although written by someone far too literate to have been the cottager in question it represents accurately the feelings of those involved.

THE COTTAGERS COMPLAINT ON THE INCLOSURE OF SUTTON GREEN[15]

1. How sweetly did the moment glide
How happy were the days
When no sad fear my breast annoyed
Or e'er disturbed my ease
Hard fate that I should be compelled
My fond abode to lose
Where threescore years in peace I dwelt
And wish my life to close

2. My eaves are few my stock is small
Yet from my little store
I find enough for natures call
Nor would I ask for more
That word Inclosure to my heart
Such evil doth bespeak
I fear I with my all must part
A fresh employment seek

3. What little of the spacious plain
Should power to me consign
For want of means I cant obtain
Would not long time be mine
The Stout may combat fortunes frown
Not dread the rich and great
The young men fly to Market Town
But where can I retreat

4. What kind of feelings must that man
Within his mind possess
Who from an avaritious Plan
His neighbours would Distress
Then soon in pity the every case
To reasons ear incline
For on his heart it stamps disgrace
Who form'd the base design

Chorus, after each verse:

Oh the time the happy time
Which in my lot I've spent
I wish the Church-yard was his doom
Who murders my content.

In contrast, Byfleet was an 'open' village, without a resident lord, with a diversity of landowners and occupations, and free of the feudal atmosphere which characterised Sutton. Here the lord, King George III (The Crown) was able to acquire only 23 per cent of the waste, and his son Frederick, Duke of York (soon to be granted the lordship) a further 13 per cent, a total of only 36 per cent of the newly enclosed lands. In Byfleet the lands were more equitably divided, so that the small and medium landowners received a fair share, and the parish poor were granted 6 per cent of the newly enclosed lands for turf-cutting and grazing.

In all three manors the fragments granted to cottagers in compensation for lost common rights were probably quite inadequate, particularly where the soils were

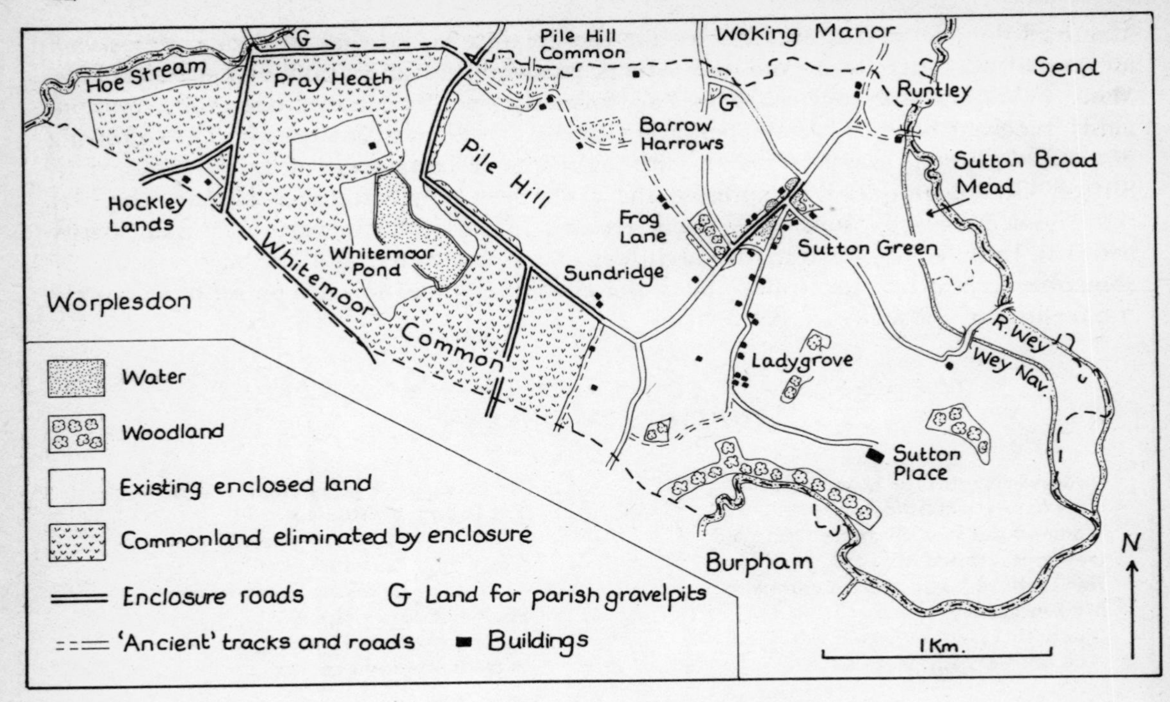

Fig. 9. Enclosure in the Manor of Sutton.

poor. The table below shows the distribution of the land between the various categories of owner.

Table 7. The Distribution of Enclosed Lands

	Byfleet		*Pyrford and Woodham*		*Sutton*	
Lord of the Manor	23%		46%		63%	
Vicar for tithes	15%		6%		15%	
Parish lands	8%		5%		2%	
Large allocations[a]	13.5%	(1)	14.5%	(4)	—	
Medium allocations[b]	26.5%	(9)	24%	(19)	4%	(1)
Small allocations[c]	9.5%	(15)	3.5%	(15)	14%	(7)
Fragments[d]	4.5%	(12)	1%	(15)	1.5%	(13)

a. Over 50 acres to one individual excluding the Lord of the Manor or Vicar.
b. 10–49 acres. c. 2–9 acres. d. Less than 2 acres.
(Figures in brackets refer to the number of recipients of land in each category.)

The Commissioners attempted to concentrate the fragments in particular areas. In Pyrford, the Townsley and Walsham Meads, Coldharbour Lane and Woodham Lane were used, whilst in Sutton the small parcels were carved out of Pile Hill Common and the long, narrow strips of former roadside waste. This was not for the convenience of the cottagers – Woodham Lane, for example, was distant from dwellings – but because it solved the problem of disposing of small or awkward corners of waste. It also placed in single ownership the substantial areas of heath and moor where fencing and improving could be too expensive for the smallholder.

Thus the expanses of Pyrford and Woodham Heaths, between the Woking road and the Bourne, were almost entirely given to or bought by Lord King, whilst in Sutton the Webb Weston family acquired most of Whitmoor and Pray Heath. These families were able to add to their estates hundreds of acres of land which were now denied to the poor.

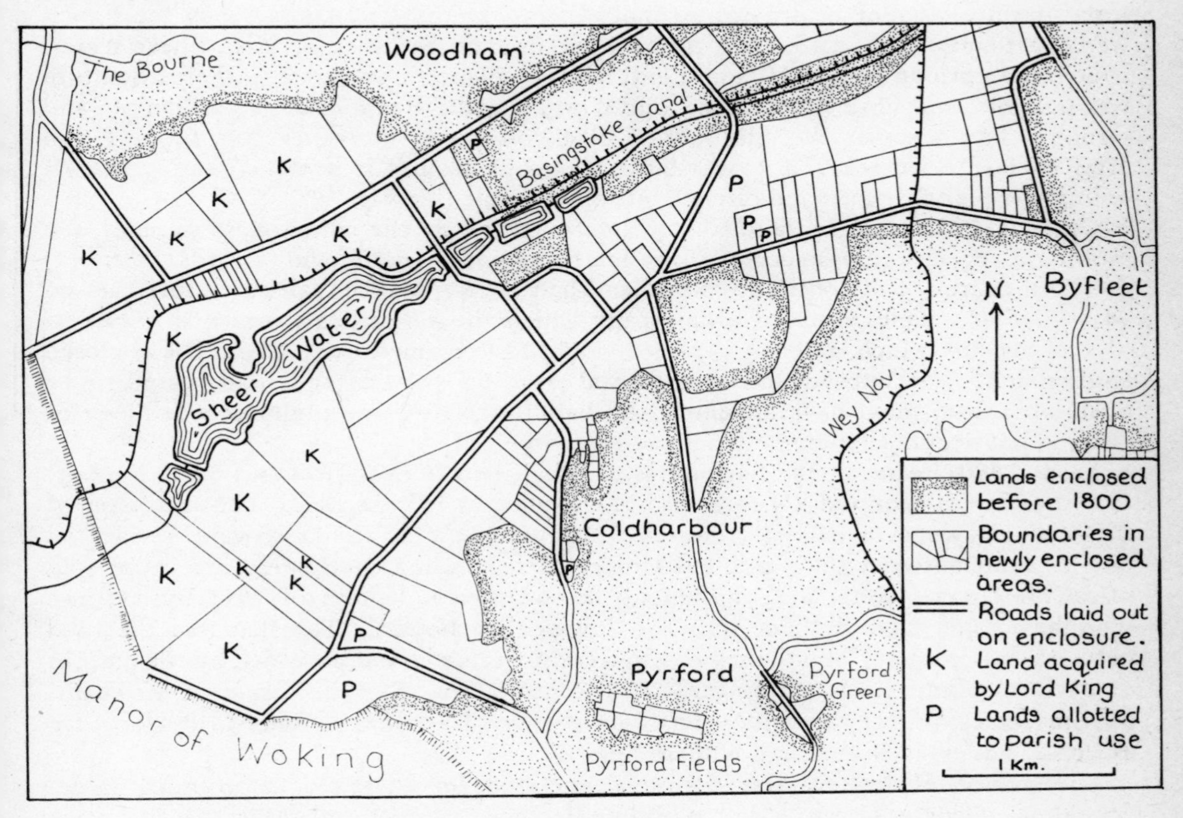

Fig. 10. The Enclosure of Byfleet, Pyrford and Woodham.

The Geography and Landscape of Enclosure

Across the empty heaths the surveyors plotted straight roads and geometric property boundaries, which bore little relation to the topography. Some existing tracks were adopted, straightened and widened, but in several cases the roads were completely new additions to the network. East Hill was one of the latter, laid out by the Pyrford highway surveyor along the parish boundary with Woking, whilst Prey Heath Road, Old Woking Road and Woodham Lane are examples of older routes improved after enclosure. There is a sharp contrast between the first of these and the adjacent winding section of Guildford Road, past Beech Hill in the unenclosed manor of Woking.

The value of the enclosed land for agriculture was far less than had been anticipated. With the end of the Napoleonic Wars much of the economic incentive for improvement faded away, and since the soils were poor and acid the usefulness of the former heaths was limited. The Weston family undertook improvements in Sutton manor, and spent large sums on draining the district around Whitmoor Pond, but the only land uses which were economically viable were rough grazing, pine plantations and some pasture; a poor return for so much effort. In the Rive Ditch valley the results were particularly unsatisfactory. Lord King drained the shallow lake, Sheer Water, which had covered some 110 acres, and laid out plantations, but no other agriculture was possible, and until after the Second World War the area remained waterlogged and scrubby. To the south, the hillslopes of Blackdown were more suited to farming, and after enclosure Norfolk Farm was built here, but around it stretched large tracts of unimproved land, fenced and ditched but unworkable (*see* Fig. 10).

Gradually, because the land was no longer grazed by the commoners' animals, the moorland vegetation was succeeded by birch and willow scrub, and towards the end of the 19th century full coniferous woodland had developed. The tall pines, interspersed with heathery glades, formed a landscape which the Edwardians regarded as typical of Woking but which a century earlier would have seemed quite alien. The enclosed land, much of it unused and unimproved over 50 years after it had ceased to be common waste, must have appeared as a liability to its owners, almost worthless for farming but needing expensive fences and ditches.

From 1880, however, the beginnings of urban growth in Byfleet and Pyrford meant that these areas acquired a greatly increased value, as building land. The successors of the original owners reaped rich rewards as this became a favoured high-value residential district, and between then and 1939 most of the unimproved enclosures were sold off. Golf courses were laid out among the heather and pines of West Byfleet and Woodham, and around them sprawled low-density housing. The shape of the road network and property boundaries was to a considerable extent governed by the pattern of enclosures and roads of the early 19th century, and even the names of the roads, in some cases, reflect the landowners who received land at that time: in Pyrford, for example, Susannah Bolton and William Tegg (*see* Fig. 19).

The manor of Bridley was privately enclosed by its three landowners, James Boudillon, George Greenfield and John Heather, in 1820–40. Most of the work involved fencing large plots on the former waste and here, as elsewhere, the poor soils discouraged serious agricultural use. The first Ordnance Survey map (1816) shows most of the area north of Berry Lane as unenclosed. In 1842 the Woking Tithe Map indicates that it had been enclosed, but it was still described as 'rough' or 'waste', whilst on the eve of the First World War the Ordnance Survey showed that much of the area was still woodland or rough grazing land.[16]

Woking and Horsell manors were never formally enclosed. This explains the fortunate survival of the attractive heaths and commons in Horsell, Westfield, Mayford and Brookwood. The London Necropolis Company acquired all common rights in the manor of Woking in 1854 (*see* Chapter Four) so that the effect on the poor was similar, but the authorising Act did not oblige the company to subdivide and enclose the land. This process was therefore undertaken in a piecemeal fashion, in the area around Woking station, as the new town grew. The commons in the south of the manor, which were less subject to pressure for building, were not enclosed, and survive. In Horsell there is no evidence that enclosure was ever seriously considered, and the time-honoured method of small-scale, piecemeal reclamation from waste continued into the present century.

Quite why there was no parliamentary enclosure in these two manors is not clear. Both were 'open' villages, without a dominant landowner and with absentee Onslow Lords of the Manor, yet Byfleet, which was similar, *was* enclosed. The interesting survival of the open field in Woking until the end of the last century does suggest that there was a strong commoners' interest in the manor, which may have been able to prevent early enclosure, and which undoubtedly fought hard, and with some success, for adequate compensation from the Necropolis Company in 1853–56.

The Unrest of 1830

During the autumn of 1830 West Surrey was involved in the civil disturbances which swept the countryside from Kent to Dorset, beginning in East Kent in the summer, and spreading west into Surrey and Sussex. Ricks and farm buildings were burned, machinery smashed, and labourers assembled in violent riots and demonstrations. Early in November there were incidents of arson against farm property in Byfleet, Egham, Cobham and Guildford.

Tithe day was traditionally 19 November: at that time the payments for the forthcoming year were set, and because the payment of tithes was so unpopular it was inevitable that, in the atmosphere of discontent which prevailed, there would be trouble. On that day in 1830 a large number of labourers and small farmers gathered in Woking village to oppose tithe payment. They were led by a man who wore a smock-frock, and shouted such slogans, as 'To Dorking! To Dorking!'. The meeting was then addressed by the radical local magistrate, Henry Drummond (later M.P. for the area, *see* Chapter Four), and he persuaded the men to disperse without violence.

Some of them later explained that they had been intending to march to Dorking to free prisoners held in the county gaol there, and that they had been forced to demonstrate by men from Horsham, of whom they were very much afraid. Horsham was a notorious centre of radical feeling, and presumably agents had been sent to Woking for the purpose, but it is apparent that there was a good deal of genuine, if non-political, local discontent: the use of the 'Horsham connection' seems to have been an effective means of exonerating the local men from involvement, and thereby avoiding severe punishment for riotous assembly.

In the Woking area unemployment was high, and increasing, wages were low, and the price of basic foodstuffs had risen sharply, enough to explain the underlying dissatisfaction. Woking Vestry officers had for some years been expressing their concern over these matters, and there is little doubt that these were responsible for the potentially violent confrontation in November 1830.[17]

Local Government in the Early 19th Century

Until the mid-19th century the parish was the major unit of local government: it was administered by the parish vestry, a 'council' which was so-called because it originally held its meetings in the vestry of the church. Vestries were, at least nominally, open to every ratepayer, and also included church and parish officers. Their business was very varied, and ranged from the administration of the Poor Laws and the upkeep of the highways, through the maintenance of the church fabric, to such miscellaneous matters as the payments for 'Taking Sparrows 6d pr Dozzen from Michs. to Lady Day & 3d. do from Lady Day to Michs.' recorded in Woking Vestry minutes for January 1820.[18] It is unfortunate that in the Woking area almost all the documents and minutes of the four parish vestries have been lost, whether through carelessness, ignorance or the ravages of time: only Woking Vestry minutes for 1818–30 appear to survive.

Except in the smaller parishes the connection with the church was, by the early 19th century, tenuous. Woking Vestry occasionally met in the church, but as if to emphasise secularity it was more usual to meet in a public house: the *Bird in Hand* at Mayford, or the *White Horse*, *White Hart* or *Crown and Anchor*, Woking village. Because so much business was connected with the poor, the Workhouse was also used.[19]

From the limited evidence available it seems that Woking Vestry was anxious to provide food and lodging of a reasonable standard for the inmates, although there was reliance, too, upon the generosity of individuals. In September 1818 'The late Mr. Brisks' willed 'a Feather Bed, Stead & Covering to the Children in the Workhouse',[20] and in January 1830 Mr. Robertson of Hoe Bridge gave '£5 for Bread for the Poor of this Parish at this Inclement Season of the Year'.[21] The Vestry made grants to the poor for clothing: 'Towards Shoes', 'for a shirt', 'Wm Baileys two Boys a Roundfrock each'.[22] Each year it advertised for the supply of 'Meat, Drink, Clothing and Lodging to those poor Persons as shall be from time to time in the Workhouse',[23] whilst in 1826 it asked for 'Persons willing to bake Bread of the Best Household Flour' for consumption there.[24]

The poor were often housed in cottages in the parish, as the above extract, which refers to 'Lodging', suggests: the Vestry paid the rent, but the private citizen accommodated the pauper. There were also cottages owned by the parish for this purpose. Horsell Vestry owned five cottages at Dunford Bridge, Byfleet, three at Camp Hill, and Pyrford two, on the edge of the Common. In October 1818 the Woking Vestry considered going into the housing market, by 'Building Cottages for the Reception of Parishioners', but it is not known whether this early form of council housing was in fact adopted.[25]

Woking Vestry regularly assessed the number of people who were eligible for poor relief. There were fluctuations according to the season, but from the early 1820s the underlying trend was upwards. In May 1819 there were 164 people, of whom 57 lived in Kingfield tithing alone. As the population of the parish was then about 1,750, it is clear that almost 10 per cent were so poor as to need assistance.[26] Ten years later there were 246 receiving poor relief, some 13 per cent of the total, and an Assistant Overseer was appointed 'To manage the Poor of the Parish, their Labour & the Workhouse'.[27]

Medical needs were not neglected. George Daborn of Woking agreed in September 1820 to attend the poor, charging the parish £2 for a birth and £1 5s. (£1.25) for a death.[28] In January 1822 William Freeman undertook, for £45 a year, to be 'Doctor for the Poor within 7 miles of the Town of Woking . . . including Broken Bones &c (but with the Exclusion of Midwifery)'.[29] The dangers from epidemics amongst the ill-fed, ill-housed and overcrowded poor were considerable. In the summer of 1830 Woking Vestry bought Thomas Sanders' house in Westfield for £65 to use as an isolation hospital, 'the Parish Officers having recently felt the dangers & inconvenience arising from the want of such a necessary asylum'.[30]

Before 1820 Woking Vestry had regularly hired out the able-bodied inmates of the workhouse to local farmers, to provide cheap labour and to reduce the rate burden. In October 1826 it was decided to extend the scheme to include those on relief but living outside the workhouse. 'Weekly Parish Meetings should be regularly held . . . by Tything in Rotation . . . or a Committee of a Given Number of Persons (should) meet on Tuesday in every week for the Purpose of furnishing Employment to the Different Labouring Poor who may Apply for it at Such Meetings'.[31] Thereafter, under the system known as 'out relief', the poor were regularly given such parish work as 'Diggin Gravel' and 'Diggin Ditches on the Roads'.[32] The problem of unemployment was not solved by this, and in the late 1820s the Vestry frequently expressed its concern over this matter, which, because it increased the number of paupers, was responsible for constant rises in the rates. It was an important underlying cause of the civil unrest in the area during 1830.

In January 1822 Woking applied for Select Vestry status under an Act of 1819: this meant that the existing system, whereby any ratepayer could attend meetings and vote, was abolished and replaced by what was in effect a committee of certain ratepayers and the officers of the parish. It was thus possibly less democratic, but potentially more efficient. The Select Vestry came into operation in December 1822, and by 1826 was meeting almost every week, because business had grown so rapidly.[33]

The Poor Law Amendment Act of 1834 deprived the parish vestries of their powers over poor relief and the operation of workhouses, and transferred these to Poor Law Unions, groups of parishes controlled by Boards of Guardians. Woking, because the old hundreds were used as the basis of the Unions, came within the Guildford Union, which built a new workhouse at Stoke. Byfleet, Horsell and Pyrford came within the Chertsey Union, which also built a central workhouse, at Ottershaw. The parish workhouses were closed, and reverted to parish property, although in October 1839 the Chertsey Guardians 'agreed to take the Poor House at Pyrford for the use of the Women and Children suffering from Opthalmia [*sic*]'.[34] The loss of the powers over poor relief was the first step towards the reform of the vestry system and the creation of a more efficient local government system, a process which was not completed until the end of the 19th century.

The Coming of the Railway

The first three decades of the century thus saw some major changes in the Woking area. Most of the open heaths and commons disappeared in the south and east of the district, whilst in the west the rise of nurserying for the first time gave the area a significant 'export' business, and increased its links with the capital. The business of local government became more complex, and in 1830 the riots and disturbances which swept Southern England brought Woking, for the first time since the 16th century, into contact with national political trends. More important than any of these, though, was the railway to Southampton.

In February 1831 plans were announced for a line between London and Southampton, with a branch from Basingstoke to Bristol and large new docks at Southampton itself.[35] The original plan proved to be over-ambitious, and in 1834 a revised scheme was submitted to Parliament, involving only the main line, and without the branch or docks. It received the strong support of army, navy and commercial interests; in the summer the London & Southampton Railway Act was given Royal Assent. A renewed proposal for the branch was defeated in Parliament a year later, after competition from the infant Great Western Railway, and so the main line was the only part of the original scheme completed.

Work began in the autumn of 1834, and proved to be much more expensive than estimated. Francis, writing in 1851, noted that although the original capital raised was £2,000,000 the eventual cost was almost £2,500,000, more than twice the intended sum.[36] The line crossed the Wey at Brooklands on a long embankment and the original (1831) route then followed the Basingstoke Canal, in places running along the bank, and crossed it four times in the Woking area.[37] In the 1834 Act this line was altered to run about half a mile south of the canal, to avoid bridging costs and to ease gradients. In consequence there were very substantial engineering works. Goldsworth Hill, a spur of Hook Heath, was cut through by a deep and long cutting, in which rare marine fossils were discovered, whilst massive and impressive embankments crossed the shallow valleys, just west of Woking station, at St Johns and between Brookwood Lye and Pirbright. These works were a barrier to north–south movement in the district, and are controlling factors in the road pattern of Woking.

This route was selected in preference to a more direct southern course along the Wey and Itchen valleys. As built, the line served only Basingstoke, a small market-town, between Kingston and Winchester, whereas the southern route would have passed close to the important towns of Guildford, Farnham, Alton and Alresford. The chosen route was, however, intended as a base for extensions to the West country, for which Basingstoke was an ideal 'springboard'. Perhaps more significantly it crossed great expanses of uninhabited and uncultivated heath, which were bought very cheaply. The landowners of the rich agricultural lands of the Wey valley were reluctant to sell, and Edward Ryde recalled that a route 'parallel to the old Turnpike Road passing through Esher, Cobham, Ripley, Guildford, Farnham, Alton and Winchester' had been seriously considered 'but the landowners opposition in those places was so great that the application . . . was unsuccessful'.[38] As a result the empty heaths which formed the spine of the Woking district were chosen instead, with profound consequences for the future of the area (*see* Fig. 11).

Construction work was slow, and the first section to be completed, the 23½ miles from Nine Elms to Woking Common, was not opened until 21 May 1838. For the opening there was a special train to carry dignitaries, directors and their guests, and a

1. Woking church and village from the south, 1820: to the right of the church can be seen the tall tower or beacon, above Hoe Place, which was blown down in 1868, and gave its name to Monument Hill.

2. 17th-century cottages in High Street, Woking village: this view was taken in April 1907, just before the demolition of the whole row. See Fig. 7 for their precise location.

3. The *White Horse* and Send Corner, Woking village, *c.* 1900: this scene has now been drastically changed, for the worse, as most of the buildings have been demolished for road-widening.

4. Old Woking High Street looking east, 1931: the scene has not changed greatly in the last half-century, except for the demolition of Bedfords' Garage, and the improvement of the road surface.

5. Old Woking High Street looking west, 1931: this and the previous view can be dated by the newly erected electric lamp standards, since the conversion from gas lighting took place in that year.

6. Gonger's Lane, Westfield, *c.* 1905: this country lane is now Westfield Road, and the view is looking from the site of the junction with Granville Road eastwards towards Loop Road and Woking Village.

7. Kingfield Green, *c.*1905. The plane trees which dominate the green today were not yet planted when this photograph was taken. Instead there was a magnificent elm at the junction with Stockers Lane. In the distance are the chimneys of Kingfield House, home of the Smallpeice family.

8. Connaught Road, Brookwood, *c.*1905. The arrival of a photographer was evidently something of an event at this time. Brookwood was only partly built up, and although there were some new villas near the junction with Station Approach the road to Knaphill still passed through scrub and woodland.

nkerman Barracks, *c.* 1900: the tall square tower dominated the entire complex and was ›minent local landmark. In front of the main block is the parade ground, once the prison :ise yard.

The main entrance to Inkerman Barracks, 1913: the high quality of the architecture is apparent; the entrance block ecently been converted to houses. The message on the reverse of the postcard says that 'we stood at the corner by the ıgs watching "Kitchener's Army" march into the barracks the other day'. The date is October 1914: the men were o France.

11. Reconstructing Hermitage Hill, 1922: To provide work for the local unemployed, Woking Council undertook several road schemes in 1921-22. Amongst these was the widening and deepening of the cutting on Hermitage Hill, St Johns.

12. (*opposite below left*) Anchor Hill, Knaphill, *c.*1919: looking westwards from the junction with Barley Mow Lane. On the left can be seen the brick-yards, which closed some five years later.

13. (*above*) Horsell church and High Street, *c.*1897: this view captures the rural atmosphere of Horsell in the late 19th century: children played in the road, and a heavy farm cart, laden with timber, stood outside the church.

14. (*below*) Plough Bridge, Byfleet, *c.*1905, showing the old ford across the River Wey, on the left. In the distance are the wooded slopes of St George's Hill. The bridge was rebuilt in 1906-7.

15. The old *Blue Anchor Inn*, Byfleet village, *c.*1898: this attractive 17th-century building was demolished shortly after the picture was taken, and replaced by the hotel which later became notorious for its role in the 'Bluebeard' murder case.

16. The Byfleet parish workhouse, 1968 Byfleet Vestry established a small poor-house early in the 18th century, to house paupers and other people on relief. The building closed in 1835, and became a cottage, which survived until the early 1970s. It was at Stream Close, Rectory Lane (formerly known as Workhouse Lane).

17. Oyster Lane, Byfleet, early 1900s: looking northwards, with the lodge of Petersham Place on the left. After 1919 the land on the right was used for housing by Chertsey R.D.C.

18. Byfleet Corner (West Byfleet), *c.*1900: a view taken before the construction of Rosemount Parade and the widening of the Old Woking Road, looking west.

BYFLE

19. (*left*) Inaugurating the Byfleet motor fire engine, June 1923. Giving the address is Ebenezer Mears, the local building contractor. Behind him (*left to right*) are Mr. Lock (headmaster of Byfleet church school); the Rector, Rev. H. V. Johnson; Leonard Stevens; Mrs. Anne Stevens (first woman chairman of the Parish Council); and Mr. and Mrs. Frederick Stoop of West Hall, prominent local benefactors.

20. (*opposite below*) Maybury Heath Lane, *c.* 1900. This rutted, muddy and tree-hung country lane is Oriental Road, which originally crossed the open heathland near Heathside Farm. It was renamed about this time, to commemorate the Oriental Institute.

21 and 21a. The medal struck to commemorate the laying of the foundation stone of the Royal Dramatic College by Prince Albert, on 1 June 1860. The obverse (left) shows the college buildings as they were to appear, and the reverse has a bust of Shakespeare, with figures representing Youth and Old Age. Around the edge is the legend, from *As You Like It*, 'All the World's A Stage & All The Men & Women Merely Players'.

22. Woking railway station, *c.*1900. The station was rebuilt in the 1880s when the line was widened. In this view, looking towards London, the very large canopy which covered three platforms is easily seen.

23. A birds-eye view of central Woking, *c.*1900: taken from the spire of Commercial Road Methodist church, with Commercial Road in the left foreground. In the distance are the electricity power station chimney and the gasworks. The white dome of the mosque peeps above the trees south of the railway, and on the extreme right is Woking Lodge, home of the Rastrick family.

24. (*opposite above*) Courtenay Road, Woking, *c.*1904: this fine picture was taken just before the road was made up, and a team of Woking Council workmen engaged in that task can be seen in the distance. The deplorable state of the streets in central Woking at this time is clearly visible.

25. (*opposite below*) Chertsey Road canal bridge, Woking, in 1922: the wooden bridge was erected in 1910 by Woking Council, on the abutments of the brick structure of 1792. The bridge was rebuilt in 1922-23.

26. Chertsey Road, Woking, *c.*1905. In the early 1900s this was the main shopp street. The photograph is looking north-east, towards Walton Road. On the left i Chobham Road, with the old *Red Hous Hotel* in the angle of the two streets.

27. Commercial Road in 1928, lookin east. Gammons' store is on the left, beyond the World's Stores; the car park was soon to be replaced by Commercial Buildings. Not one of the buildings in th view is standing today.

28. Chobham Road, Woking, *c.*1900. Looking north from the junction with Commercial Road. On the left is J. F. Gammon's store, now the site of British Home Stores. Every building in this view has since been demolished, and the street is a paved pedestrian area.

. Wheatsheaf canal bridge, 1910:
: bridge was demolished soon after
: photograph was taken. The decay-
; brickwork is clearly seen, as are
: various tie-bars holding the struc-
'e together. In the background is
›king Victoria Hospital.

Chobham Road and the canal bridge, 1910: this view illustrates the narrowness of the old Wheatsheaf Bridge
r the Basingstoke Canal: note, too, how the road surface was being broken up by the passage of cars and horse-
wn vehicles.

31. Christ Church and Church Street, Woking, *c.* 1905: at this time the street was still almost entirely residential, but today all but the church has been replaced by shops and offices.

32. Commercial Road and public buildings, *c.* 1908: (*left to right*) Woking Public Hall, later the Grand Theatre (1895); Woking U.D.C. offices (1904); Conservative Club (1898); and Commercial Road Methodist Church: all are now gone, replaced by Maples, the Post Office, Cawsey Way and Boots' respectively.

buffet lunch was provided in marquees pitched on the heath beside the line at Woking. The station did not long remain a terminus; the line was extended to Shapley Heath (now Winchfield) on 24 September 1838 and to Basingstoke on 10 June 1839. The last section, Basingstoke to Winchester, completing the through route to Southampton, was opened on 11 May 1840. The railway was an instant success, exceeding all expectations: at the board meeting on 30 August 1838 it was reported that the average number of passengers each week had been 7,586, almost four times the number predicted, and a working profit of £8,770 had been made in the first three months of operation.[39]

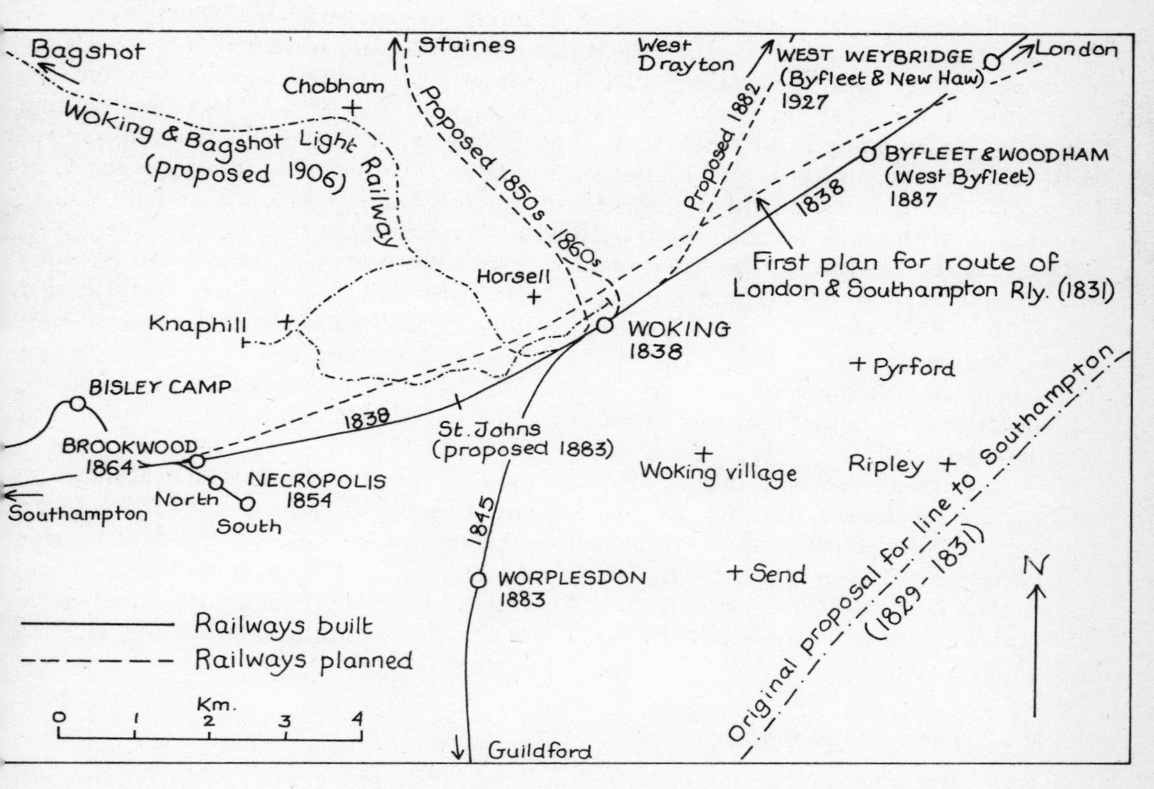

Fig. 11. Railways Built and Proposed.

The Effect of the Railway

Woking Common station immediately assumed a considerable importance as a generator of passenger traffic, since it acted as the railhead for Guildford, Godalming and much of rural West Surrey. There was no other station between Weybridge and Farnborough, and as the main road to Portsmouth was not far distant the stagecoaches which operated along this route were diverted to connect with the trains from and to London at Woking.

Previously they had used the present A3 through Ripley, and 'Woking people would meet these . . . at what is called Fell Hill . . . at the junction of the road from Woking at Sendhurst Grange'[40] but after May 1838 they ran via Stoke and Mayford. The increased traffic which resulted was the cause of serious congestion:

> 'the roads in many places were too narrow for such traffic, it being only with the greatest difficulty that two stage coaches could pass each other in many places: and there was an entire absence of stable accommodation at Woking station. In addition to the public conveyance the whole of the inhabitants of Guildford who possessed horses found that their best way to get to London was to arrive at Woking station'.[41]

Locke suggests that the coaches were actually driven onto the trains, taken to London and there driven off, an early version of 'Motorail', but there is no evidence to support that claim.[42] Equally without foundation is the persistent story that the original name of the station was 'Horsell for Woking' or vice versa. The name 'Woking Common' was employed in early years, but by the middle of the 1840s the second word was usually omitted, and in the early 1860s this became official. In the later 19th century the station (and the new town around) was occasionally called 'Woking Junction', but this was never adopted by the railway company.

The first station was a plain square building with two storeys, on the south (Woking village) side of the line. There were two platforms and rudimentary facilities for freight, but little else. The station was surrounded on all sides by empty heathlands, dotted with a few trees and with clumps of gorse, and there were no houses within half a mile. Across the canal, to the north, could be seen the tower of Horsell church, but the prevailing impression was of barren and uncultivated commons, and an almost complete isolation.

To cater for the sudden influx of traffic and people to this lonely heathland an enterprising local man, Edward Woods, bought a parcel of land at the crossroads, a quarter of a mile south of the station, where the track from Goldsworth to Heathside crossed the road from Chertsey to Guildford. At this spot, known as Harris' Lane, he built the *Railway Hotel*, opened in 1840, which supplied refreshment, accommodation and stabling for travellers. The hotel was the first building of what was later to become 'New Woking'.

Railway Expansion and Proposals

As the railway passed to the north of Guildford the company intended from the start to build a branch line from Woking Common station. In March 1838 plans were put forward for a 5½-mile line, and two years later these were revived, with the addition of a short extension to Farnham Road, Guildford. The 1840 plan involved an entirely level route, and to achieve that there were to be ambitious engineering works, notably a huge embankment, 42 feet high, across the valley of Hoe Stream at Mayford. We can appreciate the scale of this if we realise that the line would have been carried 22 feet *above* Smarts Heath Road and Hook Hill Lane.[43]

In 1843 a separate company, the Guildford Railway, applied for powers to build a line on the same route, but without the extravagant cuttings and embankments. The company was a protégé of the London and South Western Railway (to which the

London and Southampton had changed its name in 1839), and although it was approved by an independent Act in 1844 it was absorbed by the L.S.W.R. a year later. The line, which had no intermediate stations, was opened for traffic on 5 May 1845. In October 1849 it was extended to Godalming, and in January 1859 to Havant, when it became the main line from London to Portsmouth. Woking station was then a major junction, and was partially rebuilt to cater for the increased traffic.

In the later years of the century were several abortive projects for other railways to serve Woking. The Staines & Woking Railway proposed in 1851 to build a line from Victoria Arch to Egham, via Wheatsheaf Bridge, Kettlewell Hill and Horsell Common, with a separate Woking station in the future Commercial Road.[44] Variations of this plan were revived by different companies in 1853, 1857, 1859 and 1863, whilst a similar line, from Woking to West Drayton, was proposed in 1862. In 1882 the Staines, Chertsey & Woking Railway was a thinly disguised attempt by the Great Western Railway to invade the territory of its great rival, the L.S.W.R. It would have given Woking a train service to Paddington, but the opposition of the L.S.W.R. unfortunately secured its rejection by Parliament.[45]

The L.S.W.R. expanded its local services after 1860 with a series of new stations serving rural communities or areas where development was confidently expected. The short branch line into Brookwood Cemetery, described in Chapter Seven, was opened in 1854, but to cater for other traffic to the cemetery a small station was opened on the main line on 1 June 1864, using land donated by the Necropolis Company. For many years Brookwood station was used by few travellers unconnected with the cemetery, but after the late 1880s the village of Brookwood began to grow parallel with the railway to the north, and traffic increased slowly.

Byfleet & Woodham station, now West Byfleet, was opened in December 1887, to serve the district around Byfleet Corner and North Pyrford, where housing development was about to begin, and also to cater for passengers from New Haw and Byfleet village. Worplesdon station, which is distant from Worplesdon village and not even in the same parish (it is in Woking), opened on 1 March 1883. It was, and continues to be, the least used and most rural of the five stations in the present borough, and retains its pleasant but unexceptional L.S.W.R. wayside station buildings. At the time of its construction, and again in the late 1890s, there was agitation for a station to be provided for St Johns, either off the Lye or in the deep cutting below Hook Heath Avenue. The L.S.W.R. rejected the petition from local residents, claiming that Woking and Brookwood stations were too close to make the scheme viable.[46]

In 1902 proposals appeared for a tramway-type light railway to link Woking and Bagshot stations, via Bullbeggars Lane, Parley Bridge, Millbrook, Chobham and Lightwater. The Woking & Bagshot Light Railway Order of 1906 authorised construction, together with a depot and generating station at Horsell Birch. The line was to be electrified, and was to include a street tramway network at the Woking end: the routes proposed for this were Monument Road – Walton Road – Commercial Road – St Johns – Knaphill; and *Garibaldi Inn* – Anchor Hill – Littlewick – Horsell Birch. Although it was announced in October 1906 that work on the 12½-mile system would shortly be started, nothing was ever accomplished, and by 1910 interest had faded away completely.[47]

The Impact of the Railway

It is impossible to underestimate the impact of the railway on the Woking area. Whereas previously the district had been bypassed by major national transport links, after 1838 it was bisected by one of the most important and successful of the nation's railway lines, providing a fast and direct connection to the capital and later to much of the south and west of England. The consequences of the coming of the railway were not immediately felt: twenty years after its opening there were still only two buildings within a half-mile radius of Woking station. However, the railway provided the essential means whereby urban development took place; it was not its direct cause, but without it the growth of the town would have been impossible.

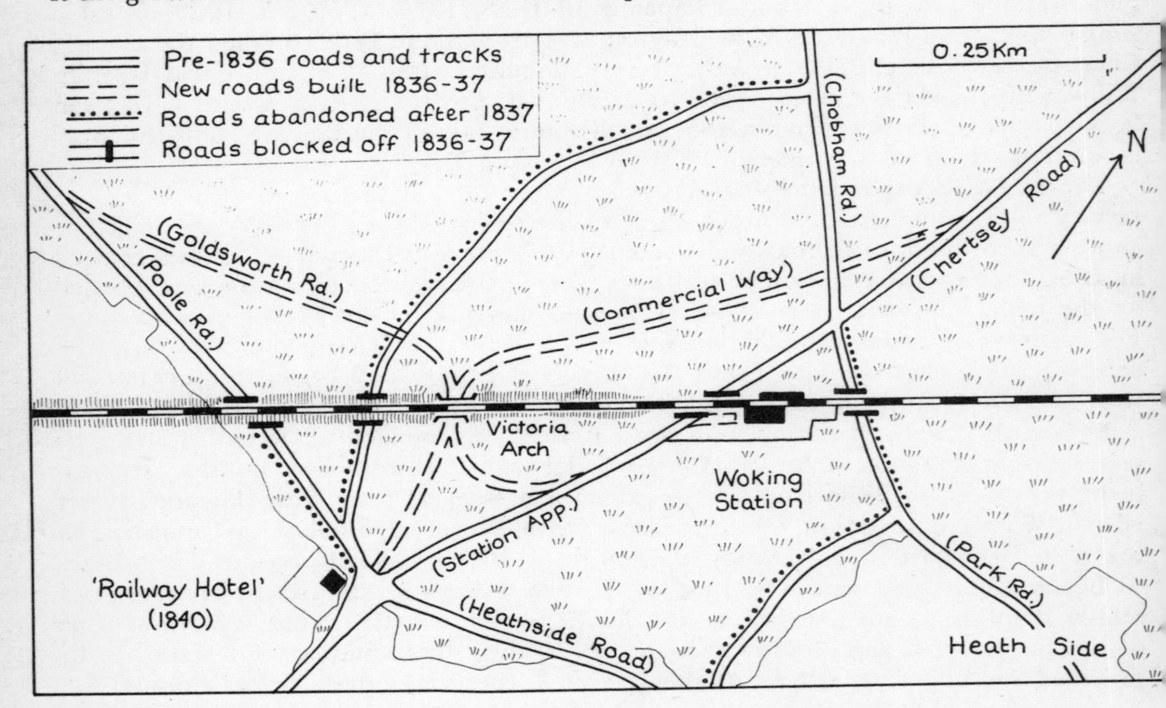

Fig. 12. Road Diversions on Woking Heath as a Result of Railway Construction.

Like the canal, therefore, the railway predated the development of the town, and as a result the shape and pattern of growth was in large measure dictated by these two features. For example, when the line was built the old tracks across the heath were diverted, and concentrated upon a single railway bridge, now Victoria Arch. As the town sprang up around the station this bridge became a point of congestion, for all the main roads of the centre now focused upon it (*see* Fig. 12). Had the plans for a line to Staines ever come to fruition the problems of the town would have been even greater, for the centre might then have been further divided, by a railway running across the site of today's Town Square and Central Library. As it was, the massive railway embankment to the south and the canal to the north hemmed in the central area and posed many difficulties for planning, traffic and the environment.

In few other towns has the railway been so significant in determining the geography, economy and character, but Woking was not a railway town. There was never any attempt by the railway company to develop a Swindon, an Eastleigh or a Crewe on the heaths of West Surrey. The railway was vital as a cause of urbanisation, but Woking was the child of a company far more bizarre. No other place in Britain can lay any claim to be a town which began in a cemetery!

Chapter Four

THE LONDON NECROPOLIS & NATIONAL MAUSOLEUM COMPANY

Its Origins

BY THE MIDDLE OF THE 1840s London was experiencing serious problems in burying its dead. A rapid increase in the population since the late 18th century had combined with appalling conditions amongst the poor, which had led to a rising death rate, to produce such numbers of bodies that the existing burial-yards could not cope. Cremation was illegal and secular cemeteries were almost non-existent, so that churchyards were crammed with bodies. Contemporary writers have left harrowing descriptions of the conditions in these places, where semi-decomposed bodies were removed to make room for new interments, where bones were piled in heaps in makeshift graves, and where the stench of decay was pervasive. Most churchyards were disgusting to look at, and posed a serious threat to health since disease and decay polluted adjacent wells. The cholera epidemics of the 1840s served to emphasise both this health risk and the lack of space for new burials.

After much outside pressure the government established in 1848 a General Board of Health which immediately began to review this disgraceful state of affairs. The result was the 1850 Burials Act. It required that, with certain minor exceptions, all burials in churchyards within the metropolitan area should henceforth be banned, and these places closed and made fit. To replace them new cemeteries with ample space and proper management should be opened outside the built-up area of the metropolis so that the same conditions would not develop in future. The Board of Health was also permitted by the 1850 Act to acquire – in effect to nationalise – privately owned cemeteries outside the capital. Encouragement was also to be given for commercial enterprises to establish approved cemeteries under Board of Health auspices.[1]

As so often happened in the 19th century there was no shortage of ambitious projects, but the translation of these into reality through the medium of government action proved to be more difficult. There had already been suggestions from individuals that a small number of enormous cemeteries, collecting the dead from large areas of the country, would be preferable to many local burial grounds. The Board of Health, in 1849, followed this example and proposed two huge cemeteries for London, the first based on an existing private one at Kensal Green and the second at Erith, Kent, whilst it also gave serious consideration to a giant national cemetery, or 'Necropolis' (City of the Dead) away from London. It was suggested that this should be at Woking, regarded as a particularly suitable place because it was one of the few unenclosed areas near to London (the source of most potential business), and because the parish was bisected by the main railway line and by the Basingstoke Canal. The common land here was extensive, and well suited to interment because it had a light sandy soil. The Woking Necropolis would be owned by the state, and managed by the General Board of Health. It was intended that the corpses of the nation would travel to the Necropolis by rail and water, a vast and never-ceasing procession of funerals which would be handled by an army of clergy, labourers and administrative officers.

Hostility to such an ambitious and authoritarian concept was immediate and vociferous, and it soon became evident that this costly and interventionist proposal was politically unacceptable in the golden age of *laissez-faire* attitudes. The Board of Health suggestion was therefore abandoned, and indeed the Board itself was abolished in 1854 because it represented state interference. The idea of a national cemetery was still favoured in several quarters, though, particularly since the Act of 1850 had banned churchyard interment in London, but had not provided an alternative.

In the spring of 1851 the original Board of Health plan was espoused by a group of businessmen, landowners and philanthropists, who proposed to provide a Necropolis at Woking, but one which would be owned and operated by a private concern. It would thus be politically more palatable, avoiding accusations of state interference, and would also be, it was hoped, profitable. Making money out of death did not seem to be repugnant, whereas public involvement in burial was an anathema.

The London Necropolis & National Mausoleum Company was registered in London on 3 October 1851, and incorporated 20 days later, with a nominal capital of £250,000. Its impressive title reflected both its origins in the Board of Health plans, and the grandiose nature of the concept. A single cemetery to serve perhaps the whole of England was an idea characteristically Victorian, at once visionary yet founded in the spirit of profit. It was expected that most of the income would be derived from the burial of the wealthy, who would pay a premium for the privilege, whilst the poor, numerically far more significant, were to be buried at parish expense under contracts with vestries and local authorities. However, the company first had to acquire the commonlands in the parish of Woking to provide the site for the Necropolis.

It was necessary to seek a private Act of Parliament because the effect of acquiring the commonland and common rights was the same as that of enclosure, and because government policy was affected. This also gave the legislature a chance to debate the proposal and to argue for or against the concept of private cemeteries on this scale. The London Necropolis & National Mausoleum Company Bill was given its formal first reading in the Commons on 18 February 1852 and the second reading on 27 February.[2] The latter involved a lengthy and acrimonious debate about the allegedly dubious character of the company, and the wisdom of its plans. Henry Drummond, Member for West Surrey, the constituency which included Woking, was particularly hostile. He declared that 'no question of local or general interest was involved in the Bill, but the promoters, he should shew, contemplated a direct fraud on the public'. They had obtained 2,600 acres, according to their prospectus, but all they had in reality accomplished was to offer Lord Onslow £33,000 for his manorial rights, and to consult nobody else. Particularly interesting, in view of subsequent events, was Drummond's categorical statement that 'the promoters intended to take powers to purchase 2,600 acres, while they themselves calculated that 400 would be necessary for the purposes of the cemetery, and they proposed to let on building leases the remaining 2,200 acres as a more commercial speculation'.

Speaking in favour of the Bill, Sir James Duke said that the scheme was deserving of support, because of the acuteness of the burial problem. He believed, too, that 'the promoters had no intention whatever to devote the ground . . . to speculation', but a note of uncertainty was evident when he added that he trusted the House 'would take care not to allow anything of that kind'. The M.P. for Guildford, James Mangles, said that the people of Woking did not object to 'a moderate portion' of their common land being taken for the cemetery, but did object to this Bill, which would 'take every acre of common land, and either convert it into a cemetery or to private purposes'. The opponents, moreover, were 'small freeholders and copyholders of Woking, living around the common, and it was futile to suppose that men in such humble circumstances could bear the cost of opposing this Bill in Committee'.

Mr. Bethell, supporting, claimed that the copyholders (manorial tenants) had at first readily assented to the proposal, and only objected when their financial compensation appeared to be inadequate. In any case, he said, they had no rights. He also stated that all railway Bills included clauses which permitted sales of surplus land. To this Henry Drummond demanded to know of a single instance where a railway company had bought 2,600 acres intending to use 400. He asserted that this 'was not a cemetery company. They meant to make their money by their building leases, and it was in fact a building society under the mask of a Necropolis'. The second reading was carried by the narrow majority of 12: 92 votes against and 104 in favour.

During the third reading, on 21 May, the most remarkable feature was that Henry Drummond, the vehement and prescient critic of the Bill in earlier debates, declared his support. Although evidence is not available it is hard to avoid the conclusion that, in some way, pressure or influence had been applied to make him change his mind. This would have been quite in keeping with the unquestionably shady and doubtful character of the company and its promotors. Viscount Ebrington, the Lord Chancellor, asked the Commons to delay the Bill until new government policies on the whole question of burial had been clarified. He felt that 400–500 acres ought to be quite sufficient, and considered 'private operation of such an extensive site suspect and undesirable, and that the Company were planning to speculate'. However his request was rejected, and the Bill passed its third reading.

The Lords approved the Bill with little hesitation. It was strongly supported by the highly influential reformist, the Earl of Shaftesbury, although he objected on the grounds of propriety to the idea of central collection of corpses at Waterloo station, and to mass pauper graves. The Bishop of London was also a powerful advocate of the Woking scheme. The record of the debate notes, amusingly, that the Earl of Chichester 'who was quite inaudible, was understood to support the Bill'. The Bill was passed in all stages, and received Royal Assent on 30 June 1852.[3]

The 1852 Act

The new Act was fully titled 'An Act to Incorporate the London Necropolis & National Mausoleum Co. and to enable such Company to establish a Cemetery in the Parish of

Woking, in the County of Surrey, And for other Purposes'. It comprised 27 clauses, most of them relating to the establishment of the cemetery itself and to restrictions on the powers of the company. An attached schedule authorised the company to purchase by agreement the whole or part of the waste or commonland in the parish of Woking, together with 101 cottages, gardens and other parcels of land. Most of these were piecemeal enclosures from the waste, and would in theory be required if the whole of the commonland was to be laid out as a cemetery, because otherwise isolated properties would have been completely surrounded. These purchase powers were to lapse after five years.

All the footpaths, highways and watercourses across the lands in question could be stopped up or diverted, although it was apparently intended that the major public roads from Guildford to Bagshot, Chertsey and Knaphill would be kept open. The cemetery was to be surrounded by a wall eight feet high and was not to be laid out within 300 yards of houses except with the consent of the owners. Charges could be levied for burials, religious services, carriage of bodies, headstones and the reopening of graves, and fees could be paid to incumbents for their assistance. The London & South Western Railway Company could contract for the carriage of bodies and other Necropolis business, and was empowered to run special trains for this purpose, whilst the Railway and Necropolis Companies, jointly, could erect special facilities for cemetery traffic at Waterloo and Nine Elms.

The most significant part, inserted after the strong expressions against land speculation during the Commons debate, was Section XVI, which stated that:

> 'The Company shall not, without the sanction and authority of Parliament, sell any lands, which they may acquire under the authority of this Act, and shall not erect, or cause, or permit, or suffer to be erected on such lands any buildings other than such as may be required for the purposes of this Act, or the residence of the officers and servants of the Company'.

The Acquisition of Land

Discussions with the Onslow family over transfer of common rights began in February 1852. These centred on the price which would be appropriate for the purchase of the Lordship of the Manor of Woking and the land affected, which the Earl of Onslow owned. On 27 April 1852 a provisional contract was signed, giving an agreed price of £38,000 for the 2,328 acres involved.[4] In the spring of 1853 a committee, formed of five members of the Woking Vestry, began negotiations with the Necropolis Company as to the amount of money which would be made available to freeholders and copyholders of the parish in compensation for the extinguishing of their traditional common rights. No agreement could be reached, for the vestry committee felt that the amount offered was inadequate. In addition the Necropolis Company, with astonishing effrontery, suggested that since it had already bought a number of freehold properties it was itself exercising common rights, and could thereby claim back part of the compensation which it would be due to pay! This suggestion, which was likely to be very damaging to public relations, was technically legal, but it reflects most unsympathetically upon the directors and encouraged belief that this was a less than socially responsible concern.[5]

The dispute was sent to arbitration. On 4 October 1853 the Sheriff of Surrey was asked by the company to call a special jury to assess claims for compensation under the Land Clauses Consolidation Act 1845. This met at Guildford on 20 October and after hearing the claims of the interested parties decided that a sum of £15,000 should be made available to the commoners in compensation for their rights. The money was handed over to the vestry committee on 10 April 1854.[6] To divide the sum in question another private Act was necessary. This was entitled 'An Act for the Distribution of the Compensation paid under the London Necropolis & National Mausoleum Act 1852, for the Extinction of the Commonable or other Rights over and in Woking Common' and it received Royal Assent on 29 July 1854. Usually known as the Woking Commons Act (1854), it appointed the Inclosure Commissioners to supervise the payments, and may be regarded as the second stage in the enclosure of the manor of Woking.[7]

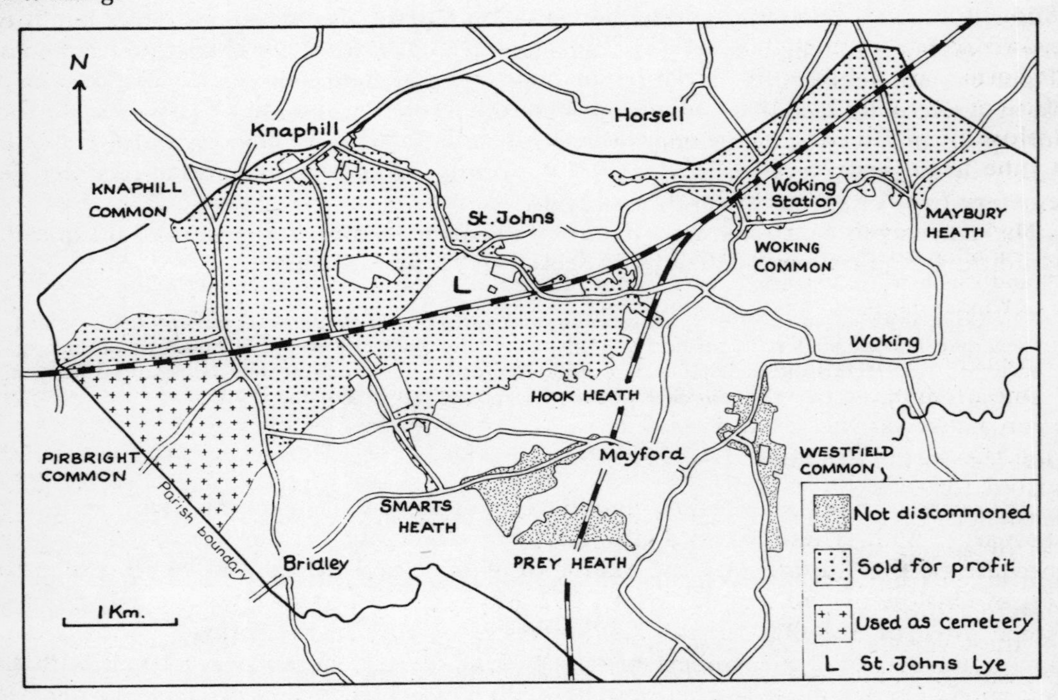

Fig. 13. Land Acquired by the London Necropolis Company

On 14 October 1854 an agreement was signed between the Rector of Woking, the Onslow family and the Necropolis Company, whereby the company took possession of all rights and lands of the commons of the manor of Woking. By this agreement the company acquired from Lord Onslow a total of 2,118 acres of land which had already been discommoned under the terms of the 1852 Act, and a further 150 acres to which they were given title, but which had not been discommoned. That meant that the land remained available to the local people for grazing animals, and gathering fuel.[8]

Westfield Common, Prey Heath and Smarts Heath, the lands in question, were of little value for speculative building, being detached and distant from the main area of company property, and so they remain as heathland even today. Their common status has been assured, by the transfer of rights from the company to Woking Borough Council. The 60 acres of St Johns Lye were also excluded from the sale of October 1854, so that the land could be used in perpetuity for recreation and for the exercise of common rights by the people of Woking (*see* Chapter 10). This had followed pressure from the Vicar of Woking, who feared the loss of amenity and income for the poor which would have resulted from the enclosure of the Lye. After the exclusion of the 60 acres the price was reduced to £33,944, or just £14.96 per acre, a bargain even in those days!

When the formalities of sale were completed the money had to be divided amongst the claimants, a process which took several years. It was decided by the 1854 Act that money should be available to freeholders and to copyhold tenants of the manor (those whose tenancy was copied into the manor court books), the former by right and the latter by custom. It was also intended to compensate those who could establish other convincing claims to exercise common rights. The Earl of Onslow himself made a claim, since as landowner he had held common rights. He wrote in June 1855 that

> 'My intentions are to put in my claim for what I may appear to be entitled to . . . not with the view of appropriating it to myself or my family after me but with the sole object of creating a fund which will affort [*sic*] a small annual supply of fuel to the labouring poor of the Parish of of Woking during the winter months.'[9]

There is no evidence that this laudable aim was ever put into effect.

One of the greatest difficulties in achieving an equitable settlement of the compensation issue was the existence of illegal enclosures (*see* Chapter Two), or 'land stolen from the waste'. The Onslow solicitors noted that some of these were known to have existed for over 60 years, many for over 20, and many others were of recent date. The length of time during which common rights had been exercised by the occupants was of course equally varied. There were legal difficulties over whether possession of land taken from the common illegally would, after sufficient time, be held to amount to actual ownership. 'Can compensation for loss of rights be paid to those who are not the owners of the land but who have for many years exercised these rights?'.[10] The Inclosure Commissioners decided eventually that it was impossible to compensate all who had taken land from the waste without permission, but that 'claims of 30 years uninterrupted use of rights' should be regarded as representing permanent possession, and thus justified compensation. This had for those concerned the incidental but considerable benefit that it gave them a *de facto* legal title to their properties. Disputes between claimants continued until 1857, for on 2 April 1857 a meeting was held at the *White Hart*, Woking, to hear claims over the compensation for the Earl of Onslow and others, and to decide whether further arbitration might be needed. The last claims were settled in the autumn of that year.[11]

Later Amending Acts

The 1855 Act

The 2,268 acres acquired by the Necropolis Company were divided into five distinct areas. Westfield Common, Smarts Heath and Prey Heath have already been mentioned. There was also a large detached portion, Woking Common (also known as Maybury Common and Frailey Heath), the area around the railway station and eastwards to the Byfleet–Woking village road. This covered some 400 acres. The fifth and major part of their acquisition, about 1,750 acres, consisted of much of the western part of the parish (*see* Fig. 12), including Hook Heath, Knaphill, Brookwood and West Hill.

Outline maps produced by the company in 1852 show that the initial plan was to close or divert most of the public highways or footpaths which crossed the former heaths. The maps also show an alternative road and path network, designed by the company architect, Henry Robert Abraham. It is doubtful, however, whether the company ever intended that this design would be implemented and it was probably produced to emphasise the apparent seriousness of their plans.[12] The first stage of the cemetery was opened in November 1854, after very rapid construction and landscaping work. It is described in Chapter Seven and covered the entire area west of the Guildford–Worplesdon–Bisley road (now A322) and south of the railway line from Woking to Basingstoke, approximately 400 acres.

It is unquestionable that the fears expressed by opponents of the company during the passage of its Parliamentary Bill three years before were justified. The remarkable prescience of Henry Drummond, in anticipating a cemetery of 400 acres with no attempt being made to turn the remainder into a necropolis, is striking. The company had adopted in theory the 1849 scheme of the Board of Health almost in its entirety, but it is improbable that it was every seriously interested in putting this into effect. Almost certainly the basic motive was financial; to take advantage of the burial problem and the proposed cemetery as a way to speculate in the land around Woking station. Anybody with enough foresight could have expected the land to appreciate in value, and this was a convenient means of acquiring it cheaply, at a price below its real worth. That the cemetery was included in the plan was laudable, and the directors no doubt believed sincerely that this type of solution to the burial problem was needed, but it is difficult to accept that they ever really proposed to use 2,300 acres for a cemetery.

Various facts point to that conclusion. The opinions of the M.P.s who opposed the 1852 Bill are of value, for they were speaking on the basis of confidential information about the company. In addition, the initial wish of the directors to include a clause allowing them to sell surplus land suggests that they were already anticipating just such a policy. There was no necessity for the company to buy more land than it needed, since enclosure acts (as this was, in effect) were often passed for parts of manors or parishes, rather than for the whole area. Perhaps as important is the decision to build the cemetery at the western extremity of the parish, without rail or water access and as far as possible from habitation. The logical site for the first phase was around Woking station, which was easily accessible from London, the West Country and Guildford, and would obviously become more so as the railway network grew.

Brookwood was the least attractive area for speculative building, whereas the vicinity of Woking station would clearly have the greatest potential for profitable land sales.

The 1852 Act required the company to build an eight-foot high wall around the cemetery. Although the aim was allegedly to use all the heathland for cemetery purposes, the first phase at Brookwood was completely surrounded by the wall, implying that there was no intention to extend beyond its limits. The most convincing evidence, though, is that in the autumn of 1854, even before the first stage of the plan was completed, the company was preparing a new Bill for submission to Parliament, to allow it to sell its 'surplus' lands. This was initiated in the Lords on 22 May 1855, and received Royal Assent very quickly, on 23 July.

During its passage there was a short debate, in which Lord Berners, for the opposition, stated that the proposed sales were 'completely contrary to the recent Burial Act', whilst Lord Redesdale, in support, told the House that 'all the promoters wanted to do was to "dispose of certain detached portions of land they had purchased which could never be properly appropriated to the purpose of the cemetery"'. If that was in truth the case, it is difficult to understand why the lands had been bought in the first place.[13]

Lord St Leonards was clearly unhappy about the Bill, and could not come to a decision in his mind. He said that if speculations were in progress he would be strongly opposed to the Bill, but that if the original purchase had been in good faith it would be wrong to oppose the company's application. The company was able to convince that its intentions were honourable, although with hindsight this does not seem to have been the case, and it thus succeeded in obtaining 'An Act to amend "The London Necropolis and National Mausoleum Act, 1852" and for other Purposes'.

The preamble stated that 'the lands mentioned and described in the schedule to this Act are not required by the said Company for the purposes of the said undertaking, and it is expedient that the said Company should have powers to dispose of the same'. By the Act the compulsory and other purchase powers of the company were extinguished, and for a period of ten years, to 1868, had the authority to sell for any purpose the Hermitage estate (27 acres) described as 'Hermitage of Rookwood', which had been acquired in 1852, the 400 acres of Woking Common around the station and in Maybury and Bunker's Hill, and lands in Knaphill and St Johns. The Act specified (Section V) that the company should build and maintain in perpetuity a road 60 feet wide from the railway bridge at Hook Heath to Wych Street corner. This is now called Hook Heath Avenue; the wide verges on each side reflect the original 60-foot requirement. Most importantly the future town centre was foreshadowed in Section VI, which required that five acres, within 600 yards of the booking offices of Woking Station, should be set aside for a 'Church, Church Yard, Parsonage House and Schools for the Poor', if the Bishop of Winchester approved of the site.[14]

The 1864 and 1869 Acts

The sale of land began immediately but interest in the area was considerably less than the company had hoped. There was comparatively little demand at this stage, and when the ten-year limit imposed by the 1855 Act expired only 343 acres had been sold, for £31,000. Much of this was in Knaphill, where the War Department had bought the sites of the new prisons, and the County Justices land for the asylum. This was a serious disappointment to the directors and shareholders, who viewed this as a money-making enterprise. In 1864 they were granted a five-year extension of the time by Parliament, having submitted a short private Bill for this purpose.[15]

This expired in 1869 and yet another Act, the fourth in 15 years, was then sought, and approved by Parliament. It virtually freed the company from any constraints where land sales were concerned. The position was clearly stated:

> 'and whereas the Company have laid out and enclosed for burial purposes a sufficient space to meet the estimated requirements of their undertaking for the next hundred years, but they have received no adequate return for their outlay and it is only just that the Company should be permitted to deal with their surplus lands [but] they have not been able to dispose of the whole of the same and a forced sale of the unsold lands within a limited time would entail great loss upon the Company'.

The last sentence shows quite clearly that the company now regarded the sale of land as its source of profit. The cemetery business, as might have been expected, had given no rewards, and as yet the shareholders had received no dividend. It is apparent that the need to seek Parliamentary approval for land sales had forced the company to declare its real interests and business. Had this emerged in 1852 it is virtually certain that the Bill would have been rejected, particularly since in the event it had only succeeded by a margin of 12 votes.

The main part of the 1869 Act was Section II which repealed Section XVI of the original Act of 1852. The only exceptions to this were the existing cemetery, west of the Bagshot road, and about 160 acres to the east of this, bounded by the L.S.W.R., the manor boundary to the south, and Blackhorse Road, which were not to be sold. The company, by this Act, was therefore free to dispose of any properties apart from those already in cemetery use and a comparatively small area adjacent which might conceivably be needed for such purpose in the distant future. It thus completed the transformation from a cemetery company to a land company, as anticipated in the debate of the House of Commons 17 years earlier.[16]

Its Character

The character of the company was apparent to some contemporaries from an early date, whilst others felt that the ambitious idea of developing a cemetery of over 2,300 acres was unlikely to succeed, however honourable the initial intentions. Behind the idealistic yet materialist notions of a profit-making cemetery company, publicised by colourful and romantic descriptions and calculated to appeal to Victorian sentiments, were businessmen anxious to make large profits out of development in the Woking area. The potential for profit was known to others. In 1851, for example, Edward Ryde told a meeting of the copyholders and freeholders of the manor that the lands which the company wished to acquire would, in the future, be worth at least £200 an acre, compared with £10–£15 per acre in 1851. This, he said, was because of the development opportunities afforded by the railway. His advice was not heeded, and he was regarded as a laughing-stock. A local man told him that 'if they broke up the common and sowed it with wheat they would not grow the seed they sowed upon it'.[17]

The sale of the land and its consequences are described in the following chapter. It seems that the doubtful character of the company was evident for many years. In the 1880s, for example, it was selling land cheaply to its own directors. At other times extensive tracts were sold to development companies with which the Necropolis Company had links, presumably for financial benefit.

The London Necropolis & National Mausoleum Company continued in existence until the 1960s, when it was absorbed by the Great Southern group, a holding company. By this time it had divested itself of almost all the lands acquired in 1852–54, with the exception of the areas excluded in the 1869 Act, and the lordship of the three commons in Westfield and Mayford. The business was, by this time, highly unprofitable, and attempts have regularly been made since the early 1950s to develop any remaining land not in cemetery use. These have all failed, because the green belt restrictions no longer permit house-building on this scale in rural areas. The cemetery is now part of Brookwood Park Ltd., a subsidiary of another holding company, Dundonian Ltd. of Banstead. Most of the records of the company were destroyed in the 1941 blitz.

The company was unique in Britain. It may be held responsible not only for the founding of the present town of Woking, but also for many of the deficiencies in its layout and character. Whilst it undoubtedly performed an extremely useful and necessary service in providing a 400-acre cemetery to serve the metropolis, it must be regarded as lacking in any social responsibility or consideration for the needs of the town which it spawned. The major interest of the directors from the 1860s onwards until the early years of this century appeared to be making quick profits, and to accomplish this they made no attempt to sell their vast land holdings in a sensible or far-sighted way. It was this which was primarily responsible for the great inadequacies of the new town.

The company can therefore be seen as, at least in part, a gigantic fraud. It secured the approval of Parliament for the purchase, at very low prices, of the commonlands of the parish of Woking, which had historically been available for the use of the community, and within two years was starting the process of sale and speculation with these assets. The ostensibly public-spirited aims of developing a cemetery to relieve the metropolis of the burdens of burials were soon forgotten and in later years no attempt was made to disguise the view that the cemetery was a liability. The directors thus deceived Parliament (which, perhaps, ought to have known better) and cheated the poorer people of Woking. Had the company adopted a responsible approach to the disposal of land, such condemnation might have been avoided but this was not to be. Woking was founded by a means unique in Britain. No other town originated in this bizarre and unusual way. The following chapters show how the town developed and what was the role of the Necropolis Company and other landowners in shaping its growth.

Chapter Five

BUILDING A NEW TOWN

Background

APART FROM THE *Railway Hotel* of 1840 and the station itself, Woking Common remained undeveloped, a great expanse of heather and gorse, for over 20 years after the opening of the railway in 1838. It was common waste, and therefore not readily useable for building, but there was little incentive for development. The station was not of great importance until it became an important junction in 1859, and the extension to Guildford had robbed it of its long-distance coach traffic, so recently acquired. Not until the passing of the Necropolis Company's Amendment Act in 1855 were the circumstances suited to development.

By this Act the company was presented with an exceptional, and exciting, opportunity to design and lay out a fine new town, covering some 400 acres of virgin land. Untrammelled by existing buildings, it could have produced architectural and town-planning features of the highest quality. This chance was completely wasted, and the opportunity thrown away in the interests of immediate profit, at the great expense of the future town of Woking and its inhabitants. Many of the problems and deficiencies which affect Woking today, and which are so much criticised, may be traced to the short-sighted irresponsibility of the Necropolis Company in the 30 years from 1855.

Three major criticisms of their policy may be made. First, with some exceptions, the company made no effort to produce a rational road pattern or town plan, and failed to co-ordinate the development of the various parts. The result was a sadly inadequate road system, and a straggling and incoherent built-up area. Second, land sales were conducted in a piecemeal and often illogical fashion, and no control was exercised over the quality of buildings erected. This resulted in an architectural heritage which, with the exception of a handful of examples, was at best dreary and mediocre, at worst appalling. Third, there was a complete absence of civic responsibility. Although the company was quite aware that it was creating a town, it did nothing to provide the attributes of urban status. Until the last years of the century there were no public buildings, no drainage or sewerage, no water supply, no street-lighting and no made-up roads. No provision was made, when designing street patterns or dividing the land into lots, for any public open spaces or focal point. When civic and public buildings were built they were scattered at random and untidily across a central area, mixed with housing and small businesses.

All these factors contributed to the failure of Woking to develop a commercial status concordant with its population, and to the generally uninteresting appearance of large parts of the town. It is impossible not to condemn the behaviour of the Necropolis Company,. for the 19th century provided many examples of individuals or companies planning and building new towns with care and vision, whilst covenants and sale agreements could, at the very least, have ensured that services and land uses were regulated.

In consequence outside opinion of the appearance of the town has been unanimously hostile. Nairn called it 'a period piece, though not a very creditable one . . . a Victorian gridiron mushroomed around [the station] . . . its mean and joyless public buildings, offices and chapels'.[1]

In fairness to the company there were some attempts, later in the century, to provide townscapes of a higher quality, but these were concerned primarily with expensive housing areas. It should also be said that much blame must lie with the local government structure, or the lack of it. The parish vestry was weak, financially restricted and anachronistic, the Highway Board was internally divided and rurally based, and the Sanitary Board was similarly riven with discontent and, in addition, was engaged in interminable disputes over the problems of Woking with the unhelpful and distant Local Government Board. Had there been a form of urban government for the parish from the middle of the 1870s, when it first became a possibility, matters would undoubtedly have been improved, but there was a delay of 20 years, until 1893, before this came about, and by then it was too late.

New Woking

The first building in what is today the centre of Woking was the *Albion Hotel*. This was erected in 1856–57 by Reuben Percy (after whom Percy Street was named), the landlord of *The Wheat Sheaf* since 1849. He bought a plot of land immediately opposite the north entrance of the station, and there built the hotel to rival the *Railway Hotel* south of the arch. North of the *Albion* towards the Chertsey road (now Commercial Way), were livery-stables and other facilities for rail travellers.[2]

Early in 1859 the Necropolis Company made the first of several sales to John Rastrick, a wealthy railway builder who was responsible for, amongst other lines, that from London to Brighton. Eventually he owned over 40 acres south of the railway, including the land where the telephone exchange and Oriental Parade are today, and built himself a large house, Woking Lodge, which was approximately on the site of the present Oriental Road car park.[3]

Following these two sales, and four years after the amending Act, the company made its first important auction of land on Woking Common. This took place on 20 October 1859 in London, and involved 60 acres around the railway station, in the heart of what was to become 'New Woking'. The company architect, Henry Abraham, had laid out a road network and divided the land into 89 lots, ranging in size from 0.15 acre to 3.6 acres. This initial sale had very significant consequences, because it established the character of the two parts of the town, north and south of the railway.[4]

The road pattern adopted was clumsy, because there was no attempt to alter the existing network of tracks across the heath. New streets were fitted around these, and the result was a series of awkward junctions and odd-shaped plots. North of the railway

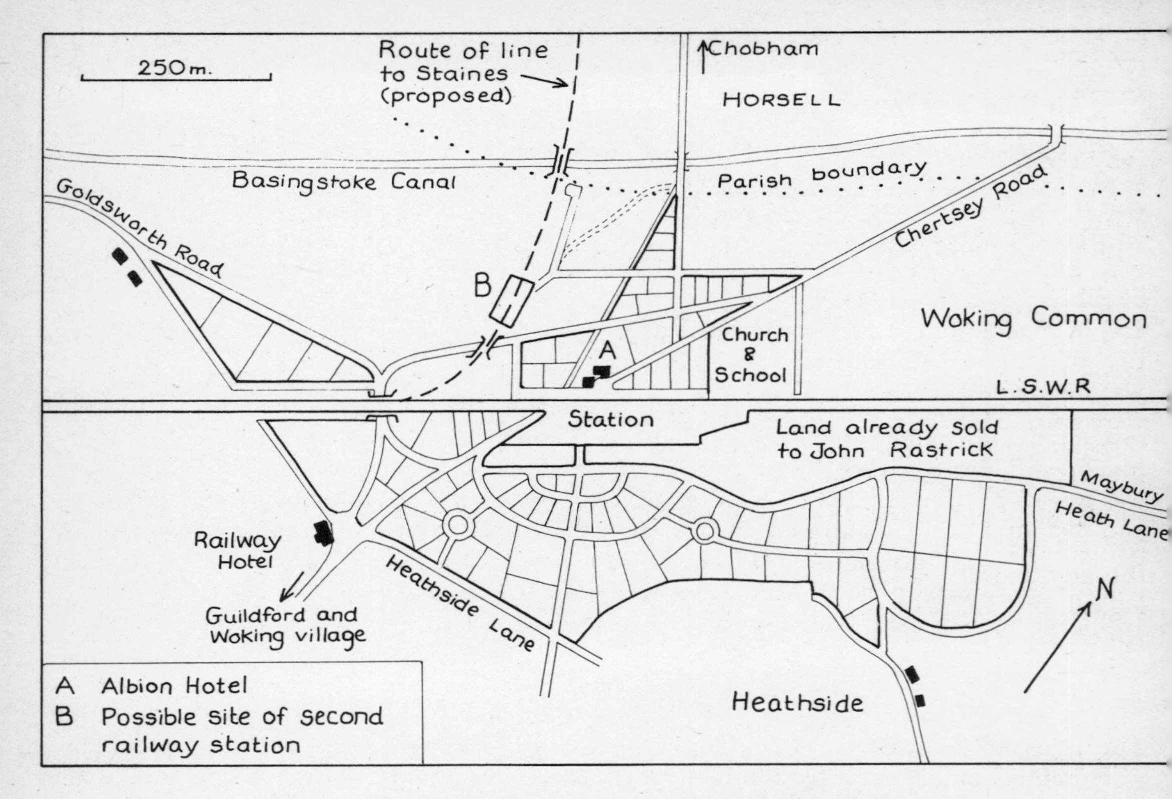

Fig. 14. The Plan of the New Town, and the Land Sale of 1859

Abraham favoured a grid pattern of roads, but the present Chertsey Road and Commercial Way, which already existed, cut across the grid and this led, most notably, to a difficult junction by the railway arch. In addition the old footpath from the station direct across the heath to Wheatsheaf Bridge was retained, and further divided the grid. This was, in the long term, fortunate for the town because as Church Path it has long formed an attractive feature, but it did not assist in the sensible planning of a new town.

South of the railway Abraham chose a rudimentary pattern of radials and concentric links, focusing on the station, but he did not have the courage to divert existing tracks. Therefore Heathside Road (then Lane) and the present Oriental Road fit uncomfortably into the new pattern, which is exemplified by Station Approach, White Rose Lane and Oriental Crescent. He also designed two 'circuses', clearly inspired by Regency town planning in Bath and Brighton, but neither of these has survived (*see* Fig. 14).

The sale of October 1859 was not a great success, and as late as 1890 much of the land remained undeveloped. Its importance is that it created the street pattern of central Woking and fixed the location of the town centre. Under the terms of the 1855 Act the Diocese of Winchester had acquired a site of three acres in what was later to become Onslow Crescent, on which to build a church, vicarage and school. This strongly suggests that at this early date it was assumed that the town centre would be south of the railway.

By October 1859, however, the company had proposed that the church land should be a 5-acre site between the present Chertsey Road, Stanley Road and Duke Street, and it showed this on the sale plan.[5] The change seems to indicate that the Company wanted the town centre to be north of the line. The construction of the *Albion Hotel* may have been partly responsible for this, but of much greater significance was the likelihood that higher prices could be obtained for land to the south. This was elevated, and in places commanded wide views across the Wey valley, and would thus be attractive to middle- and upper-class buyers. The 1859 plan reveals that the southern area was divided into large plots, indicating a 'high-class' market, whilst north of the railway were small plots suitable for low-value housing and commercial properties.

This would not in itself have been harmful to the future of the town, but the company did not try to produce a town centre to complement the superior areas south of the station. The crude and ill-conceived grid pattern gave no focal point, and since the Church did not want the Stanley Road site there was no land set aside for any public buildings. A central square or focus of key roads would have been logical and valuable, but none materialised. Whether or not shops or public facilities appeared, and where, was to be left entirely to individuals.

The Reversed Station

The Rastrick family, and particularly George, the second son of John, is popularly blamed for the unusual position whereby the main entrance of Woking station faces south, away from the town centre, whilst on the north side there is a small and cramped access. There is no doubt that George Rastrick, a solicitor, was something of an eccentric, and had little interest in the town which was growing up around his large estate, but it was not due to him that this curious position arose.

The main entrance was on the south side from the earliest days, long before the town was founded, because the two main sources of traffic, Guildford and Woking village, lay to the south. Access was by the truncated remnant of the old Chertsey road, now Station Approach, and the original station had no northern entrance. It is said that the Rastrick family bought their 40 acres south of the line and then refused all offers to purchase, until the death of George in 1904. This is so, and of course there was no reason why they had to sell the land if they did not wish to do so, but it did not prevent the development of the town centre on the south of the railway.[6]

The evidence of the 1859 map shows that the Necropolis Company had already made the decision to allot the area south of the station to high-value residences and to place the town centre to the north of the railway. Had there been any wish to develop commercial functions in the White Rose Lane district it would have been quite easy to do so, for almost all the Rastrick lands lay to the east, along Oriental Road, and only a narrow strip was to the immediate south of the station. Therefore the location of the town centre on 'the wrong side of the tracks' was the decision of the Necropolis Company, and the Rastrick family may be exonerated.

When the railway was widened, and the station rebuilt, in the 1880s, the L.S.W.R. wanted to acquire more land on the north side to provide a worthy entrance for the town centre, then growing. The Rural Highway Board refused to sell any of their land, and so the opportunity was lost. The last chance to provide a full-sized entrance on the north came in 1897, when the *Albion Hotel* was being rebuilt. Local dignitaries, including Dr. Leitner of the Oriental Institute (*see* Chapter 7) proposed that the area around the hotel should be redeveloped, and a civic square laid out in front of the station. It was to be called 'Victoria Square' in honour of the Diamond Jubilee, and would have formed an excellent focus for the town centre, and a northern entrance to the station more in keeping with the expanding town. The proposal was rejected by an unimaginative town council which disliked the idea of spending public money, even on so worthwhile a project.[7]

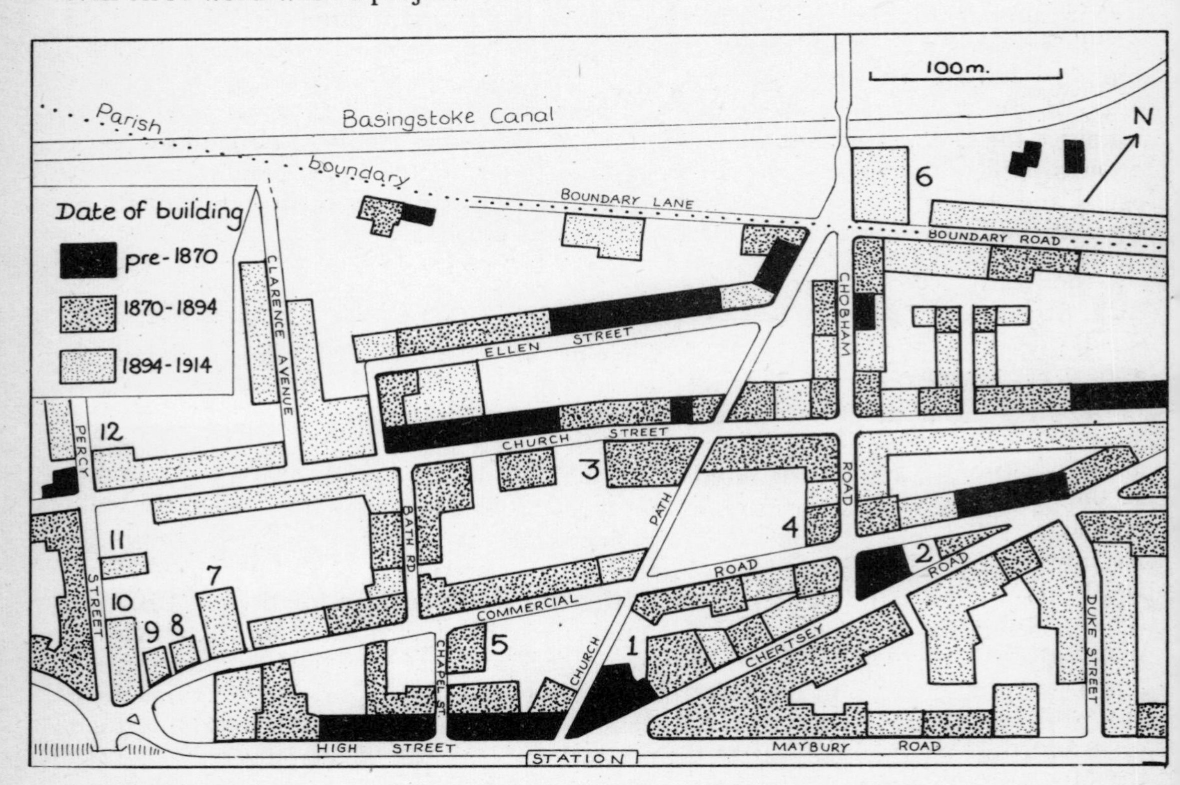

Fig. 15. The Development of Woking Town Centre 1870–1914

1. The Albion Hotel
2. The Red House Hotel
3. Christ Church
4. Gammon's store
5. Baptist chapel
6. Victoria Hospital
7. Commercial Road Methodist church
8. Constitutional Club
9. Woking U.D.C. offices
10. Woking Public Hall
11. St Dunstan's Mission church
12. Co-operative store

The Town Centre 1860–1914

The central area grew only slowly in the 1860s and 1870s, and in a most haphazard fashion. Although it attracted the attention of speculators, and in May 1863 the West Surrey Mutual Benefit Building Society opened an office at the *Albion*, potential residents did not seem to be enthusiastic about the prospect of moving to the district. In 1870 the only properties, apart from the *Albion* itself, were a row of new houses in what became High Street, facing the railway, and, in Providence Street (later Church Street), a few detached and semi-detached houses, with a little row of small villas behind these in Ellen Street (West Street). To the east there were no roads at all, and Bridge Road (Chobham Road) and Chertsey Road had only a few scattered cottages[8] (*see* Fig. 15).

Already, though, the future importance of this part of the parish was becoming clear to some. In January 1870 the *Surrey Advertiser* reported that:

> 'There are those who believe that the neighbourhood of the railway station will become, ere many years, covered with buildings, and that the erections now known as the town of Woking, will be designated the *old*, as distinguished from the new town of Woking to spring up at the railway station.'[9]

This seems to be the first use of the name 'Old Woking'.

There was little commercial development until the late 1870s (*see* Chapter Twelve) but then the pace quickened, and almost by accident a shopping area evolved along High Street and Chertsey Road, with offshoots in Chobham Road and Maybury Road (not officially renamed 'Broadway' until 1923). The retailers and workshops were scattered amongst the houses, and the centre remained straggling and inadequate. The architecture was invariably mediocre at best, and the High Street was dominated by the massive railway embankment which made it a one-sided street.

The church was built in 1884–93 on Providence Street, amongst the houses, whilst, at the western edge of the centre, on Commercial Road (a very depressing name typical of the period) a few public buildings appeared in the 1890s and 1900s. All are now demolished, swept away in the radical replanning of the centre during the 1970s. The best of the group was probably the Woking District Conservative Club (1898), tall and of red brick with white stone dressings, and designed by Henry Whitburn, an architect who was Chairman of the Urban District Council in 1913–14.[10]

On one side of this was Commercial Road Methodist church, in similar materials but with the addition of a tall slender spire which was a landmark on the featureless town centre skyline; the church was destroyed by fire in 1966. On the other side were the Municipal Buildings (1904) and the Woking Public Halls (1895), later the Grand Theatre. These buildings formed a little group (Plate XXXII) which faced the junction of High Street and Commercial Road, remodelled in 1903–4 with a small public garden and underground lavatories. It was a strange town which was content to have its very modest public buildings staring across some lavatories at a massive and dominating railway embankment. Such were the results of the negligence displayed by the Necropolis Company.

By 1895 most of Commercial Road, Chapel Street and Bath Road had been built up, and in the next year Duke Street was constructed across the land that had once been reserved for a church and schools. The lower part of Chertsey Road was developed in stages from the early 1880s, with the largest single scheme being the Woking Station Estate, sold by the Necropolis Company in 1892. This occupied the east side of the road, between Addisons Road and Duke Street. Covenants required that the developers should not use the land for 'a Tavern, Beerhouse or Shop for the sale of Intoxicating Liquors . . . a Factory or a Bank'.[11] The evils of drink and money were clearly equated!

Clarence Avenue, which was in the vicinity of the present Library, was developed as a lower middle-class residential area, with small semi-detached villas, from the mid-1890s. It was named after Prince Albert Edward, Duke of Clarence and Avondale, who died in 1892. This was the only residential area which was not largely converted to other uses by the middle of the 20th century. Commercial Road, which in its central section was at one time entirely occupied by houses, soon lost most of its residents as business uses took over. By 1914 the plan of the town centre was virtually complete, but in terms of appearance and the facilities which it offered it was scarcely satisfactory.

Walton Road and Goldsworth

The decision of the Necropolis Company, in 1858–59, to move the nascent town centre across the railway and to associate the new site with small cheap plots ensured that the long narrow belt of land, rarely more than half a mile wide, between the railway and the canal, would assume an inferior social status. Although there were attempts in the late 1870s to publicise Goldsworth as a 'superior' district these failed and by the 1890s this area, like its twin to the east of the centre, was regarded as suitable only for artisans and clerks.

In 1870 Goldsworth had included a scattering of recently built houses and a few small farms nearer to the canal, amongst them Oaks Farm and Vale Farm. Thereafter it grew in a very haphazard fashion, partly because the Necropolis Company was not the only landowner. Plots were sold off piecemeal by the different owners and were developed independently of each other. This is reflected in the shape of the road network. The central spine route, Goldsworth Road, winds because it was the ancient trackway across the heath from Woking village and Heathside to Knaphill. When the area was built up no attempt was made to improve its alignment. On either side there are short streets and pathways, unconnected with each other and not forming a network. Thus Poole Road and Cherry Street were not linked to Butts Road or Kingsway. Much of the building was of an inferior quality, and in the late 19th and early 20th centuries Goldsworth was known as an unhealthy and overcrowded district.

To the east of the centre there was only poorly drained and scrubby heathland until the early 1870s, with no buildings and no roads other than dirt tracks. In 1869 the Necropolis Company began to lay out a grid pattern of roads on this part of the common, before selling it off for house-building.[12] The area was constricted by the railway to the south and by the parish boundary to the north and east, the latter marking the edge of the land purchases of the early 1850s. These factors dictated the shape of the road pattern, and the need to avoid crossing the boundary was responsible for the curve in Boundary Road near the gasworks and the tuning-fork shape of Arnold Road and Eve Road, crammed into the corner of the Necropolis Company lands at the edge of the parish (*see* Fig. 16).

From the mid-1870s the company held regular auctions of plots in the east end of Woking and building operations began in 1879. Substantial areas were sold, for resale after subdivision, to a shadowy undertaking, the United Land Company, one of several speculative development firms with which the Necropolis Company had connections. The intention of both companies was that the district should be built up as a lower middle-class sector of the town, contrasting with the more expensive properties to the south of the railway. The plots were therefore large enough only for the terraces, semi-detached and tiny detached residences of that income group.

Even within this limited area there was to be social grading. When, in 1888, the Necropolis Company disposed of the last large portion of what it was marketing as the 'Woking Common Estate', it advertised the land as suitable for 'small villa-type

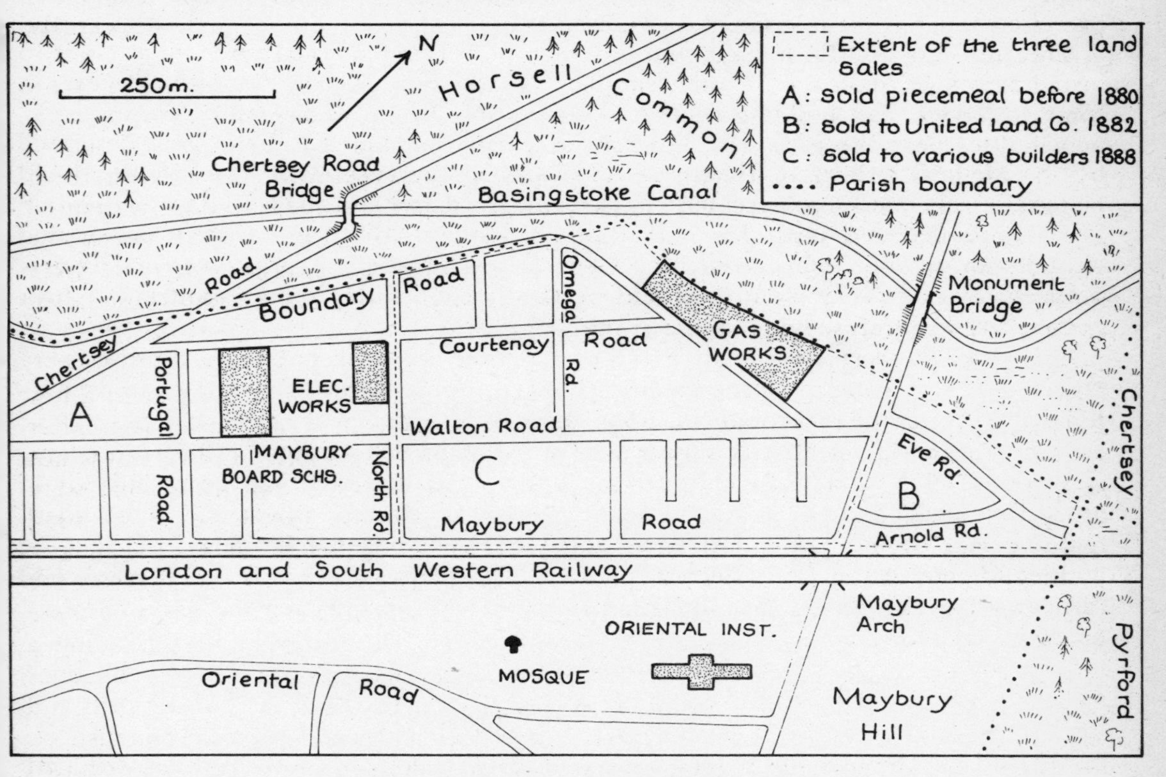

Fig. 16. The East End of Woking 1870–1914

residences'.[13] It offered 201 plots covering most of the area between the railway, Boundary Road and Board School Road. Frontages increased from north to south, those on Boundary Road being 30 feet and those on Maybury Road and Monument

Road close to the Railway Arch were 60–80 feet. All had a 15-foot depth of front garden except those close to the Arch, where 22 feet 6 inches was allowed. The implication was that Maybury Road would be more exclusive than the streets to the north, with the peak property values being by the Arch itself. This might seem surprising, in view of the noise and dirt from the road and the railway, but perhaps the company felt that having the better properties in sight of the railway was a good advertisement. The transition between the small detached properties opposite the railway and the terraced houses on Boundary Road is still very marked, although ironically the situation is now reversed, and the more desirable residences are those facing the common on Boundary Road.[14]

Most plots were bought, eventually, by small private builders, who proceeded to erect cheap and shoddy housing. Although there were by this time bye-laws to control the worst excesses of unplanned and unserviced development, many of the regulations were openly flouted by the builders, and the local authorities were unable, before 1893 when the Woking Urban Sanitary Authority or Local Board was formed, to exercise enough force to compel their observance.

The land was poorly drained, and the Necropolis Company had made no attempt to install sewerage, drainage or water supplies. Roads were unmade for over 20 years in some instances, and building standards were poor. In November 1897, for example, new houses near the gasworks, built by a speculator named Cohen, were described by the Medical Officer of Health as 'the worst property in Woking . . . built of old materials, very badly constructed . . . exceedingly damp and inadequately drained'.[15] They were declared unfit for habitation in January 1899 and Cohen was forced virtually to rebuild them before the Council was satisfied. Nearby, an area of new property in Courtenay Road was said in March 1906 to be 'quite insanitary . . . wet and muddy with refuse lying on the ground'.[16]

This from the very start of its life, and at a time when other local authorities were taking the first steps towards slum clearance, the east end of Woking was characterised by substandard properties, poor environment and physical deterioration. The construction of the electricity power station in Board School Road (1889) and of the gasworks (1892) in Boundary Road, the latter on land which had been laid out in plots for small houses, accelerated the process of decline which the substandard building had begun. Other industries appeared, including the Woking Laundry, the Woking Mineral Water Co., Glosters' corn-crushing plant and several timber yards and carpentry workshops. Already by 1914 this was without question the 'working-class' quarter of the town.

South of the Railway

Confirmed in 1859 as the higher-quality residential area of 'new' Woking, the land south of the railway acquired a completely different character from that to the north. It was designed to contrast with the dull geometric street pattern and regular plots of the centre, and its layout bore a close resemblance to the curving paths of Brookwood Cemetery. They were designed by the same architect, and the pleasant wooded glades with unexpected vistas and shady corners which were to create a peaceful and beautiful resting-place for the dead were to be equally suitable for the living of Heathside and Maybury. The design was intended to avoid monotony and regularity, and its winding roads and plots of differing sizes helped to achieve this. The retention of the lanes which had crossed the heath assisted, by producing a more varied road pattern. Most notable in that respect was the ancient trackway which followed the edge of Woking Common, along the top edge of the slope above the Hoe valley. It has survived, as Heathside Road, Pembroke Road and Park Road East, and the sharp bends in its central section reflect its origins.

The scale of building was limited until the late 1870s, for the 1859 sale was not a success in this area. Several large properties, including Heathside House and Wergs Cottage, were built in the White Rose Lane district, but, although an extensive road network was laid out across the heath, most of the remainder stayed as heather and gorse. The construction of the Royal Dramatic College (1860–65) brought renewed interest, and houses were built on Maybury Rough (around the present Shaftesbury Road). In 1869 the *Surrey Advertiser* noted that 'The disposition to erect Dwellings

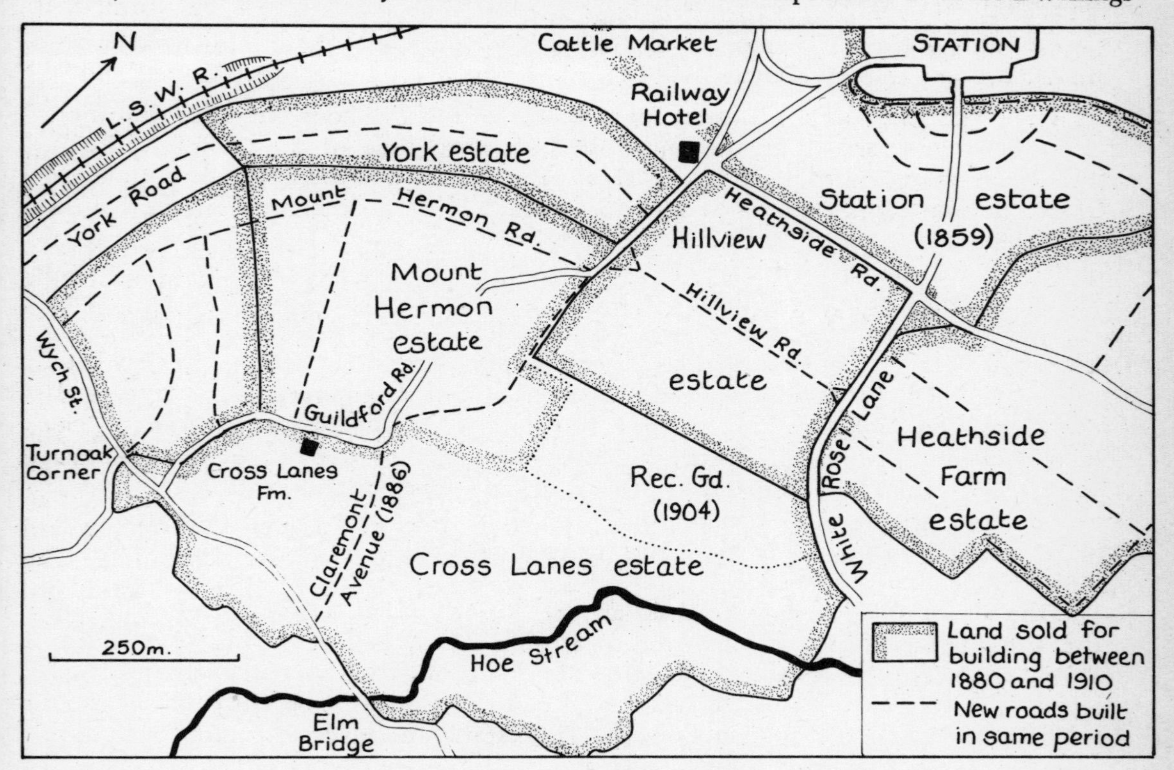

Fig. 17. Mount Hermon District 1860–1914

in this neighbourhood is becoming more manifest',[17] and from the late 1870s the land between the *Maybury Inn*, the railway and Heathside Farm was gradually sold and built on.

In 1882 came the first major sale of land by the owners of Heathside Farm, involving 16 acres between Park Road West and Heathside Road, and this was followed in 1883 by the largest of the various land sales south of the station. The Fladgate family sold their 136-acre Cross Lanes Farm, covering all the area between Elm Bridge, the *Railway Hotel* and White Rose Lane, and westwards to Wych Street. The farm was sold for building, not as a going concern: 'from its being so admirably situate between Main Roads, and from its beauty and healthfulness, [it] offers an Opportunity for Investment Seldom met with'.

The sales catalogue extolled the virtues of the property, and of Woking:

> 'It is in the heart of one of the loveliest parts of the country, and from its commanding position all the beauties of the neighbourhood are open to it . . . its surroundings of large heath covered Commons constitute it one of the healthiest spots in the Country, a fact well known to the leading physicians who strongly recommend it to their patients, . . . railway communication, which is exceptionally good . . . is another feature in its desirability to city men and gentlemen whose daily occupations require their presence in the metropolis . . . the Estate is ripe for development and so admirably situated . . . that it lends itself most readily to many excellent schemes for subdivisions . . . it offers altogether an exceptional opportunity to Capitalists and others of making a most genuine and profitable investment.' [18]

This sale was of great significance for Woking, for the area concerned was the whole of the southern approach to the new town, on either side of the Guildford Road, whilst its development from 1885 onwards was a major contributor to the population increase. Several large estates 'of superior character' were developed on the former Cross Lanes Farm, with distinctive features of their own. The portion west of Guildford Road was divided into large plots along gently curving roads, as the 'Mount Hermon estate', across the hillslope towards Turnoak Corner. To the north a small block was sold separately, and christened 'the York Estate' in 1893. The Duke and Duchess of York (later King George V and Queen Mary) were married in that year. It was described as 'adjoining the favoured Mount Hermon area . . . in a most advantageous position on high ground surrounded by superior residences'.[19] The railway which ran along the entire northern boundary of the estate was not mentioned! York Road was laid out on the land, and was built up with a mixture of detached and large semi-detached properties; there are some excellent examples of Edwardian suburban building here, and many houses still have their attractive white-painted wooden balconies.

On the other side of Guildford Road the Suburban Land Company bought the entire tract between Hoe Stream and Heathside Road, and marketed it, after subdivision, as the Hill View estate. For once the claims of extensive vistas were justified, for from the south of the estate (Hillview Road and Constitution Hill) the sweep of the North Downs could indeed be seen. The estate was made still more attractive after 1904, when the land sloping down to the Hoe Stream was sold to the Council and laid out as a public park: it was thus preserved from further building (*see* Chapter Eleven).[20]

At the southern end of the Cross Lanes estate the land was sold to several different builders, and so there was a greater diversity of house-types. The existing road network was inadequate, and a new road was built to cut out the diversion to Turnoak

Corner for traffic to Woking village and Kingfield. The road linked Elm Bridge with the foot of Guildford Hill, and was completed in 1887. It was called Claremont Avenue, after the home of the Duchess of Albany, who in that year laid the foundation stone of Christ Church.[21]

Building on the various division of the Cross Lanes land continued until the First World War. Many of the houses are excellent examples of their type, large and expensive but not in the most superior category. They were built by or for the professional people for whom Woking was becoming a magnet. Redevelopment since 1960 has meant the loss of all the Hillview estate and much of Mount Hermon, but there are good and scarcely altered original examples in Constitution Hill, in York Road as already mentioned, and at the lower end of Claremont Avenue. In Brooklyn Road and West Hill Road there are many of the larger properties. It is essential that care should be taken to protect some of the better examples, particularly those with ornamental woodwork. The charming 16th- and 17th-century Cross Lanes farmhouse, on the south side of Guildford Road, is a fortunate survival, its existence little suspected by many of those who daily use the busy road.

Hook Heath, the highest part of the Borough of Woking, is now one of the most exclusive and beautiful parts, with its fine conifers, quiet roads and large houses. During the 17th and 18th centuries it was the haunt of tinkers and squatters, and around College Lane and Wych Hill there was an untidy collection of poor cottages, sandpits and smallholdings. The area was somewhat isolated by the railway lines in their deep cuttings, and it was not until the end of the 1880s that the Necropolis Company attempted to sell land in the area.

Using experience gained from the development of expensive residential areas elsewhere in Woking, the company used more subtle marketing techniques, and emphasised the seclusion, the attractive setting and the fine views from Hook Hill southwards to the Hogs Back and the North Downs. It established an estate office in Hook Heath itself, to provide a more personal service to prospective purchasers, and enticed them with the promise of membership of the new and exclusive Hook Heath Golf Club.[22]

The plan of the new district involved three wide, straight and tree-lined roads, Hook Heath Avenue, Holly Bank Road and the significantly named Golf Club Road, with Hook Heath Road winding along the edge of the hilltop plateau. To the west was the golf course, to the south and east the open fields sloped down to Mayford, and to the north the railway, in a deep cutting, preserved the 'separateness' of the area. Plots were very large, almost all being at least an acre, and the houses were correspondingly impressive, hidden behind tall holly hedges and surrounded by pines and firs. The main period of building was 1895–1914, although further development took place after 1920. The dominant character, though, is of Edwardian opulence: several of the houses were designed by architects of international repute. Fishers Hill and Fishers Hill Cottage are by Lutyens, with gardens by Gertrude Jekyll.[23]

West Woking

The choice of the heathland south of the old squatter village of Knaphill as the site of a Convict Prison and a Lunatic Asylum (*see* Chapter Seven) reinforced the historic tendency for this area to be largely lower-class and artisan in its social composition. After the 1860s the village expanded in a piecemeal and unplanned fashion, adding to the incoherence of its appearance. The patches of common and the smallholdings of the old village were infilled with short rows of cottages and with single dwellings, and by the end of the century they were interspersed with some shops and workshops, brickpits and small market-gardens, producing the untidy and confused character which is still typical of Knaphill.

During the 1870s and 1880s the remainder of Knaphill Common north and west of the asylum was sold by the Necropolis Company, and developed with terraced cottages and small semi-detached villas. The quality of much of the building was poor, necessitating some slum clearance after 1950, although many of the inhabitants were originally employees of the institutions, and as such rather higher on the social scale than labourers and other artisans. The land north of the boundary with Horsell, because it was in agricultural use and ownership, was not developed until the middle of the present century, and until the 1930s the built-up area stopped sharply at the border.

West of the main road from Guildford to Bagshot there was little building until the last two decades of the century, although Brookwood station was opened in 1864. The narrow belt of land between the railway and the canal was not obviously suitable for development until the pressure on the more desirable sites, towards Knaphill, increased as suburban growth from Woking began. In the 1880s the first houses of Brookwood village were built, and gradually, but in a characteristically unplanned way, the elongated community grew, scarcely more than one house deep, along the Knaphill to Pirbright road. It has remained isolated, with the railway and canal to the north and south, the cemetery beyond the railway, and heathlands to the west and east.

St Johns, at the southern end of Knaphill Common, shared in the building boom provoked by the construction of the prison and asylum. It provided housing for employees and there was some commercial growth encouraged by the income brought to the district. The earlier community, centred on the canalside at Kiln Bridge, and comprising labourers working in the brickfields, farms or nurseries, by the late 1830s had grown sufficiently to be given a separate chapel-of-ease and, from the mid-1840s, the name of St Johns.

In the 1870s and 1880s terraced housing was built on both sides of the canal with small and cheap villas in Barrack Path and Copse Road, whilst the village began to extend outwards along the roads towards 'The Hermitage' and Goldsworth. The steep rise of St Johns Hill marked a rapid transition between lower- and higher-value properties. On the upper slopes the wealthy built their homes, attracted by the extensive views across the valley to Chobham Common and, after 1893 when the Jackman family sold 40 acres of tree nurseries on the hill, by the potential for beautiful and secluded woodland settings.[24]

Horsell

The village of Horsell stagnated until the early 1880s, and the ancient core remained almost unscathed by modern development until that time. It was surrounded by fields, heathlands and nurseries, and despite the proximity of Woking station it still appeared entirely rural in character. Such a quality could not survive indefinitely, however, and from the middle of the 1880s the village came increasingly within the suburbanising

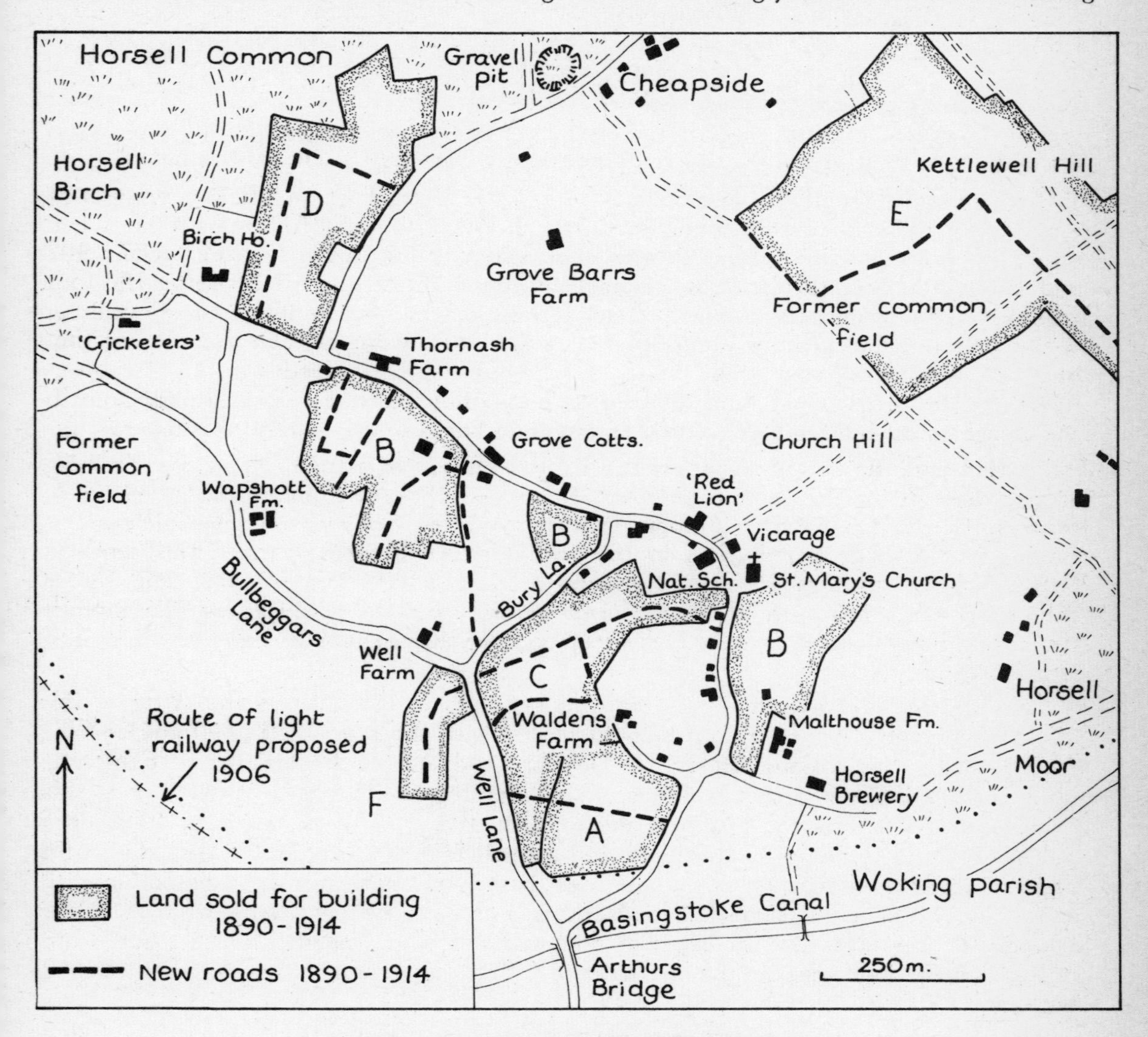

Fig. 18. Changes in Horsell Village 1890–1914.

A Abbey Farm
B Horsell Nurseries
C Waldens Park estate
D Horsell Common estate
E Horsell Rise and Kettlewell Hill
F Woking Co-operative Society Garden Suburb

influence of Woking. Land to the south and west of the main street was sold for housing, and a tentacle of development extended from Woking, over the canal at Wheatsheaf Bridge, and along Chobham Road towards Kettlewell.

The land ownership in the vicinity of the village was unusually fragmented, with several small farms and market gardens, and this produced a piecemeal and uncoordinated development. Each piece of land was separately sold and built over, with its own access road, which accounts for the complex road pattern west of Horsell High Street. Abbey Farm was sold in 1890, Horsell Nurseries in 1899, and Waldens Farm in 1900. The last was described as 'most eligible and ripe for development as a small Building Estate. Woking Station is a very rapidly growing Town, and this Estate must greatly increase in value'.[25] Abbey Road was built in two stages in 1892 and 1896, Waldens Park Road in 1898, and Ormonde Road from 1901. The houses ranged from very small semi-detached properties on the low-lying and unfashionable Arthurs Bridge Road, to middle-class detached houses on the Waldens Park estate.

To the north of the village Russell Road was laid out in two phases during 1902 and 1904. It was marketed as the 'Horsell Common Estate', with 125 plots of 20-foot frontage. The promoters claimed, falsely, that it was 'within 20 minutes' walk of Woking Station' and, more accurately, that the plots were 'suitable for the erection of small Villa Residences . . . or Cottages, which are urgently needed in the neighbourhood'.[26] The proposed Woking & Bagshot Light Railway, which was to pass close to the village, and would improve access to the main line station, was also mentioned.

Further east the new housing around Kettlewell was of a superior quality, for here as elsewhere in the district the builders of expensive houses shunned the older village centres. The National Land Company, another of the shadowy concerns which undertook speculative property deals in the area during the early years of this century, bought up several large tracts of farmland in East Horsell before 1914. These were then subdivided into plots, roads were marked out, and the land was resold. Amongst the farms bought were Potters Corner (Woodham Road), Castle Farm and parts of Horsell Grange.[27]

The most interesting of all the housing schemes in Horsell was the 'Woking Cooperative Society Garden Suburb'. It originated with the purchase in 1908 of land off Well Lane by the Woking, Horsell & District Co-operative Society. At first this was used for grazing the Society's horses, and later for allotments, but in 1911 it was decided that it should be put to a more productive use. Work began in 1912 on a £9,000 scheme to build 30 dwellings and a small branch store, as the first stage of a more ambitious design. The scheme was based on 'garden city' principles, with attractive and spacious semi-detached cottages along a crescent, with a green at the far end. It was intended for lower-income families which needed housing but could not afford the high rents in the district, and it thus served as a substitute for municipal building.

The later phases of the plan were never started, but the Garden Suburb, now called Holyoake Crescent, survives almost unaltered, its architecture and plan bearing a close resemblance to the more famous 'garden city' designs at Letchworth and Hampstead. At the entrance, an inscription in brick on the gable of a house bears the proud title: 'W.C.S. Garden Suburb 1912'.[28]

So Horsell grew in two ways, as an expensive low-density suburb in the Kettlewell district, and with medium-density middle and lower middle-class housing around the village itself. Sadly, too little attention was paid then, and after 1918, to the retention of the many attractive features of the ancient main street. Writing in 1963 Nairn judged the place harshly: 'swamped by Woking. A few battered cottages remain from the old village'.[29] Horsell still has charm, and time has mellowed the rawness of the buildings dating from the last century, but much of its character was lost in the processes which began then.

Byfleet and Pyrford

Byfleet village, unlike Horsell, was comparatively unscathed upon the outbreak of the First World War. It was not easily accessible from a railway station, the nearest being Weybridge or Byfleet & Woodham, and road access was poor. It also lay in the damp lowlands of the Wey valley, and so was less attractive to the speculative builder than the slopes of St George's Hill or Woodham. The village scarcely grew between 1800 and 1860 and after this date the housing development was markedly less concentrated than in, for example, Horsell or Knaphill. The main change was the construction of several very large houses in extensive grounds, north of High Road. All have now disappeared, but they are recalled by street names today: Weymede, Shrapnells and Grasmere, for example.

These houses were built by wealthy Londoners who no longer needed to live in the city, and could afford to spend most of the week in their 'country residences', but who still wished to be within easy reach. Their tastes are reflected in the description of Petersham Place, sold in 1888: 'A Freehold Residence with 5 acres 2 roods 17 perches, with charming Pleasure Gardens and Grounds Formed with great Judgement, taste and originality'.[30]

Elsewhere in the village some small villas and terraces were built for lower-income groups, and these frequently lacked amenities. By the late 1890s the conditions of housing in the village were heavily condemned, and somewhat later the practice of building cheap, inferior properties led the Chertsey Rural District Council to attempt to 'prohibit the building of dwellinghouses upon sites so lowlying and waterlogged as to be absolutely unsuitable for the purpose and a constant source of danger to the health of the District'.[31]

The greatest change in Byfleet, and one which was traumatic for the entire lower Wey valley, was the building, in 1905–6, of Brooklands race track. This was strongly, but unsuccessfully, opposed by the parish and district councils, and straddled the borders of Byfleet, Chertsey and Weybridge. It entailed the diversion of the Wey and the demolition of two ancient farms, Brooklands and Wintersells. Its high embankments and noise could not fail to impinge upon the village, whilst during its construction there was constant trouble from traction-engines damaging roads.[32]

The owner of the race-track, the Hon. Henry Locke King, was the best known local resident and largest landowner, who also gave generously to the parish, so too much criticism could not be made. The Parish Council was, however, unhappy about the interference with public footpaths, and this resulted in a protracted dispute, eventually resolved in favour of Locke King. He was a pioneer aviator as well as motor enthusiast, and Brooklands became one of the earliest airfields in the country. The Byfleet Parish Council sent a letter in September 1913 asking him 'to stop the practice of Aviators practising with their Machines over the Village on account of the danger to life & property'.[33]

The relationship between Byfleet and West Byfleet was very similar to that between Old Woking and Woking. In the years before 1800 West Byfleet did not exist but was simply a road junction, known as Byfleet Corner, with a few scattered cottages and houses towards Pyrford and New Haw. It was largely waste (even though it had been enclosed in 1805) because the land was poor. The Surrey Industrial School (*see* Chapter Seven) arrived in 1879 and this stimulated some building, whilst in 1884 the L.S.W.R. agreed to build a new station to serve Byfleet, Pyrford and Woodham. After considering sites at Camphill Road and Sheerwater Road it settled upon Byfleet Corner, and in December 1887 Byfleet & Woodham Station was opened.[34]

By this date the opening of a station on a main line close to London was an almost infallible guarantee of increased land values, whilst the mere mention of a possible opening could excite speculation in property. The first sales in the West Byfleet area were in 1881, when Sheerwater Court was auctioned, and the land between the railway and the canal from Old Avenue to Camphill Road was acquired by developers. This was followed in 1883 by the 10½ acres between Byfleet Corner, Camphill Road and the railway, 'very agreeably situated . . . on high ground, with fine views, and therefore

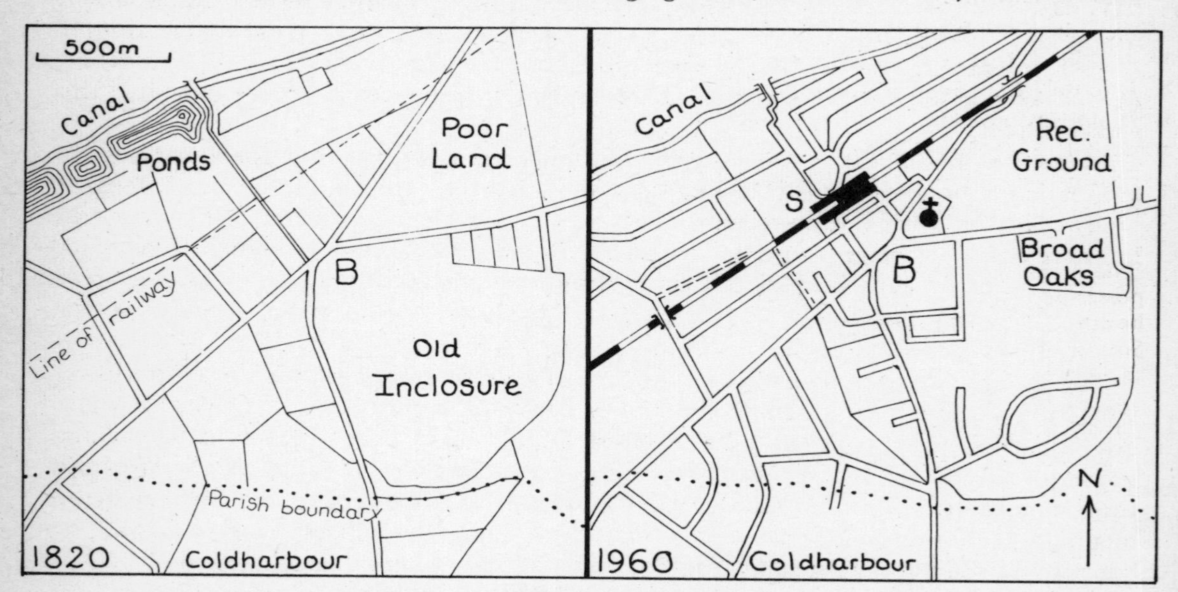

Fig. 19. West Byfleet: the Enclosure Landscape and its Effect upon Later Development.

B Byfleet Corner S Railway Station

admirably suited for the Erection of small Residences. Undoubtedly the best site for the proposed New Station'. The views are not apparent today![35]

Between 1887 and 1914 the land around the new station was built over. The road pattern was dictated in large part by the earlier property boundaries and field shapes, themselves laid down by the Enclosure Commissioners nearly a century before (*see* Fig. 19). West Byfleet was thus an excellent example of an urban area moulded by the features of the rural landscape which preceded it. Partly for this reason the plan was not very logical, and as with Woking there was no attempt to produce a community which had a focal point. The station was on the edge of the centre, the church (1912) likewise, and the shopping area was small and an afterthought.

Some higher-density housing was built north of the railway, in Station Road and Claremont Road, and in Camphill Road and Lavender Road to the south (the name of the latter refers to the lavender which was once grown there, to supply the essential oil distillery in Pyrford). Most of this housing was of the standard 'small villa-' type, on plots of 20–30 feet frontage. Elsewhere, the growing 'village' was almost entirely at low densities, with large houses in tree-lined streets, and much of the natural woodland retained. In the vicinity of the station such extravagant use of land rapidly succumbed to the pressures of commerce, and redevelopment took place in the early years of this century, with properties only 30 years old being pulled down to make way for shops and businesses. In 1906–7, for example, the extensive grounds of 'Rosemount' were used for road-widening and for the main shopping parade which bears that name.[36]

Between Byfleet and West Byfleet is Dartnell Park, one of the best of the many expensive low-density estates so frequently found in Woking. The land was enclosed in 1806, but was never used for agriculture, and by 1870 it had become thickly grown with conifers; it was called, after its owner, Dartnell's Wood. It was then renamed, and as Dartnell Park was subdivided into building plots and sold off in 1884–98. The sales were in several phases: the ambitious 1887 scheme involved 43 plots of 1¼ to 3½ acres, although later divisions were usually smaller.

Extensive publicity centred on the theme of 'a country residence near to town', and upon the natural landscape qualities:

> 'The estate is adorned with Majestic Timber . . . giving richness and beauty to home new . . . possessing so many advantages that it is probably without equal in the country . . . the dry healthy soil and air, varied drives and walks amidst some of the most beautiful Pine and Sylvan Scenery [fulfil all] the requirements of a country gentleman, or those whose vocations call them to town.'[37]

Later sales were accompanied by persuasive descriptions of the tennis club and boat club which would be provided for the fortunate few who lived there, and one brochure announced that the plots offered 'excellent sites for full-sized tennis lawns at no great expense'. The developers even chartered a special train from Waterloo, and provided free tickets and luncheon in a marquee by the canal for prospective buyers. Designs were produced for possible houses, one showing a bizarre Gothic Romantic building, with overtones of the neo-vernacular; it had tall chimneys in the Tudor style, high tile-hung gables, Gothic windows and half-timbering.

Pyrford remained rural until the First World War, and was comparatively little affected by the changes going on elsewhere in the district. The exceptions to this were the Old Woking Road and Coldharbour, where the influence of West Byfleet was felt, and growth spilled over the parish boundary. This was particularly so after the St

Nicholas Waifs & Strays Home was built in Floyds Lane in 1906. Some 'suburban' houses were erected, such as those in Aviary Road (1910–12) and elsewhere the properties were large, detached and secluded.

South Woking

When the focus of development moved to the vicinity of the station, from the 1860s onwards, the ancient village of Woking and its attendant hamlets of Kingfield, Shackleford and Westfield stagnated. They grew very slowly during the later 19th and early 20th centuries, despite the industries which existed there, and in 1914 the historic linear form along High Street was almost unaltered. Houses were, even at this date, only one deep, and such growth as there had been consisted primarily of filling in gaps along the street frontage itself, producing a complex pattern of buildings of different centuries. Examples of pre-1914 housing along this road include New Forest Cottages, Kingfield Green, and those opposite the Manor House in Old Woking. There had been a little development off the main street at Kingfield, where Stockers Lane and Loop Road both have pre-1914 houses, but the linearity was otherwise remarkably well preserved.

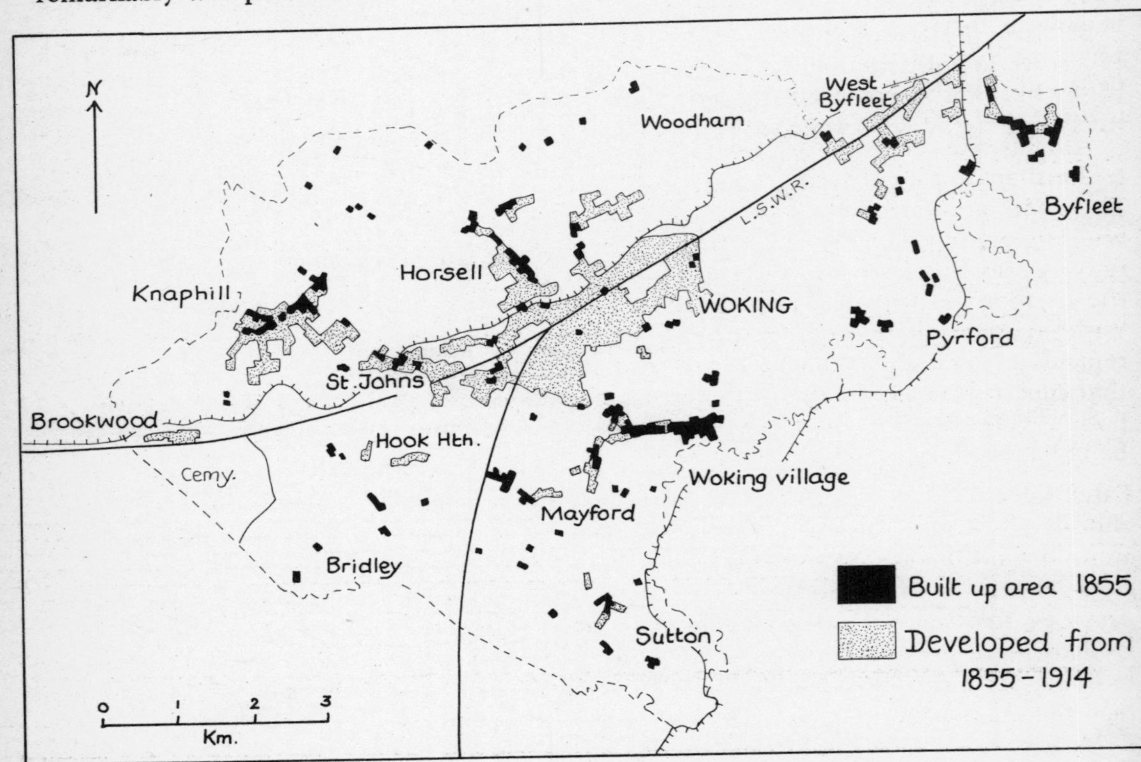

Fig. 20. The Growth of Woking 1855–1914

Elsewhere in the southern part of Woking there had been equally little growth, because agriculture had declined and these places were remote from railways, whilst the break-up and sale of estates had not taken place on the scale of the process in the urban area. A notable exception to this was between Sutton Green and Mayford, where the 122½-acre Frog Lane Farm was sold in 1894. It was offered either as a single going concern, or in 14 different lots, and eventually the latter method was selected.[38]

The farm was said to be a choice site 'for the erection of Country Residences in a beautiful part of Rural Surrey within easy reach of London: the sites are elevated and command delightful views; the soil is dry and the situation must be very healthy'. These very large plots, some of 7½ acres, were sold, and only one, covering 40 acres, remained in farming use. The resulting housing was, of course, at unusually low densities and particularly select. It was built along Pyle Hill, a private road on the line of an enclosure lane of 1811. The 'y' in Pyle was used instead of 'i' to indicate good taste.

The New Town

Between 1860 and 1914 a new town grew up on the bleak heathlands of Woking Common, and the process of urban development transformed the neighbouring villages. The change had been astonishing, for within half a lifetime a peaceful rural area had become a thriving, multiplying urban community. As we have seen it was, in many ways, an inadequately planned and poorly serviced town, but a town it was, without question. Further expansion and the remedial measures of later generations have made it the largest town in Surrey, and a major commercial centre.

All this may be traced to two factors, the choice of a northern route for the London & Southampton Railway in 1834 and the burial problem of the capital in the 1840s. The latter produced the bizarre solution of a giant cemetery, and the location of this was largely determined by the railway. Woking was not a railway town, although the railway was fundamental to its growth. It was a cemetery town, and the influence of the London Necropolis Company upon its shape and character was extremely strong. Without the railway and necropolis it is likely that Woking village would have remained comparatively small, perhaps not unlike Chobham or Odiham today, but that must, of course, be pure hypothesis. The planting of a completely new town in a barren heathland by a cemetery company is fascinating enough for such fancies to be unnecessary.

Chapter Six

LOCAL GOVERNMENT REFORM AND SERVICES 1860-1914

THE RAPID GROWTH of the town, described in previous chapters, made the provision of such basic services as gas, water, and sewerage a matter of increasing urgency. During the second half of the 19th century public and private enterprise made slow and often uncertain progress towards satisfying this demand, whilst over the same period the structure of local government itself changed considerably in response to the ever-widening scale of its tasks, and to take account of the development of a completely new town in the Woking area.

Local Government to 1890

The first reform in the local government of the area had been the transfer of Poor Law functions from the parish to the Unions in 1834, and the recognition that vestries were also inadequate for the administration of other services was responsible for a series of national reforms, and the establishment of new authorities, in the 1860s and 1870s.

In April 1864 Surrey was divided into Highway Districts under the terms of the Highways Act of 1862. By this measure the parishes lost the powers over roads which they had held since the reign of Elizabeth I, and were amalgamated for this purpose into larger areas, administered by Boards which were elected by the vestries. Geographically, the Highway Districts were based on the Petty Sessional Divisions, themselves derived from the ancient Hundreds, so that Woking was included in the Guildford Highway District, and the other three parishes within that of Chertsey. Since the Borough of Guildford, which possessed its own highway powers, was excluded from the Highway District, Woking was the largest of the 13 constituent parishes in the Guildford Highway District, with four of the 17 members of the Board by 1880.

Highway Districts were usually unpopular, because they had deprived the parish of one of its oldest and most significant powers. Dissatisfaction with their performance increased as costs rose, particularly when former turnpike roads were returned to public control. As early as 1869 the Board of the Guildford Highway District voted for a partial return to parish control, and in 1873, by a majority of ten to four, it asked the Surrey County Justices to allow its dissolution. After some hesitation the request was refused, and so the discontent continued, to be exacerbated after 1878 when another Highways Act introduced the principle that the financial contributions of each parish were to be in accordance with its rateable value, and not, as previously, with the length of public road within its bounds.[1]

In Woking parish there was particular opposition to the Highway District, because it failed to meet the needs of the growing town. The rural parishes, which had a disproportionatly large voting strength, considered that they were subsidising the two urban parishes, Woking and Stoke next Guildford, with their greater road mileage and heavier traffic, and hence their need for larger sums of money. The rural members therefore used their majority on the Board to block the more costly schemes for road improvements in Woking and Stoke, and would only allow minor works, such as filling in potholes. The special needs of Woking were thus neglected for over 30 years, resulting in a large backlog of essential works for the town council which took over in 1893. In the Chertsey District there was a more even balance between rural and urban interests, so that this inequitable situation did not arise.

The 1862 Highways Act was inspired by the inefficiency of the parishes in dealing with road matters. The 1872 Public Health Act was, in contrast, motivated by the complete absence of any provision for health and sanitation measures in rural areas. It established Rural Sanitary Authorities, which were to administer sewerage, drainage, lighting, building regulations and public health. The R.S.A.s were closely related to the Poor Law Boards of Guardians, who automatically became the Board of the R.S.A. The Woking area was split between Guildford- and Chertsey-based authorities, as with all other local government at this time. The former, including Woking parish, met at Stoke Union Workhouse, and the latter, which covered the other three, met at Ottershaw. There was no connection with the Highways Districts of the same names, and the areas of each were different.

Woking was always the largest constituent of the Guildford R.S.A., with almost twice the population of the next largest parish, Godalming Rural, in 1872, and providing nearly 30 per cent of the rate income of the Authority in 1892.[2] In Chertsey R.S.A. the three parishes in the area remained in a minority, with only 11.1 per cent of the rateable value in 1894, compared with 31 per cent in Walton-on-Thames and 26 per cent in Chertsey.[3] Woking was unquestionably badly served by the Guildford R.S.A., which was a conservative body, ill-equipped to cater for the pressing demands of a fast-growing town. In part the deficiency is explained by the same rural bias as affected the Highway District, but neglect was also due to protracted and wasteful bickering between the R.S.A. and the Local Government Board, the Ministry which supervised its affairs. In contrast, the Chertsey R.S.A. was known for its progressive character,[4] and, although most of its efforts were directed towards its urban parishes, Byfleet in particular derived some benefit. These rural areas were certainly better served than most in the county during the later 19th century.

By the early 1890s, therefore, the local government structure of the Woking area was confused and complicated. There were two Highway Districts, two Rural Sanitary Authorities and four parish Vestries. In addition, Woking and Pyrford had School Boards (*see* Chapter Eight) and the Surrey County Council had been established in 1888 to replace the County Justices. Although there was now a town of 12,000 people there was no form of urban government, and scarcely any evidence of the attributes of a civilised urban community. From 1890 a series of reforms was at last introduced, and a more efficient and straightforward system was created to carry out the task of providing adequate services for the town.

The Woking Urban Sanitary District

The increasingly urban character of the parish of Woking made it an anomaly within the Highway District and Sanitary Authority from their earliest years; a problem of which the Vestry was acutely aware. From the mid-1870s it made a series of fruitless attempts to persuade the Local Government Board to permit the separation of the parish and its constitution as an Urban Sanitary Authority, which would have highway powers in addition to those of health and sanitation, and would be in control of its own destiny. The L.G.B. would only concede the right of the Guildford R.S.A. to treat Woking, in certain specific respects, as though it were an urban area.[5]

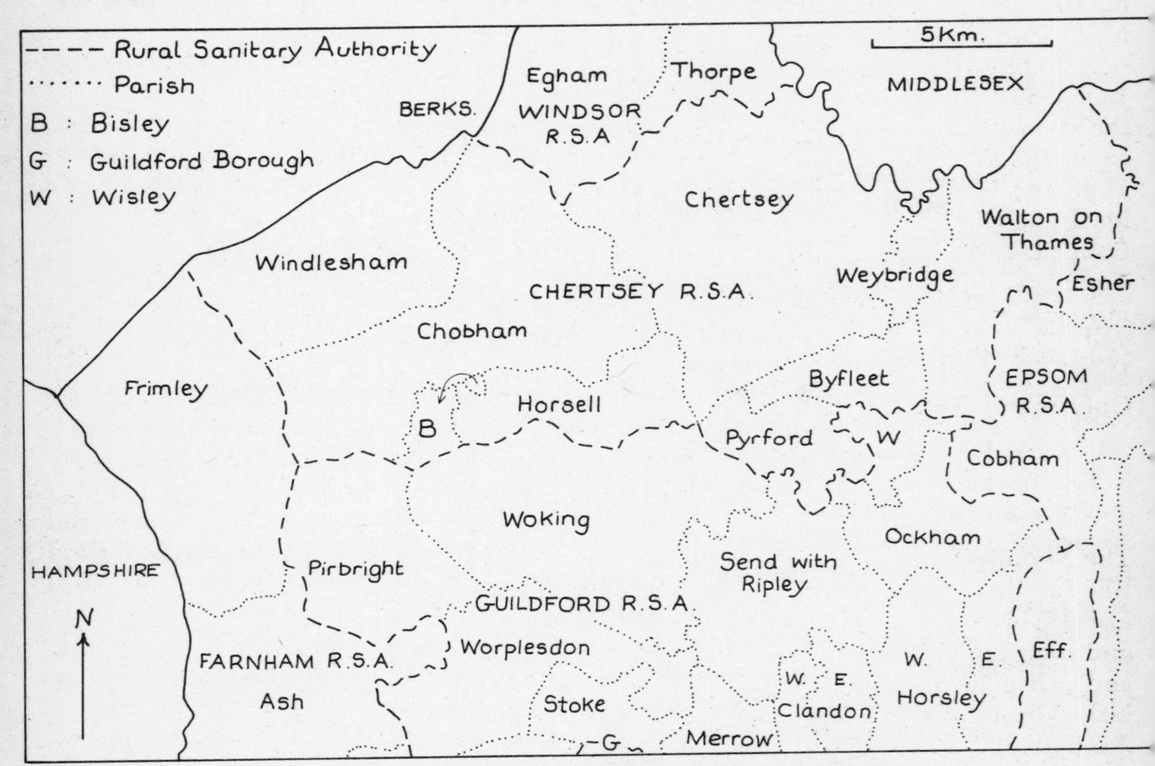

Fig. 21. Local Government in the Woking Area 1890

Under the Public Health Act of 1875 the R.S.A. could levy an additional special rate to provide a service in a single parish which it did not provide over its whole area. The procedure for acquiring such powers was lengthy, and each service had to be treated separately even for one parish. Thus, a rate could be levied to provide lighting, or fire services, or drains, but each of these would have to be individually approved and administered. In 1880 the Guildford R.S.A attempted to establish a 'Woking Committee', to which all the powers of the Authority would be delegated. That would effectively have separated the administration of Woking, although it would nominally have remained part of the R.S.A. However, the L.G.B. quashed the plan, stating that it was contrary to the terms of the 1875 Act, and was therefore illegal.[6]

The sewerage and drainage issues which came to the fore in the late 1880s led to a revival of separatist agitation, and Woking Vestry applied unsuccessfully for urban status in the summer of 1890. In the spring of 1892 the application was resubmitted, following a further delay in plans for the building of a sewerage system, and this time the L.G.B. was more sympathetic. The R.S.A. was not, because it feared the loss of one-third of its rateable value. It put forward a proposal that the parish should be split: the area around the station and the town centre would be granted urban status, but the remainder, including Woking village, St Johns and Knaphill, would become a new parish of Woking Rural, and stay within the R.S.A.[7]

A public inquiry into the Vestry plan was held at the Woking Public Hall on 20 June 1892. It revealed strong local support for urban status, and great opposition to the division of the parish on the lines suggested. The Local Government Board decided to accept the arguments of the Vestry and its supporters, and therefore on 1 October 1893 the Woking Urban Sanitary District came into being, with full powers over all local government matters except those reserved to the School Board and the County Council. It was governed by a democratically elected Local Board, or Council, and the Vestry was abolished for all civil purposes. For the first time the parish was divided into wards: Woking Village & Mayford, Sutton & Bridley, St Johns & Goldsworth, and Knaphill & Brookwood, returning three councillors each, and Woking Station & Maybury six. The full Council of 18 held its first meeting on 4 October 1893, at the Goldsworth Hall.

The Reforms of 1894

The Woking Local Board had a life of only 15 months, for at the time of its birth a Bill for the general reform of local government was passing through Parliament. The Local Government Act of 1894 provided for the abolition of most existing authorities and their replacement by a uniform system of councils for civil parishes, rural districts and urban districts, which would be directly elected, all-purpose and geographically rationalized bodies. Under the Act, from 1 January 1895, Woking Urban Sanitary Authority and Local Board were replaced by the Woking Urban District Council. The change was one of name only, for the new Council controlled the same area and had the same powers as its predecessor, and included most of the former councillors and officers.

Chertsey Rural Sanitary Authority presented many more problems. In April 1894 it had stated its desire to remain identical in area and merely to change its name to Chertsey Rural District.[8] Surrey County Council, however, favoured the separation of the urban parishes of Walton-on-Thames, Weybridge and Chertsey, and their assumption of urban status, as had recently happened to Woking. Thorpe, which due to the complexities of history had been administered by Windsor R.S.A. (Berkshire) although in Surrey, was to be added to the proposed Chertsey R.D.C. in partial compensation. Since the County Council was responsible for the implementation of the 1894 Act, this arrangement was the one adopted, and which came into effect on 1 January 1895.[9]

Chertsey Rural District Council bore all the marks of a 'rump' authority, since it was composed of those parishes left over after the excision of the three Thames-side towns. It was a geographical absurdity, with seven parishes divided into three separate portions: Thorpe, over four miles from the nearest point of the remainder of the district; Byfleet and Pyrford; and Bisley, Horsell, Windlesham and Chobham. The logical centre was Chobham, but the Council met at Chertsey, outside its administrative area. With the loss of the three towns Byfleet had acquired a

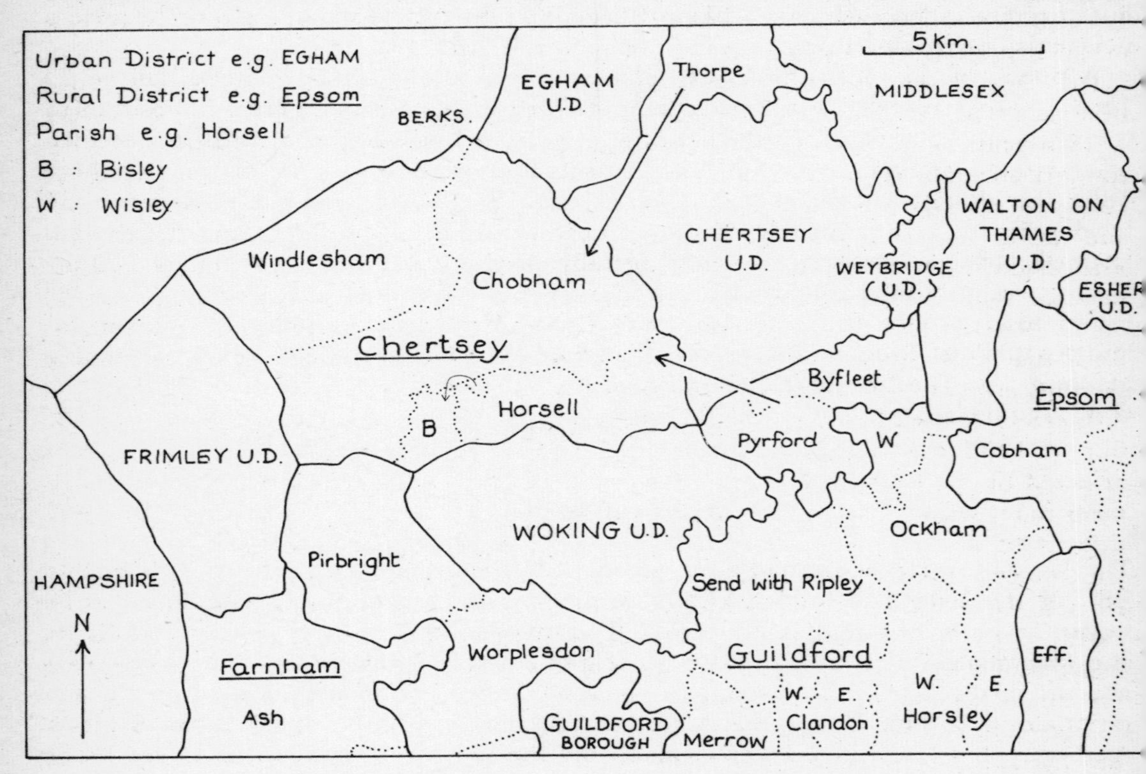

Fig. 22. Local Government in the Woking Area 1900

considerably increased importance, as the largest component of the R.D.C. apart from Windlesham. In 1895, the first year of its existence, the Council received 23 per cent of its rate income from Byfleet, 13 per cent from Horsell and 9 per cent from Pyrford. Nevertheless, Byfleet was under-represented, with only two of the 12 members, whereas four would have been appropriate.[10]

By the Act of 1894 the old system of vestries was also abolished, and in its place the civil parish was introduced. This was administered by a democratically elected parish council, to provide for small-scale local needs and, in the case of larger parishes, to act as agents of the rural district council in certain matters. The new parish councils of Horsell, Pyrford and Byfleet each met for the first time in the New Year of 1895, providing a third tier of local government beneath the county and the rural district.

The Union of Woking and Horsell

Even before the new system came into operation there had been talk of the possible amalgamation of the parishes of Woking and Horsell, which seemed to have common interests and were beginning to form a single built-up area. In April 1894 the Woking Local Board proposed to Horsell Vestry that the two parishes should unite to form one urban district from January 1895, and it would seem that the response was favourable.[11] For reasons which remain obscure the plan was not implemented, and Horsell became a separate civil parish.

Two years later Woking Council inquired of Horsell Parish Council whether it would support an application for the revision of their mutual boundary. This followed the old course of the Rive Ditch, its memory being perpetuated today by Boundary Road, and it was suggested that a more sensible line would be the canal between Arthurs Bridge and Monument Bridge.[12] Horsell parish stood to gain, in terms of area and rateable value, but the Parish Council opposed the Woking plan at the public inquiry on 31 March 1900. Surrey County Council therefore modified the proposal, and from 31 March 1901 only that part of Horsell lying south of the canal was transferred to Woking, an area of 58 acres with 23 people.[13]

In 1895 Horsell had contributed 13 per cent of the rate income of Chertsey R.D.C., but in 1902 this had increased to 18 per cent as suburban growth from Woking affected the parish. The failure of the Rural District Council to provide services commensurate with this expansion of population and rateable value produced much discontent locally. The lack of any mains drainage was a source of particular annoyance, and the possibility of providing that service independently encouraged Horsell Parish Council to consider breaking away from Chertsey R.D.C. Windlesham Parish Council proposed, in April 1903, to seek urban powers, and this fired the imaginations of Horsell councillors. In August 1903 the Parish Council voted to apply for separation, and the establishment of a Horsell Urban District Council.[14]

The County Council held an inquiry into the application on 31 December 1903 at the Horsell Parish Institute. Chertsey R.D.C. expressed its strong opposition to the plan, which would inevitably have led to the break-up of the whole district, and the County Council eventually decided against allowing the application. The proposed Horsell U.D. would have been one of the smallest in the country, and its population and rateable value could not have given it a sufficiently strong financial base for the provision of a wide range of services. More significantly, though, its destiny was clearly inextricably linked with that of its larger neighbour.[15]

Following the failure of its application, and still frustrated in its aim of providing a sewerage system for the area, Horsell Parish Council began to make overtures to Woking Urban District Council. The attractions of Woking's much greater resources, and its own enthusiasm for union, proved compelling. On 22 January 1906 a Parish Council committee was formed to approach Woking Council 'with a view to ascertaining upon what lines and on what conditions they would be prepared to consider the question of amalgamating with the parish of Horsell'.[16]

Woking U.D.C. offered generous terms, centred upon a guarantee of the immediate and subsidised construction of a full network of sewers. In a parish poll on 1 October 1906 the ratepayers of Horsell voted 195 to 118 in favour of union. At the ensuing public inquiry the Rural District Council and Bisley and Chobham Parish Councils opposed the amalgamation, the latter two because they feared that the territorial ambitions of Woking Council would not stop at the borders of Horsell.[17] The County Council, which had supported the union during the previous three years, rejected their pleas, and approved the proposal. On 1 October 1907 the parish of Horsell was united with the Urban District of Woking, and the old Parish Council was dissolved. On the enlarged Urban District Council there were four Horsell members, twice the representation on Chertsey R.D.C. The parish was divided into two wards, the North or Rural ward returning one member and the South or Village ward three.

The Future of Chertsey Rural District

The loss of Horsell and the imminent separation of Windlesham were to remove 45 per cent of the rateable value of Chertsey Rural District, and to leave it even more anomalous in shape. Therefore in the autumn of 1907 the Council decided that it was more sensible to reorganise the pattern of local government in the area, to make it more efficient and rational. It voted for its own abolition, and asked the constituent parishes for their views on the future. All expressed concern at the prospect of being absorbed by adjacent urban districts, but were equally doubtful about the value of the existing arrangement.[18]

Byfleet, by now greater in population and rateable value than Windlesham, was obviously large enough to become a separate urban authority. With this in mind a parish meeting of ratepayers voted in March 1908 for the establishment, at the earliest opportunity, of a Byfleet Urban District Council. The Parish Council was less ambitious, and after considering but rejecting some suggestions for union from Weybridge U.D.C., itself threatened by Walton-on-Thames, decided to support union with Pyrford only, as a small rural district, since 'the area [is] essentially rural in character and likely to remain so for many years to come'.[19] Pyrford Parish Council preferred independence, as Pyrford Rural District, which with just over 300 inhabitants would have been amongst the dozen smallest in England, and was clearly impossible. It therefore agreed to the Byfleet proposal.[20]

A public inquiry into the dissolution of the Rural District was held at Chertsey Town Hall on 8 October 1908. As a result of this the County Council decided to reject the application for dissolution, claiming that it did not wish to undertake a major reorganisation of local government in North West Surrey. The peculiar Chertsey Rural District thus survived against its own wishes. It was now reduced to five parishes in three separate pieces. Byfleet was by far the largest, with 47 per cent of the rateable value in 1909, and it became even more dominant as the years passed. Finally, in 1929, the administration of the Council was moved from Chertsey to West Byfleet, but in 1933 the long overdue radical reorganisation took place, and Chertsey Rural District was abolished.[21]

The Services

Roads

The condition of the roads in the Woking area was the cause of constant complaint throughout the half-century before the First World War. In Byfleet, Pyrford and Horsell the problems were those of many rural parishes, but in Woking the rapid growth of the town, and the neglect by the Highway District Board, combined to create a particularly serious deficiency in standards of maintenance and construction. Around the railway station the old tracks across the heath were subject to intensive use, and quickly became notorious for their inadequacy.

The real need was for a concerted attempt to level, surface and drain the roads throughout the built-up area, but the Highway Board would not approve the considerable expenditure involved. Filling in the deepest potholes, mending fences, and fighting off innumerable attempts by adjacent landowners to encroach upon verges and banks were useful, but did not touch the heart of the matter. To add to the problems, damage was regularly caused by floods, the new traction-engines and by military exercises on the nearby commons, and claims for compensation were rarely successful.

The Minutes of the Highway Board are full of reports and complaints about the appalling state of the roads. In 1871, for example, a resident described White Rose Lane as 'in so rough a state as to be impassable',[22] and in 1890 the inadequacy of the drainage led one observer to suggest that there was 'a natural course of surface water in Church Street and Percy Street',[23] in the very centre of the town. In the same year the Highway Board had to purchase chemicals to spray in Mount Hermon Road and Brooklyn Road, which were 'overgrown with weeds and grass'. The residents themselves contributed to the conditions, since they emptied foul effluent and waste into the streets, broke down fences, and even dug up the roads, as in 1871, when the Highway Board threatened prosecution after 'James Woods had taken a cartload of sand and gravel from Wych Lane'.[24] In July 1886 complaints were received that the road outside Woking Station had been blocked 'by Fishmongers and Butchers Stalls being placed thereon'.[25]

During the 1880s the Highway Board at last began to make some attempt to remedy the worst deficiencies, by adopting a few of the main roads and making them up to a more acceptable standard, and by requiring private developers to pay attention to the quality of estate roads: the latter power was not used to its full effect. In 1869 the 45 miles of public road in Woking parish had been allocated only '3 Wheelbarrows, 3 Rakes, 4 Scrapers and 1 Pump',[26] but in 1887 a steam-roller was bought from Aveling & Porter for use in the parish, and a second one was added in 1890.

The Woking Local Board and the Urban District Council were faced with a huge backlog of work bequeathed by the Highway District, and regarded road improvement as a priority. In the summer of 1894, for example, Walton Road, Maybury Road, Church Street and Bath Road were at last made up and adopted, but ruts and mud remained typical of many urban roads, and of almost all those outside the built-up area, until the First World War.[27]

Bridges

Unmade roads were a nuisance, but unsafe bridges were a positive danger, and this aspect of highway repair caused many difficulties for the local authorities during the period before 1914. Attempts to compel the London and South Western Railway Company to widen the railway arches involved a great deal of fruitless negotiation throughout the 1880s and 1890s. All the arches resembled short tunnels through the massive embankments, and with the growth of road traffic they had become major bottlenecks; the unwidened examples at Blackhorse Road and Brookwood still reveal this problem. The Railway Arch in Woking town centre, to which the name 'Victoria' was added in 1898, was only 20 feet wide, and had to cope with all traffic to and from the centre, as well as on the main Guildford–Chertsey road. It was also unlit and had no footway, and so was a danger to pedestrians and road traffic alike. It was only in 1906–7 that the Council was to reach agreement with the L.S.W.R. on the provision of a new 40-foot arch with lighting and footways.[28]

The river bridges, many of which were wooden and all of which were old, were also becoming dangerous by the 1880s. The traffic growth which resulted from urban development imposed severe strains upon their structures, and in 1883, for example, it was noted that Ell Bridge (Elm Bridge) was in an 'unprotected state' because the parapets had fallen down. The old name 'Ell Bridge' means 'plank bridge', and it was the ancient wooden structure, only 12 feet wide, which was still carrying all the traffic between Woking village and the station: it was finally rebuilt in 1891–92 with a 30-foot brick double arch, for £670.[29]

Chertsey Rural District Council spent £1,700 on rebuilding Plough Bridge, Byfleet, in 1903–4, after it had been declared unsafe following flood damage and general decay, and the Parish Council had made persistent complaint. The R.D.C. also rebuilt and resurfaced the causeway between Pyrford and Newark, in co-operation with Guildford R.D.C., and renewed the bridges over the Bourne at Mimbridge and Dunford.

The most pressing problems were those associated with the canal bridges, for these were complicated by the vexed question of ownership and responsibility for repair. The Basingstoke Canal bridges had been built in the 1790s, and were, a century later, structurally weak and too narrow and steep for the increased traffic. The Wheatsheaf and Chertsey Road bridges in the centre of Woking were notoriously bad, and during the 1890s were several times the subject of dispute between the latest of the canal owners and the local authorities. The canal company held that the local councils were legally required to keep the bridges in repair, a view which was hotly contested by the councils, and with good reason.

The issue remained unresolved by 1905, although notice to repair had been served on the company without effect; since it was in precarious financial circumstances it always seemed unlikely that the work would be done. In 1906 the situation became even more serious, because the deterioration of the brickwork meant that Woking U.D.C. and Chertsey R.D.C. had to impose restrictions on the use of all the bridges, including their closure at night, and in the autumn it was necessary to close the Arthurs Bridge and Chertsey Road Bridge completely. Since the latter carried the main

Woking-Chertsey road its closure could not be tolerated, and the two councils therefore made temporary repairs to the bridges during 1907 and 1908.[30]

The repairs involved the demolition of parapets and the arch of the bridge, and the erection of a wooden superstructure. Woking U.D.C. then promoted a private Act of Parliament which entitled it to take all necessary steps to recover the costs of bridge works from the owners of the canal. When this failed, a long and complex court case was initiated, but although this found in favour of the Council the costs were never recovered, not least because nobody connected with the canal had any money to hand over. After the First World War Woking U.D.C. abandoned the attempt to enforce payment, and in 1922–24 undertook the total reconstruction of the bridges at Brookwood, Hermitage, St Johns, Chobham Road, and Chertsey Road. Of the old-style bridges that at Harelands survives.[31]

Sewerage and Drainage

This prosaic subject is of the greatest importance in explaining the history of the Woking area. It was the basic issue in the long and difficult struggle to achieve a satisfactory local government system and provoked more complaint, controversy and criticism than any other matter. Once the final plans had been approved it accounted for by far the largest single item of expenditure by both Woking U.D.C. and Chertsey R.D.C. in the years before the First World War.

Until the end of the 19th century no part of the present Borough had mains drainage, and a sizeable new town had arisen without any provision whatsoever for efficient and hygienic sanitation. In the low-lying parts it was usual to dispose of household waste and industrial or agricultural effluent directly into streams or ditches. In the more elevated areas, away from natural watercourses, cesspools and soakaways were ubiquitous. Solid refuse was piled in the streets and lanes, dumped on middens, or carted away to fill old clay pits. Such conditions were of course far from unique, but it was particularly regrettable that they should have been allowed to develop in a town which was new. This was the result of the negligence of the Necropolis Company and the feebleness of the Rural Sanitary Authority.

The lack of sewerage was unhealthy as well as unpleasant. In the late 1870s there were repeated outbreaks of typhoid and cholera in the district, and these were traced to polluted drinking water. The absence of efficient sewerage, and the equally deplorable lack of piped water supplies, meant that wells for the supply of household water were sunk adjacent to soakaways and cesspools. In January 1874, for example, it was reported that a new row of cottages near Woking station was supplied from wells into which sewage was leaking from an overflowing cesspool. This danger was reduced from the mid-1880s as piped water was introduced, but cases of polluted well water were recorded in Sutton Green and Bridley even after the Second World War.[32]

The 1875 Public Health Act entitled Rural Sanitary Authorities to provide sewerage, drainage and scavenging services by the levying of special rates, but the powers were voluntary, and many chose to ignore them. Guildford R.S.A. did nothing to implement the Act in Woking, although it repeatedly discussed the problem. In June 1875, for example, the Clerk drew to the attention of the Local Government

Board 'the Serious want of drainage in the District around Woking Station',[33] and as a consequence a Parochial Committee, consisting of members of Woking Vestry and their representatives on the R.S.A., was formed to consider possible solutions.

It was agreed that the parish should be divided for sewerage purposes into an undrained area and three Special Drainage Districts, for Woking village, Woking Station and Knaphill. These were areas within which an extra drainage rate could be levied, so that ratepayers in those parts not to benefit would not have to contribute.[34] The L.G.B. refused to sanction the necessary expenditure, and claimed that the application was premature because no detailed designs had been submitted. This refusal began a protracted and frustrating series of disputes over sewerage which lasted until the end of the century.

In September 1880 the L.G.B. relented so far as to allow the R.S.A. to enforce a set of bye-laws for Woking parish, under the Acts of 1872 and 1875. These were designed to control the provision of water supplies, the location and efficiency of cesspools and refuse disposal facilities, and the design of buildings, but as long as the town was without any mains drainage most of their provisions remained useless.[35] The pages of the Highway and Sanitary Authority minutes, the reports of the Medical Officer of Health, and a wealth of private opinion and comment, bear eloquent testimony to the primitive conditions which prevailed throughout Woking just one hundred years ago.

In January 1883, for example, there were complaints about 'house and shop drains discharging into Chertsey Road',[36] whilst between 1890 and 1892 a legal battle was fought between the owner of the *Red House Hotel* and the Rural Sanitary Authority, culminating in the former being fined £2 for 'allowing waste and filth to flow onto the road from his premises'.[37] The London & South Western Railway Company was a regular offender: in December 1889 it was fined for permitting 'manure water' to drip through the Railway Arch at Woking onto the road beneath,[38] and five years earlier had been held responsible for a most unsavoury incident, when there was an 'overflow of sewage and liquid filth from their premises, and . . . the company's servants had emptied the contents of cesspools into a ditch and allowed it to flow into the highway' at Goldsworth Road.[39] As late as 1895 developers were still submitting plans for houses without any sanitation other than the most rudimentary: a scheme for Arthurs Bridge Road in that year involved 'nothing but buckets for sink waste', and was rejected.

In the villages conditions were no better. It might have been expected that Byfleet, drained by the Wey and several small watercourses, would have suffered less, but in warm weather its ditches became stagnant, foetid pools. The stream flowing through the centre was normally flushed by the overflow from the Wey Navigation, but a survey conducted in May 1890 for Chertsey R.S.A revealed that it was also fed by 'offensive matter from the brewery . . . sink and urinal waste from the Plough Inn . . . slops and privy drains, and . . . offensive liquid manure'. All the inhabitants questioned had complained about the stench. The same survey noted that the Rive Ditch on Horsell Moor was noxious because 'the drainage from houses in Woking parish flows into the watercourse, the occupiers of which [presumably the houses!] appear to use it as a common sewer'.[40]

These medieval conditions were intolerable, and in 1889 the Guildford R.S.A. tried once more to designate a S.D.D. for the station area, but as before it failed to produce a detailed design, and once more the L.G.B. refused the application. Only in November 1890, 15 years after the first serious discussion of the issue, was a design drawn up and submitted.[41] The engineer responsible, E. R. Lailey, proposed a 15½-acre sewage works beside the Hoe Stream just north of Elm Bridge. This, and the sewer network to serve the station area only, would cost £12,000. The site, which is today part of Woking Park, was unpopular, and in March 1892 it was turned down by the L.G.B. after a public inquiry. An alternative site, in Tinkers Lane, Kingfield (now Elmbridge Lane), close to the present Leisure Centre, was then suggested and proved equally unpopular, as might have been expected since it was merely on the opposite bank of the river. For this we may be very grateful, for had either site been adopted it would have had a ruinous impact on the environment, destroying forever the attractive Hoe valley.

Building a sewerage system. As one of its earliest acts the Woking Local Board opened a competition for the design of a proposed sewerage network, and received no fewer than 23 entries. In September 1894 approval was given to the scheme of the 2nd-prize winner, W. H. Radford. It involved the laying-out of a 28-acre sewage farm at Scotchers Farm, Horsell, with the outflow to the Bourne. The total cost of £30,000 was to be payable by the ratepayers of Station & Maybury ward, which would be a Special Drainage District.[42] At the public inquiry it was revealed that the scheme had serious flaws: the sewage works would be at a higher level than much of the area to be drained, and expensive pumping was thus required, whilst its limited capacity would not allow extension of the network to other parts of the Urban District. In addition, the site was outside the Council's area, and this had proved to be unacceptable to Chertsey R.D.C.

The L.G.B. therefore refused to sanction the scheme, as it had done so often before, and in July 1895 the Urban District Council adopted instead the design of the 4th-prize winner, John Taylor & Son & Santo Crimp.[43] This firm was appointed engineer for the project, which required the Council to buy 42½ acres at Woking Park Farm for the sewage works and outfall. The farm was the lowest point in the Urban District, and so was suitable for gravity flow rather than extensive pumping, and its larger area would permit the construction of 24½ miles of sewers instead of the 12½ proposed under the previous scheme.

Lord Onslow, the owner of the land, was strongly opposed to the plan. At a public inquiry on 30 January 1896 his agent stated that there would be serious damage to the surrounding farmland, and 'much greater damage will accrue to the estate when looked at as a prospective building estate . . . the best sites might well look down directly onto the works'.[44] At the time the entire Hoe Bridge estate, from Old Woking to Pyrford, was being planned as an exclusive residential area, with very large building plots for expensive houses. The implementation of the sewerage scheme may therefore have been partly responsible for saving from development the expanse of open hillside at Sheepwalks, with its fine views across the Wey Valley to the sweep of the North Downs, which is such an attractive feature of this part of Woking.

The Council eventually acquired the land for the works by compulsory purchase for £8,250. The last building work on the main project was finished in November 1899, and operation began in December, almost 25 years after the idea was first raised. It was the thirteenth separate attempt to build a sewerage system for the town, and had cost a total of £64,000. That the delay occurred was regrettable, but there is no doubt that the final version was much superior to any of its predecessors, and but for the delay the sewage works would almost certainly have been located where Woking Park is today.

As soon as the basic network of sewers had been completed, work began on extensions to the outer parts of the district. St Johns was reached in 1900, Maybury Hill in 1903, Knaphill, Kingfield and Woking village in 1905 and Hook Heath in 1906. By the autumn of 1900 all but 26 of the premises in Woking Station & Maybury ward had been connected to the mains, and cesspools, soakaways and earth closets were virtually eliminated.[45] At last one of the major obstacles to civilized urban living had been removed, and there was an immediate improvement in the health, appearance — and smell — of the town centre.

Horsell, Pyrford and Byfleet. When the possibility of Horsell becoming an urban district was being discussed in 1903, Chertsey R.D.C. somewhat belatedly approved a design for a sewerage scheme in the parish. This was so that the public inquiry could be told that the matter was in hand. Although the separation of Horsell did not happen, the sewerage plan was reaffirmed: it was to involve the purchase of the entire 65-acre Deep Pool Farm, Mimbridge, and the use of 15½ acres for a sewage farm, the remainder being leased for agriculture. The system would thus drain in entirely the opposite direction from the new Woking network.[46]

In October 1904 the L.G.B. refused permission for the project, because the estimated cost of building would be greater than the rateable value of the parish, and because there had been objections to the siting of the works. Instead it recommended that the Rural District Council should negotiate with Woking U.D.C. for the sewering of Horsell by the latter. A year later the scheme was resubmitted without alteration, and the L.G.B. issued a strong reprimand to the R.D.C. for ignoring its instructions. This dissuaded the R.D.C. from further efforts, and as an alternative Horsell Parish Council began the discussions which led to union with Woking in October 1907.

Woking kept its promise, and immediately applied for, and received, powers to extend the existing network of sewers into Horsell, the cost to be borne by the entire Urban District. Work began in the summer of 1908, and in September 1909 the first section became operative, using new connections to the Woking sewers at Vale Farm Road and Maybury. The scheme as finished had cost £7,000 less than the Chertsey R.D.C. plan, and sewered almost twice as many streets, so Horsell residents derived major and immediate benefits from union.[47]

Plans were drawn up in 1904 for the Byfleet area, to ward off similar moves for separation. Initially the Rural District Council wanted to use 10 acres at Brooklands, but the site was not suitable, and was later incorporated within the new race-track. In April 1906 a report described the sanitary conditions of Byfleet village as totally unsatisfactory, but further delays occurred whilst the R.D.C. tried to persuade

Weybridge U.D.C. to treat Byfleet sewage at its new works. A third plan, for a 25-acre sewage farm at Sanway Fields, was postponed and then abandoned during the period in 1908 when the future of Chertsey Rural District seemed uncertain. Only in October 1908, after this question was resolved, was a fourth, and ultimately successful, plan approved by the Parish Council and the R.D.C.[48]

Ten acres were purchased from the Countess of Lovelace in the parish of Wisley, south of the Wey. Guildford R.D.C. opposed the application at the public inquiry, held in January 1909, but objections were overruled by the L.G.B. in its decision. As a condition of approval the Board stipulated that the design should included 'the planting of trees and shrubs and the tasteful laying out of so much of the land as is not required immediately . . . to preserve the present character of the river',[49] an early example of concern for the environment.

Work on the £32,000 project, designed by Messrs. Elliott & Brown, began in September 1910, and in the same month Pyrford Parish Council asked the R.D.C. and the engineers to design an extension to link the populated parts of their area to the Wisley works.[50] This was approved in April 1911, the cost being £7,800, and shortly afterwards Guildford R.D.C., forgetting its original hostility, arranged for Wisley parish to be connected. The Byfleet and Pyrford sections were completed in September 1912, by which time extensions along Old Woking Road were already in progress. The rapid development of housing in the north of Pyrford and in West Byfleet resulted in an unexpectedly large volume of sewage, and as early as 1913 it was necessary to extend the Wisley works, the river being diverted for that purpose.[51]

By the outbreak of the First World War, therefore, modern and efficient drains and sewers had been built in most of the urban areas of Woking. The total cost had been about £150,000; without the slightest doubt money well spent, and an invaluable investment. The installation of sewerage was fundamental to the progress of the town and to the well-being of its inhabitants, and this, together with the size of the sums involved, explains the contemporary preoccupation with the matter.

Scavenging

The removal of solid refuse, including street litter and trade waste, was an early concern of the Woking Local Board, and in December 1893 John Brown was awarded a six-month contract for scavenging and cesspool-emptying. His work was unsatisfactory, and his habit of dumping the foul contents of cesspools on land near new houses in Maybury Hill led to many angry complaints. When the contract expired John Wilson was given the work, at a rate of £108 10s. for six months of refuse collection duties, and an additional £3 2s. 6d. (£3.12½) per cesspool emptied. Although his work was better, there was still doubt as to the efficiency of private contractors, and in July 1898 the Urban District Council voted to buy horses and equipment and carry out the tasks using direct labour.[52] With characteristic indecision it then reversed this vote, and reappointed Wilson. Private contractors continued to do the work until the 1920s, although the Council began to buy vehicles and lease them to the individuals concerned. After 1903 the scavenging service was operating in all the built up parts of the

Urban District, and to reduce time the first 'motor dust cart' was bought, secondhand, in 1908 at a cost of £45 10s. 0d.[53]

Chertsey Rural Sanitary Authority began a scavenging service in Byfleet village in August 1894, using 'night carts' operated by direct labour, as was its custom.[54] The service seems to have been efficient, and in February 1897 was extended to cover West Byfleet. Four years later, after requests from Horsell Parish Council, equipment was bought to provide refuse collection and cesspool-emptying services for Horsell village: a cart for £33, a pump for £12, and £5 for shovels and a hose.[55] In October 1907 Woking U.D.C. took over responsibility for Horsell, and the job was given to private contractors.

Finally, in February 1909, Pyrford Parish Council decided to sell the old parish gravel pit in Coldharbour Lane, and with the proceeds it bought a 'sanitary cart and appliances' for refuse collection and cesspool-emptying.[56] As the sewers were gradually extended into the more remote parts of the area the need for cesspool-emptying diminished, and by 1914 most of the scavenging operations were concerned, as they are today, with the collection and disposal of dry refuse and rubbish.

Water Supplies

The absence of piped water until the mid-1880s gave the new town of Woking a peculiarly primitive character, for by that date almost every other town of its size had at least some provision for a public supply. In the late 1870s, as pressure for a water and gas supply grew, several schemes were put forward. After a public inquiry in the spring of 1881 the Woking Gas & Water Co. was incorporated by Act of Parliament.[57] It had been successful over a rival, the Woking & Horsell Gas, Light & Coke Co., largely because it proposed to supply both water and gas. The gas powers were, however, never used, and the company soon became known as the Woking Water Co.

By its Act it obtained powers to make deep borings into the chalk aquifer near Clandon Crossroads, below Newlands Corner, and to build a covered reservoir there. It was empowered to supply pure piped water to the parishes of Woking, Chobham, Send, Ripley, Pyrford, Wisley, Ockham, Bisley, Horsell, East and West Clandon and Merrow. The work was started at once, and from the last months of 1883 the water mains were gradually extended throughout the urban parts of Woking, Horsell and Pyrford, the last named being reached by the mid-1890s.

The South West Suburban Water Co., by an Act of 1869,[58] was authorised to supply a wide area of the Thames Valley, including the parishes of Byfleet and Chertsey. Progress was slow, and it was not until the late 1890s that the whole of Byfleet was served with piped water.

Gas and Electricity

Although the Convict Prison (1859) and the Lunatic Asylum of 1867 (*see* Chapter Seven) had small private gas plants of their own, there was no public supply of gas in the parish of Woking until the early 1890s, and the town was thus one of the last in the country to acquire such a facility. The earliest serious attempt to provide a supply was in August 1866, when a meeting at the *Anchor Inn*, Woking village, discussed the idea, but nothing came of it. in September 1869 Edward Ryde recorded in his diary that he had presided at a public meeting at the *White Hart*, 'called to hear a proposal from Messrs. Holmes & Co. to construct a Gas Works for Woking'.[59] The plan was for a small gasworks near Maybury Arch, to supply the town centre and Woking village. The response was favourable, especially since street-lighting would be made possible, but few local people were prepared to subscribe money, and once more the idea faded away.

In 1881 the issue was revived, with the rival applications of the Woking Gas & Water Co. and the Woking & Horsell Gas, Light & Coke Co., leading to the success of the former. In its 1881 Act the Company received powers to build a gasworks on a two-acre site at Tinkers Lane, Kingfield, owned by one of the directors, George Smallpeice of Kingfield House. It is clear that the ownership of the land was the major factor determining the choice of site, for in every other way the land at Tinkers Lane (approximately where the Leisure Centre is today) was eminently unsuitable, being low-lying, flood-prone, and remote from the railway or canal which would be used to transport the coal. It is probable that the realisation of this discouraged the company from using its gas powers.[60]

A new Woking District Gas Company held its first meeting in December 1891, following its incorporation by Parliament in the previous session.[61] Its directors included the same George Smallpeice who had promoted the 1881 scheme, and also G. B. and B. D. Holroyd, members of the well known Byfleet milling, landowning and political family. The new company, with a capital of £16,000, was authorised to supply gas to the parishes of Woking, Horsell, Pyrford, Byfleet, Send and Ripley. It purchased 1½ acres of former commonland in Boundary Road from the Necropolis Company for £649 10s. 7d. (£649.53). The land had been intended for house-building, and was already laid out in plots: local residents were opposed to the scheme, fearing pollution and a fall in property values, but it had the great advantage of being very close to the canal, on which a coal wharf was built.[62]

The gasworks, with a capacity of 70,000 cubic feet and a 60-foot high gasometer, were opened on 9 June 1892, and the enterprise proved an immediate success, paying a dividend of 3½ per cent to 5½ per cent regularly from the first year onwards. The increases in industrial demand and in the number of domestic consumers were most satisfactory, and a profitable sideline was developed, supplying ammonia, ashes and tar to the local authorities for highway and sanitary use. In 1901 and 1905 the works were extended to increase production, and in 1909 a tramway was built between the wharf and the works to cope with coal traffic.

The success of the gas company contrasted with that of the electricity supply company. Although amongst the last English towns to be provided with gas, Woking was one of the first to have a public electricity supply. Godalming was the earliest (1881) but when in 1889 the Woking Electricity Supply Co. was incorporated few other places had followed suit. By Parliamentary Order in the spring of 1890[63] the Company was empowered to supply electricity for domestic use and for public lighting. By the same Order undertakings were authorised for Bournemouth, Oxford, Derby and Portsmouth, so in this respect, at least, Woking could consider itself the equal of some of the great cities of the land.

The new power station, built and operated by Messrs. New & Maynes, was in Board School Road, and the original mains extended from there through the town centre to the *Goldsworth Arms* and the top of Constitution Hill. Work on building the station progressed very rapidly, and power was first supplied in November 1890.[64] Almost all of the output was used for public and domestic lighting, and the company therefore shut the power station during the hours of daylight. This proved to be uneconomical and a disincentive to prospective customers, and so enthusiasm for the service was extremely limited.

The first six years of operation saw the connection of only 179 business and domestic users, and as late as 1910, after 20 years, there were only 1,500. Finances suffered accordingly, and in 1898 the directors seriously contemplated going into liquidation. To build up new business the company extended the area within which it could operate, and a succession of Parliamentary Orders brought additional parishes within its sphere: Horsell and Woodham (1892),[65] Chertsey, Byfleet, Pyrford and Wisley (1900),[66] and Cobham, Laleham, Littleton, Ockham, Pirbright, Ripley and Thorpe (1908).[67]

Between 1897 and 1910 the gas and electricity competed to extend their mains to new parts of Woking and district, the former reaching Horsell in 1897, West Byfleet in 1899, Mayford and Hook Heath in 1902, and the latter Woking village in 1907, Knaphill in 1908 and, by 1914, Pirbright, Ripley and Bisley.

Street-Lighting

Their main area of competition, though, was in the lighting of the streets of Woking. This was a priority of the Woking Local Board as soon as it was established, in part because of the danger associated with unlit streets but also so that residents were better able to avoid the streams of sewage, the deep ruts and the pools of mud which then characterised the streets of the town. A few oil lamps were sited at road junctions, and private individuals in some instances provided lights outside their property, but the parish and its neighbours were otherwise completely in the dark.

In November 1893 the Sanitary & Lighting Committee of the Local Board asked to two companies to submit tenders for the 100 street-lamps which it proposed to erect, and to quote prices for their maintenance. In July 1894 the contract was awarded to the Electricity Supply Co., after tests had shown that it could provide brighter lighting at a cheaper rate. The seven-year contract was for a basic rate of £310 16s. 0d. (£310.80) for the lighting and repair of 100 lamps each year, with an additional payment of £513 15s. 0d. (£513.75) for the initial installation. The lights were to be lit from sunset until midnight, and only in the winter months. Light therefore came to the dark streets of the town centre on 28 January 1895, making Woking one of the earliest towns to have electric street-lighting.[68]

Unfortunately the supply proved to be unreliable: interruptions were frequent, standards of upkeep were low, and the financial instability of the company was scarcely encouraging. Complaints from the public were numerous, and when the lighting resumed in October 1895 it was noted that 21 of the 111 lamps were inoperative. In the autumn of that year the Council awarded a new contract for the lighting of St Johns and Woking village to a local firm which intended to use oil lamps, even though the Electricity Company offered to extend its mains to those areas so that electric light would be available. The reputation of the company plummeted still further in December 1895, when the entire system failed just before a meeting of the Finance & General Purposes Committee which, the fates being unkind, had been due to discuss lighting expenses.[69]

So unsatisfactory was the performance of the company that in November 1898 the Sanitary & Lighting Committee debated the possibility of making a compulsory purchase order for the entire undertaking. This would have been a remarkable step for so timid and conservative an authority, yet the motion to acquire was lost only by the casting vote of the Chairman when it came before the full Council in March 1899, an indication of the irritation felt by councillors.[70]

When the contract expired in the autumn of 1900 the Council rejected the tender of the Electricity Supply Co., and instead approved that of the Gas Company. The former, angered by this, threatened the Council with an injunction if it attempted to interfere with the lamp-standards. The directors stated that they were 'astonished at the manner the Council had treated them in the matter'.[71] But their protests were to no avail: gas-lighting began on 1 August 1902, in part using secondhand equipment purchased from Battersea Borough Council which, ironically, was in the process of converting from gas to electricity. So Woking, after seven years of electric-lighting, went against the national trend and opted for gas light.

During the next few years most of the outlying areas were provided with street-lighting, usually in response to requests from residents. In 1910, for example, Oriental Road was lit after there had been complaints that it was 'unsafe for women after dark and . . . frequented by tramps and loafers of the worst class'.[72] In Byfleet there were attempts, after the formation of the Parish Council, to introduce street-lighting, but with no success. Motions for the erection of three oil lamps were rejected by a parish meeting in 1895 on the absurd grounds of excessive cost, and a plan for 11 lamps failed a year later. Further abortive proposals were made in 1901, 1911 and 1913, but on the outbreak of the First World War the villages of Byfleet and Pyrford remained almost entirely unlit.[73]

The Fire-Brigades

Woking had no fire service until 1896, and before then relied on the time-honoured but inadequate method of chains of buckets from a pond or stream, or upon the distant and minimally effective town brigades of Guildford and Chertsey. The increased rateable value of the parish led to pressure for local protection, but an attempt to set up a volunteer force in 1870, using the private manual engine owned by Ernest Hilder of Hoe Place, did not receive enough support.

In April 1894 the Local Board formed a committee to supervise the formation of a fire service, and in May it recommended the purchase of a steam fire-engine, hoses and uniforms, to be distributed amongst the four 'urban' wards.[74] The Local Board was reluctant to spend the money, and in August rejected the idea of buying an engine. In May 1895 the new Urban District Council reversed the decision of its predecessor, and provisionally accepted the tender of Merryweathers for an engine and accessories. The decision caused a split in the Council, between those members who supported municipal assistance for services such as fire-protection and those who were opposed to public expenditure and wanted to leave the work to private enterprise. As a result there was yet another reversal, when in October 1895 the vote to confirm the tender and its acceptance was rejected.[75] Therefore only £300 was spent on equipment, to be housed in corrugated iron sheds (unkindly compared with bathing huts) at Kiln Bridge, Hipley Bridge (Old Woking), Knaphill High Street and Chertsey Road, Woking. Each site was equipped with '1 Jumping Sheet, 1 35-foot ladder and 2 short ladders'.[76]

The arrival of the equipment caused much local interest, and the leader writer of the *Woking Mail* was inspired to write an execrable verse in celebration:

> Now, my boys, give a shout! 'tis a noted occasion
> For at last we have got, after no end of persuasion
> Our fire apparatus, with hose of good leather,
> And men willing to turn out in all sorts of weather
> The engine's p'raps ordered, or 'tis the money delaying
> While for safety from fire all Woking keeps praying!

The poet then turned comedian: 'I pictured how nice it would be for Woking to possess in such sad weather one of Merryweather's engines'.[77]

A 20-man volunteer brigade was formed in December 1895, with Charles Sherlock, an early supporter of the idea, as its first Captain. His task was not easy, for he lacked adequate equipment, his men were untrained volunteers, and the manual pumps were inefficient. In each report submitted to the Fire Brigade Committee he bemoaned the absence of a steam engine, and this created an intense personal antagonism between himself and the chairman, Councillor Kittredge, a St Johns shopkeeper and vehement opponent of council spending. In August 1897 the Committee dismissed a petition from the entire brigade asking for a steam engine to be bought, and in November the Captain and 17 of his men resigned, leaving the town without a fire service.[78]

The Clerk of the Council, Robert Mossop, persuaded them to return, but they did so reluctantly, reiterating their belief in a steam engine as the only means of providing adequate fire-protection. With astonishing lack of wisdom the Fire Brigade Committee then gave them a public reprimand, even though all were volunteers, and in consequence the Knaphill section resigned again, this time permanently. At the elections of March 1898 the issue of whether or not to buy a steam engine was dominant, and several anti-engine candidates were defeated, whilst Kittredge lost the chairmanship of the now vital Fire Brigade Committee.

On 11 May 1898 the new council voted once more to buy an engine, to cost £430, and after a further delay, during which Messrs. Rose, the manufacturers, sold the Woking engine to Ipswich Corporation, a steam engine was eventually delivered in August 1899.[79] In February 1899 a permanent fire station, near the present site in Church Street, was approved to house the new engine. The poor relations between council and brigade continued until the delivery of the engine: in July 1898 Sherlock wrote to the Committee that 'Councillor Kittredge... proved his incapacity as Chairman ... to such a marked degree that it became a bye-word and reproach in the district ... he has gained the ridicule of the Council and the Ratepayers, as well as my contempt'.[80]

The activities of the Woking Fire Brigade occasionally bordered on the farcical. At a fire in Woking Laundry on 26 April 1900 sparks from the steam engine set light to the Fire Brigade handcart and equipment, and in their anxiety to save their property the members ran the cart over the hosepipes, bursting them and cutting off supplies to the fire. Telephone communication was so poor that a year later only the village manual engine arrived at a fire in Walton Road timber yard, which was destroyed with £2,000 of damage, despite being less than half a mile from the Chertsey Road depot.[81]

Byfleet had a volunteer brigade, organised from the mid-1880s by Sir James Whittaker Ellis, a leading local resident, and this used his private manual engine. In December 1893 Chertsey Rural Sanitary Authority approached the Local Government Board to ask whether Byfleet Vestry might assume control of the brigade, whilst retaining its voluntary status. This arrangement was permitted under Section 171 of the 1875 Public Health Act, and involved the levying of a special rate to pay for the brigade. From February 1894, therefore, the parish rented the engine and uniforms for £10 a year, and after 1896 also rented the newly built fire station in High Road. With its 11 men and engine Byfleet for several years had a fire service superior to that of Woking.[82]

In 1902 the fire station was bought by Byfleet Parish Council for £310 from Sir James, and members considered replacing the ancient and inefficient manual engine. The meeting of the Council in July 1906 agreed that a steam engine should be bought, but did not agree to a rate rise to pay for this. Instead it was decided to raise the money by voluntary contributions. Local people gave generously, and the new engine entered service in April 1908. The history of the Byfleet brigade contrasts with the troubled early life of its neighbour in Woking.[83]

Woking U.D.C. signed an agreement with Horsell Parish Council in 1902, whereby Horsell would be covered by the Woking brigade in return for a fee of £25 per year.[84] In 1906, after rejecting a similar arrangement with Woking, Pyrford Parish Council agreed to pay a retainer of just £5 per year for the services of the Ripley Volunteer Brigade.[85] The rapid growth of the northern part of Pyrford soon made this arrangement inadequate, and in March 1910 an agreement was signed with Byfleet Parish Council whereby the latter gave Pyrford equal coverage with its brigade, in return for £25 annually (soon increased to £50). This was a further indication of the growing links between the two parishes.[86]

This review of the major developments in local government in the half century before the First World War reveals the striking contrast between the neglect and inefficiency of the period up to 1893 and the rapid changes of the years after that date. The new authorities which were established in 1893-95 were faced with a tremendous backlog of work, and their energy in attacking this was most commendable. Even though the detailed implementation of the policies was rarely smooth, in only 20 years they succeeded in improving the quality of life in the four parishes to a remarkable degree, and of that they were justifiably proud.

Chapter Seven

THE INSTITUTIONS

THE SECOND HALF of the 19th century saw the construction of a series of public and private institutions in the Woking area. Some were short-lived, but of great interest, whilst others have survived to the present day and have had a significant impact upon the development and character of the district. In the 1870s and 1880s Woking showed signs of developing into a working-class, institutional–industrial town. It was only the enthusiasm amongst the middle and upper classes for the area as a fashionable place to live, which prevented this from evolving further.

Curiously, the factors which attracted these people were also those which had led the various government and philanthropic bodies to consider Woking as the site for their institutions. Foremost amongst the advantages was the freely available, undeveloped and cheap land. At this stage there was no obvious alternative use, and the Necropolis Company with its vast land holdings was only too anxious to sell at the earliest opportunity. The empty heathlands were also elevated above the damp and allegedly unhealthy lowlands. Their fresh breezes and salubrious air were regarded with equal favour by the wealthy and fashionable and by those who proposed health institutions. Transport was also a significant factor, since there was an excellent rail service to London giving easy access for businessmen and officials alike.

The institutions played a fundamental role in the development of the district, and in particular of the parish of Woking. They were amongst the earliest and largest purchasers of Necropolis Company land, beginning shortly after the passing of the 1855 Amendment Act, and at their peak in the early 1890s they occupied almost 10 per cent of the area of Woking parish. Their presence brought increased income to local businesses and gave employment to labourers displaced from the land by agricultural decline. They were responsible for a large part of the 1861–81 population growth, and it would be fair to say that, with the railway and the Necropolis Company, they brought the infant town into being.

Brookwood Cemetery

The earliest and greatest institution, if it can be described as such, was Woking Necropolis, from the 1860s more commonly known as Brookwood Necropolis or Cemetery. Brookwood village did not then exist, and the name was derived from the ancient Brook Wood, which was in the vicinity of the present mental hospital. The work of building the cemetery began in November 1852, immediately after the London Necropolis & National Mausoleum Company had acquired title to the land.

The original intention, if early engravings are to be believed, was to include the land north of the railway at least as far as the canal. A new station would serve the cemetery, and act as the focus of radiating avenues. As built, the necropolis stopped short at the L.S.W.R. main line so that the station, which did not open until 1864, lay at one edge and was not central to the design.[1]

Originally, too, the old trackway from Knaphill to Pirbright was to be closed, as were all other public rights of way across Woking Common except the Bagshot–Guildford and Knaphill–Crastock roads. In their place the company proposed a new and almost straight road from Triggs Lane to Pirbright Arch, along the south side of the L.S.W.R. From this, at Hook Heath Bridge, straight roads would link with Saunders Lane and Mayford. Another road would wind along the southern edge of the heath from Wych Street to Blackhorse Road. Of all these routes only the last (now Hook Heath Road), and the Mayford link (Pond Road) were actually constructed. The Knaphill–Pirbright track was instead retained, straightened and christened Cemetery Pales: it thus bisected the new cemetery.[2]

As explained in Chapter Four, the land chosen for the cemetery, about 450 acres off the Bagshot to Guildford road, was the least suitable for speculative building, and this accounts for the choice of site. In 1852 it was a great expanse of heath, with gorse, bracken and a few pine trees, wind-swept and lonely. The Necropolis Company set out to transform this into an oasis of beauty and peace, a laudable aim and one which was achieved with considerable success.

Responsibility for the design and its implementation lay with three people. Henry Abraham, the company architect, was almost certainly the man who planned the network of radiating and concentric paths and avenues. It bears a close resemblance to the pattern of streets around Woking station which he produced seven years later. The cemetery has both a grid of paths and a sequence of curving concentric avenues, and these parallel the 1859 town centre design so obviously that the link must be presumed.

For the buildings in the necropolis the company employed Sir William Tite, the architect of the L.S.W.R. stations at Nine Elms, Gosport and Southampton, who had been involved with the earlier great cemetery at Norwood, South London. His precise contribution is not known, but his name was certainly connected with the work and it is probable that the two cemetery stations and the Anglican chapels were his.[3] Robert Donald, the nurseryman of Goldsworth, was responsible for planting and landscaping in the cemetery. He was a specialist in such work, and as an associate of the influential J. C. Loudon had already seen the latest in cemetery design. Following this example Donald made much use of shrubs, such as rhododendrons and azaleas for which his nurseries were famous, and planted extensive groves of conifers.

The cemetery was divided by the paths and avenues into separate 'grounds' which were allotted to different London parishes and to various religious denominations, for, as befitted a national necropolis, this was to cater for all classes and faiths. Between the L.S.W.R. and Cemetery Pales were Catholic and Noncomformist areas, and later Mohammedan and Parsee. To the south was a larger Anglican section. In the 1920s a large new military cemetery was laid out north of the road, and was later extended to cater for Second World War dead. The military section is also subdivided into national zones, including American, Canadian, Turkish, Dutch and French.[4]

The wealthier occupants were housed in tombs and mausolea, and a remarkable variety of memorials and monuments can be seen. Few are of great individual merit, but together they represent an exceptional collection of funerary designs from the past 130 years. The pauper burials, in contrast, were unrecorded and unmarked, and although these were the great majority, they have left little trace. The company designed an 'earth-to-earth' coffin for parish burials, one which would quickly disintegrate and permit early re-use of the site. An 1879 report noted that 'the pauper graves average 7 feet in depth & the private graves from 10 to 20 feet'.[5]

On 9 November 1854 the cemetery was consecrated by the Bishop of Winchester at a ceremony which included a luncheon for the shareholders and directors. The first burial was of the 'stillborn male twins of Mrs. Store of the Boro', at exp. of parish', on 13 November.[6] This set the tone for the remainder of the century, for although the well known provided the income and the impressive headstones, the poor provided most of the business.

In 1860, only five years after the opening, there were 3,020 burials, and the peak was recorded in 1866 with 3,842, an average of about ten funerals each day. Every one was carefully recorded by the cemetery manager in a series of great leather-bound volumes; unfortunately the location of most was not mentioned! After 1880 the rate of use began to slacken as other cemeteries opened nearer to London, and by 1914 the growing use of cremation had further reduced demand. Nevertheless 201,000 burials had been made by the end of 1939 and today the figure is almost 300,000.[7]

Perhaps the most remarkable feature of the cemetery, and one which reflected its origins in the 'national necropolis' concept, is that it was served by its own private railway, opened in November 1854. This was a 1-km branch leaving the main line at a point known as Necropolis Junction, just west of Brookwood Station. There were two stations within the cemetery, built of white painted wood and each with a 'courtyard' plan, the fourth side being the platform. The line crossed Cemetery Pales by a level-crossing close to the present offices, and there was also a short siding into the stonemasonry works operated in conjunction with the cemetery. The Necropolis Company had a special station at Westminster Bridge Road near Waterloo, to handle the shipment of corpses at the London end.

Every day at 11.35 a.m. or 11.45 a.m. a train left London and arrived at Necropolis Junction 50 minutes later, conveying the dead, their mourners and other visitors. A stop was made at North Station, and arrival at South Station was at about 12.50 p.m. with a return journey starting at 2.15 p.m. The company owned the carriages used, but the L.S.W.R. provided the locomotive and crew. On Saturday, the busiest day, the train would carry a full complement of 30 to 35 funeral parties. The service continued until 1941, although by then it operated only twice a week, but in May of that year the train and station were destroyed during an air raid on London. After the war it was uneconomic to restore the service, and the cemetery railway was dismantled.[8]

Brookwood Cemetery is a place at once bizarre, beautiful and melancholy. The landscaping of the 1850s has matured to give precisely the character which the promoters wished. Nairn describes it as 'a sombre complex landscape unlike anything elsewhere in the country', whilst Pevsner is reminded of 'a garden suburb with all the houses become mausolea'.[9]

It is now an anachronism. The number of burials has fallen to an average of two a week, and there are only five staff to look after 450 acres when at one time there were 160. Decay is well advanced, assisted by vandalism, and monuments are broken or crumbling. Large tracts are overgrown and impenetrable with rampant shrubs and self-sown conifers. Both stations have been destroyed, one deliberately in the 1950s and one by vandals in 1972, and the chapels are locked and derelict.

No capital is available to remedy these problems, and there seems little chance of any substantial restoration work being carried out. Green Belt restrictions mean that the cemetery cannot be built on or otherwise developed, and so it is probable that the physical deterioration will continue unchecked. It would be a tragedy if the unique character of this fascinating place, the largest cemetery in Western Europe, was to be lost, but at present it is difficult to be other than pessimistic about its future.

Woking Crematorium

Woking has a special place in the history of death in Britain, for as well as the largest cemetery it also possesses the oldest crematorium. Although this method of disposal was widely practised before the Christian era it was not used between then and the middle of the 19th century, and was regarded with abhorrence on religious and moral grounds.

The growth of secularism, the desperate lack of burial space, greater interest in hygiene and a reinterpretation of the meaning of 'Christian burial', including the phrase 'ashes to ashes', combined in the 1860s to produce a movement in favour of cremation. During the next decade it was legalised in Italy and Germany and a Cremation Society was established in England.[10]

The Society decided to build a crematorium, to be used initially for experiments with animal corpses. This would allow different methods to be tested, and would help to convince sceptics and opponents of the effectiveness and hygienic nature of cremation. A particular objection had been that smoke would be emitted, creating an offensive nuisance, and it was hoped to prove otherwise.

In 1878 a small plot of land on the south side of Hermitage Road was purchased, and building work began that autumn. In January 1879 the *Sanitary Record* reported on the project, noting that the site was 'in a secluded part of Woking parish, admirably suited for the purpose, and sufficiently remote from habitations . . . no better site could have been obtained, nor will many of the large towns which are eager to avail themselves of the coming reform be able to suit themselves as well'.[11] The general advantages of the Woking area were clear, but it cannot have been coincidence that two miles away was the largest, busiest and most impressive cemetery in the country. The contrast was certainly in the minds of the Cremation Society members.

Although cremation was not technically illegal there was no precedent for its use, and the Society was anxious to carry out a human disposal as a test case. It was told by the Home Secretary in 1879 that, whilst he was in favour, Parliament would have to consider the issue before it was accepted in law. Local opposition was strong, and many clergymen were vehemently antagonistic to the idea. The Vicar of Woking regarded the whole concept as an anathema, and his lawyers prepared a memorandum on the subject.[12]

This recited the usual moral and social objections, and added that 'the proposed establishment is regarded with the greatest abhorrence by the inhabitants of the district, who in addition to their dislike of such a method . . . are filled with not unreasonable fears that the value of their property will be seriously injured by it'. It was claimed that 'one schoolmaster has lost a Pupil through the Parents reading of the Crematory in the papers, and the wife of a Warder at the Gaol refuses to live in a nearby house'. The Revd. G. F. Saxby told a meeting of clergy that 'our gratitude is due to the Vicar of Woking for successfully resisting the first attempt to intrude the funeral power in our midst'.[13]

In 1882 there was a private cremation in Dorset, and in 1884 the famous Price case led to a judgement in favour of the method, provided that no nuisance was created. The Vicars of St Johns and Woking, and Lord Onslow, Lord of the Manor, then made desperate efforts to prevent the Society from operating its St Johns Crematorium, which had been in readiness but unused since 1879. 'We at Woking . . . are most strenuously opposed to anything of such being carried on so near to us & we will do all in our powers to prevent it . . . the society especially ought never to be allowed to use the apparatus at St Johns'.[14]

But it was to no avail. On 26 March 1885 'the cry went round the neighbourhood, "A woman to be burned"',[15] and accompanied by this unattractive call the body of Mrs. Pickersgill, a member of the Society, was conveyed from Woking Station to St Johns. There it was cremated by officials of the Society; the first legal cremation in Britain in modern times. The new method was slow to achieve popularity. By 1900 only 1,340 disposals had been carried out at Woking, and the local press continued to report cremations as exceptional events. After 1918 there was a rapid increase in its use and in 1968 the number of cremations in Britain for the first time exceeded that of burials.

The original Woking crematorium was plain and utilitarian but in 1889, once the method had been accepted, it was replaced by a red brick building with stone dressings, 'in the style of the early 13th century'. The architect was E. F. Clarke. It stands in extensive grounds which have been attractively landscaped, with a pool, lawns and gardens.[16]

The Convict Prisons and Barracks

One of the infamies of the English penal system of the early 19th century was the rotting prison hulks moored offshore at Woolwich and elsewhere. In their later years the ships had been used primarily for invalid prisoners, and when the last convicts were transferred from the *Defence* to Lewes Gaol in 1853 it was realised that some more satisfactory alternative was needed for these people. They could not withstand the harsh régimes of conventional gaols, and in any case these were already seriously overcrowded. The Home Office therefore decided to build a new prison specifically for invalid and infirm convicts.

After a survey of possible sites the Government selected Knaphill, where the Necropolis Company had recently offered for sale the entire Common. In 1858, 64¾ acres, between Robin Hood Road and the Knaphill–Crastock road, were purchased for £6,487. The new prison was designed by Sir Joshua Jebb and the better known Arthur Blomfield, and was built by Messrs. Myers & Co. of London. On 28 April 1859 the north-east part was opened for the reception of prisoners by a detachment of officers from Lewes, Carisbrooke and Dartmoor. The official opening was on 22 March 1860, and in the intervening year almost 300 invalid convicts were transferred from Lewes.[17]

The prisoners who could undertake manual work were given labouring jobs in the buildings and grounds. The Governor reported in the autumn of 1860 that:

> 'the prisoners have been most industrious and their conducts generally very good . . . [many] have been employed . . . in digging foundations for the prison walls, gas works, gas and water mains and drains, also in the formation of exercising grounds, paths and roads. Latterly a gang has been placed at the disposal of the farm bailiff for the purpose of clearing the brushwood and raising a mud wall to enclose the property'.[18]

The prison was dominated by a clock tower 190 feet high, which bore a strong resemblance to the Italianate campanile of St Barnabas' Church, Oxford, designed by Blomfield in the late 1860s. The west wing of the prison was specifically for the care of the chronically sick and insane, the east for those who were able to work and did not require constant attention. It was an austere, functional and impressive building, and because of its hilltop site was a prominent feature of the landscape of west Woking.

Prison reform also led to the idea of segregating male and female prisoners, and in the mid-1860s it was decided to use the extensive site at Woking for a second gaol, to house female convicts. Work began in the autumn of 1867, using labour from the existing prison to reduce costs. The first stage was opened on 5 May 1869 and by the end of that year the buildings housed their full complement of 700 women, most of whom had come from Millbank Penitentiary. This gave a total prison population of 1,400.[19]

The women prisoners were not given labouring tasks, but were widely used for menial tasks, including cooking, sewing, cleaning and gardening. They sewed mailbags and made clothes for male convicts, prison uniforms and school uniforms for the boys of Greenwich Hospital. Some women worked in the craft workshops, making mosaic tiles and designs: their products were used in local churches, St Paul's Cathedral and various museums.[20]

A company of the 40th Regiment was dispatched to Knaphill from Aldershot to guard the prisons, in 1868 and 1869, when several Fenians were housed there. This caused much disquiet locally, as Knaphill residents feared that an attempt might be made to release the prisoners. The female prison had its share of notoriety. Constance Kent was there for several months, and in August 1889 it admitted its most famous inmate, Mrs. Maybrick, immediately after her reprieve from execution in Liverpool. She arrived 'careworn and haggard in appearance' at Woking station, 'where a crowd of over 100 people greeted her and chanted slogans in her support'.[21]

The fall in prison populations in the later 19th century and the development of an improved system of care for the criminally insane produced a surplus of places in Woking's two establishments, and in 1886 it was decided that they should be phased out over a period of ten years. This seems surprising, because the female prison was only 18 years old, but the availability of alternative uses must have been the deciding factor. During 1888 the prisoners in the male prison were transferred to other places, and on 21 March 1889 it was closed when the last batch was moved to Wormwood Scrubs. The female prison remained until October 1895, when the remaining inmates were taken to Holloway.[22]

In 1889 it was suggested that the army should take over the male prison for use as a military hospital, because facilities at Aldershot were inadequate. Although seriously considered this was rejected, but in November 1889 ownership was transferred from the Home Office to the War Department, and in 1895 the remainder of the site and buildings was conveyed. Both prisons were converted by the army and were renamed the Inkerman Barracks.[23] Their new function was associated with the major expansion of military activity in West Surrey and North East Hampshire in 1888–1902, including the acquisition of most of the common-land in the adjacent parishes of Pirbright, Bisley, Frimley and Chobham.

After the Boer War there was a brief revival of the previous function, when part of the barracks became a military prison, but this ceased after 1918. The barracks survived for another 50 years, and were extended by the construction of married quarters in the grounds.[24] With the reduction in Britain's military commitments and the end of national service Inkerman Barracks became surplus to requirements and were gradually run down from 1955 until their eventual closure in 1965. The married quarters were retained as an adjunct to the nearby camps at Pirbright and Blackdown, but the former prison buildings were demolished and the site cleared. Most of the land was sold to Woking U.D.C. and has been used for local authority and housing association residential development, for public open space, and for the projected St Johns bypass.

Brookwood Hospital

The third of the trio of institutions which occupied over 25 per cent of land in Brookwood and Knaphill was the County Lunatic Asylum, latterly and more sympathetically known as Brookwood Hospital. In 1841 the Surrey County Justices opened a County Asylum at Wandsworth, under the terms of the County Asylums Act of 1828. This was to replace a wide range of private institutions where physical abuse and harsh treatment were rife. The Wandsworth asylum became known as a model establishment, noted for its advanced and humane conditions and high standard of administration.

By the late 1850s population growth and the wider use of asylums had stretched the capacity of the Wandsworth building to its limits, and the Justices agreed to build a second asylum to serve the west of the county, but taking patients from the east if necessary. They felt that a large open site with a healthy atmosphere and pleasant landscape was preferable to a congested and unpopular urban location. Moreover the land had to be cheap to reduce the rate burden, and this ruled out good agricultural districts. The former heaths west of Woking were an obvious choice, especially since the convict prison, an institution of comparable size and character, was already under construction there.[25]

In 1860 the Justices bought 150 acres between Knaphill village and the Basingstoke Canal for £10,500. The site sloped gently to the south and was drained by a small stream which rose in Knaphill and fed the canal. It was hoped that this would provide a suitable water supply. Construction work began in 1863 and the first patients were admitted on 17 June 1867.[26]

The asylum was designed as a self-contained community, in accordance with the contemporary philosophy of segregating mental patients from the outside world. There were no public services available in the parish of Woking, and so it had its own gasworks and sewage farm. The latter employed a patent system whereby liquid wastes were sprayed onto eight acres of ryegrass near the canal to be broken down organically. The small stream was soon found to be inadequate, and in 1869 four reservoirs, with a total capacity of 0.4 million gallons, were constructed at the upper end of the site. In the summer of 1868 the building was provided with central heating after a number of elderly patients had almost died of hypothermia in the asylum hospital. The overall cost to the end of 1881 was £104,855 17s. 1d. (£104,855.85½).[27]

As in the Wandsworth asylum a progressive régime was operated. There was undoubtedly some harshness but by contemporary standards discipline was relaxed and many efforts were made to provide a congenial environment. In September 1867, for example, a 'Concert & Ball was attended by over three-quarters of the Patients'. Cards, dominoes and draughts were provided in each ward, whilst 'objects of interest such as framed pictures, birds &c are gradually being added. The cheaper forms of illustrated periodicals are regularly circulated, and a library is being instituted. A brass band is also being formed'.[28]

Those patients who could do so worked in the various departments of the asylum, cooking, cleaning, washing and carrying out repairs. A Home Farm was started and in 1886 this was growing four acres of vegetables and eight of cereals and potatoes. Other occupations included cobbling, basket-weaving and rug-making. All this was therapeutic, but it also made a major contribution to the reduction of running costs.[29]

Unfortunately many potential benefits were not realised because of the attitudes of the Boards of Guardians of the Poor Law Unions. These bodies could send patients either to their own workhouses or to the County Asylums. In their first Quarterly Report the visitors of Brookwood Asylum noted with concern that 'the great majority of the Patients are of the incurable class; and in not more than 5 per cent of the whole number is there any reasonable prospect of recovery'.[30] Six months later they again deplored this aspect of the system, saying that the main function of the asylum should be 'as a Hospital for the treatment of the recent and Curable Class . . . Quiet and harmless Chronic Cases should be sent to Wards attached to Union Workhouses'.[31] Despairingly, in midsummer 1868, they reported the high mortality rates: 'some . . . arrived in such a hopeless condition that they appeared as if they were sent here only to die'.[32]

Eventually these faults were remedied, although as late as 1884 only 94 of the 242 admissions were deemed 'curable'. By then, though, the death rate of 8.69/1,000 per annum was less than that for the country as a whole (9.85/1,000) and this represented a considerable achievement.

In the middle of 1875 there were 672 patients, about half being women, but by the end of the century the numbers had grown and the ratio of men to women was about 40:60. The 1921 Census recorded 1,188 patients and that of 1931, 1,477. With such numbers the asylum made a great impact upon the Knaphill area, and was responsible for a large part of the 1861–71 population increase in Woking parish. The sprawling red brick Gothic buildings, now surrounded by later extensions, are not obtrusive because they are in a shallow valley amidst trees, but the extensive grounds have acted as a barrier to the southward growth of Knaphill and help to separate this village from Brookwood. The building of the asylum and prisons stimulated local trade and industry, particularly in the construction and retailing sectors, whilst their employees contributed to the substantial development of working-class housing in Knaphill and St Johns.[33]

By the late 1970s the asylum was becoming obsolete. Its main buildings were over a century old, and were regarded with increasing disfavour as a place for the care of the mentally ill. Modern ideas reject large segregated institutions, and in 1981 the Surrey Area Health Authority announced that the hospital was to close, and its patients were to be transferred to smaller modern units. This would free the extensive and valuable site for comprehensive redevelopment, with housing, industry and open space. As it is the last large area of developable land in the Borough this is an exciting opportunity.[34]

The Royal Dramatic College

The two most unusual institutions in Woking used the same site, on the south side of the railway line at Maybury. The first was the Royal Dramatic College, an ambitious but ultimately unsuccessful attempt to establish what might have become a permanent centre for the dramatic arts.

It has its origins in a meeting at the Princess Theatre, Oxford Street, on 21 July 1858. Amongst those present were Charles Dickens and William Makepeace Thackeray.[35] They discussed proposals to build an institution which would provide a home for retired actors and actresses who might otherwise have been destitute, and which could include a school for members of the profession. The outcome of the meeting was the formation of a trust, to raise finance and to carry out the building work. It was intended that the money should be found from voluntary subscriptions and donations, and this aim received an important boost in the autumn of 1858 when Prince Albert conferred his patronage upon the plan.

A Royal Charter, incorporating the Royal Dramatic College, was granted on 8 June 1859, and the trustees then looked for a suitable site.[36] This had to be within easy reach of London, the centre of the theatrical world, but it was essential that the land should be as cheap as possible, because money was restricted. Woking was the obvious choice, with its excellent rail service and large expanses of heathland for sale. Early in 1860 the trustees purchased ten acres of Maybury Common for £750 from the Necropolis Company. The site was adjacent to Maybury Arch, and alongside the railway line.

On 1 June 1860 a special train brought the Prince Consort from London to a temporary platform which had been erected beside the site at Maybury. The Prince was welcomed by the prospective Master of the College, Webster, who was one of the trustees, and at a short ceremony laid the foundation-stone of the new building. He then heard a loyal address, thanking him for his invaluable assistance, and in reply expressed his best wishes, and those of the Queen, for the project.[37]

The first residents were admitted in September 1862, well in advance of the official opening which was not until 5 June 1865. Prince Albert had died in 1861 and his place as patron of the College had been taken by Edward, Prince of Wales, whose interest in the theatre, and in actresses, was well known. At the opening the Prince toured the buildings and received the customary address, and in reply described the objective of the College, 'to cheer the evening of [the] life . . . of those who are entitled to seek shelter in this asylum'.[38]

The residents, and others associated with the College, observed a day of celebration every 23 April. That day, by happy coincidence, was the anniversary of the birth of William Shakespeare and of Thomas P. Cooke, a wealthy actor who invested his money to support the College 'because he had private means himself but knew that other members of his profession had not'. Cooke also endowed a 'prize drama', a competition in which the winning playwright received £50 in return for giving all rights and royalties of his work to the Royal Dramatic College Trustees.[39]

His generosity was the principal means of support for the College, but was supplemented by a wide variety of fund-raising activities. Fêtes and fairs were held, an annual dramatic performance was given at a London theatre, and members of the acting profession, writers, dramatists and cultural patrons were approached and asked to donate. Cooke died in 1867, and by his will another large sum was left to the College.[40]

The Royal Dramatic College was designed by T. R. Smith in a curious mid-Victorian interpretation of the 'Tudor' style, and was constructed of red brick, the standard local material. Terracotta reliefs were employed to ornament the building. It had a large central hall, surmounted at the western end by a tower with a small 'spire', and along the front was a pillared arcade or cloister. This was to provide an area, protected from the weather, where the aged residents could sit. There were two wings, one on either side of the main hall and entrance. Each had five self-contained 'houses', individually subscribed by organisations or benefactors and accommodating two persons. There was thus room for 20 residents, ten of each sex.[41]

It is likely that this number was never reached, for the 1871 Census records only 16 old people together with Webster and his wife, who acted as matron. There were nine actresses and seven actors, one of whom rather pathetically described himself as a 'retired tragedian'. The youngest was 60, the eldest 85. It seems that the Master and his wife ran the entire complex without any permanent assistance, presumably to reduce expenses.[42]

In March 1870 it was said locally that the College was 'in need of funds' and in the following years, the financial position became increasingly precarious. Building costs had been higher than anticipated, and the cost of running such a substantial building with its extensive grounds was too great. Public and private interest in the project was waning, and Thomas Cooke, its greatest benefactor, was no longer there to provide more money. In the early months of 1877 emergency meetings were held to consider the future of the College, and on 12 November the governors and trustees reluctantly decided that it must close immediately.[43]

The Charity Commissioners instructed that the building, land and moveable assets should be sold to cover expenses and repay debts, but it was not until the end of June 1880 that this was completed. Messrs. Farebrother, Lye & Palmer of London put the property up for auction, but the reserve price of £5,000 was not reached. It was then sold by private contract to Alfred Chabot, a land and property speculator.[44]

The Oriental Institute

Chabot determined to sell his newly acquired 'white elephant' as a single property, for a different institutional purpose, since it would not be marketable for house building in view of the freely available development land in the vicinity. In the spring of 1884 it was purchased by Dr. Gottlieb Wilhelm Leitner.

Leitner was born at Pest, Hungary, on 14 October 1840. As a child he showed an extraordinary ability in languages, and by the age of ten was fluent in Turkish, Arabic and most European tongues. At 15 he was appointed Interpreter (1st Class) to the British Commissariat in the Crimea, with the rank of colonel. When the Crimean War ended he went to London to study at King's College. When he was 19 he became lecturer in Arabic, Turkish & Modern Greek, and at 23 was appointed Professor in Arabic and Mohammedan Law.

Three years later he was asked to become Principal of the Government College at Lahore, now in Pakistan, and soon succeeded in raising this in status to the University of the Punjab. He founded schools, literary associations, public libraries and academic journals, whilst at the same time dedicating himself to the study of the cultures of the Indian subcontinent.

He returned to Europe in the late 1870s to pursue research at Heidelberg University, and also undertook work for the Austrian, Prussian and British Governments. His ambition now was to found a centre for the study in Europe of Oriental languages, culture and history. On his return to England in 1881 he sought a suitable site for his proposed institution, and in 1883 came upon the vacant Royal Dramatic College in Woking, a building admirably suited for the purpose.

He bought the college and set about converting it into the Oriental Institute, decorating the interior with priceless objects which he had collected during his travels in Asia. Part was made into an Oriental Museum, said to contain probably the most interesting collection in the possession of any private individual in this country. The Institute trained Asians living in Europe for the learned professions, undertook studies of linguistics and culture, and taught languages to Europeans who wished to travel to the East.

It was an ambitious and fascinating project, and Leitner himself remarked upon the strange circumstances whereby Woking had become a centre for Oriental Studies. It remained comparatively obscure locally, and Woking people seemed unaware of the precise nature of the Institute. As Leitner said, 'There is no place in the world where the Institute and its publications are less known than in Surrey'. Leitner hoped that the Oriental Institute would in time be granted full university status, and by the late 1890s it was already awarding degrees under the University of Lahore, with which it had very close ties. He intended that it should be the acknowledged centre for this field of study, a role which was later acquired by the London University School of Oriental and African Studies.[45]

Sadly his ambitions were not fulfilled, for the Institute relied too heavily upon Leitner's personal enthusiasm and wealth, and it did not survive his early death. In 1898 he fell ill, and in January 1899 travelled to Bonn, on medical advice, to bathe at Godesberg spa. He contracted pneumonia during a cold spell in February, and on 22 March 1899 he died at Bonn, aged 58. His body was returned to England, and he is buried in Brookwood Cemetery.

The death of its director and founder meant the end of the Oriental Institute, and it closed in the summer of 1899. The treasury of artistic and historic objects and the library were sold. The contents were dispersed and soon the buildings stood vacant once more. Had it succeeded the project might have had a profound effect upon the town. It is realistic to suppose that by 1914 there would have been an Oriental University of Woking, making the town a cultural centre of importance, and giving it an identity and status which it has tended to lack. But this remains hypothetical, and the Institute is now all but forgotten. It has only two permanent memorials. Maybury Heath Lane was renamed Oriental Road in the 1890s, and beside the railway near the site of the former Institute is the most exotic and delightful of all the buildings of Woking, the mosque.

Woking Mosque

To cater for the spiritual needs of those Moslems who were studying at the Institute, and to provide for any others of the faith who lived within reach, Leitner built a mosque, which was opened in October or November 1889. It is the oldest mosque in the British Isles, and probably in Europe, and is thus of considerable historic interest.

Within a few years it had naturally become a centre for British Moslems, and was the venue for religious and social festivals which attracted visitors from a wide area. Amongst the worshippers in the 1890s were 'Her Majesty's Indian attendants at Windsor'.[46] Although mosques have since been built in many British towns and cities, and the Regents Park Mosque is now the centre of Islam in this country, Woking Mosque is still one of the senior places of worship. The town also has a large resident Moslem population.

The design was based on drawings and paintings of other mosques, chiefly from India, and is thus of Indian rather than Arabic appearance. Its architect was W. I. Chambers, and it was paid for by donations from the faithful in Britain and India. The most generous benefactor was Her Highness Shah Jehan, the Begum of Bhopal, a friend and patron of Leitner and his university at Lahore. In her honour it was officially called the Shah Jehan Mosque.

It has a green onion dome, white walls and minarets, and a great deal of delightful blue and gold ornamentation. Nairn describes it as 'extraordinarily dignified . . . especially by comparison with other mock-Oriental buildings of the same date . . . as pretty as the Brighton Pavilion'.[47] Contemporaries were intrigued and charmed by this curious addition to the landscape of Woking, and the obituary for Dr. Leitner referred to 'the beautiful mosque which is such a conspicuous object near the railway'.[48] It is still visible from the train, although trees have grown up around, and to the traveller it is one of the few remarkable features of an otherwise conventional town.

In 1917 the government paid for and built a Moslem Cemetery on Horsell Common, near the Six Cross-roads, for the burial of the Indian soldiers who had been killed whilst fighting in Europe.[49] At this time Woking Mosque was still the only one in Britain, and it was perhaps felt that nearness to the spiritual centre of their faith was appropriate. The Mosque had been closed and empty between 1899 and 1912, while the Institute was vacant, but in the latter year it was re-opened by a mission from the Punjab.

Other Institutions

The Industrial School. In 1867 the Surrey County Justices opened an Industrial School at Wandsworth. This was a new approach to dealing with the unemployed and destitute youths who were so numerous on the streets of the capital and other large towns. The Surrey Industrial School was officially intended for 'Destitute Boys not Convicted of Crime', although some boys who had committed minor offences were later admitted.[50] The school gave boys accommodation and education, and undertook to teach them a craft or trade, such as shoemaking, tailoring or carpentry. It was financed from the rates and from the sale of goods and produce. The Wandsworth School, on a congested urban site, was soon inadequate and in 1870 the Justices leased Coldharbour Farm, 250 acres between Byfleet Corner and Coldharbour, Pyrford. The school moved there in 1871, and the 1881 Census recorded 247 occupants, of whom 41 were staff. They accounted for no less than 70 per cent of the population growth in Byfleet parish from 1971 to 1881.

There was still a need for a permanent home. In the autumn of 1886 an ideal opportunity was presented when Mayford Farm came up for sale. It covered 27 acres of pasture between Mayford Green, the railway and Hoe Stream, and the cost was £15,000; The school moved here in August 1887. It is still there, renamed 'Kinton' and operated by the Greater London Council.[51]

St Peter's Home. The St Peter's Sisterhood, an order of Anglican nuns based at Kilburn, opened a small convent and convalescent home at Sandy Lane, Maybury, in 1885. It was intended for 'respectable sick women suffering from illnesses which require skilled treatment and nursing, often for much longer periods than the rules of general hospitals and ordinary convalescent homes allow them to receive'.[52] The Home was enlarged in the 1890s, and was able to accommodate about 60 patients with 40 nuns and other members of staff. A fine chapel, in a Byzantine style with mosaics, was built in 1897-1901, to a design by J. L. Pearson.[53]

The Railway Orphanage. The London and South Western Railway Servants Orphanage was founded in 1885, and in 1907 the trustees and governors acquired an extensive site beside the railway line near Woking station. Here a large new orphanage, accommodating 200 children, was opened in 1909, having cost £24,000. It is now called Woking Grange, and serves the Southern Region of British Rail.[54]

The Waifs & Strays Home. The St Nicholas' Home for Crippled Children was opened in Pyrford Road, Byfleet in about 1893. In 1906 it moved to impressive new buildings in Floyds Lane, Pyrford, and was renamed the St Nicholas' Church of England Home for Waifs and Strays. The buildings were designed by E. J. May and have been described as 'Half Lutyens, Half Voysey, and half as attractive as their Academy elevations'. The Home is now the Rowley Bristow Orthopaedic Hospital.[55]

Chapter Eight

THE WELFARE OF THE COMMUNITY

Religion

UNTIL 1927 WOKING, with most of non-metropolitan Surrey, was part of the vast Diocese of Winchester. In that year the county was detached to become the new Diocese of Guildford, a plan which had first been mooted in the 1530s. From 1829 until 1887 the parishes of Byfleet, Horsell, Pyrford and Woking had been included in the Deanery of Stoke (next Guildford) but in the latter year this was divided, to cope with a rapidly increasing population. A new Rural Deanery of Woking was established, comprising the present Borough together with Bisley, Chobham, Frimley, Ockham, Pirbright, Send, Ripley and Windlesham. The Church of England was thus the first body to recognise that Woking was destined to become the leading town in North West Surrey.[1]

The four ancient parish churches were sufficient to cater for the district until the 1840s, whilst it remained primarily rural and agricultural. They all survive today, and are the oldest extant buildings in the Borough, but suffered considerably during the middle years of the 19th century at the hands of 'restorers'. The activities of these people resulted, in some cases, in the loss of much that was of interest or beauty, and so diminished the ancient and remote character of, in particular, St Mary's, Horsell and St Mary's, Byfleet. Of the former, where the work was designed by W. F. Unsworth (who later undertook Christ Church, Woking), Nairn says, 'a sorry mess of restoration and enlargement . . . all new or renewed to extinction'.[2]

Pyrford church was restored in 1868-70, and during the course of this work the first of the ancient wall-paintings were discovered as later plaster was removed. Here the restoration work was sensitive and appropriate, and, by upgrading the quality of the fabric itself, ensured that the distinctive and delightful character of this little church would survive. The architect was Sir Thomas Jackson. Munby described the work as it was in progress; it will be noted that the wall-paintings were not regarded with much favour!

> 'The interior was a heap of rubbish; all the old pews and seats gone or waiting rearrangement. A few scraps of rude old fresco, scraped bare, showed on the walls. Outside, the ivy is gone from tower and gable and wall; and within the ancient porch . . . barrels of mortar were standing a-row. In the churchyard . . . the ivy torn from the church lay about in heaps.'[3]

By the late 1830s it was becoming apparent that Woking parish was inconveniently large as a single ecclesiastical unit. St Peter's Church is in the extreme east, and the growth of the Knaphill–Kiln Bridge district at the opposite corner had made the existing difficulties of access a problem for increasing numbers of parishioners.

In 1840 work began upon a new chapel-of-ease at the foot of Hook Hill south of Kiln Bridge, to serve the area.

It was a simple aisleless building, in Kentish Ragstone with Bath Stone facings, designed by Sir George Gilbert Scott and dedicated to St John the Baptist. In view of its rather humble origins it was perhaps to be expected that St John's would not be a work of merit, although one of the earliest buildings by a subsequently outstanding architect: 'Not in Scott's own list of his early "ignoble" churches. It ought to be'.[4] The chapel was enlarged several times, and thereby lost its original appearance, but time has had a mellowing effect, and its pleasant setting beside St Johns Lye adds to its character. In 1883 it became a fully-fledged church when the ecclesiastical parish of St John's was formed from that of St Peter's. The church gave its name to the surrounding community; properly, the church and parish are spelled 'St John's' whilst the ward and district name has lost its apostrophe, and is always spelt 'St Johns'.

With the development of the new town around Woking station from the late 1860s, another church became necessary, but it was over 20 years before this was provided. As already shown (Chapter Five) the Necropolis Company had been obliged by its Act of 1855 to allocate land near the railway station for a church and school, and the Diocese of Winchester had acquired three acres in the future Onslow Crescent. The site was never used for the intended purpose, although Christ Church Vicarage was later built there. Instead, a plot of land 255 feet by 138 feet on the south side of Providence Street (Church Street) was chosen by the diocesan authorities in 1861.

It was not formally conveyed by the Necropolis Company until 1870, and in the meantime services were held in the back room of a new shop in Chertsey Road. A temporary iron chapel was opened on the Providence Street site in 1877 by James Titcombe, Vicar of Woking, and later first Bishop of Rangoon. By 1885 it was uncomfortably cramped and 'in a rusty and leaking condition', and the Parochial Church Council voted to build a permanent structure, rejecting a suggestion that yet another site should be found elsewhere in the town centre.

William Unsworth was commissioned to design a church, and on 10 November 1887 the Duchess of Albany laid its foundation stone. Although it was only partly finished the building was opened for worship on New Year's Day 1889 and the final stage, the construction of the flèche, was carried out during January 1893. At a service conducted by the Bishop of Winchester on 14 June 1893 the building was consecrated and dedicated, Christ Church. A new ecclesiastical parish, covering the town centre, Maybury and Mount Hermon, was created on 28 August.[5]

Christ Church, a simple and unambitious building in plain red brick, was described by Nairn as 'big in scale, honest . . . Inside, a big kingpost roof above a big apsed space with tiny ambulatory aisles . . . as with so many late Victorian architects, the cheaper the building, the better the design'.[6] The reference to finance is significant, for serious problems were encountered in raising the money during the six years of construction, and the original designs were modified to reduce costs. Initially Unsworth proposed a brick tower at the eastern end, but it was abandoned and the slender copper-sheathed flèche substituted. Christ Church was surrounded by the typically drab and dreary buildings of 'New Woking', and although in the heart of the town had neither the setting nor the character of an important urban church. In the late 1960s it, alone amongst its neighbours, was spared demolition in the comprehensive renewal of the central area, and now stands beside the Town Square, which forms the focal point of the new design: unfortunately its orientation did not accord with that design, and the main entrance to the church faces away from the Square.

The suburbs of the growing town were also provided with separate churches. St Paul's, Maybury Hill (1895) was followed by Holy Trinity, Knaphill, and St Mary of Bethany, York Road, both in 1907.[7] The last was designed by Caröe, and is clearly influenced by the distinctive 'vernacular' style evolved for domestic architecture at this time. A similar influence is apparent at St Saviour's, Brookwood (1909), where J. H. Barr designed 'a neat church . . . with Lutyenesque details'.

A separate ecclesiastical parish of Woodham was carved out of Addlestone in 1893, when the new All Saints' Church, Woodham Lane, was opened. The architect was the ubiquitous William Unsworth, who lived nearby at Woodhambury, the house which he had designed for himself. In contrast to Christ Church, Woking, the design for All Saints' was in an imitation 'Old Surrey' style, with perfectly replicated medieval details. It has been described as 'frigid and expensive . . . joyless and stone-dead', but today, standing in its quiet close surrounded by conifers, it forms an attractive scene.[8]

In 1872 a small iron mission church was built near Byfleet Corner, to serve this developing area which was remote from St Mary's, Byfleet. The iron church survived for 40 years, until 1912, and eventually ended up as the headquarters of a rifle club at Bisley. It was superseded by the new St John's Church, designed by Caröe and built at a cost of £12,000. This has an attractive exterior, in the 'Surrey' style, with a short shingled steeple, but Nairn is uncomplimentary about the interior: 'a complete specimen of the fussily-detailed, genteelly-roofed type of design which has been the bane of English church architecture for nearly fifty years'.[9]

There were no Catholic churches in the area until 1876, when the Salvin family of Sutton Place spent about £2,000 on building St Edward's, Sutton Green; before then worshippers used private rooms and chapels. In the new town an iron mission church was erected in Percy Street in the late 1890s, to accommodate 150 people, and a presbytery was built close by at the junction with Church Street. In 1924–25 a new church was built, St Dunstan's, at the corner of Oriental Crescent and White Rose Lane. It has an uninteresting sub-Gothic design and accommodates 450.[10] The presbytery was then incorporated into the old fire station, demolished in 1980.

Nonconformism in Woking dates back at least as far as the middle of the 17th century, for in 1668 the Guildford Monthly Meeting of the Society of Friends attracted members from 'Godalming, Guildford, Sheere, Myrrow, Warnbarrow, Pirbright, Warplesden and Oakinge . . . ', whilst in 1681 and 1682 Quakers from Woking were imprisoned at Guildford for refusing to pay tithes.[11] An Independent Baptist Chapel was established in Kingfield, close to the present church, in the mid-1770s, and by this time, too, meetings were being held in Horsell.

In 1809–10 an old cottage on the edge of Horsell Common was adapted for worship 'after the order & according to the doctrines of the sect of society called Particular Calvinistic Baptists', and in 1815–16 a new Chapel was built there at a cost of £206 14s. 3½d. (£206.71½). It was attended by worshippers from as far afield as Albury, Egham and Horsley.[12] A mission was opened in a cottage near Woking station in 1879, as a branch of the Addlestone pastorate, by Henry Gloster, one of the leading figures in Woking public life during the 30 years from 1875. In 1886 it moved to its present site on Goldsworth Road, the pastorate having been transferred to Woking in 1883. In 1885 another mission was established by the Rev. E. W. Tarbox of Woking at Anthony's on Horsell Common. He claimed that 'it was like working in a heathen land, for many of the little folks had never even heard of the name of Jesus', an interesting reflection of education in the Woking of a century ago.[13]

Education

Until the early years of the last century there was almost no provision for education in the four parishes of Woking. There were a few 'informal' establishments, such as dame schools, which provided the rudiments of instruction to a small number of pupils, but virtually no records survive from these.

Horsell was a centre of nonconformism by the late 18th century, and at some time in the 1790s a school was established in the village by this community. It later became the Horsell Baptist School. There was also a small Church of England school, maintained by voluntary payments from parents. The church school was expanded in the early years of the 19th century, and a survey of 1818 noted that it had an average attendance of 165. Of these more than half (87) came from Woking parish, which did not have its own church school. The same survey reported that in Byfleet there was a voluntarily maintained day school for 24 pupils, but no other provision, whilst in Pyrford parish there was no school at all, and 'the poorer classes are entirely destitute of means of education, though desirous of obtaining them'.[14]

A second survey, carried out for the government in 1833, after it was realised that standards of education in Britain were deplorably low, revealed that there had been only a small improvement in provision in the Woking area. Horsell Church school, then a voluntary day and Sunday school, was staffed by a master and mistress at a joint salary of 50 guineas a year. It had an average of 209 pupils, of whom 91 were from Woking, 38 from Pyrford and 80 from Horsell. It had thus been enlarged substantially, and some Pyrford children were now receiving education, but at a long distance from their homes.

In Byfleet there were then three day schools, all supported entirely by donations, but they accommodated only 49 children between them, so that many were still left without any education.[15] A newer, and larger, voluntary school was founded in the village in 1840. By 1838, too, the Vicar of Woking, Charles Bowles, had set up a small voluntary school in Woking Village, where educational facilities were surprisingly inferior.

The provision of education had hitherto been essentially unorganised, but in the 1840s the government began to make grants to the National Society for the Promotion of the Education of the Poor in the Principles of the Established Church (founded 1811) for the building of schools, usually known as National Schools. The earliest in the Woking area to be described as a 'National School' was that opened at Pyrford in 1847, the first in the parish, with 32 places. It was followed, in 1848, by the Church Street School in Woking village and in 1849 by the Westfield National Schoolroom.

The Church Street school was enlarged in 1899-1901, but still survives although it closed in 1981. The Westfield National School has been superseded, but the building remains. It is the attractive little hall and mission church on the edge of the common opposite the present Westfield Middle School.

Small church schools were opened in St Johns and Sutton Green in the late 1850s, and another in Knaphill in the early 1860s to serve the increasing population of this corner of the parish. Horsell Church School was adopted by the National Society and rebuilt in 1851 with only 81 places, since children from adjacent parishes no longer came. Byfleet School was similarly adopted, and reopened after extensive rebuilding in June 1856, with 146 pupils.[16]

Private education continued to supplement the public sector, although its relative importance diminished as the latter was developed. Some private schools were ambitious, and in the later 19th century several were founded in the Woking area which survive to the present. One which seemed likely to flourish was Woking College, founded in September 1869 by the Rev. Charles Arnold at Woking Grange. It was advertised as 'a private school to provide education of the highest class, and . . . conducted on the principles of the Church of England, the system being based on that of the public schools'.[17] By 1871 the school had 60 pupils from all over the country, but its founder died in 1885, and it did not long survive this blow.

As urban growth began in the late 1860s the existing system of National Schools in Woking came under further strain, because the 'New' Woking had no educational provision. The 1870 Elementary Education Act made 'primary' schooling compulsory, although not free of charge, and also permitted the local authorities to make improvements in facilities where these were inadequate. The increased school population, combined with the deficiencies of the National Schools, made this latter power essential for Woking.

The School Board

There had been a growing public concern over the shortage of school places even before 1870, and the Woking Vestry immediately held meetings at Church Street School to discuss the questions arising out of the new Act. In June 1872 it was decided by the Vestry that 'new school accommodation is required at Woking and that the same can best be provided by a School Board'.[18] These were autonomous bodies directly elected by the ratepayers but responsible to the new Department of Education, and were intended to administer and develop education in districts where provision was inadequate. A meeting in December 1870 had heard that at least 200 children in the parish were unable to find a place at school, an indication of the severity of the problem.[19]

The proposal for a school board divided the parish politically, between the older areas such as Westfield and the Village, which already had schools, and the growing communities of Woking Station and Knaphill, which were lacking in educational facilities. A poll was taken in February 1873, and the results reveal that this split was responsible. (*See* table top of page 123).

Vote on School Board Establishment 1873[20]

	For	*Against*
The Village	9	50
Woking Station	60	10
Goldsworth/St Johns	3	50
Knaphill	42	14
Mayford/Westfield	28	31
	142	155

In the following year the decision was reversed and on 30 April 1874 elections were held for the Woking School Board, the ninth of its kind in Surrey. The first meeting was held at Church Street on 21 May.

The Board was the first local government body to give an effective service in the parish. Because of its importance and its considerable spending power it always attracted controversy and interest, and its elections were often hotly contested. The rift between the two halves of the parish lasted into the 1890s, although the newer areas, with their larger population and greater needs, eventually gained the ascendancy. Election to the School Board was said to be determined by the status and occupation of the candidates rather than by their abilities or concern for education, as the poem below makes clear:

WOKING SCHOOL BOARD ELECTIONS, 1880 [21]

1. As I went down the Station-road
   I saw a funny Bill:
   It tells us how the coming Board
   The Voters they should fill.

2. A Parson, he the first should be
   A Farmer he came second
   A Publican the triple X
   And Fourth a Doctor, reckon'd.

3. An Undertaker, he's the next,
   'Cause why? The reason's plain
   In boards he'll pack the present Board
   So opposition's vain.

4. A Minister dissenting next
   Because he won't agree
   A Tradesman closes up the list
   The "General" to be.

5. And "that's the list that's best for me",
   Says rising Woking Station!
   "Ah lack-a-day! There's no Fair play",
   Says Mistress Education.

In the early days the feud within the parish was enlivened by Ebenezer Smith, a maverick who was much disliked by the 'Old Woking' members, yet very popular with the electorate. In April 1877 he topped the poll (of 12 candidates for seven seats) with 431 votes, almost 100 more than the next candidate.[22] In 1876 he had been described as 'in a state of unmistakable intoxication' at a meeting of the Board, and in 1878 was largely responsible, by his continued objections, for a stormy debate over the election of a Chairman and a new member to fill a vacancy. The member was to be co-opted, and the Vicar of Woking, Oliphant, was proposed. Smith objected, and the 'New Woking' members supported him, with the result that the nomination was approved only by the casting vote of the Chairman: 'Smallpiece said it was a farce'.[23]

The new School Board set about its tasks with an energy and enthusiasm that made a sharp contrast with the inertia and inadequacy of the other local government bodies in the area. Within a month of its election it had purchased, for £600, an acre of land on Maybury Common, north of the railway, from the Necropolis Company. Work on the new school here, to serve the fast growing areas of East Woking, began in October 1874, and it was opened for instruction on 6 September 1875, with places for 70 infants and 180 older children. The importance attached to the Maybury School may be gauged from the naming of 'Board School Road' in its honour. The first master was Thomas Rushforth, who had formerly taught at St Johns; he was assisted by his wife and daughter. In June 1878 all three were dismissed 'in consequence of the very unsatisfactory Report of H.M. Inspector of the Maybury Board School',[24] Rushforth had also been reprimanded several times for the ill-treatment of infant pupils.

The School Board, after some acrimony, also took over the running of most of the schools operated by the National Society, which retained the freehold. Westfield was transferred in December 1874, Church Street and St Johns in July 1876, and Knaphill in March 1877.[25] The premises were usually inadequate for the increasing numbers; in May 1879, for example, H.M. Inspector said of Knaphill School that it had 'crowded and unsuitable premises, and satisfactory results could hardly be looked for'.[26] The School Board thus began a sustained programme of new building and enlargement.

A new Knaphill Board School was built at a cost of £2,090 (including Master's House) in 1880–81. Maybury School was enlarged by 200 places in 1881 and by 1891 had 192 pupils in the Infants Section and 488 in the Mixed Junior. The old school at Westfield was replaced in 1897 by a new Westfield Infants School (now the Middle School), on land bought for £350 from Gustav Wermig, the first Chairman of Woking U.D.C. Goldsworth School, which cost £6,362, was built in 1897–98 to cater for this fast developing residential area, and had places for 350 juniors and 188 infants. Finally the Board bought land for a 240-place school at Brookwood in 1901, and the building was opened in 1903. At the time of its dissolution, therefore, the School Board operated six schools, some of which had separate Infant and Junior sections, and had approximately 1,800 pupils on its roll.[27]

The Board also attempted to regulate education in the private sector. In February 1884, for example, the Board of Education was asked to send 'a competent person to assess the efficiency of the non-Board National School at Sutton Green',[28] as a result of which the school was closed and its pupils transferred to Westfield. Three years earlier it had taken steps to prevent children from 'attending Mrs. Lilley's school, which is inefficient and therefore illegal'.[29]

In the other parishes there was little need for completely new schools, but enlargements were made as population grew. In 1902 Byfleet National School had 385 children and that at Horsell 133. Neither parish had felt the need for the school board, and the National Society continued to provide all facilities. In contrast Pyrford had been badly served by its small and overcrowded school of 1847, and by the late 1880s there was serious concern about the poor standards. The 1889 Local Government Act allowed the new county councils to make compulsory declarations of school boards, and to enforce elections, in parishes where facilities were inadequate. Surrey made use of this power, and on 19 December 1891 a Pyrford School Board was elected, to undertake the replacement of the old school. The new building, at the junction of Coldharbour Road and Engliff Lane, was opened in the spring of 1893 and had places for 62 children; it was enlarged in 1909.[30]

The 1902 Education Act made free primary education compulsory, and also required that, with exceptions for large cities, county councils should take over all education functions. It thus swept away the multitude of school boards and other *ad hoc* bodies which had proliferated over the years; there were 29 of the former in Surrey alone by this time. In 1903, therefore, the County Council took over the functions of the Woking and Pyrford Schools Boards and of the National Society in Byfleet and Horsell. The Boards had laid solid foundations for education in the parishes of Woking and Pyrford, and their effectiveness had contrasted markedly with the feeble and inadequate attempts of the other local government agencies in the last quarter of the 19th century.

Secondary Education

Apart from the sending of a very few children to attend secondary schools in neighbouring towns there was no provision for education beyond primary level until the early years of this century. The only exception was the Woking Mutual Improvement Society, founded by the Vicar in 1867. This gave instruction to adults in a wide range of subjects including foreign languages, and included a small lending-library, with newspapers and periodicals.[31] In June 1893 the Woking School Board, having completed much of the work on elementary education, adopted a scheme for the provision of evening classes to be held in Board Schools. This was started during the winter of 1893–94.[32]

In March 1894 the Woking Local Board, which had no education powers, set up a Technical Education Committee to press the School Board for improvements in secondary education. As a result practical classes were added to the evening class scheme, and the County Council was urged to provide a secondary school for Woking, by then the largest town in the county without such a facility.[33]

In 1909 the County Council purchased a large, central site on Station Approach for a Boys' Secondary School. The imposing red brick and stone buildings of the County School for Boys were opened in 1914. Eight years later the County School for Girls was established in a converted house in Park Road, at a cost of £6,500. The school moved to spacious purpose-built premises in Old Woking Road, on the edge of the town, in 1959. The comprehensive system was introduced in the Woking area in 1975 and both schools were later closed. Their sixth-form pupils were transferred to the new Woking College at Rydens Way, Old Woking.

Libraries

The 1892 Libraries Act had given local authorities power to raise rates and to use public funds for the provision of free libraries. Hitherto they had been required to seek special permission for that purpose. Woking Urban District Council did not attach much importance to the idea, being preoccupied with the more urgent matters of the fire-brigade, sewerage and roadworks. However in November 1902, after several members had expressed an interest, the Council debated a proposal that it should apply to the Andrew Carnegie Foundation for a grant to provide a free library in the town, and to adopt the 1892 Act for its administration. The plan was accepted, but in January 1903 a meeting of the full Council reversed this resolution, yet another example of the fatal indecision which characterised the authority before the First World War.[34] In October of that year the proposal was again debated. Carnegie had most generously offered a gift of £5,000 for the building of a new library in Woking, but the councillors rejected his offer on the grounds that a penny rate would be needed to raise money for stocking the library.[35] It is interesting that £4,500 was at that time being spent on building new council offices.

This parsimonious decision delayed the introduction of library facilities for over 20 years. In February 1924 the Council debated a resolution that a public library should be established in Woking, and received representations to this effect from local churches, women's organisations and educational bodies. The only dissenting voice was that of a resident who objected to the 'spread of infectious disease through books and newspapers'.[36] It was decided that the Urban District should provide its own library service, with accommodation being made available in the civic centre then proposed at the junction of Church Street and Percy Street.

This scheme was abortive, and the Council therefore asked Surrey County Council to assist. A new site was agreed, and in 1928 the Urban District Council acquired the disused Baptist Chapel in Commercial Road for conversion to a Library. It opened on March 1929, with Mr. G. R. Wells as the first Librarian. Although Woking U.D.C. at first operated the library the County Library Service became ever more closely involved, until by 1939 it was, in effect, absorbed by the latter.[37] In 1974 the old, and hopelessly cramped, library was closed and replaced by the large new building on Town Square. Surrey County Council provided branch libraries in Pyrford and Byfleet in 1928, after requests from the Parish Councils.

Justice

Traditionally law enforcement was carried out, with variable success, by unpaid constables appointed by the manor courts. Thus in Woking, a large parish there were usually four constables for Woking manor and one for Sutton, whilst Byfleet had two and Pyrford and Horsell one each. In later years they were sometimes 'taken over' by the vestries when manor courts fell into disuse, but often were not replaced. The 1851 Census recorded only one full-time policeman, in Woking village, for the whole of the present Borough, although voluntary unpaid men would have been available when needed.[38]

In 1850 the County Justices established the Surrey Constabulary, a paid and properly organised police force. There were six divisions, and the four Woking parishes were included in the one based on Chertsey. Initially this was sufficient, and the growth of the town was accommodated by additions to the ranks of parish constables: in 1871 Byfleet had two, Horsell one and Woking three.[39]

By the early 1880s, however, pressure was growing for better local facilities, and in 1885 the Chief Constable received a petition from Woking residents urging that the town should be separated from the Chertsey division. The arguments were accepted, and in 1886 a site in Harris' Lane (now Heathside Road) was purchased for £300, and a new police station built there. This opened in 1887, with facilities for three officers and cells for four offenders, at a cost of £2,750.[40]

In November 1895 Woking Urban District Council asked the County Council to allocate more police to the town, after there had been 'unruly scenes in the streets'.[41] After a perplexing delay, the request was agreed in July 1896. In other parishes provision was generally adequate, but in January 1896 Pyrford Parish Council asked for a policeman to be appointed for the parish, where there had been no resident constable for many years.[42]

The Woking area was included in Chertsey Petty Sessional Division, but in December 1901 the County Magistrates proposed that, as it was by then a substantial town, it should be separated. The proposal reappeared, with the support of Woking U.D.C., in August 1905. Chertsey Rural District Council and the parish councils of Byfleet and Pyrford were extremely hostile to the idea, seeing it as the prelude to a wider administrative reform which would expand Woking Urban District. Nonetheless the scheme went ahead, and in the spring of 1906 the new Woking Petty Sessional Division was created, including the four parishes together with Send & Ripley, Ockham and Wisley. The courthouse was built beside the existing police station.[43]

Hospitals

Until the 1890s there was no hospital near Woking, and all patients except those with highly infectious diseases were catered for by the Royal Surrey County Hospital at Guildford or, more probably, were treated at home. In 1882 Guildford Rural Sanitary Authority built an isolation hospital, for patients with infectious diseases, at Wood Street Common, Worplesdon; this took people from the Woking area. Patients from Horsell, Pyrford and Byfleet were not provided for until 1892, when Chertsey R.S.A. opened a similar hospital at Ottershaw.[44]

The need for such institutions is revealed in the reports of the Medical Officer of Health, for epidemics were frequent in the Woking district until after the First World War. In the autumn of 1901, for example, diphtheria closed all the schools in Knaphill and Brookwood for eight weeks, and in November 1905 the same disease caused the deaths of 22 children, all aged seven or under, in the Woking Station ward.[45] Every year brought outbreaks of scarlet fever and measles, and in November 1898 most of the families in Goldsworth were affected by a mystery illness described as 'Sore Throat', but which was eventually found to be a form of cattle fever: the Goldsworth Dairy herd was discovered to be the source of the trouble, and infected milk had been distributed for several days before the authorities traced the problem.[46]

With such unpleasant and insanitary conditions the provision of a hospital for the town, which by the mid-1890s had almost 15,000 people, was long overdue. In

November 1893, as a temporary measure, the Woking, Horsell & Woodham Cottage Hospital was opened in Bath Road. It occupied a converted house, and had a nominal staff of eight.[47] In 1899 it was replaced by the Woking Victoria Hospital, next to the Wheatsheaf Canal Bridge. This purpose-built cottage hospital had cost £4,200, and was named in commemoration of the Diamond Jubilee of 1897, the year in which work began. An extension was built in 1901–3, costing £7,000 and paid for by the Urban District Council and the people of Woking as a memorial to the late Queen.[48]

The Guildford and Godalming Borough Councils had opened a new isolation hospital at Woodbridge in 1893. The newly formed Woking Local Board asked for permission to participate in its management, and this request was repeated in 1895 by Woking U.D.C.: a Parliamentary Order of August 1896 established the Guildford, Godalming & Woking Joint Hospital Board for that purpose.[49] In 1933, following the reorganisation of local government, Woking U.D.C. agreed to co-operate with the councils of Walton & Weybridge, Chertsey, Egham, Bagshot and Frimley & Camberley, to develop a comprehensive health and hospitals service for North West Surrey. The result was the formation, in October 1935, of the Ottershaw Joint Hospital Board, which began work on building the complex later known as St Peter's Hospital, at Chertsey.[50]

In 1934 plans had been put forward for a new Woking District Hospital, to replace the Victoria. A site at Kettlewell Hill was chosen, and in 1937 the project was given outline approval and planning permission, but the war broke out before building work could be started.[51] The National Health Service, which inherited the plan in 1948, decided to concentrate local hospital facilities at St Peter's, and so the scheme was abandoned. Since then the Woking Victoria Hospital has several times been threatened with closure, under rationalisation proposals, but at the time of writing it has managed to survive, as a result of very strong local opposition to such a move.

Chapter Nine

THE PEOPLE AND THEIR WORK 1850-1914

The People

THE REMARKABLE CHANGES of the 19th century were not evenly spread among the parishes of the Woking area. Although the overall trend was upwards, there were periods during the century of stagnation or decline, which interrupted this growth. The appendix gives a table of population figures whilst the table below shows the rate of change in each decade to 1911.

Table 8. Percentage Intercensal Population Change [1]

	Byfleet	*Horsell*	*Pyrford*	*Woking*	*'Borough'*
1801-1811	8.3	14.4	14.8	17.8	15.4
1811-1821	8.9	9.4	11.4	14.7	12.5
1821-1831	19.4	9.1	4.4	9.1	10.1
1831-1841	31.8	13.8	8.5	25.7	22.8
1841-1851	2.2	–0.5	9.6	14.3	9.3
1851-1861	12.1	3.4	4.4	34.6	23.8
1861-1871	18.8	13.8	–6.3	72.5	52.1
1871-1881	37.8	0.3	–3.9	29.9	26.3
1881-1891	9.8	13.4	25.7	14.3	14.1
1891-1901	22.0	108.4	22.5	65.9	63.1
1901-1911	75.4	42.2	85.4	34.3	39.8
1801-1911	717.6	513.8	325.6	1,525.9	1,085.4

During the early years of the last century population growth rates were comparatively high, and evenly spread geographically, although it should be remembered that the actual populations were small. During the 1820s and 1830s the agricultural depression was a major factor in the slackening of growth, for there was increased out-migration as unemployment became serious. Towards the end of the 1830s, however, the area received a substantial boost with the coming of the railway and other industries. Brayley reported in 1840 that 'since the introduction of the Printing establishment and Paper Mills here [Woking] and of the fixing of a Railway Station at Woking Heath, the population has of late years increased considerably'.[2]

Just as significant was the temporary influx of labourers and other workers employed on building the main line and the Guildford branch. By 1851 these people had moved further along the railway, and new lines were no longer being built in the Woking area. The 1851 census therefore showed a sharp fall in the rate of growth in both Woking and Byfleet, where railway workers had been recorded in 1841.[3]

After the mid-1840s there was a renewal of the agricultural depression, this time exacerbated by the mechanisation of farming, which had not reached the district during the earlier recession of the 1820s. Rural communities throughout Southern England began to stagnate, and from the 1850s entered into a long period of decline. In the 1840s the population of Horsell parish fell slightly, and in the following decade there was scarcely any increase here, or in Pyrford and Byfleet. The natural increase was almost balanced by the loss of people moving elsewhere to find employment.

This served to highlight the contrast with the parish of Woking, where the construction of a prison and an asylum between 1859 and 1869 provided a catalyst for major population growth. In the 20 years from 1851 the population of the parish increased by 3,750, or 132 per cent, and 1861–71 was marked by the fastest growth rate in the history of the parish. This was, however, deceptive, for of the 1871 population about 3,000 were inmates of institutions, officers and warders, or their families. These people thus accounted for by far the greater part of the rapid increase. Had the institutions not been built the growth over these two decades would have been of the order of 25 per cent, a level quite comparable with those of neighbouring parishes. It is clear that the institutions performed a vital role in encouraging the development of the new town.

Perhaps the most striking feature of the period, 1861–81, apart from the growth of Woking, is the decline of Pyrford, which, already the smallest parish, lost almost 10 per cent of its inhabitants in these 20 years. Whilst Byfleet had started to experience some growth as a consequence of suburbanization, its neighbour was becoming a depressed and declining community, still sunk in rural isolation. Even Horsell, which was less remote, saw a complete stagnation in the decade after 1871. Although less than thirty miles from the capital these, and other West Surrey parishes, shared many characteristics of rural areas in Wessex during this period.

In Byfleet there was a sudden spurt of growth after 1871 as a result of the transfer of the Surrey Industrial School for Boys, from Wandsworth, in 1879. The 1881 census noted that there were 247 inmates and staff, who accounted for 20 per cent of the population of the parish, and thus about three-quarters of the inter-censal increase.[4] Without the school the growth rate would have been some 9 per cent and some stagnation might have been expected.

This trend was dramatically reversed during the 1880s as large-scale urban growth began. In Woking there was a lull after the institution development of the previous decade, but in Pyrford and Horsell the decline was ended. The boom period for the Woking district was 1891–1901, when Horsell more than doubled its population, and Woking nearly so. This growth, of 63.1 per cent over the 'Borough', was due to the suburban development in areas such as St Johns, Maybury, Brookwood and Knaphill, and around the newer centre of West Byfleet, spilling over into North Pyrford. During this decade the parish of Woking grew so rapidly that it eclipsed Egham and Chertsey to become the largest town in North West Surrey, a position it has held ever since, whilst in the following decade it overtook Guildford, and thereafter was the most populous town in the county outside the metropolitan area.

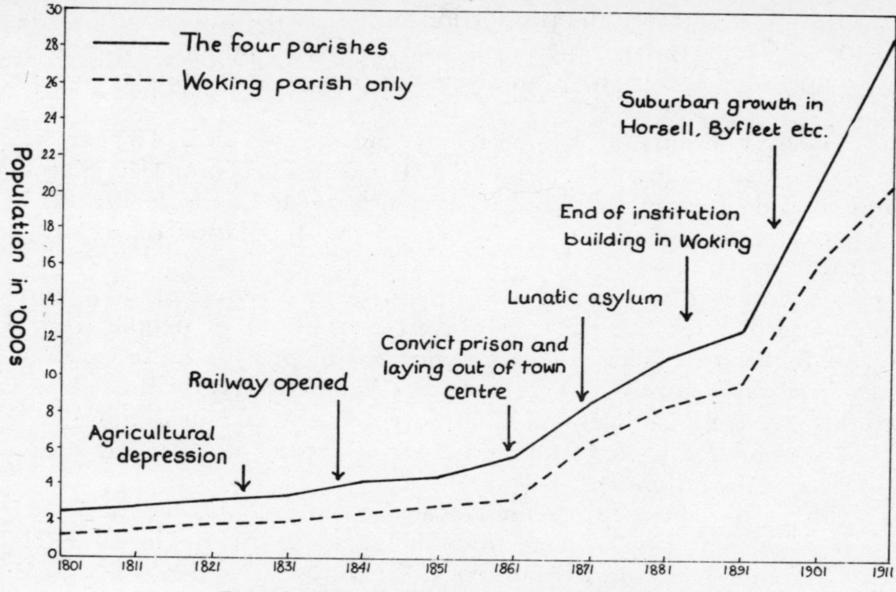

Fig. 23. The Population of Woking 1801–1911

The Origins of the People

The census returns of the 19th century, from 1851 onwards, include information relating to the place of birth of the people. These have been analysed for 1851 and 1871, to determine the origin of the inhabitants of Woking and its constituent parishes. The results are summarized in Table 9 below.

Table 9. Birthplace of Inhabitants[a] 1851 and 1871[5]

Place of Birth	*1851*		*1871*	
	No.	*% of total*	*No.*	*% of total*
The Borough of Woking	2,916	62.8	3,182	49.8
Adjacent parishes[b]	578	12.4	657	10.3
Remainder of West Surrey	329	7.1	422	6.6
South East England	276	6.9	655	10.3
Greater London	265	5.7	580	9.1
East Anglia	73	1.6	188	2.9
South Midlands	57	1.2	142	2.2
South West England	40	0.9	216	3.4
Remainder of England	54	1.2	145	2.2
Remainder of British Isles	24	0.5	122	1.9
Miscellaneous	34	0.7	76	1.2

a. Excluding inmates of asylum and prisons. b. Chobham, Chertsey, Weybridge, Wisley, Ockham, Ripley, Send, Stoke, Worplesdon, Pirbright, Bisley.

It is apparent that a major change took place over the 20 years, since in 1851 almost two-thirds of the people were born in the four parishes, whilst in 1871 the proportion was less than half. Furthermore the proportion born in adjacent areas of West Surrey fell from 19.5 per cent to 16.9 per cent over the same period. There was thus a tendency, growing over the years in question, for people to migrate to Woking from further afield.

In this they were undoubtedly helped by the railway, which in 1851 extended no further westwards than Basingstoke but by 1871 had reached into Devon and Dorset. It was then a great deal easier for people to move towards London, and this helps to explain the sizeable increase in the proportion of the population of Woking born in the five south-western counties.

The same ease of travel, and the decline of agriculture in these predominantly rural areas, were responsible for the very significant new flows of people from Sussex, Hampshire and Berkshire. Woking, as a growing town, provided alternative employment, and as a railway centre could easily be reached. The reverse flow, a movement outwards to this area from London and Middlesex, was also encouraged by the railway, which made it possible for some to commute to the capital and also led to the choice of Woking as an area for retirement.

There is evidence of some interesting localised movements, for in 1871 of the 54 residents born in Suffolk, 21 came from the adjacent small villages of Cockfield, Bradfield and Stanningfield, south of Bury St Edmunds. A similar flow occurred in movement from Sussex, where 36 of the 136 migrants came from Kirdford, Wisborough Green and Billingshurst. The reason may be that landowners had connections with these places. The Locke King family had estates in that part of Sussex, whilst the elder members of the Hilder family of Hoe Bridge were born in Cockfield, and presumably brought workers with them, whether deliberately or not, when they moved to Woking.

In many cases, though, moves were over a short distance, and close relationships existed between neighbouring parishes. There were obvious links across the boundary between Bisley and Chobham and Horsell, or between Woking and Send. The association between Woking and Byfleet, however, was tenuous, as an indication of the lack of ties between the constituent parishes of the Borough at this time. The local movements are shown in Table 10 (page 133).

It can be seen that links between Woking and Horsell were, even at this stage, very strong. Almost 12 per cent of the population of Horsell was born in its larger neighbour. We may therefore visualise major movement from the immediate vicinity of the Woking parishes associated with smaller flows of migrants from more distant counties. The result was a greater diversity of people in the Woking of the later 19th century than was found in earlier years. Unemployed agricultural workers from Sussex and Wessex, prison officers and their families from the Isle of Wight and London, poor labourers from Scotland and Ireland, and wealthy families from the metropolis were all attracted by the opportunities for work or housing offered by the new town.

Images of Woking

The wealthier residents came because Woking offered space and beauty, to contrast with the congestion, noise and dirt of London. In their writings, and in some of the

Table 10. Local Birthplaces 1871[6]

Born in:	*Byfleet*	*Horsell*	*Pyrford*	*Woking*
Bisley	—	23	5	29
Byfleet	336	6	8	16
Chertsey	41	13	6	29
Chobham	2	65	6	64
Horsell	7	391	5	103
Pirbright	2	11	—	47
Pyrford	33	3	163	26
Ripley	11	7	16	24
Send	8	1	11	62
Stoke next Guildford	1	—	1	23
Weybridge	5	—	1	1
Wisley	8	—	9	2
Woking	22	106	33	1,923
Worplesdon	1	15	3	49
TOTAL	829	893	357	5,316

literature of the time, we may discover their impressions of the area, and so recapture images of Woking in these years.

Land was cheap, and it was possible to purchase large plots on upper slopes, away from the damp lowlands which were alleged to be unhealthy. Natural growths of woodland had softened the bleakness of the former heaths, to produce an attractive combination of tall, scented pines and heathery glades, amongst which houses could be built with views of distant hills across wide green valleys. In the later years of the century West Surrey was a land of great and as yet unspoiled natural beauty: some still remains.

The Victorian diarist, minor poet and amateur sociologist A. J. Munby was enchanted by Pyrford. Between 1864 and 1868 he made frequent visits to Wheelers Farm; Sarah Carter, the daughter of the owner, provided a further incentive! In 1878 he bought the 'grey old gabled farm with quaint little garden in front' and lived there until his death in 1910.[7] On his first visit he described the view from Pyrford Church: 'there was a melting yellow sunshine over all the valley . . . diffused through a warm and fragrant haze. And the abbey, grey beyond a yellow belt of corn, and the elms and firs of Warren Wood, and the long waving lines of willows by the water, and under their green & their silver grey stood groups of red and white cattle'.[8] He appreciated most 'the freshness and quiet, & the sense of infinitude . . . that the remote heaths and meadows of the Wey can give'.[9]

A more eccentric enthusiasm was that expressed by a character in Virginia Woolf's novel *Night and Day* (1919), set in the Edwardian period. The delightfully overbearing Mrs. Cosham says 'deliberately and elaborately',

> 'I come from Woking, Mr. Popham. You may well ask me, why Woking? and to that I answer, for perhaps the hundredth time, 'because of the sunsets. We went for the sunsets, but that was five-and-twenty years ago. Where are the sunsets now? Alas! There is no sunset now nearer than the South Coast.'[10]

The combination of rural peace and easy access to London attracted some famous residents. Sir Charles Dilke, the Liberal Cabinet Minister ruined by a notorious divorce case, bought a large plot at Pyrford Rough from the Earl of Onslow in 1894, and built a bungalow for himself and his wife. This was to have been the most exclusive part of Woking, with great houses in extensive grounds on the south-facing slopes commanding panoramic views of the Wey valley, but the estate was sold to the Guinness family (the Earls of Iveagh) in 1902, and the plans were abandoned.[11] Instead, the new owners built one of the last of the large English country houses, Pyrford Court, in 1908–10, and the use of the land for expensive private housing was no longer possible. This has been a great benefit, for the land in question is particularly attractive and worthy of protection.

In 1898 Dilke wrote to the Earl of Onslow recounting a clash between two cultures, those of the new wealthy residents and of traditional West Surrey.

> 'A fire broke out when a poaching party was collecting from three pheasant nests in the young self-sown pines to the west of us [Pyrford Rough] . . . they [the keepers] got it out by hard work, though the spot is a specially dangerous one. The ex-policeman did not appear and the cottagers looked on and jeered. Sunday is the . . . only poaching day, so I doubt if the ex-policeman does his duty . . . pheasant egg shells everywhere shew what an extraordinary natural game country it is'.[12]

In 1898 the Hon. Gerald Balfour, M.P., brother of Arthur Balfour the future Conservative Prime Minister, moved to the house 'Fishers Hill' at Hook Heath, designed for him by Edwin Lutyens. He was active in local community life, whilst his wife, Lady Betty, helped in relief organization and charity work during the First World War. In 1919 she was elected as councillor for St Johns Ward, and so became the first woman member of Woking Urban District Council. Until her resignation in 1923 she played a major part in council housing and public health policies, and Balfour Avenue, Westfield, is named after her.[13]

One of her closest friends was the remarkable Dame Ethel Smyth, composer and suffragette, who bought a plot of land at Hook Heath in 1908 and built herself a cottage, 'Coigne'. She lived here until her death in 1944, with a housekeeper and a succession of Old English Sheepdogs all named 'Pan'. Dame Ethel was President of the Woking branch of the National Union of Women's Suffrage Societies. At the height of the suffragette agitation before the First World War she gave lessons in 'guerrilla action' to Emmeline Pankhurst, whom she once took 'at nightfall to a deserted spot on Hook Heath to throw Stones at a Tree'.[14] She was a familiar and eccentric figure in Woking for many years, as she strode about the streets. Vera Brittain recalled that Dame Ethel once told a public meeting that the title she would most prefer was 'Ethel, Duchess of Woking'.[15]

An indication that Woking was a popular and fashionable place to live was that Conan Doyle used it as the setting for one of the Sherlock Holmes short stories. In *The Naval Treaty* the Mount Hermon district is accurately described:

> 'We were fortunate enough to catch an early train at Waterloo, and in a little under an hour we found ourselves among the fir-woods and the heather of Woking. Briarbrae proved to be a large detached house standing in extensive grounds within a few minutes' walk of the station . . . through the open window . . . came the rich scent of the garden and the balmy summer air'.[16]

A more important claim to literary fame is that H. G. Wells lived in Woking between the summer of 1895 and autumn 1898. His house was 'Lynton', a small detached villa in Maybury Road, then a respectable middle-class address, although today rather run-down. The house was cramped, and, because it faced the railway, was also noisy, so that it proved unsatisfactory for the writer, but whilst there he wrote several short stories and three of his best known novels: *Wheels of Chance*, *The Invisible Man* and, most famous of all, *The War of the Worlds.*

The last of these, published in 1898, is actually set in Woking, and the invading Martians land on Horsell Common, in the old sandpits. Their first major move is to destroy most of the town. Wells wrote that he wrecked Woking, and killed his neighbours in painful and eccentric ways. The book reveals an intimate knowledge of the town and its surroundings, and from it we can gain a valuable impression of how Woking looked in the mid-1890s.

Some aspects have changed little: 'the undulating common seemed now dark almost to blackness, except where its roadways lay grey and pale under the deep-blue sky of the early night',[17] but no longer can we see 'over the Maybury Arch a train, a billowing tumult of white, firelit smoke, and a longer caterpillar of lighted windows',[18] for the undramatic electric trains have replaced the steam locomotives of Wells' era.

He notes small details: 'there was a noise of business from the gasworks, and the electric lamps were all alight'.[19] At that time Woking was one of the few towns which had the latter amenity. In contrast, a survival from the rural past was 'the little one-roomed squatters' hut of wood, surrounded by a patch of potato-garden' at Bunker's Hill (near College Road).[20] The semi-rural character of the town only 80 years ago is described:

> 'We were spanking down the opposite slope of Maybury Hill towards Old Woking. In front was a quiet sunny landscape, a wheatfield ahead on either side of the road, and the Maybury Inn with its swinging sign ... The scent of hay was in the air through the lush meadows beyond Pyrford, and the hedges on either side were sweet and gay with multitudes of dog roses'.[21]

We may be glad, though, that Woking has been spared the fate of which Wells so gleefully wrote:

> 'the town became a heap of fiery ruins ... the valley had become a valley of ashes ... Where flames had been there were now streamers of smoke; but the countless ruins of shattered and gutted houses and blasted and blackened trees that the night had hidden stood out now gaunt and terrible in the pitiless light of dawn'.[22]

Employment 1850–1914

Changes in employment were far-reaching during the second half of the 19th century, as the Woking district was transformed from a rural backwater to a thriving town. The decline in the agricultural labour force was rapid, and it was compensated for by the equally fast growth of the service sector, which by the First World War had achieved a dominant role in the economy of the town. The following table (page 136) summarizes these changes for the parishes of Woking and Horsell: comparable 1911 data for Byfleet and Pyrford are unavailable.

Table 11. Employment Change 1851-1911[23]

Sector	1851 No.	1851 Per cent	1871 No.	1871 Per cent	1911 No.	1911 Per cent
Agriculture	858	57.0	847	40.9	962	9.0
Crafts/Trades	129	8.6	232	11.2	1,658	15.5
Retailing	87	5.8	145	7.0	874	8.2
Services	242	16.1	400	19.3	3,296	30.8
Public employees . . .	11	0.7	296	10.9	1,258	11.7
Industry	120	8.0	82	4.0	599	5.6
Professions	33	2.2	68	3.3	580	5.4
Transport	26	1.7	72	3.5	847	7.9
Miscellaneous	—	—	—	—	638	6.0

The most remarkable change is that in the agricultural sector, which in 1851 provided 57 per cent of jobs but in 1911 only 9 per cent, even though the numbers employed increased slightly. This was due entirely to the growth of nurserying, and on the farms the decline in employment was even more acute. As the town grew there was no comparable increase in the industrial sector, which actually declined between 1851 and 1871 because the printing industry left the district, and which remained small in 1911. Similarly the retail sector had not kept pace with the growth of the town. If it had increased in line with the population there would have been almost twice as many employees in 1911 as there actually were. The deficiency reflects one of the greatest inadequacies of the new town, that it lacked a shopping area suitable for its population.

The remainder of this chapter considers in detail various industries and other sources of employment which were significant in the second half of the 19th century.

Agriculture

Chapter Two showed how, in the early years of the century, Woking was almost entirely an agricultural area. Despite the development of small industries and the advent of the railway age the same was true when, in 1852, the Necropolis Company put forward its plans. The 1851 census recorded 2,113 workers in the four parishes, of whom 1,294, or almost two-thirds, were engaged in agriculture. All but 61 of these worked on or owned farms, the others being nurserymen (53) and foresters (8). In the parish of Pyrford agriculture accounted for no less than 91.5 per cent of the workforce and, even in Woking, with its greater diversity of employment, 47.5 per cent. In reality, the proportions were even higher, for women and children generally did part-time or seasonal work on the farms, including reaping and fruit-picking.[24]

During the 1850s it was customary in this area for boys to begin farm work at 12 or 13, although most would already have had experience of harvesting. In the more remote areas, such as Sutton and Bridley, where there was no nearby school, boys began work at 10 or 11; the youngest farmhand in 1851 was a nine-year-old boy at Westfield. However the census records many children as 'scholars' even though they attended school infrequently or only on Sundays, so even younger children were doubtless employed unofficially.

Female labour was similarly under-recorded. The 1851 census does indicate some, such as three at Bunker's Hill (aged 25, 24 and 19) and a family of three at Kingfield (a widow of 56 and her daughters of 22 and 16) but other sources show that the use of women on farms was more widespread and socially acceptable than this would suggest. A. J. Munby had an obsessive interest in working women, and his copious diaries contain details of numerous conversations with them. In May 1864 he observed the female labourers in the fields between Woking and Pyrford where Pyrford Court is today, but then known as Blackdown Farm:

> 'At the other end of the field, two women, clad in what seemed white garments, were moving as if from work, each with a hoe upon her shoulder. One of them turned, and came towards me . . . She looked hard & wide-eyed at me, as one who sees not strangers often. But she stopped readily to talk . . . Her fellow, she said, had gone to pick up faggots among the felled timber under the wood; and she had brought her hoe as well as her own. They had been hoeing carrots, since eight this morning . . . There's many women, she said, and girls too, married and unmarried, that work afield about here hoeing, and couching, and reaping with the sickle . . . a woman's work is tenpence a day; a man's twelve shillings a week. Men and women don't work much together: the female labourers will hoe on one side of a field, the male on the other . . . Hoeing is not hard work at all, says she, and its healthy is field work . . . Lots of the girls that works in the fields come from Maybury, & from Bunker's Hill'.[25]

Local farmers employed casual labour as well. In this area the tradition of vagrants, travelling people and wandering labourers continued until the beginning of this century, a survival of the old 'roughness' and of the illegal squatting so widespread a hundred years before. Munby's woman labourer exclaimed, 'We've no Irish about here, oh no', but other workers were clearly employed casually. The 1851 census records an itinerant agricultural labourer of 43 years, with his wife and six children, living 'in a tent on the common' at Hook Heath, whilst at Wych Street (now Wych Hill) a vagrant labourer was 'sleeping in the Barn'.[26] As late as 1911 Woking and Horsell had 76 people living in tents, sheds, barns or caravans.

By 1871, just 20 years after the 1851 census recorded the prosperous rural economy of Woking, the character of agriculture had been transformed, and profound changes were taking place in the rural communities. Over this period total employment in the four parishes increased by 24 per cent, but in agriculture it fell by 15 per cent, from 1,294 to 1,096. This concealed a substantial growth in nurserying, and so the fall in farming alone was some 22 per cent.

Locally the consequences were even more serious. Horsell experienced a 13.8 per cent loss in this sector, Byfleet 30.6 per cent, but most dramatic was Pyrford, where the number of workers engaged in agriculture fell by 60 per cent over the two decades. This parish was least able to cope with the problem, and the result was a fall in overall population between 1851 and 1881, as a classic 'drift from the land' took place.

Nursery employment, already expanding, increased sharply in Woking, and to a lesser extent in Horsell, from the 1890s and in 1911 there were almost twice as many nursery workers as farm employees. By 1921 there were 890 nurserymen and women in the two parishes, and these increases had absorbed many of the displaced farm-workers, but in Byfleet and Pyrford, which had virtually no alternative agricultural employment, there had been much distress. The table below summarizes these changes.

Table 12. Agricultural Employment 1851–1921[27]

	1851		*1871*		*1911*		*1921*	
	No.	*Per cent*	*No.*	*Per cent*	*No.*	*Per cent*	*No.*	*Per cent*
Byfleet . . .	222	58.9	154	40.9	–		–	
Pyrford . . .	214	91.5	95	54.0	–		–	
Horsell . . .	217	70.7	187	62.8	962	9.0	1,315	6.7
Woking . . .	641	53.8	660	37.2				

The Brick Industry

The origins of the brick industry of the Knaphill area have been described earlier. After the construction of the railway there was a fall in demand, but the building of the asylum and prison, followed by urban growth, ended the contraction of the industry. The 1851 census recorded 21 workers, with 17 in 1871 and 25 in 1911, but it is certain that many more were employed in the brickfields and were described only as 'Labourer' in the returns.

The brickyards were located on the slopes of Goldsworth Hill, Hermitage and Knaphill, where beds of clay occurred among the Bagshot and Bracklesham sands. Those near to Kiln Bridge were the earliest to open and had closed by the 1890s. A description of Brickfield Cottage, St Johns, which was built in the late 18th century and demolished in 1907, suggests the conditions in which the brickmakers lived: 'an old mud cottage with a straw roof. The walls were crumbling down'.[28] These brickpits were used, from 1894 onwards, for refuse disposal, the rubbish coming not only from Woking but also, by canal, from Kingston and Richmond.

The claypits and brickfields along the St Johns–Goldsworth road, near the canal, dated from the building of the waterway. They were acquired in the 1870s by the Slocock and Jackman families who operated them in conjunction with their nursery and landscape-gardening businesses, and later with property speculation. The works served purely local markets, although in the 1880s unsuccessful attempts were made, in co-operation with the Surrey & Hampshire Canal Corporation, to develop a trade with London. Deliveries were made, by horse and cart, as far as Woodham, Woking village and Pirbright.[29]

The Jackman-owned Goldsworth brickworks, near the *Rowbarge* public house, operated between 1877 and 1889. They produced the bricks for Westfield Board Schools (1879–81) and for many houses in New Woking and Knaphill. Output reached a peak, 867,000 bricks, in 1882 but profits never exceeded the £419 of 1880, and competition from the large brickworks of the Midlands was always strong. The owners negotiated cheap contracts for the transport of coal by canal from Radstock in Somerset, and from Warwickshire, but costs remained high, and the works could not survive.[30]

At Knaphill in the middle of the century extensive brickfields were developed between Robin Hood Road, Anchor Hill and Victoria Road, with kilns close to the *Queens Head* public house. In 1916 there were 14.6 acres of pits, with a further 25.4 acres available for extension in the area known as Fulk's Orchard. These were the largest of the Woking brickworks, and had operated since the building of the convict prisons in the 1860s. The 1921 census showed 44 brickworkers in Woking, most of whom, presumably, worked in this area. The Anchor Hill brickworks, owned by Cook Brothers, closed in 1925, as a result of the depression in the building industry, but the brickworks off Robin Hood Road were able to weather this recession, and remained in business throughout the inter-war period. Their closure in 1942 ended brickmaking in Woking after more than two centuries.

Paper and Printing

In 1835 Woking Mills closed, after a continuous history of at least 800 years. They were vacant for three years, but in 1838 Alderman Venables of Guildford bought them to convert for paper manufacturing, 'the meandering stream of the Wey affording great opportunities for such a purpose'.[31] Venables died in 1840 and his business was taken over by Henry Virtue Bayley & Co.

The Woking Mills produced paper from rags, using two machines. Women were employed to sort and bundle rags, and men undertook the heavier jobs, including bleaching and boiling. Power was provided by a steam engine, although in later years the company produced its own gas from a small plant. In 1851 there were 54 paper workers in the parish of Woking and in 1871, 55, although other workers lived elsewhere, for in 1861 it was noted that 'the increase of population in Send parish since 1851 is attributed to the erection of houses for the workmen of a large paper-mill situate in the parish of Woking'.[32] A. J. Munby recorded in 1868 that walking from Woking station to Pyrford in the late afternoon, at Hoe Place he 'passed the paper-mill girls on their way home from work'. These women lived in the poor squatter cottages at Bunker's Hill.[33]

During the late 1860s the industry went through a difficult period, and many similar small mills closed. In April 1870 it was reported that 'Messrs. Bayley the well known paper manufacturers of Woking have given a fortnight's warning to the whole of the hands employed in their mills, numbering 136. If the mills are closed it must have a most disastrous effect on the trade of the town of Woking'.[34] This particular closure was not carried out; instead the business was sold to the Woking Paper Co. Ltd. Henry Bayley moved to Ripley, to become the miller at Newark, where he died in November 1879. The brief revival in Woking under the new ownership was not very successful, but it lasted until falling profits led to the closure of the mill in 1894.

A complementary industry was printing, established at Church Street, Woking village, in 1837 by John B. Bensley of Andover.[35] After some years of financial troubles the business was sold in April 1843 to Joseph Billing of London. He expanded it, and by 1851 employed 35 Woking people and others from Send and Ripley. The site, opposite St Peter's Church, was cramped and afforded no room for expansion, and as the business grew it became clear that it would no longer be adequate.

In March 1856, therefore, new premises in Guildford were purchased, and in July the Woking works were closed.[36]. Most of the employees moved to Guildford so that in 1871 only three printers were recorded in the parish of Woking.[37]

In November the Chilworth printing works of Unwin Bros. were destroyed in a spectacular and expensive fire. An urgent search for alternative premises led to Woking mills, abandoned a year earlier, after the paper industry failed. This site was selected because Unwins held a strong belief in the value of water power: its use at Chilworth had given them 'a wholly mistaken idea of its importance for the future'.[38] The Woking mills had 'a sufficient volume of water to drive two turbines and raise a total of 100 h.p. [but] all the surrounding land was low lying and perilously liable to flooding after snow or in prolonged wet weather . . . Housing accommodation in the nearby village was not plentiful, and the railway station was a full two miles away'.[39]

Despite these disadvantages the mill was bought and rebuilt with 'a handsome, somewhat Flemish style . . . facade in warm red brick'.[40] Willows were planted by George Unwin along the access causeway from Hipley Bridge, and care was taken to maintain the beauty of the river. The first workers moved in during May 1896, only six months after the Chilworth fire. After floods in February 1900, when the turbines were made useless because there was no fall of water, a gas-engine was installed, and in the 1930s the works were converted to electricity.[41]

There were 200 workers in 1906, mostly from the Woking area but including several from Guildford and Wonersh. 'One stalwart walked twelve miles there and back from Guildford six days a week, and was never late or absent . . . life was more leisurely and an apprentice could slip off occasionally in summer during working hours for a swim in the river'.[42]

Unwin Brothers are now part of the Staples Printing Group, and their Gresham Press imprint still carries the name of Old Woking to all parts of the world. They continue to be a major local employer, and their works, standing on the site of the Saxon corn-mill of Woking, is a prominent landmark in the flat fields beside the Wey.

The Railways

The railways, in addition to their profound impact upon the character of Woking, also generated a substantial amount of employment. Initially this was mainly of a temporary nature, concerned with railway-building, and this led to an influx of labourers and their families. The small size of Woking station meant that few staff were needed, and in 1851 only 24 railway employees were resident in the four parishes, representing just 1.1 per cent of the workforce.

As the system expanded Woking became a station of importance, particularly after the opening of Portsmouth Direct Railway (Godalming–Havant) in January 1859. The widening of the line in the late 1880s, to give four tracks, meant that the station was rebuilt with improved facilities, whilst the growth of the town around it had increased the amount of traffic handled, and made it necessary to employ extra staff. The locomotive depot at Woking, situated on the south side of the line at the London end of the station, was transferred to Guildford in January 1889 as part of the rebuilding programme. It had formerly employed up to 60 men, but the move had no serious consequences for the town. In 1871 there were 71 railway workers living in the four parishes of Woking, but by 1911 the figure had risen to 361, when they represented 3.5 per cent of the workforce of the Urban District. The opening of the stations at Brookwood and Worplesdon, each with a full complement of staff, had contributed to the increase.

In 1851 the great majority of the railway workers had been born in Surrey or Middlesex, but the extension of the L.S.W.R. network into Dorset, Devon and Cornwall allowed workers to move to Woking from these areas in search of employment, a trend apparent among railway employees. The 1871 Census records L.S.W.R. staff living in Woking but born in towns such as Honiton, Crediton and Exeter: the places of birth of their children show that some migrated gradually eastwards along the main line, towards London. In 1871 over a quarter of all railway workers recorded in Woking came from the four western counties.[43]

Other Industries

Nineteenth-century Woking had a variety of smaller industries, often short-lived and employing only a few people. Although economically unimportant they are of considerable interest. Perhaps the most unusual was the distillery beside the *Sun Inn*, on the road from Byfleet Corner to Pyrford. It produced rosewater, lavender water, flower and herb essences and fragrant oils, using locally grown ingredients. It appears to have opened in the early 1850s, and in 1872 the original owners, the Collins family, sold it to John Newland, who operated it until closure in about 1905.[44]

During the 1880s Messrs. Woodward & Co. manufactured liquorice in Westfield, but nothing more is known of this enterprise,[45] whilst in 1895-1908 the Owens Artificial Stone Co. operated a small works close to Worplesdon station. Sapoline, a type of liquid soap, was produced by C. T. Tyler & Co. near Woking station from the late 1860s. They had moved there from Breaston, Derbyshire, but the works closed in about 1885. The Tyler family then established a wine and spirits business, and in this role they were active in Woking until recent years.[46]

As stated in Chapter Two, brewing had been of local significance for centuries. In Woking village the brewery founded in 1715 was taken over from the Strong family in 1870 by Henry Charrington. He rebuilt the brewery, but sold it in 1887 to John Lovibond & Co. Ltd. The new owners were in Woking for only three years, and closed the business in 1890; it was never reopened.[47] John Stedman, maltster and brewer, carried on a small business, from the late 1860s until just before the First World War, from premises in Brewery Road at the foot of Church Hill in the village of Horsell. He proudly advertised in local newspapers that he grew all his own hops, and most of his own barley, and produced beer of the highest quality.[48]

Byfleet Brewery, the largest of those which operated in the Woking district, flourished during the late 19th century, at first under the ownership of Henry Dennett. From him the business passed to the Holroyd brothers, who carried it on for many years. They were also active in local politics and were millers and landowners. Holroyd Breweries amalgamated in the 1890s with Friary Ales of Guildford and Healey's of

Kingston, but continued to function until 1905 when the need for larger and more modern premises made the Byfleet brewery obsolete. Friary Holroyd & Healy's Breweries Ltd. later evolved into Friary Meux.[49]

The Institutions

The population of Woking parish grew by 34.6 per cent between 1851 and 1861 and the census reported that this was 'attributed to the erection of the Invalid Convict Prison, the officers and their families alone amounting to 202 persons'.[50] In 1871 of the 1,774 employed persons in the parish 10.6 per cent were engaged in prison or asylum work, whilst the inmates themselves formed no less than 33.7 per cent of the total population.

Although the relative importance of the institutions diminished as the town developed further they remained a significant source of employment, and continued to account for a substantial proportion of the population. The four institutions listed in 1901 (the Barracks, St Peter's Home, the Asylum and the L.C.C. School) had a total of 2,050 inmates, or 12.6 per cent of the population, whilst their 527 employees still accounted for 7.6 per cent of the workforce. As late as 1931, despite the reduction in size of the barracks, 6.7 per cent of the population of Woking U.D. lived in institutions.[51]

Many of the original staff at the prison came from existing penal establishments, and so birthplaces such as Carisbrooke, Holloway and Lewes are recorded in the census returns. The staff lived in the vicinity of the prison. Special housing was provided for many of them, in the roads bearing the singularly depressing names, Prison Street, East and West Prison Street, and Main Street. Their presence, however, resulted in considerable prosperity for St Johns and Knaphill, and accelerated their growth, for, with about 1,000 people amongst the staff and their families, local shopkeepers and farmers had a large new market. Other existing residents found service jobs and labouring work at the prison or asylum, and this helped to alleviate the distress of the agricultural depression. Such, perhaps, was the Kingfield man who in 1871 gave his occupation to the census enumerator as 'Scaffold Labourer at the Female Prison'.[52]

The table below shows the growth and decline of the institutions as recorded by successive census returns. It does not include the staff and other employees.

Table 13. Institutions 1871–1931[53]

	1871	*1881*	*1891*	*1901*	*1911*	*1921*	*1931*
Asylum	635	1,041	1,062	1,104	1,119	1,118	1,447
Prisons	1,431	1,291	285	–	–	–	–
Barracks	–	–	–	795	724	462	242
Military Prison . . .	–	–	–	–	64	–	–
St Peter's Home . .	–	–	44	61	63	85	93
L.C.C. School . . .	19	206	176	138	181	59	138

Chapter Ten

CONTINUED EXPANSION 1914-1939

Overview

THE FIRST WORLD WAR checked the growth of the town and its neighbouring parishes, because new building was virtually ended to concentrate on the war effort, and because movement of people from other areas was not generally possible. Over the district as a whole the population grew by only 10.5 per cent in 1911-21, compared with 39.8 per cent in the previous decade.[1] The sole exception to this slackening of growth was Byfleet parish. Here the construction of the Vickers aircraft works at Brooklands, mainly within the parish, attracted labour from outside the district. To cater for this influx of workers the company, in co-operation with Chertsey R.D.C. and Byfleet Parish Council, built a special model housing estate on Brooklands Road.[2] Byfleet increased its population by 1,213 during the war decade, a rate of 41 per cent which may be contrasted to the 5.8 per cent growth in Woking parish.

When house-building resumed after the war the expansion of the district accelerated once more. Initially the increase was rather slow, and over the four parishes the decade 1921-31 saw a 13.8 per cent population growth, not inconsiderable but substantially less than before the war. In the late 1920s the pace quickened, and towards the end of the inter-war period the growth rate once more approached pre-war levels, being 27.3 per cent during the 1930s. During the 20 years to 1941 some 13,000 people were added, about the same number as 1891-1911. The increase was unevenly spread across the four parishes: Woking, which was already a large urban area, experienced lower growth rates than the other three, and over this period Horsell, which almost doubled its population, had the highest increase. Pyrford grew steadily, at 18.8 per cent in 1921-31 and about 20 per cent in 1931-41, whilst Byfleet, which showed a slackening after the wartime boom, to 15.5 per cent in the 1920s, doubled its rate of increase in the 1930s.

There was no census in 1941 because of the war, but the Registrar General estimated the population of the enlarged Woking Urban District as 42,000: this excluded residents on active service, so had normal conditions prevailed a population of perhaps 45,000 might have been expected. The overall rate of increase had thus been about 40 per cent, or 14,000 people, since 1921. In 1891-1911, the period of extraordinarily rapid expansion, a 132 per cent increase was recorded, involving 16,000 new residents. It is clear that some of the initial momentum of growth was lost in the 1920s, but this had been overcome in the 1930s, only to be halted abruptly by the outbreak of the Second World War.

The reduced rate of increase after 1918 may be attributed to a variety of factors. The large institutions, which had made a significant contribution in the late 19th century, had reached their maximum size by 1914 and some had begun to decline. Railway services were deteriorating in quality and attractiveness, particularly when compared with the newly electrified routes nearer London, and this, with the additional distance, undoubtedly dissuaded potential commuters from moving to the district. Until the late 1920s, too, Woking had few industries of any size apart from the aircraft works at Brooklands, and so there was nothing to bring those from the depressed areas who, looking for work, migrated to the South-East in large numbers between the wars.

After 1936–37 the railways to Portsmouth and Alton were electrified, giving the town a vastly improved service, with frequent fast (and often non-stop) trains to Waterloo. This enabled it to develop as a commuter area of major importance. The growth of industries during the 1930s also encouraged in-migration. Vickers at Brooklands increased output during the 1930s with the rearming of the military forces preparatory to the war, whilst two firms which acquired more than local significance, James Walker Ltd. and the Sorbo Rubber Company, both opened in the late 1920s. Already by 1921 Woking had overtaken Guildford to become the largest town in Surrey outside the metropolitan area, a position which it has held ever since, reinforced by major expansion in 1930–70.

Town Planning

As shown in earlier chapters the second half of the 19th century saw the rapid creation of a new town of Woking without any attempt to plan such expansion. Many problems resulted from this failing, some of which are still apparent today. In 1909 the first national legislation in this field, the Town Planning, Housing, Etc. Act, gave local authorities permissive powers to prepare planning schemes, but the response was poor; neither Woking U.D.C. nor Chertsey R.D.C. chose to adopt the Act. Until the mid-1920s therefore, the only means available for either council to influence the shape and quality of urban growth was the bye-laws of the 1880s, which gave limited powers over house design and the siting and size of new roads and services. These were quite inadequate for larger-scale ordering of development and for the effective zoning of land uses.

The Town Planning Act 1925 required that all urban councils with a population of over 20,000 should, by January 1929, submit a Town Planning scheme, to ensure the better arrangement of new housing, industry, open space and roads. Two years earlier Woking U.D.C. had added 'Town Planning' to the title and functions of the Housing Committee, partly in response to the council's own building (and therefore planning) activities.[3] This revised committee began consideration of a scheme for the Urban District under the 1925 Act. There was also at this time considerable enthusiasm for regional schemes embracing all or parts of several adjacent authorities and giving voluntary guidelines for the future pattern of development over larger areas. In October 1926 Woking U.D., Chertsey R.D.C. and five other councils established a North West Surrey Joint Planning Committee.[4]

Adams, Thompson & Fry, a firm of consultants, were appointed to advise upon and design a plan for North West Surrey, and this was completed in March 1928. It aimed to present 'in broad outline a considered policy for future development . . . to secure and maintain the best possible conditions in matters of health, economy, convenience and amenity'.[5] There were four aspects: the zoning of undeveloped land to guide its future use; the designation of routes for new or improved roads; the protection of land with scenic quality or recreational value; and the preservation of 'amenity' by the regulation of advertising and roadside land uses and the adoption of a progressive policy towards architecture and antiquities.

The scheme proposed that there should be three distinct urban areas in Woking: Knaphill–Brookwood, Woking town, and Byfleet–Pyrford–Addlestone. These would be separated by 'rural' zones, but a large new industrial development was suggested for the Sheerwater valley, north of the railway line between Woking and Byfleet.[6]

Woking U.D.C. approved the basic plan but was unhappy about the details, and in April 1928 it established a separate committee for Town Planning, to produce a local zoning and planning scheme.[7] A full-time officer, Henry Tame, was appointed as the first Town Planning Assistant in July 1931.[8] Producing the scheme was a frustrating and lengthy process, although there is no evidence that the council was over-anxious to bring it to completion. After March 1933 its scope was extended to include the newly acquired parishes of Byfleet and Pyrford, and it was not until October 1938, nine years after the initial target date, that the Woking Planning Scheme was formally adopted.[9] Shortly afterwards it was made redundant by the outbreak of war, which ended all building operations.

The scheme was nevertheless important, because it acted as an outline guide for council planning policies from the late 1920s, and thus helped to shape the growth of the town for the decade before the Second World War. Those pleasant but unexceptional rural landscapes north and south of the town and around Pyrford were not considered as worthy protection from building, and councillors were unwilling to prevent landowners from developing their property if they wished. In fact their powers to do so were limited; their main weapon, the purchase of land for protection, was not available because financial constraints were so tight. The main concern was to foster the future of the town as an increasingly high-class residential area, and in order to achieve this preference was given, where appropriate, to low-density housing developments. Much of the rural area was therefore zoned for building at four houses per acre or less. The existing higher-density districts would be allowed to expand, but were to cover a smaller area than these new, low-density zones.

As part of the development of rural areas the council wished to protect certain lands which would form public open spaces, mainly along riversides, and to reserve routes for proposed new roads. The central area of Woking would be extended and redeveloped to cater for the greatly increased population of the town, whilst smaller improvements were anticipated in older shopping areas such as Knaphill and West Byfleet. Industry was regarded with mixed feelings, for although it was desirable to provide manufacturing employment there was no wish to see industrialization detract from the residential character of the town: extensions of the high-density 19th century areas were to be avoided. Therefore the Joint Committee scheme for the Sheerwater

Valley industrial zone was accepted. The council even gave serious consideration to the idea of providing a Woking Municipal Airport, although the plan never came to fruition.[10]

Had the 1938 plan been implemented in its entirety the appearance and character of Woking would have been radically altered, for the population, about 36,000 in 1931, was to grow by 300 per cent by 1970, to exceed 140,000 (that is, almost twice its actual 1981 population). The older core area, in these proposals, might have been an island in a sea of low-density housing lapping at and spilling over the borders of the Urban District, so that Woking would coalesce with Guildford and Bagshot, as it does now with Addlestone and Weybridge in the east. The Second World War prevented the further implementation of the plan, and afterwards the imposition of tight planning controls, including the green belt, necessitated the abandonment of the pre-war proposals. Since it allowed the retention of much of the open countryside south of Woking, and northwards towards Chobham, this was to the advantage of the town.

The Geography of Growth 1918–1939

We may distinguish three categories of residential development in the period between the wars: low-density private estates; higher-density speculative schemes; and municipal projects. The history of the last is recounted in Chapter Eleven. Geographically, council housing was concentrated in four areas, the old-established villages of Knaphill, Horsell, Old Woking with Westfield, and Byfleet. In these districts land was cheaper than elsewhere because they were rather 'unfashionable' and less attractive to developers than the slopes of Hook Heath or the pinewoods of Woodham. The land ownership was more fragmented so that smaller parcels came onto the market regularly and could be developed comparatively easily by the councils, which did not have the resources to undertake ambitious projects or to purchase high-value sites. Since money was limited it was essential that services should be readily available, to reduce installation costs, and thus all of the inter-war council housing schemes were situated close to roads which already had gas, electricity and water mains.

Large parts of the district were immediately excluded from consideration due to cost restrictions, and such areas as Hook Heath, Woodham and West Byfleet were never regarded as suitable for council housing by the authorities concerned. Although about 18 per cent of all inter-war houses in the Urban District were built by the two councils the impact of this on the appearance of the town was comparatively small. There were no fewer than 20 separate sites (some adjacent) and 35 major contracts were involved, so that the vast estates found in other towns are not seen in Woking. In addition the municipal schemes were interspersed with private housing, which used designs often not greatly dissimilar, so that they were not prominent. In very few cases were the council houses built along major roads, but were usually tucked away on backlands, which further concealed their presence. Only in Westfield, which had 35 per cent of the entire council house stock in 1939, could it be said that this type of housing affected the appearance of the district in a substantial way.

Higher-Density Speculative Housing

This was likewise found close to the older parts of the district, although there was some building of the type on the fringes of the new centre, and a smaller amount within the rural area. Particularly significant between the wars was the extension of those areas which had been growing before 1914, by the infilling of vacant or derelict land and the acquisition and development of deteriorating farmland on the fringes. This helped to give these districts their somewhat untidy, piecemeal appearance and was without question to the detriment of their ancient plan and their architectural qualities.

The higher-density private developments were frequently the work of local builders, who did not have the resources to cater for large-scale projects. Typically a firm or an individual would purchase two or three fields close to a road, or between earlier housing schemes, and then lay out a small estate with a central cul-de-sac. The councils did not attempt to control such schemes except insofar as they conformed to byelaws. Consequently there was often no co-ordination between adjacent sites, and a wasteful duplication of roads and access to major highways.

The process of breaking up and selling farmland had started before the First World War. In Woking village, for example, a single row of small semi-detached villas, Hipley Street, now isolated in the incongruous surrounds of the Manor Industrial Estate, was built just after the war on land formerly part of Fords Farm, and disposed of about 1910.[11] During the 1920s the changes were more rapid, and in this same area Kingfield, Shackleford, Howards and Fords Farms were all sold in piecemeal plots between 1920 and 1950. Small estates were developed on the former fields, such as the 42 houses and short parade of shops built by A. & J. Simmons Ltd. of Old Woking on the new Shackleford Road in 1935–39.[12] The property of Kingfield Farm, an attractive early 19th-century building which still survives although in a much altered setting, was sold in the mid-1920s. A ribbon of housing replaced it along Kingfield Road, between Elmbridge and Kingfield Green. More private houses were built along the adjacent Tinkers Lane, which in 1928 was widened, made up and given the more decorous but less interesting name Elmbridge Lane.[13]

In Horsell the extensive lands of Horsell Grange were similarly sold and broken up, to disappear beneath a sea of speculative housing. Wheatsheaf Close and Orchard Drive were built on the site of the former orchards in 1934–39.[14] Around Horsell village itself the lands of Grove Barrs Farm came under the hammer in the late 1920s and 1930s, and the new road, Meadway Drive, was built across the area: it was once intended to be part of the Woking Western Bypass, but that scheme later faded away. On Horsell Common the old enclosure known, for its elliptical shape, as Roundabouts, was built over in 1936–38 by E. Hicks of Horsell. It was taken from the waste in the late 18th century, and is now a single street of houses, Common Close, isolated on the heath.[15]

Byfleet village, perhaps because it was low-lying and damp, and close to the noise of Brooklands, was less attractive to the developers of expensive housing, and so was instead more favoured by speculative builders aiming at the lower end of the market. The land between Rectory Lane and Church Road was covered in the 1930s, consolidating the previously straggling shape of the village, and in the process erasing most of its open character and appearance of antiquity. There were many small estates, including the Clock House development of 1934; the construction of Foxlake Road, Binfield Road and Hopfield Avenue on the lands of the former Foxlake Farm (their names now recall the vanished rural past); and the 'Summermeades' estate of 1938, on Church Road, the name which typifies the pseudo-rustic publicity of many 1930s' speculative builders.[17]

In the later 1930s plans for more ambitious projects began to appear. They bore a close resemblance to the suburban estates nearer to the capital, and often involved builders and developers from outside the district. The first was approved in July 1934. It was the initial phase, involving some 183 houses and six shops, of a more extensive project for the Hermitage estate. This had been the grounds of The Hermitage, an 18th-century mansion lying north of the Basingstoke Canal on the hillslope west of St Johns. The house was sold in 1933 and demolished two years later. Work on building the new estate began in 1937, and was completed, to a different plan, in the late 1950s.[18]

During the 1930s Davis Estates Ltd. developed the grounds of Woking Lodge, once the property of the Rastrick family: it occupied a prime site along Oriental Road, south of the railway. The construction of 73 houses at Floyds Lane, Pyrford, was authorised in 1935, and in 1937 Councillor Griffin was permitted to build 93 houses off Rectory Lane, Byfleet, a development later known as Winern Glebe.[19] Councillor Tarrant, a building contractor who had been awarded the contracts for most of the council houses in the late 1920s and 1930s, received permission in 1938 to develop 12 acres in the Coldharbour district of Pyrford, and in the same year the Council gave outline planning permission for what was to become one of the largest building schemes in the town after the Second World War, the Pyrford Woods estate, between Coldharbour and the Old Woking Road, with over 600 houses.[20]

The smaller projects frequently ignored planning considerations, although few were rejected by the Council. Exceptionally, conditions were laid down to ensure a rational use of the land, but often the road system and division of the land were poorly conceived, and awkward junctions and wasted space resulted. If two or more small estates were developed next to each other it was rare for them to have a shared access, and so there was unnecessary duplication of roads, as each had a separate network. In a few cases the Council itself built roads to avoid that problem, or to conform with the regional plan. Westfield Avenue, for example, was built in 1934–37 as a cut-off route from Elmbridge to Westfield, bypassing Kingfield and providing an alternative to the road through Mayford for traffic to Guildford. In that aim it was a failure, but its origin is reflected in its greater width, wide verges and sweeping curves. On either side, the houses and bungalows are entirely typical of the private housing of the 1930s.[21]

The largest inter-war development was on the site of the old Woking Town Field, between Old Woking High Street and the Hoe Stream. It comprised 440 houses and a row of shops, and there were further plans for a cinema, more shops and about 250 more houses. The estate centred on the proposed Old Woking bypass, part of the dual carriageway which was to link Woking with the A3 at Ripley. Originally called Hoe Bridge Road, it is now known as Rydens Way. A wide central reservation was left to accommodate the bypass, with narrow service roads beside it.[22] Today, 50 years later, it is still in that state, awaiting the dual carriageway which was regarded as essential half a century ago, and which is still scheduled to be built 'in the future'. To the east a grassed strip marks the line of the unbuilt road, and at the western end the service roads fade into the unmade dirt track of Stockers Lane.

The Low-Density Estates

As noted in Chapter Nine, the late 19th century had seen the start of the 'fashionable' image for Woking, and the development of the first low-density estates aimed at, or built by, high-income families. Between the wars this tendency was accelerated, helped in part by the attitude of the council, which wanted to foster and maintain a more exclusive and higher-status image for the town. Hitherto it had seemed to be a combination of institutions for the undesirable and a squalid frontier settlement – or so one would believe from the reports of the conditions in Woking at this time.

Some 2,500 acres, or almost 15 per cent of the present Borough, were sold for low-density building between 1919 and 1939, or were already designated as such at start of the period.[23] A further 2,000 acres or thereabouts were zoned for such use in the future. The term 'low-density' was used to represent a maximum of four houses per acre and preferably only two houses.

Five districts in Woking attracted such development: Hook Heath–Bridley, Pile Hill (tastefully renamed Pyle Hill)–Prey Heath, the Heathside–Maybury area, Kettlewell–Woodham, and West Byfleet–Pyrford. They had many common features, including remoteness from the old-established and deteriorating village centres, and a varied topography. The hills, ridges and slopes were an immediate asset, giving potential for attractive landscaping and views: in the case of Hook Heath and Maybury the impressive sweep of the North Downs could be seen across the broad Wey valley. Most important, perhaps, was the presence of tall pines and abundant heather, to provide secluded and well wooded grounds. Thus the factors regarded as desirable before 1914 continued to exert a powerful influence after the First World War.

The earliest of the inter-war estates was The Hockering, south of the not dissimilar late 19th-century developments in the Park Road–Pembroke Road area of Maybury. It was promoted by the Smallpeice family, the owners of the land, who were prominent local residents, solicitors and farmers for much of the last century, and lived at Kingfield House. In 1904 they laid out four estate roads (subsequently Hockering Road, Cleardown, Daneshill and Knowl Hill) curving gently down the wooded slopes of the Hoe valley towards White Rose Lane. One hundred and seven plots, covering 130 acres in all, were marked out 'for the erection of high class residences'. The name of the new development was taken from the small village of Hockering, near Norwich, where the family had its origins in the 17th century. Little had been achieved by 1914, but during the 1920s every plot was purchased and individuals built their own large houses, to produce the exclusive and secluded environment that we see today.[24]

In 1932 Woodham Hall and its 67 acres of wooded land were sold for building and the house was demolished. It was partly surrounded by Horsell Common and close to the New Zealand Golf Club, and so was admirably suited for a low-density scheme.

Gravelled roads were built from 1935 onwards, curving amongst the trees and carefully landscaped. The scheme was finished in the 1950s. The road names 'The Gateway' and 'The Riding' reflect the status of the area, whilst 'Woodham Waye' is an example of the self-conscious mock rurality of the typical 1930s' low-density estate.[25]

Dartnell Park and the Coldharbour district of West Byfleet and Pyrford were both extensively developed during this period, although here the process had been well under way before 1914. North of the railway the 54-acre Old Avenue estate was laid out after 1925 on land which had formerly been part of Sheerwater Farm, and was, in the early years of the previous century, unenclosed scrub and marsh. Trees screened the estate from the railway line, but the developers could not have foreseen that after 1948 the L.C.C. overspill estate would abut on the north of their expensive suburb. In this area the West Byfleet Golf Course was an attraction to would-be residents.

In a similar way the development in the west of the district, between the main railway lines to Guildford and Basingstoke, was closely associated with golf; Hook Heath even has its Golf Club Road. There were two large courses in the area, and in 1939 golf courses covered no less than 14 per cent of the entire Urban District. This western sector was perhaps the most superior of all, and has remained so, with large houses approached by gravel drives, hidden amongst the trees and scarcely visible to the public eye. Hook Heath had begun to grow in the 1890s, but during the 1920s and 1930s a high proportion of the non-golf course land to the south-west was also developed, including the significantly named 'Fairway' scheme (from 1936) and its neighbours in the Worplesdon Hill area, north of Fox Corner on the Bagshot Road.[26] Surprisingly, one name remained to recall a radically different past: Clodhouse Lane and Hill derive from the small huts built on the heath by the poor to protect their turf, or 'clods', from the rain and thereby to keep it dry for fuel.

The low-density housing areas of Woking have a distinctive character and appearance, and retain many of the qualities which contributed to their early popularity. Indeed, the subsequent tree growth and the maturing of the landscape have added to their beauty and charm. Unfortunately in recent years there has been some thoughtless and obtrusive infilling. There is an obvious temptation to subdivide the extensive grounds to capitalise on the high value of land in Woking, but this is often to the detriment of the character of the area. Although in theory these districts are protected against unsuitable development this is not always the case in practice, and more needs to be done. Perhaps the designation of some parts as a Conservation Area would be appropriate, in view of their social, historical and aesthetic importance.

The Impact of Expansion

In terms of the growth of the built-up area the two inter-war decades were most eventful. By 1914, despite the rapid expansion of the previous 30 years, the town still consisted of the new and densely populated central area, with its suburbs of Maybury and Mount Hermon, and the separate villages of Knaphill, 'Old' Woking, which had only tenuous physical connection with the Woking Station area, Horsell, and Byfleet and Pyrford. There were also the outlying hamlets such as Mayford, Sutton and Pyrford Green and more recent and scattered development including

Brookwood, Hook Heath, Woodham and West Byfleet. Woking, Byfleet and Pyrford were still quite distinct, separated by semi-rural belts of open land, whilst the town of Woking itself was unplanned and straggling.

During the next 25 years the ancient villages were consolidated and grew outwards. Old Woking and Westfield coalesced as new council and private housing spread along Vicarage Road and Westfield Road. Horsell had expanded eastwards towards Woodham, and southwards had become physically united with Woking. West Byfleet, focusing upon the small nucleus of the 1890s, extended outwards into the north of Pyrford parish. Beyond this increasingly coherent urban area were recent

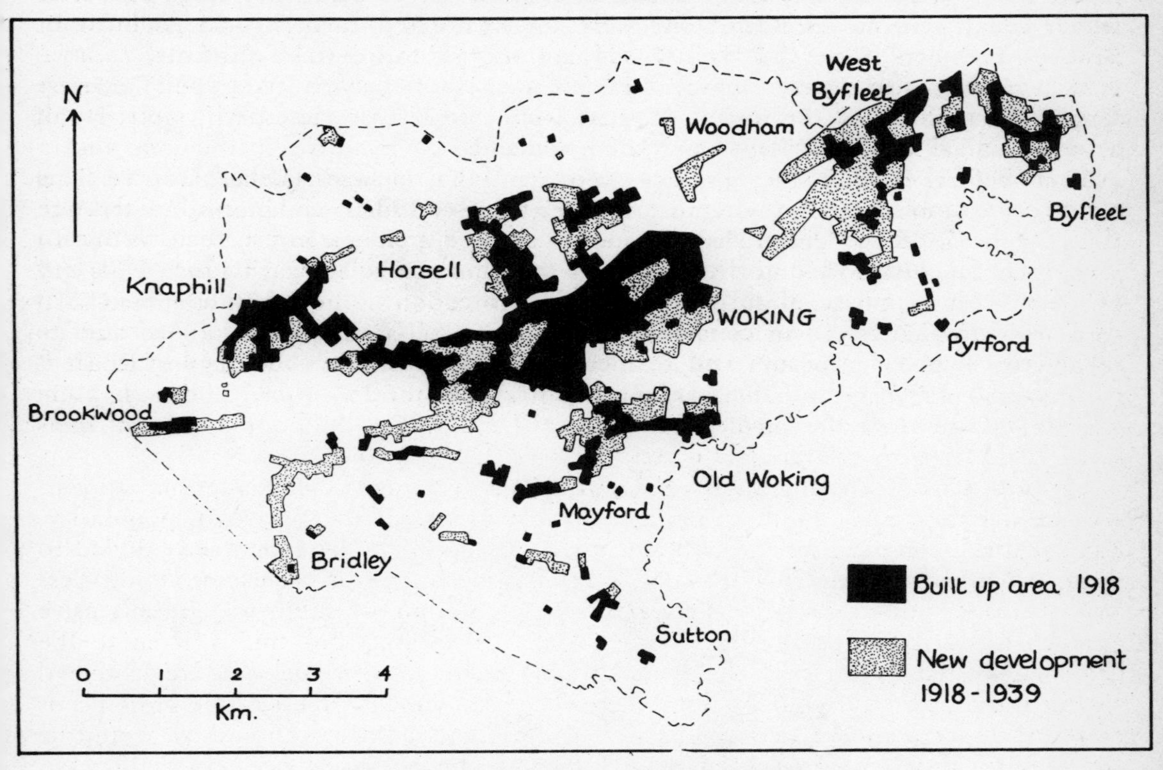

Fig. 24. The Growth of Woking 1918–1939

developments in the rural zone: Sheets Heath, Fox Corner and Woodham Hall, for example. Byfleet and Pyrford had evolved closer ties, physically and socially, and in turn Woking and Pyrford had crept closer to each other as housing was built along the Old Woking Road, a physical representation of the administrative union operative from the spring of 1933.

Woking and its villages were changing their character, as well as expanding. In 1944 Byfleet, once a pleasant, rural community, was described as 'a scattered overgrown village with no real centre and a lot of mean development and cheap shop blocks . . . a more or less isolated township [which] has little in common with West

Byfleet (a well-to-do suburban residential area)'.[27] The town of Woking, as its council had hoped, was being transformed, at least in part, into

> 'expensive London dormitory areas for the "managing director" type of resident with a good sprinkling of retired business people occupying large houses with chauffeurs' and gardeners' cottages attached'.[28]

The impact of growth might have been much greater had the war not intervened. By 1970 Woking could have had 150,000 people, almost twice its present size and equivalent to Reading or Oxford today. The built-up area, according to the more ambitious suggestions, was to be about 50 per cent larger than it is today. The areas which today remain open land but were then expected to be developed included Bridley, Saunders Lane, Pyrford Court and the Pyle Hill–Westfield–Sutton Green district in the south. Martyrs Lane, Carthouse Lane and the vicinity of Hill Place were targets for building in the north. All that would be left undeveloped were strips of amenity land along river valleys and some woodland.

Even before 1939, however, there were signs that changes in national and local attitudes to unrestricted growth might affect these confident and ambitious suppositions. In 1937–38 the Urban District Council showed greater concern than before for the loss of amenity which might result if all this land was built over. Its lack of money prevented the purchase of suitable sites as a protection against development but it was becoming interested in concepts such as green belts and chains of parkland to safeguard valuable landscapes and to increase the amount of public open space. It is quite probable that even if the war had not intervened the 1930s projections of future growth would have been scaled down.[29]

Chapter Eleven

LOCAL GOVERNMENT AND SERVICES 1914-1939

THE GEOGRAPHY of local government altered little between 1894 and the early 1930s, although there were localised changes such as those which affected North West Surrey in 1907-9. As the functions of local authorities became more complex, and involved increasingly large expenditure, many small districts were unable to provide a full range of services, and in the late 1920s central government decided to undertake a reform of local government areas, to provide larger units. Between the wars councils took responsibility for more aspects of service provision, and the more important of these are described below.

The Reform of Local Government 1929-36

After Windlesham became an urban district in 1909 there were no more changes in the local government pattern of North West Surrey until 1933. Woking U.D.C. wrote to Chertsey R.D.C. in 1928, asking to annex any areas close to their mutual borders which were not easily serviced by the Rural District Council.[1] This attempt to extend the Woking boundaries was emphatically rejected, but together with the reforms proposed by the Local Government Bill then passing through Parliament it seriously worried the Rural District Council.

In June the council resolved to apply for urban district status, and for extensions to its own boundaries. Surrey County Council was opposed to this scheme, which was described as 'fantastical and grotesque . . . doomed to failure' by the County Clerk, who said that it was absurd to suppose that this authority could become an urban district, whilst boundary incursions into urban districts were quite unknown. The County also quashed another suggestion, that Byfleet and Pyrford should become an urban district. This was unacceptable because national policy was against the creation of small new districts.[2]

The Local Government Act 1929 instructed each county council to prepare a scheme for rationalising local government areas by amalgamating units, extending boundaries and breaking up certain rural districts. In February 1930 Chertsey R.D.C. submitted its recommendations, suggesting that it should be extended and consolidated by the addition of parts of Chertsey and Egham U.D.s, the whole of the Horsell North ward of Woking, Windlesham (which would lose its urban status) and Wisley parish from Guildford R.D. If Windlesham was to remain an urban district, Byfleet and Pyrford, which together had a larger area, population and rateable value, and were growing more rapidly, should become an urban district.[3]

Not unexpectedly all the urban districts submitted plans for their own aggrandisement:

Table 14. Urban District Expansion Plans 1930[4]

Authority	*Areas to be annexed*
Chertsey	All parts of Windlesham, Byfleet, Pyrford and Wisley, parts of Horsell and Egham,
Egham	All of Thorpe and Windlesham, part of Chobham.
Walton-on-Thames	All of Weybridge, parts of Byfleet (Village) and Chertsey (Addlestone).
Weybridge	All of Byfleet, part of Chertsey (Addlestone).
Windlesham	All of Chobham, Bisley, parts of Chertsey (Ottershaw), Egham and Brookwood
Woking	All of Bisley, Pirbright, Send, Ripley and Pyrford, part of Chertsey (Woodham).

There was also a serious unofficial proposal to make a new urban district comprising Addlestone, Ottershaw, Woodham and Byfleet, but this involved splitting Chertsey U.D. and was rejected by the county for this reason. Surrey proposed, at first, to abolish Chertsey R.D.C. and parcel it out amongst the urban districts, Woking receiving Bisley, Chobham Village, Pyrford and Woodham. Early in 1931 the County Council held a series of meetings with local representatives, which led to a revision of these plans, and the decision to create Bagshot R.D.C., so that Woking was unable to acquire Bisley. It was decided not to interfere with the boundaries of Guildford R.D.C.[5]

The County Council proposed to divide Byfleet parish along the Wey Navigation, giving West Byfleet, with Pyrford, to Woking, and 'Old' Byfleet to an amalgamated Walton and Weybridge. This plan caused a storm of opposition, the Parish Council declaring that 'without a shadow of doubt there is a very bitter feeling against the division of the parish'.[6] It felt that Byfleet should go in its entirety to Walton & Weybridge, or as a second choice, with Pyrford to Woking. Eventually the County Council compromised, with a new boundary to run along the Wey at Plough Bridge. St. George's Hill and the whole of Brooklands would be lost, but the village and West Byfleet would stay together.

A 19-day inquiry was held into the Surrey Review Order in October 1931, two days being devoted to 'the Woodham question'. Surrey favoured the transfer of the district between the Six Cross-Roads and New Haw from Chertsey U.D.C. to Woking. Chertsey opposed this, claiming that it would lose potential rate income from future development. It would only agree to the cession of 66 acres around the Sorbo works.[7] Woking stated that Woodham had been neglected. Claiming to be motivated by 'the need for economy, efficiency and logic', it gave evidence that Woodham residents, who numbered just 136, had, 'for the last 30 or 40 years enjoyed all the amenities of Woking', and that 'improvement has [only] been accelerated since the question of Woodham coming into Woking arose'. The counsel for Chertsey U.D.C. used a dramatic metaphor in reply: 'While the plum has been ripening Chertsey has had to bear all the expense, but now that it has become ripe Woking are anxious to pluck it'.[8]

In his decision the Minister of Health broadly supported Surrey County Council. Woodham, as far as Sheerwater Road, was joined with Woking, as were Pyrford parish and Byfleet west of Plough Bridge. Woking also acquired a small area of Bisley west of the Garibaldi Crossroads, Knaphill, to rationalise the boundary, which had hitherto run through houses. Walsham Mead, the old Pyrford common meadow, was annexed by Ripley parish. On 31 March 1933 Chertsey R.D.C. was dissolved, and the Urban District of Woking substantially enlarged.

By a further amendment, in 1936, Surrey County Council returned to Byfleet parish (Woking U.D.) 14½ acres around Byfleet Mill, which had been transferred to Walton & Weybridge in 1933. This gave a final area for the Urban District of Woking of 15,710 acres.

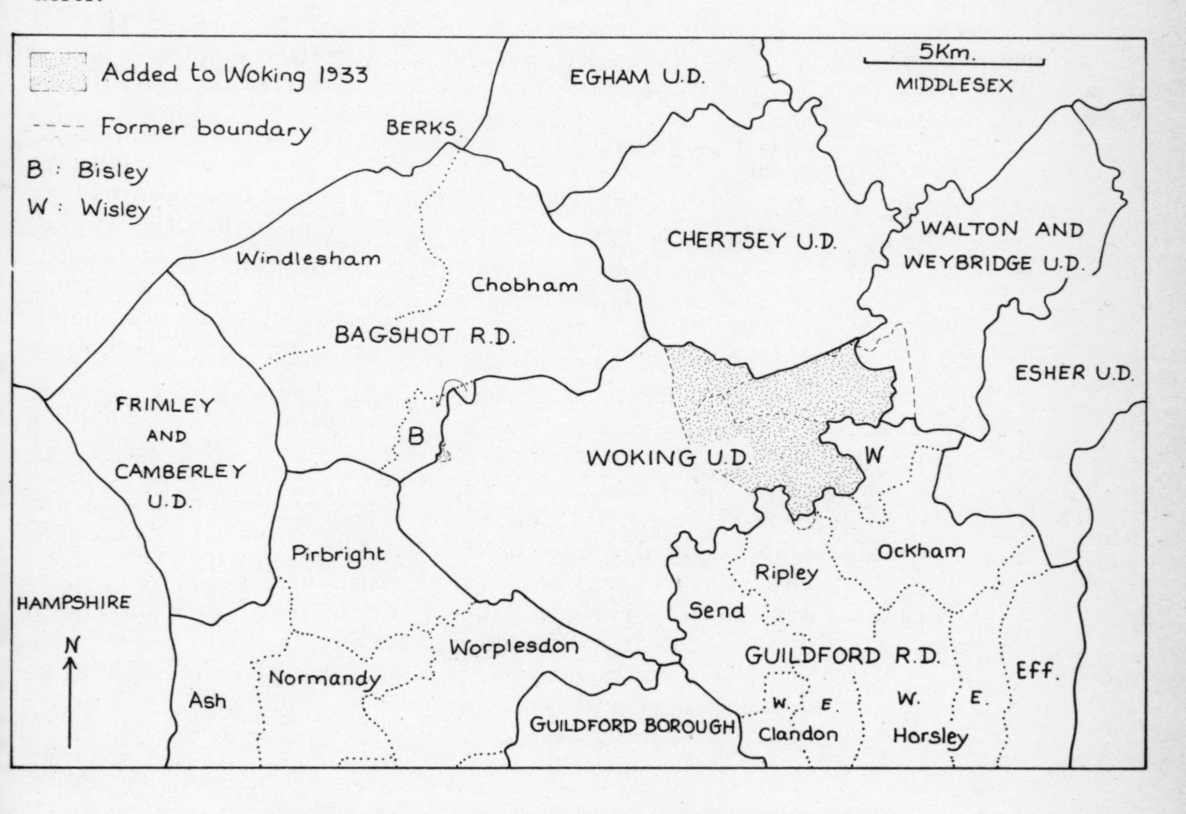

Fig. 25. Local Government in the Woking Area after 1933

Incorporation. The Woking Urban District had not been given new ward boundaries since 1908, when Woking Station & Maybury Ward was subdivided. That ward had 55 per cent of the population and 53 per cent of the rateable value of Woking parish, but only one-third of the councillors. From it, and the St Johns & Goldsworth Ward, were formed the Goldsworth, Chertsey Road, St Johns and Maybury & Mount Hermon wards, to give a council of 26 members from nine wards.

On enlargement the area should have been completely re-warded, but it was decided to defer this pending an application for Incorporation, which would establish the office of Alderman, and hence affect electoral arrangements. In 1930 Woking had been granted a coat of arms and motto, *Fide et Diligentia* (By Faith and Diligence), whilst from generous donors came a Badge and Chain of Office for the Chairman of the Council, who thus became a Mayor in all but name.[9]

In September 1935, after some hesitation, King George V was petitioned to grant a Charter of Incorporation to create a Borough of Woking. It was felt that this would be appropriate for a town of this size, bestowing civic dignity, and acting as a unifying factor. Not until May 1937, under King George VI, did the Privy Council inform Woking of its decision. The granting of borough status was to be delayed until 1942 to allow the new and old areas of the district time to develop closer links.[10] This was a strange decision, for in 1937 Epsom & Ewell, which had been extended in almost identical circumstances in 1933, was granted a Charter. In 1942 there were more important matters to consider and no more was heard until 1955, whilst Borough status was not in fact achieved until 1974.

Council Offices. The Woking Local Board at first met in any building which was available: in October and November 1893, for example, its deliberations were at the Goldsworth Public Hall, the *Temperance Hotel* and the Masonic Hall. In March 1894 it moved into a temporary home on the first floor of Ashby's Bank, at the corner of Broadway and Chertsey Road, renting the offices and strong-room for £100 per annum.[11] The new Woking U.D.C. decided, in May 1895, to build permanent offices for itself and bought a site in Commercial Road for £420. A scheme was approved in January 1897, but there was a public outcry against the expenditure of an estimated £6,000 at a time when a steam fire-engine was being refused on the grounds of cost. In January 1898, therefore, the plan was abandoned.[12]

On a hot day in June 1899, just before the steam engine was to be delivered, a spectacular blaze gutted the council offices in Bank Buildings, to the ill-concealed delight of those who pointed out the irony of an anti-engine council suffering so badly by fire.[13] The Council was forced to move, for the fifth time in six years, and rented cramped rooms over Jobson's shop at 13 Broadway, whilst replacement offices were designed. On 14 March 1906 the first meetings were held in the new Council Offices opposite the junction of High Street and Commercial Road. Built at a cost of only £4,500, and modest in scale, these were soon inadequate to cope with the growth of council business, and were supplemented by prefabricated temporary rooms in the rear yard.[14]

Chertsey R.D.C. was administered from Chertsey town, outside its administrative area, until 1928, although a Surveyor's Office was established in West Byfleet in 1908. The increased scale of council activities, and the need for efficient operation to counter the threat of dissolution, led to a decision, in January 1927, to provide separate offices within the district. Oakfield School, West Byfleet, was bought for £9,500 in the following month, and converted to office use, the formal opening being on 9 July 1928.[15] Only five years later it was closed, as Chertsey R.D.C. failed to survive the reforms of 1933, and its offices became redundant.

The newly enlarged Woking U.D.C. immediately began to search for alternative accommodation. In September 1935 it approved a report which described 'the inadequacy & inconvenience of the present Council Offices . . . their appalling overcrowding . . . congested, uncomfortable and inefficient'.[16] As a temporary measure the first floor of the Grand Theatre, Commercial Road, was leased to house the Town Planning Department. In September 1938, after several other sites had been considered, three detached houses in extensive grounds, between York Road and Mount Hermon Road, were acquired as new offices. The intention was to convert them for a short period whilst money was raised for a purpose-built civic centre. Most departments moved there in the spring of 1939, but due to the vicissitudes of war, planning and local government finance, they remained until 1982, when a new Town Hall, the eighth council building in less than a century, was completed in the centre of Woking.

The Services

Roads. Before 1914 the two authorities had expressed concern about the increasing number of motor vehicles. They were unhappy with the noise, and possible danger, and the damage caused to road surfaces. Dust clouds were raised in dry weather, and in an attempt to combat this nuisance Chertsey R.D.C. bought 400-gallon vans for watering the streets of Horsell and Byfleet, whilst in September 1906 the Clerk wrote to the County Council asking them to impose a 10 m.p.h. speed limit through Byfleet village, where 'the road is very narrow and winding and also [has] a considerable number of people moving about'.[17] In the same year Mr. H. Locke King received a claim for £152 14s. 0d. (£152.70) compensation from the Council for damage to roads 'by Traction Engines making the new Motor Track at Brooklands'.[18]

Byfleet Parish Council regarded watering as 'money thrown away', and successfully urged the Rural District Council to tar the roads. In 1910 a contract was made with the Woking District Gas Co. to buy at least 15,000 gallons of coal tar annually, at 2½d. (1.1 p) per gallon. This was sprayed onto the dusty surface to form a thin crust, which was waterproof and more stable, but could not cope with heavy vehicles. The London General Omnibus Co. was told in May 1921 that Chertsey R.D.C. could not license a Byfleet–Woking service because 'the road is not safe for the proposed traffic and the road crust is not of sufficient thickness at present'.[19]

By 1914 the urban roads were being brought up to a tolerable standard, so that after the First World War attention turned to the rural areas. Both councils made piecemeal improvements: Woking U.D.C., for example, spent £1,321 in 1921–22 on widening Hermitage Road, St Johns, as an unemployment relief scheme (*see* Plate XI), and in the following year reconstructed the water-splash near the junction of Hook Heath Road and Saunders Lane. These works did not please everybody: in December 1923 Chertsey R.D.C. received a letter complaining about the new tarred surfaces because 'horses are unable to get a foothold, and sand or grit should be spread for that purpose'.[20]

After 1924 proposals were considered for the construction of new roads, and the Regional Planning Scheme (1928) incorporated some 15 such schemes in the area. Several were small scale diversions, but some had more than local significance. The

Byfleet Loop Road, to divert the A245 away from High Road, was given formal approval in 1928 but land acquisition was still in progress in 1939 when war broke out. The scheme was not completed until 1962, 40 years after it was first suggested. Similar delays affected the eight major projects approved by Woking U.D.C. in May 1928. These included a Woking Western Bypass (Turnoak Corner–Horsell Common), a diversion of the Guildford road between Mayford and Pyle Hill, a north–south bypass of Old Woking, and a Woking Eastern Approach Road (Kingfield–A3 at Ripley). All of these are still, in some form, on the Surrey County Council roads programme, not yet begun after more than 50 years! The South Orbital Road (M25) through Byfleet was first mentioned in 1929, but was still not complete at the time of writing (1982).

In December 1930 Woking Council approved a £3,838 'traffic circus' for the busy and dangerous staggered junction at Turnoak Corner, and this, the first roundabout in Woking, was completed in the autumn of 1934.[21] It inspired a similar project for the Six Cross-Roads, on Horsell Common, but this junction was not improved for another 30 years. Another sign of 'progress' in 1934 was the introduction of the first of many one-way systems designed to reduce congestion in Woking town centre, whilst proposals for an inner relief road were first brought forward in the late 1920s.[22]

During 1925 several councillors raised the question of on-street car-parking, which was exacerbating traffic problems. The Council approved, by 11 votes to 10, a £1,075 plan for a car park in Duke Street, because 'a Parking Place . . . for Motor Cars is essential to the well-being of the Town', but in March 1926 this vote was reversed.[23] Eight years later, after pressure from the Chamber of Trade, the situation was reviewed, and as a result a plot of vacant land between Victoria Arch and the Bus Station was bought from the Anglo-American Oil Co. for £1,000.[24] It was opened as a car park in that eventful year for the Woking motorist, 1934, and doubled as a market place on Friday and Saturday in the absence of anywhere more suitable.

As part of long-term central area redevelopment plans which included the widening of Commercial Road into the major traffic artery, the Council purchased Nos. 17–31, on the north side of this street, compulsorily, in 1936. These former houses had been converted to offices and businesses; in 1937 they were demolished and their sites became a second central car park, an ugly expanse of tarmac which remained until the eventual reconstruction of the centre in the 1970s.

Street-Lighting. During the First World War the Gas Company experienced considerable problems with its lighting business. Many employees were absent on war service, and poor-quality coal supplies affected gas output. A partial blackout, imposed in October 1915, led traffic to collide with lamp standards, and most of these were then removed. After the end of the war the Company were slow to resume full lighting, replying to Council criticism of this by stating that they had 'only one lame horse, and scarcely any labour, so that it was very difficult . . . to get on'.[25] In 1929 there were coal strikes, which further delayed the restoration of lighting. During the war, too, 'rough elements' had destroyed, by vandalism, over 200 lamps in the Woking area, adding to the problems of the Company.[26]

The Electricity Supply Co. was not in a position to tender for the lighting business in 1921 and 1923 because its mains did not yet extend to the outer parts of the district and (in 1921) 'owing to the comparatively high cost of materials and the dearness of money at the present time'.[27] In 1931, however, both companies tendered for the lucrative contract. Specimen lamps were erected, and following photometric tests to determine the reliability and quality of the two systems the Woking Electricity Supply Co.'s tender was accepted. Electric light returned to the streets of Woking in October 1931 after an interval of 30 years.[28]

The question of lighting Byfleet was not revived until 1923 when the Parish Council asked the Woking District Gas Co. to estimate the likely cost of 52 lamps in the Village and West Byfleet. The Company required £305 12s. 0d. (£305.60) per annum for 12 years, and the question was deferred.[29] In September 1924 Chertsey R.D.C. accepted instead the tender of the Woking Electricity Supply Co. for 53 lamps and that of the Gas Company for a small number of lights in outer parts of the parish. The cost would be £327 per annum, to be met by raising a special rate. A parochial committee was appointed to administer the scheme, which came into operation in the autumn of 1925 and was later extended to the northern part of Pyrford parish.[30]

Both contracts expired in 1936 and Woking U.D.C., when reviewing the agreement with the Electricity Supply Co., insisted that the lamp types and voltages should be standardised throughout the district, whilst the last eight gas lamps were to be converted to electricity.

Sewering and Scavenging. Between the wars both local authorities were concerned with extending the basic sewerage network to serve the outlying or newly developed parts of their districts. The largest unsewered area was the Sutton & Bridley ward of Woking, where the small scattered population had been considered insufficient to warrant inclusion in the 1898 scheme. In June 1927 Woking U.D.C. received a report recommending that a new trunk sewer should be built along the Hoe Valley from Bridley to Old Woking. This would serve the Sutton & Bridley ward, relieve the existing sewer through Kingfield, and provide drainage for a substantial acreage of undeveloped land in and around Mayford, thereby stimulating building.

By 1934 the new sewer had reached Saunders Lane, moving westwards, but further extensions were deferred in November when the Public Health Committee ordered a comprehensive review of the entire sewerage network. The existing system was 'now running at full capacity even in dry weather' and in the future it would have to cope with large population increases.[31]

Messrs. John Taylor & Sons, the engineers, 40 years before, for the basic network, produced outlines of two designs, both involving new trunk sewers at a deep level. The first would entail the retention, modernisation and enlargement of the Old Woking and Wisley works, supplemented by a third sewage farm beside the Bourne west of Dunford Bridge. The alternative, and far more radical proposal, was for the closure of both existing works and the construction of a large new plant at Townsley Mead, Pyrford, beside the Wey opposite Wisley Gardens. This could, if necessary, be connected to a central works for the entire Wey and Mole valleys, a possibility mentioned by the Ministry of Health in 1935–36.[32]

The new system was designed to cater for, and indeed would facilitate, the development of the greater part of the open land in the Urban District, between 1939 and

1970, and anticipated an ultimate population of 140,000, perhaps more. This was a 300 per cent increase on the 1936 figure, but the war prevented the start of construction work, and afterwards the population figures were drastically reduced, making the 1936 plan unnecessary.

Woking U.D.C. continued to contract much of its refuse collection and disposal function to private enterprise for the decade after the First World War. The contractors dumped the household waste on council-owned fields adjacent to the Constitution Hill Recreation Ground. In 1928 a subcommittee which had been investigating the matter found that the amount of waste handled was becoming too great, and that 'although there would probably be no saving in the first year, still the work would be carried out more efficiently, and satisfactorily, if the whole of the work of scavenging was carried out departmentally instead of partly by contract'. The Council therefore took over the entire operation from January 1929.[33].

In April 1932 11½ acres beside Hoe Stream, south of Elmbridge, were purchased for a new dumping area, despite strong local opposition. The Recreation Ground tip, which dated originally from 1907, was closed in 1934 and landscaped, providing a site for the new swimming-bath and an extension to Woking Park. The new dump could only be a short-term solution, and by July 1938 the Public Health Committee had selected two more sites. The first extended from Elmbridge tip along the valley to Mayford Bridge, and the second covered 38 acres of water-meadows between Moor Lane, Westfield, and Old Woking. This, the favoured site, would be raised 10 feet by tipping, and was to include a rubbish destructor.[34] Surrey County Council opposed both sites on amenity grounds, forcing the Council to choose a third site, 40 acres on either side of the Bourne at Mimbridge, with capacity to take the waste of the entire district for 15 years. Bagshot R.D.C. expressed strong objections, and the landowner refused to sell.[35] Again the war intervened and afterwards, faced with this local opposition, Woking U.D.C. co-operated with Guildford Council to provide a joint destructor unit at Slyfield.

Chertsey R.D.C. which, unlike its predecessor, had used contractors for scavenging in Byfleet and Pyrford, decided in April 1925 to institute weekly collections to replace the irregular visits then made. This was successful but, because it created extra work, expensive, and in October 1926 the Council resolved to take over all scavenging, disposal and cesspool-emptying, using direct labour. A motor-lorry was bought for £245, but so effective was the new policy that, even allowing for this, there was an overall saving of £195 7s. 10d. (£195.39) in the first year of operation.[36]

A dump for household refuse was available at Camphill Road, but the contents of the remaining cesspools were deposited on Pyrford Common. This practice resulted in so many complaints that in 1929 a Special Rate was levied to purchase, for £640, a cesspool-emptying machine which would allow disposal into the sewerage system. In 1933 this was taken over by Woking U.D.C. on the dissolution of Chertsey R.D.C. and the new authority continued the work of extending the sewers to such areas as Woodham, Sheerwater and Pyrford Green, which had not hitherto been served.[37]

Recreation, Parks and Baths. In 1854 the Vicar of St John's fought successfully to prevent the inclusion of St Johns Lye in the lands acquired by the Necropolis

Company.[38] During the next half-century this area became increasingly valuable for recreation as its economic importance declined. The Woking Local Board took over the management of the Lye and regulated it, passing bye-laws to control its use, although as late as 1926 there was a case of the ancient manorial rights being exercised, contrary to bye-law restrictions. A resident cut turves in the belief that this was legal 'for stuff that was taken for use on our own premises'.[39]

This was an isolated example of protection of open spaces. Elsewhere, the loss of common rights and enclosure reduced the amount of land available for recreation, and when the densely populated new town grew on Woking Common, after 1860, there was no provision for public open space. All the land was sold to speculative builders, without a proper town plan to reserve land for such amenities. By the 1890s residents had started to demand the provision of a park or recreation ground, but the new Local Board and its successor had weightier problems to consider.

The death of Queen Victoria in 1901 prompted suggestions that an open space might be dedicated as a memorial, land in Oriental Road being proposed as the site, but the Council decided instead to give a further endowment to the Victoria Cottage Hospital in Boundary Road.[40] A garden with shrubs and trees was provided in 1904 when the junction of High Street and Commercial Road was remodelled. Although officially called Victoria Gardens this has, for many years, been known colloquially as Sparrow Park. The War Memorial was erected there in 1923, although it has since been moved to Town Square.

In 1902 a development company, the Suburban Land Corporation, offered to sell to the Council 23 acres on the southern site of the Hillview estate, then being laid out, and the sale was completed in December 1904. For £4,000 the Urban District Council acquired a valuable site, eminently suited to use as a recreation area.[41] It lay on the south-facing slopes of a shallow valley, with the Hoe stream flowing along the southern edge. Woking town centre was within easy reach, and the topography would permit attractive and easy landscaping, whilst the damp meadows along the river could not be used for building and would, in the future, provide possible extensions of the open space.

In July 1905 a layout for the Constitution Hill Recreation Ground was approved, incorporating a formal garden area, extensive planting of trees and shrubs, a sports ground, tennis-courts, a bowling-green, a small swimming-bath and a children's playground. By the outbreak of war in 1914 most of these had been provided. The terrace walks, rose-gardens, and the magnificent avenues of limes and horse chestnuts were laid out in 1910–11, and remain amongst the most attractive features of the Park.[42] The swimming-pool was opened on 1 June 1910, and comprised a timber-lined rectangle 100 feet by 40 feet beside the river, from which water supplies were drawn. It cost £588 0s. 1d. (£588.0½p) and was unusually primitive even when it was built.[43]

The low-lying meadows were used for a municipal rubbish dump, to raise them above normal flood levels. In 1920, the first stage of this refuse tip was completed, and another four acres of fields towards Elmbridge were bought for £400 from the Clerk to the Council, Robert Mossop. The former dump was then covered and landscaped as a 'Job Creation Scheme' for between 45 and 55 unemployed labourers. Rhododendrons and flowers were given by an anonymous donor, and two small ponds, with aquatic plants and wildfowl, were dug beside the river. In 1927 the whole area was officially renamed 'Woking Park'.

During the 1920s there were several attempts to build a new indoor heated swimming pool in the town centre, but these were unsuccessful because the necessary finance could not be found. After considerable delay Woking U.D.C. decided to abandon this proposal, and instead to construct an open-air pool in the Park, using the land which had been raised by tipping. Designs were approved in May 1932, and on 5 June the Duke of Sutherland opened the new pool, which comprised an open-air bath, with fountain, changing facilities and café in ferro-concrete, in a style typical of the period. The compacted waste on which it was constructed did not provide adequate foundations, so the pool 'floats' on a raft of concrete.[44]

The remainder of the dump was grassed, and a new concrete bridge built for an access road linking the Park with Elmbridge. The entire project cost £21,600 and involved extending the Park by four acres. At the same time the fields south of the river towards Elmbridge Lane were bought by the Council to add to the Park. These included a small area of woodland, and brought the total area to 43 acres.[45]

Horsell Parish Vestry laid out a nine-acre area on Horsell Common in 1893, opposite *The Wheatsheaf*, where a cricket pitch had existed since at least 1870. This was a poor parish, so expenses were defrayed by voluntary subscription.[46] Twelve years later this land was the subject of an undignified dispute between Woking U.D.C. and Lord Onslow, the holder of the common rights. The latter wished to sell his interest in the land but the Council would only agree to make up the adjacent Ferndale Road in return. Although Onslow wrote that 'it seems monstrous that I should have to give away my property to avoid having to pay for the construction of roads that will be of no benefit to me', he eventually conceded, and in 1910 Woking U.D.C. acquired full rights over this piece of common.[47] Extensions and improvements to Wheatsheaf Recreation Ground were made in 1920–21 to provide work for the unemployed.

At Boundary Road the land alongside the Canal, transferred from Horsell to Woking in 1901, was levelled and grassed between 1903 and 1910 to provide a recreation area close to the densely populated Walton Road–Maybury Road district. This was a popular site for fairs and circuses, recalling the early 19th century when Woking Common was frequented by gypsies and tinkers because of its remoteness.

Knaphill Recreation Ground was laid out in 1921–22 on a four-acre site originally acquired for housing. The Necropolis Company added another acre, as a gift, in 1923.[48] A year later 14½ acres of nursery land in Lower Knaphill were left to Woking Council in the will of the late Anthony Waterer, of the famous local nurserying family. This valuable gift was gladly accepted, and in 1925–28 the park which bears the name of the donor was laid out, a considerable undertaking because the land was 'soggy, uneven and infested with moles'.[49] Between 1928 and 1935 small recreation grounds were also provided at Old Woking, Sutton Green and Brookwood.

In 1899 the Byfleet Charities asked the Parish Council, which had discussed recreation facilities in 1895, to take over and improve the private recreation ground off Rectory Lane. This was agreed and the work was undertaken in two stages between 1900 and 1905.[50] In West Byfleet the growth of the village after 1880 had made it desirable to provide some public open space, so in 1912 the Parish Council took a lease on 12 acres in Camphill Road owned by the United Charities. This area had not been opened when war was declared, so food crops were grown there from 1914 until 1918. There was a suggestion that it should become permanent allotments, but local opposition was strong, and the site was therefore levelled and grassed, being opened on 6 June 1921.[51]

Byfleet Village Recreation Ground was extended in 1921–23 by generous gifts of land from Mr. Henry Locke King and Mr. C. Charrington of Broad Oaks. The last extension before the war was in 1936 when Woking U.D.C. paid £600 for 6.17 acres of United Charities land. A further nine acres had been offered but the Council would only give £500 for this, and the vendors then refused to sell.

By 1939 recreational facilities had been provided in all the built-up areas of the district to supplement the considerable informal recreation space afforded by heaths and commons in Woking and Horsell. The Urban District was comparatively well endowed in these respects, but attention was turning towards the purchase of more extensive areas of agricultural land to protect them from development, which was confidently expected for the future.

Council Housing. The Housing of the Working Classes Act 1890 gave local authorities powers to build dwellings for those who were unable to provide their own. By the early

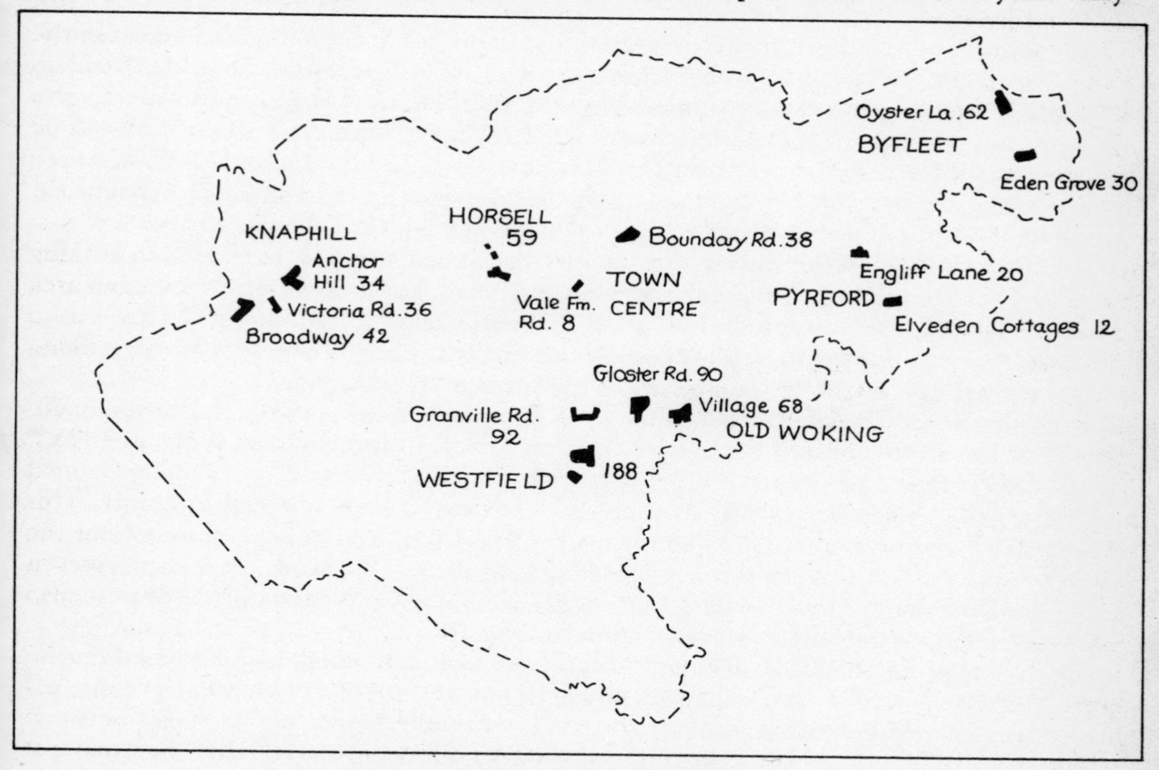

Fig. 26. Council Housing 1919–1939

years of this century most were at least investigating the possibility of entering the field of housing, although only in industrial districts was there large-scale involvement. In Woking the problem was primarily the one which is still with us today, that of high prices for land and property and high rents, so that lower-income groups, the 'labouring classes', were at a serious disadvantage.

In June and July 1910 the Sanitary Committee of Woking U.D.C. heard witnesses testify to the acute difficulties faced by working men in finding cheap accommodation. A Housing Committee was established in July 1911 'to consider the availability of land for the erection of cottage dwellings in the district whether by the Council or by a co-operative scheme'.[52] By the end of 1911, 16 sites had been surveyed, the final choice being 5½ acres at Horsell village, suitable for about 60 dwellings.

The Medical Officer of Health proposed that the estates should 'resemble a small garden suburb, the rows of housing being laid out in curves rather than in straight lines . . . the central cottages should be arranged either in a crescent or in a square . . . to allow the provision of a small playground in the centre'.[53] The Local Government Board was less idealistic: 'the Committee must not be too particular about the exact shade of bricks, and they must aim at spending no unnecessary money on appearance or ornamentation'.[54] These remarks set the tone for the whole of the inter-war period, with the Council trying to provide dwellings of a high standard whilst the Government imposed stringent economies.

In February 1914 the Council purchased 6½ acres behind Old Woking High Street for £538 from their Clerk, Robert Mossop. The Horsell site had been delayed by disputes over sale prices. An outline scheme for 76 cottages was produced for Old Woking, but work had not started when war broke out. The site was then used as emergency allotments growing turnips and potatoes.

A *Special Report on Housing* prepared in 1917 recommended that land should be purchased for a further 180 dwellings to make up the deficiency created by the cessation of building work during the war. It was agreed that the Horsell land should be bought together with 19½ acres at Gonger's Lane (now Westfield Road) and 8½ acres owned by the Necropolis Co. at Broadway, Knaphill. During 1919 slow and complex negotiations for these sites continued, and in October a 200-house programme was approved for 1920–22, comprising 42 houses at Woking Village, 78 at Gongers Lane, 40 at Kirby Road, Horsell, and 40 at Knaphill. Work on the first project, St Peter's Road (Old Woking) began in late October 1919, and the first Woking U.D.C. house was occupied in August 1920.[55]

The housing programme at first proceeded with only minor interruptions, although the laudable initial aim, to build solid, spacious and well-fitted houses, was thwarted by frequent cost-cutting instructions from the Ministry of Health. For example, in 1920 the Government insisted on thinner walls and floors and the omission of porches, whilst in 1921 serious changes were made in the Horsell houses. The installation of hot-water systems, hand basins and electric wiring was forbidden, a short term economy which proved very expensive in the long term when these essential facilities had to be provided for existing houses.[56]

In April 1921, when 100 dwellings had been completed or started, the Housing Commissioner told Woking U.D.C. that 'it is our intention to concentrate on the larger industrial areas [and] it will not be possible to allot further houses to your Council's area at present'.[57] The Council was infuriated, since the Knaphill site had only just been started, with site works partly finished and four houses built. In December, after several ineffectual protests, a letter was sent to the Minister: 'the Council [are] very disappointed . . . In addition to having the land and the necessary funds [they] also have a large quantity of bricks . . . the Council ask whether you will kindly reconsider their application: The houses are badly needed'.[58] The answer was an uncompromising 'No', and there was then no choice but to wind up the housing accounts and take steps to dispose of the 16 acres of land purchased for housing but still undeveloped.

In Byfleet and Pyrford, Chertsey R.D.C. was the housing authority. It began building cottages for the rehousing of inhabitants of slum properties in Thorpe village in 1911. In August 1917 all the parish councils were asked whether they had any views on the need for council housing. Pyrford replied at 'at least 10 cottages should be built & that suitable sites would be at Cold Arbour or Pyrford Green'.[59] The Rural District Council concurred, and in March 1919 bought 3.1 acres at Pyrford Green from the Countess of Lovelace for £300.

Byfleet Parish Council sent a letter to Chertsey R.D.C. in May 1919, asking for '20 Cottages in the Village and 20 at West Byfleet, with sufficient land to be acquired to allow for further schemes'.[60] Most of the possible sites proved to be physically unsuitable or too expensive. The final choice was for land in Petersham Avenue and Oyster Lane owned by Mrs. Rutson of Byfleet Manor. She was unwilling to sell at a price low enough to satisfy the ever-vigilant Ministry of Health. Not until July 1920 did the Housing Commissioner for the Ministry agree to a purchase price; a delay of over a year.

Chertsey R.D.C. was incensed: 'this Council . . . do hereby record their abhorrence of the methods of the Housing Commissioner . . . his multitudinous officials, and inspectors, his forms, his verbosity and vacillation, create such a barrier to progress that they are no longer tolerable'.[61] Its troubles did not end there. Although work began on the Engliff Lane, Pyrford site in April 1920, and on the Byfleet scheme in September, no more projects were authorised. Both were completed in the summer of 1921, and the Government then refused to allow any more building, this being a 'non-priority' area. Forty-two dwellings had been constructed in the two parishes, of a total of 62 in the entire Rural District.

The new Housing Act of 1923 required local authorities to submit figures on overcrowding and waiting lists. Woking indicated that there were 34 houses in the area which were unacceptably overcrowded or needed demolition because of their condition. It asked to be allowed to build at least 25 houses during 1924. The seriousness of the problem was illustrated by the report that 'there are sheds and harness rooms being used as dwellings'.[62]

Predictably the Ministry prevaricated, and in October 1924 was informed by the Council that 'it seems absolutely necessary that further houses should be provided with the least possible delay'.[63] When the Council was at last able to advertise for tenders, in January 1925, the Minister rejected its application for financial approval. The Clerk was instructed to write that 'the Council consists of a very careful body of men, and they therefore consider that you should have sufficient confidence in them to allow them to build these houses'.[64]

Work on the housing programme was eventually resumed in December 1925, and by 1933 the Urban District Council had built 513 houses, a total of 613 since 1919.[65] Almost all were two or three-bedroomed dwellings, semi-detached or more rarely in rows, set in austere estates. Both houses and landscaping showed, in their plainness, the effects of cost-cutting, although the designs show a distant relationship to the garden suburb theme suggested before 1914. They were concentrated in Woking village, Knaphill, Westfield and Horsell, older housing areas where land was cheap and easily serviced. The new, and more expensive, districts, such as Mount Hermon Road and Hook Heath were never considered.

The programme, whilst not unambitious, was inadequate to cope with the expansion of the town and its population, In 1927 there were 193 cases on the waiting list 'in dire need of amelioration', and a further 81 needed 'rehousing on the grounds of decency, common modesty, moral and physical health'.[66] The 1930 Housing Act introduced slum clearance measures, and Woking U.D.C. reported that in 1931–35 it would need to build 182 houses, of which 55 would be for rehousing families living in slum properties, mainly in the Walton Road area, Old Woking and Knaphill. Yet, although this target was exceeded, 229 houses being provided in this period, there were still 76 urgent cases on the list in June 1935.[67]

Chertsey R.D.C. also pressed for a resumption of housing activity. In May 1924 the Medical Officer of Health noted 'the deplorable and insanitary conditions' of housing in Byfleet, with cases of overcrowding such as a family of four living in a lean-to shed, and three adults and nine children in a two-bedroomed house.[68] A deputation was sent to the Minister in July 1924, and it seems to have been effective, for in December a renewal of work was authorised.

Henry Locke King, with characteristic generosity, gave a site in Oyster Lane 'in view of the desirability of keeping down the rates as much as possible'.[69] In 1925 land at Pyrford Green was purchased from Lord Elveden as a site for the cottages which bear his name. Between 1925 and its dissolution in 1933, Chertsey R.D.C. built 12 houses in Pyrford and 44, all in Oyster Lane or Eden Grove, in Byfleet. West Byfleet was an expensive area, and was not considered.

The enlarged Woking Council built only 58 houses in 1934–36, in marked contrast to the completion rate in the previous decade. Land was particularly hard to find, and the Council was regularly outbid by private companies which possessed greater resources and were not subject to price restraints. In January 1938 it was noted that 'the increased cost of building, the difficulty of obtaining suitable land at a reasonable cost, and the inadequacy of drainage facilities' had been responsible for the decline in building and its eventual end.[70]

Although the Council considered, in September 1935 and in 1938, building homes specifically for elderly people, nothing was accomplished. Woking was listed in the National Survey of Overcrowding (June 1936)[71] as having 47 cases in need of relief, whilst in the following month the Council indicated a need for at least 52 new houses as a matter of priority, but to no avail.

With more vigour and less Government obstruction more could perhaps have been done: for example, the Council never used the compulsory purchase powers which were available. Nevertheless, the total of 785 council houses built between 1919 and 1936 was, in view of the many and recurring difficulties, a not inconsiderable achievement, and it played an important role in providing accommodation for lower-income groups and those in unsuitable housing in this district of highly-priced land and property.

Fire-Brigades. In 1915 Woking Fire-Brigade, with its volunteers and one horse-drawn steam-engine, was threatened by a disaster: Captain Sherlock noted that 'on 13th October at 10.5 pm I was advised that Zeppelins were in the neighbourhood and had already passed over Weybridge. About the same time explosions were heard, and flashes seen in the direction of Guildford. Gas was started under the steamer, and the First and Second Engineers stood ready.'[72] The anticipated air raid did not materialise but when, in November 1917, Sherlock resigned after 22 years of service, his successor, Wright, requested that a motor-engine should be purchased, the Zeppelin alarm having emphasised the outdated nature of the equipment.[73]

In contrast to the stormy and dramatic events of 1897–98 the Urban District Council readily agreed, and in September 1919 a motor-engine with telescopic ladder was delivered from Dennis Bros. The arrival was timely, for in June the steam-engine had 'collapsed' whilst pumping out the swimming-pool, and was clearly at the end of its life. It was kept in reserve, but never used again, and in November 1924 it was sold for £50.[74]

Captain Wright resigned in July 1924, and was replaced by the Sanitary Inspector, Mr. Barnes. He was concerned at the inadequate fire cover provided for the sprawling town by one engine, and in 1925 began to expand and re-equip the Brigade. Members of the Council visited other brigades to inspect their facilities. As a result £2,000 was spent on a second engine and some smaller items, delivered in November 1925. In the same year Councillor Illingworth donated a Renault car which was converted into a 'fast Motor Tender for the use of the Fire Brigade'.[75]

To cater for the growth of operations the Council, after considerable confusion over new designs and possible sites, built a 'new' fire station on the site of the present building, in Church Street. The former Roman Catholic church house, 'St Dunstan's', was purchased and converted to form the basis of the station, as an economy measure. The project cost £4,900, and the new building was formally opened on 21 July 1928.

Barnes resigned, because of overwork, in July 1929 and the Council appointed Major C. H. Hudson as Captain, granting a retaining fee of £50 per quarter for out-of-pocket expenses. The men were dissatisfied with this choice, and in November most resigned, following the rejection of their request for reconsideration. This time, in contrast to the events of 1897, the Council merely appointed replacements.[76]

In November 1925 Chobham and Pirbright parish councils signed agreements whereby, for retaining fees of £50 and £40 per annum respectively, Woking U.D. would provide fire cover in their areas, whilst in 1926 Bisley signed a similar undertaking for a fee of £12.[77]

Byfleet Fire-Brigade wanted a motor-engine, but in September 1919 a previous decision to purchase one was reversed by the Parish Council. It was not until June 1923 that the £1,780 engine was delivered, and to help to defray these costs Pyrford Parish Council agreed to increase its contribution to £50 per annum. In July 1929 Byfleet Parish Council, asking for this to be increased again, to £65, pointed out that Pyrford had a bargain, for with 21 per cent of the rateable value of the two parishes they paid only 11 per cent of the costs of the Brigade.[78]

Woking U.D.C. took over responsibility for the Byfleet Brigade in March 1933 and for 3½ years administered it separately. But at a serious fire at Brooklands Aerodrome in October 1936 the Byfleet engine broke down, and an inquiry revealed disquieting circumstances. A report, in February 1937, condemned the Brigade, describing 'a lack of organisation, supervision, administration and co-operation', and the fire station was found to be 'too small, inconvenient and inadequate'.[79] In normal circumstances the Brigade would have been disbanded, but in view of the proximity of the airfield, and the threatening war, it was decided to retain it. The Woking Chief Officer took charge of a completely reorganised Brigade, with a new name, 'Woking Fire Brigade – Byfleet Section'.[80] Plans to build a replacement station in Oyster Lane were cancelled in September 1939, and the old building continued in use until the final closure of the Brigade in 1962.

Captain Hudson was made part-time salaried Chief Officer in November 1935, a first step towards ending the volunteer status of Woking Brigade, and a recognition that a town of 40,000 people could no longer rely entirely on the services of unpaid amateurs. In February 1938, the Chief Officer became a full-time employee, to cope with the greatly increased workload resulting from war preparations.

A new Fire Brigade & Air Raid Precautions Administration Committee was established in 1935, and planned a series of measures, including casualty stations, first-aid posts and fire-watching points. During 1938 it supervised the digging of trenches and the setting up of a permanent A.R.P. system, whilst an agreement was made with James Walker & Co. for the storage of 30,000 gas-masks. After plans were finalised in January 1939 work began on constructing public air-raid shelters.[81]

Under the Fire Brigade Act 1938 each local authority became responsible for its own area, but Bagshot R.D.C. and Guildford R.D.C. only had partial fire-brigade cover. With Home Office approval the agreements concerning Pirbright, Bisley and Chobham were renewed in January 1939, with a further payment of £108 per annum to provide emergency cover in the event of war.[82]

In March 1939 another agreement was signed between all the local authorities of North West Surrey whereby, although their eight brigades remained separate, they would establish joint mutual protection against wartime emergencies. It was followed, in September 1939, by the compulsory amalgamation of all brigades under County control for the duration of the war. This was a prelude to the Fire Services Act of 1947, which made the arrangement permanent. The Woking Brigade therefore became part of Surrey County Fire-Brigade in 1947.

Chapter Twelve

THE PEOPLE AND THEIR WORK 1914-1939

The People

AS CHAPTER TEN SHOWED, the population growth between the wars was unevenly spread, because at different times the focus of building activity changed. A relatively detailed analysis is possible using the statistics for electoral wards, of which there were 11 in the post-1933 Urban District. Apart from the small changes, affecting Byfleet, Horsell North and Pyrford, which resulted from the 1933 reorganisation of local government the boundaries of wards were unaltered between 1908 and 1948, and a valuable continuity of data is thus assured. The tables below show these statistics:

Table 15. Population by Ward

	1911	*1921*	*1931*[a]	*1931*[b]	*1951*
Chertsey Road	4,649	4,747	4,312	–	4,149
Goldsworth	3,524	3,731	3,569	–	3,069
Knaphill & Brookwood	3,525	3,851	4,825	–	6,695
Maybury & Mt Hermon	3,081	3,252	3,565	–	4,199
St Johns	3,458	3,068	2,932	–	3,818
Sutton & Bridley	1,277	1,510	1,701	–	1,783
Woking Village & Mayford	2,268	2,879	4,860	–	7,900
Horsell North	600	641	658	822	1,462
Horsell South	2,246	2,744	3,509	–	5,396
Byfleet	2,960	4,173	4,819	4,511	7,365
Pyrford	979	1,179	1,401	1,394	1,760
Post-1933 U.D.	28,747	31,775	36,151	35,894	47,596

[a] Population in pre-1933 admin. area. [b] Population in post-1933 admin. area.

Table 16. Percentage Change in Population

	1911–21	*1921–31*	*1931–51*[a]	*1911–51*
Chertsey Road	2.12	–9.16	–3.78	–10.77
Goldsworth	5.87	–4.34	–14.01	–12.91
Knaphill & Brookwood	9.25	25.29	38.76	89.95
Maybury & Mt Hermon	5.55	9.63	17.78	36.29
St Johns	–11.28	–4.43	30.18	10.41
Sutton & Bridley	18.26	12.65	4.32	39.62
Woking Village & Mayford	26.94	68.81	62.55	248.32
Horsell North	6.83	2.65	77.86	143.67
Horsell South	11.45	27.88	53.78	140.25
Byfleet	40.98	15.48	63.27	148.82
Pyrford	20.43	18.83	26.26	79.78
Post-1933 U.D.	10.53	13.77	32.60	65.57

[a] Calculated on the basis of 1951 area.

The two inner wards, Chertsey Road and Goldsworth, which accounted for the bulk of the low-value, working-class development in the town, both reached their peak population immediately after the First World War, and thereafter experienced a gradual decline. Taken together they lost 15.5 per cent of their population between 1921 and 1951, and whereas in 1921, 27 per cent of the population of the town lived in these two wards, in 1951 this had fallen to 15 per cent. The decline continued, so that by 1971 the Central ward, which approximately coincided with the two former divisions, had only 5,770 inhabitants, and in the early 1980s this was estimated to have been further reduced, to about 4,500, or about half the number of 60 years before.

Such depopulation, which has been typical of inner areas in most major towns since the 1920s, is particularly interesting in Woking because the areas affected were less than 50 years old. Indeed the Walton Road district was still being developed only 20 years before its decline began. The sequence of growth, stagnation and decline was telescoped into three decades.

The loss of people may be attributed to a variety of factors, of which the most important was the gradual conversion of houses in and around the town centre to commercial and business uses. This had begun almost as soon as 'new Woking' started to grow, but it accelerated after the First World War. During the 1920s and 1930s much of Commercial Road, Church Street and West Street, and the inner ends of Maybury, Walton, Goldsworth and Guildford Roads, were taken over by non-residential uses, and their occupants moved to the suburbs of the town. In addition there was some clearance of substandard properties by the local authority or private owners, and the Council also demolished some houses for future town centre renewal. The increasingly unattractive and deteriorating environment of the two wards encouraged voluntary movement out of the centre, and some population was lost as overcrowded families were rehoused in the new peripheral council estates.

St Johns ward also experienced a substantial decline in population between the early years of this century and the late 1920s. The fluctuation in the number of military personnel and their families resident at Inkerman Barracks was responsible. During the First World War many servicemen moved out of the area on active service, and the military role of St Johns was reduced as the new camps were opened further west, in Pirbright, Blackdown and Deepcut. There was no decline in the civilian population, and after 1918 the ward was popular with house-builders. The increase in civilian population was sufficient to reverse the trend by the late 1920s, and in 1931–51, with a 30.18 per cent increase, St Johns was growing at a rate almost equivalent to that of the town as a whole.

Another inner ward, Maybury & Mount Hermon, grew quite slowly in the period between the wars, and seemed likely to stagnate and perhaps even decline. The area had already been built up by the First World War, and there was thus comparatively little land available for new development. Such housing as was constructed tended to be at a low density, just as before 1914, and there were fewer new residents than might otherwise have been the case. Low increase rates were also recorded in Sutton & Bridley ward, which had a small population and was still almost entirely rural. Until the mid-1930s it was unsewered, and so was not suitable for large-scale housing development. Large areas were also protected from building because of their character or ownership: Sutton Place estate, the golf course, the commonland and the flood-plains of the Wey and Hoe came into this category.

Horsell North ward resembled Sutton & Bridley until the end of the 1930s, and had an almost static population during the 1920s. It, too, had expanses of protected land, including Horsell Common, several prosperous nurseries, and the water-meadows of the Bourne valley. In 1933, however, Woodham was added to this ward. Development had already begun in that area, and continued apace until the outbreak of war. The result was a 77.86 per cent increase in population between 1931 and 1951, the fastest growth of any ward in the Urban District during that period.

Horsell South, Knaphill & Brookwood, Byfleet and Pyrford wards all shared in the process of suburban growth during the 1920s and 1930s, as the different parts of the district began to coalesce physically. The older core areas of Knaphill, Horsell and Byfleet were surrounded by extensive new estates, at higher densities than those in the more fashionable, higher parts of Woking. The most spectacular growth between the wars, however, was that experienced by Woking Village & Mayford ward, the most favoured district for higher-density speculative housing and also the location of the majority of Woking U.D.C. council estates. This ward received a substantial proportion of the population which moved from the town centre, and also attracted people from outside the Urban District on a large scale. In the period 1921–51 the population of the ward rose by no less than 174 per cent: after the early 1950s the supply of building land began to falter, and the imposition of Green Belt controls further reduced its potential. Growth rates then fell sharply, and by the mid-1960s the increase was negligible.[2]

Councillors and Officials

Parish vestries were usually composed of church worthies, local farmers and landowners, with a sprinkling of businessmen and traders. Since only ratepayers could vote or stand for election it was impossible for the working men who formed the majority of the population to have any direct voice in parish affairs. As a result of this limited range of people from which the vestry was drawn, it was often the case that a few powerful figures dominated local government.

In Woking, for example, the Ryde family of Poundfield House, Woking village, had great influence. Edward Ryde, whose diaries have been quoted in this book, was a member of the Vestry for nearly 30 years, exercised a strong influence over the School Board from 1874 until 1888, and chaired meetings on subjects ranging from the need for a gasworks to the widening of White Rose Lane, the flooding of the road across Broadmead to the establishment of a Local Board. As long ago as the 1850s he had been advising local people on the legal aspects of the Necropolis Company plans. He owned hundreds of acres in the vicinity of Woking village, and was a pillar of the church and the agricultural society until his death in 1892.[3]

His close friend, George Smallpeice of Kingfield House, was likewise a landowner and farmer, and latterly became involved in property development and house-building. In the words of his grand-daughter he was 'a true English yeoman',[4] but unlike his forebears in earlier centuries he was an active businessman, a director of the Woking

District Gas Company, the promoter of the Hockering estate and the owner of an estate agency in Station Approach. He served for many years on the parish Vestry and School Board, and his brother, Mark, was clerk to the Guildford Board of Guardians.

The new Local Board which took office in 1893, and its successor from 1895, Woking Urban District Council, were divided internally between the representatives of the old and new parts of the town, perpetuating the split, noted in Chapter Eight, within the School Board. In 1899 the members and ratepayers of the Woking Station & Maybury ward asked the Council to increase its representation. With six councillors it had about 30 per cent of the seats on Woking U.D.C., but contributed 53 per cent of the rate income and had 48 per cent of the population.

Its councillors claimed that 'we are often in a minority on matters affecting ourselves' and that 'we wish to secure what we are willing to pay for'. Members for Woking Village & Mayford ward felt that the exact opposite was true: 'To oblige Station Ward interests several of the outside wards were included in the drainage scheme . . . [this] was forced upon the ward against its will by outside members'. The County Council, aware that Horsell would be incorporated in the Urban District in the near future, decided to await that event and then re-ward the whole area.[5]

This split gradually healed as the urbanisation spread beyond the new town centre, but the contrast between the old and new remained. The Council was increasingly dominated by tradesmen and the owners of small businesses, whose interest contrasted with the more rural ones which had predominated in the vestries. The first and only Chairman of the Local Board was William Hill Corrie of Woking Village, after whom Corrie Road is named. He was killed in an accident, shortly after his retirement, in October 1895. Gustav Wermig, the owner of Egley Nurseries on Old Hill, was the first Chairman of the Urban District Council. Only in 1920 did it become usual to limit the term of office of the chairman; to one year in the 1920s, two years in the 1930s and back to one year after the Second World War.

In the first two decades of its existence the Council was composed, in about equal proportions, of tradesmen, farmers and 'gentry' or professional people. In 1899 the Woking & District Chamber of Trade was formed, and from its earliest days nominated 'trade' candidates for local elections, with considerable success.[6] Many were given a party label, 'Woking Tradesmen's Alliance'. This practice continued until 1923. Of the nine Chairmen in the period 1895–1914 two were farmers or landowners, five were tradesmen, one was an architect and surveyor and one a sanitary engineer. After 1918 there were fewer farmers and instead a sprinkling of active or retired military men appeared. Lieutenant-Colonels were chairmen in 1927–29 and 1934–36. The only member to serve two separate terms was Henry Quartermaine, garage owner, plumber, fire-brigade officer and entertainments entrepreneur, in 1925–26 and 1930–32.

In 1919 Lady Betty Balfour was elected for St Johns ward, to become the first woman member of Woking U.D.C. She resigned in 1923 and the same ward elected Miss Frances Ogle in her place. Thereafter there was always one woman, but never more, on the Council: Enid Lakerman in 1924–27, Dr. Joan Cave in 1927–31 and Miss M. Graves after 1931.[7]

During the 1920s the Council remained basically non-political, but in 1928 this was suddenly changed by the rise of a new group, the Woking Ratepayers Association. At the elections of March 1929 this put up candidates in several wards, and was startlingly successful, winning three seats and defeating sitting councillors in each, amongst them the Chairman, Albert Foord. The Association went on to win three casual vacancies in the following year, and another three at the elections of March 1930, to give it nine seats on a council of 22. Its aims were the reduction of council spending and opposition to expensive projects, but its influence began to wane after the reorganisation of local government in 1933.[8] The effect, though, was to hasten the politicisation of the Council, so that it became more overtly Conservative. After 1945 this process continued, with the election of Labour candidates in several wards and, remarkably, a Communist in Woking Village & Mayford.

Local Councillors in Byfleet and Pyrford

The Holroyd family, which at one time owned the mill, the brewery and a large area of farmland in Byfleet, dominated local politics in the late 19th and early 20th centuries. The parish was somewhat apathetic about local government in the 1890s, and was run by a vestry similar to that in Woking. Chertsey Rural Sanitary Authority held little interest for its Byfleet and Horsell members and, for example, Major Collis Bourne of Byfleet attended only one meeting of the Authority between August 1889 and May 1892. In contrast William Shears of Lees Farm, the member for Pyrford, was a faithful councillor and went to almost every meeting.[9]

In 1895 Chertsey Rural District Council was formed, and Byfleet elected George Barron Holroyd as one of its two councillors. He was also elected to the new Parish Council, and remained on both until 1919, the controlling influence on all political matters affecting the parish. In 1897 he succeeded Admiral H. F. Egerton as Chairman of Byfleet Parish Council, and held that position continuously for the next 22 years, for some of which time he also acted as Chairman of Chertsey R.D.C. His retirement in 1919 was marked by his colleagues with heartfelt regret, and must have seemed like the end of an era.[10] Whilst this lengthy tenure by a leading landowner might suggest a feudal or reactionary regime, Byfleet Parish Council was in fact a progressive body after the First World War, when it abandoned its reluctance to spend even the smallest sums and instead installed street-lighting, improved recreation facilities and was an active campaigner for better housing and sanitation.

In April 1922 Mrs. Ann B. Stevens was elected as its first woman member, and in September she was joined by Mrs. Ada Castleman. Mrs. Stevens was elected Vice-Chairman in April 1928, and hence in April 1929 she succeeded as Chairman of the Parish Council, the first woman to hold such an office in the Woking area. Since then, indeed, there have been only two others, Mrs. Rhoda McGaw, who was the only woman and only Labour councillor ever to be Chairman of Woking Urban District Council (1963–64), and Mrs. Margaret Gammon, Mayor of Woking in 1980–81.[11]

By 1928 Byfleet had three seats on Chertsey Rural District Council, and in March 1929 was awarded another. At that election one of the successful candidates was Henry S. Cawsey, who has achieved an unequalled record of long service in local government in Woking. With the exception of a short break in the early 1930s he has been a councillor, first on the Rural District Council and then on Woking Urban District Council and Borough Council for over 52 years at the time of writing.

Officials

The driving force behind the agitation to gain urban status in the 1880s and early 1890s was Robert Mossop, a solicitor of Goldsworth Road who also owned land in Kingfield and Woking village. He represented the Vestry and other pro-separation parties at the several inquiries held into the matter, and in doing so acquired an extensive knowledge of the operation of local government. Mossop was thus the obvious choice for Clerk to the Council, and he was appointed to this position by the Woking Local Board from 1 October 1893. In January 1895 he became Clerk to the Urban District Council, and held this post for almost 34 years. Although no roads were named after him or memorials erected in his honour he did more than any other individual to guide the town through its difficult formative period and into maturity. Councillors came and went, but Robert Mossop was always there to solve problems and offer advice.

His death in 1928 was, as might be expected, a great blow to the members and to his colleagues. The Council placed on record 'their deep appreciation of the service which [he] rendered to the town for so long a period; they will remember with gratitude the conspicuous ability with which he, as Chief Administrative Officer, conducted the business of the Council, his guidance, sound judgement and urbanity . . . '.[12]

As successor to Mossop the Council appointed Mr. Fountain, but his stay in Woking was short, and he resigned in the spring of 1931. In July F. H. Smith, the Town Clerk of Basingstoke, was appointed to the job. He, too, served the town well, holding the post for 22 years until 1953, through the difficulties of local government changes, the Second World War and the post-war social reforms. Michael Shawcross succeeded him as Clerk to the Council, and his term lasted until after the reform of local government in 1974, when he became Chief Executive of the Borough Council. In 1976 he was followed, on his retirement, by Rodney Dew. In its 90 years of separate urban government Woking has had only five chief officers, a tribute to their dedication and valuable service.

Shops and Traders

Traditionally the villages of Woking, Byfleet, Horsell and Knaphill had been served by a surprising variety of retailers and craftsmen, providing for purely local needs and often using locally produced materials. Woking village, with its semi-urban character and larger population, had a greater range. In 1840 Brayley noted 'two good inns, and several respectable shops',[13] although in the early 19th century 'the tradesmen's houses and shops were all of the smaller kind', according to Edward Ryde.[14] The village had a weekly market until the late 1830s, and the annual Whit Tuesday Fair was held until the 1870s at least.[15] The following table summarizes the retailing and craft trades of the area in 1851: it should be noted that the statistics refer to numbers employed, not to establishments.

Table 17. Retailing and Crafts in 1851[16]

	Byfleet	*Horsell*	*Pyrford*	*Woking Village*	*Knaphill*	*Rest of Woking*
Baker	2	3		5	2	1
Butcher	1	1		4	1	2
Corn-dealer	4			1	1	
Draper		1		2	1	
General storeman				2		2
Grocer	3	4	3	10	4	4
Hotel/Inn staff	3	4	1	5	3	5
Blacksmith	5	4	2	6	3	3
Bricklayer	5	1		4	1	2
Carpenter	7	7		9	3	4
Cordwainer[a]	3	1		6	3	1
Painter/Glazier		1		1		
Plumber				3		
Shoemaker		2		5	2	1
Tailor/ess	4	1		18	6	3
Wheelwright	3	1		6	2	1

[a] A cordwainer worked with leather.

Pyrford thus had the bare minimum of services: the grocer, who supplied a wide range of general goods, the blacksmith and the carpenter, with the publican providing essentials of a different kind. It is clear from the table that Woking village, including Shackleford and Kingfield, was the main 'shopping centre', serving Send and parts of Pyrford as well as its own parish. Knaphill, although not a large community, acted as the centre for Bisley, west Horsell and south Chobham, and so had a considerable range of services and shops.

The table excludes the many unusual or specialised trades which flourished when the competition from mass-production was not yet a threat. Thus there were five broom-makers in Byfleet, and saddlers in Woking village and Horsell. In Woking village, too, the census recorded a coach builder, two milliners, a pump-maker, a rope-spinner, a book-seller at the printing works, and a yeast-dealer. Carrot-merchants and vegetable hawkers were listed in 1871 at Maybury, and a whip-maker at Byfleet in 1851. In the same year an 'Oyster Dealer' was living in Kingfield, apparently an unusual occupation so far from the sea, but explained by the use of oyster-shells for liming the acid soils in the area.[17]

Altogether, in 1851, the craft and retail sectors employed 272 people in the four parishes, or about 10.5 per cent of the total workforce:

Table 18. Retailing and Crafts in the Workforce, 1851

	Byfleet		*Horsell*		*Pyrford*		*Woking*	
Crafts	34	9%	19	6%	3	1%	110	9%
Retailing	15	4%	13	4%	4	1%	74	6%
Total workforce	377	100%	307	100%	234	100%	1,191	100%

Development around Woking station after 1860 meant that the existing shopping facilities of the parish became quite inadequate. The Necropolis Company had failed to make any provision for shops when it laid out the street pattern and sold off the land, and shopping areas thus grew up without planning and haphazardly, a problem which has bedevilled the town ever since. The late 1860s saw the loss of the opportunity to create a worthy town centre.

The first business premises near the station, apart from the *Railway Hotel* of 1840 and the *Albion Hotel* of 1856–57, was the coal and timber yard owned by the licensee of the *Albion*, Reuben (or John) Percy. It dated from 1860, but as late as 1870 there were no other shops or businesses in the area. In that year, though, the *Surrey Advertiser* noted that:

> 'Mr. Wells, who has recently erected a pretty line of houses near the station [is] to convert them into shops . . . [he] has determined to meet the more pressing wants of the district, by erecting in the first place shops for the business of a butcher and a draper . . . At present railway employees and others have to go to Guildford for meat and other articles of consumption.'[18]

The conversion of newly erected houses into shops is an indication of the arbitrary and ill-conceived process by which the new town grew. These houses-cum-shops were a row along High Street, facing the railway between the *Albion Hotel* and what is now Chapel Street. In 1871 they were occupied, from the eastern end, by the Post Office, a grocer, a carpenter, a butcher, a draper and milliner, another carpenter and builder. The emphasis upon the construction trades, inevitable in a new town, where property development was booming, was repeated elsewhere. Providence Street (later Church Street), which was just being built-up, had two smiths, a carpenter and a joiner, and in Helen Street (West Street) there were a bricklayer, a gardener, two more smiths, two carpenters and a boot-maker.[19]

Elsewhere, by 1871, there had been some further diversification of crafts and trades. Woking parish had acquired two chemists, an egg-dealer, a poulterer, a hairdresser and a photographer, and amongst the trades represented were two farriers, a basket-maker, a stay-maker, an upholsterer and a well-digger. Horsell had an umbrella-maker, Byfleet a knitter and a whip-maker.

Gradually the centre of 'New' Woking achieved a dominant position. A sure sign of its rising importance was the move, in 1876, of Glosters the Corn-Merchants from the Market House, Woking Village, to new premises, grandly styled 'The Corn Exchange' in Chertsey Road. The firm described itself as 'unique in combining . . . the oldest business in the trade of Old Woking and the first in New Woking', a pardonable exaggeration. Henry Gloster, a prominent local Baptist, was County Councillor for Woking in the 1890s and Chairman of Woking U.D.C. in 1904–5. His move must have had a significant psychological impact amongst those who were still doubtful of the future of the growing town.[20]

By the end of the century the centre was thriving, with a wide variety of shops and businesses and a genuinely urban character. Many names well known in Woking today, or which survived until recently, had appeared by this time. Thus in the Directory of 1899 are listed, amongst others, Boormans the Carriage-Builders of Guildford Road: Tylers, wine-merchants of Chertsey Road; Albert Pocock, the tobacconist, of

Chertsey Road: Maxwell & Sons' music shop in Maybury Road or Broadway; James Gammon, draper, at the corner of Chobham Road and Commercial Road; and Dowsett & Mann Ltd., estate agents. Skeet's ironmongery business was founded in 1891 and in 1901 amalgamated with Mr. Jeffe's enterprise to produce one of the best known of all Woking traders, one which still flourishes today.[21]

At this stage the shopping area consisted almost entirely of small family businesses, and there were only three concerns owned by companies and not based in the area. All were in Chertsey Road: The International Tea Company; the Home & Colonial Stores; and Freeman, Hardy & Willis, 'bootmakers'. More typical was the store run by an individual, such as Mrs. A. Gunning of 3 The Pavement, Chertsey Road. She advertised 'art needlework of all kinds, fancy goods, plain & fancy stationery in the latest designs, well assorted stock of bibles, prayer books, toys in great variety'.[22] In the villages the old-fashioned, all-purpose shop still recalled an older lifestyle: William Lucas of Byfleet called himself 'grocer, draper & stationer; books and shoes in great variety; patent medicenes [*sic*] & garden seeds'.[23] Personal service of a different kind was offered by Charlotte Goodall, who in September 1888 was sentenced to three months' hard labour for keeping a brothel in Church Street, Woking.[24]

The shopping area in 'New' Woking was centred upon Chertsey Road, between the station and Walton Road. This was the only part where shops were purpose-built from the start, and this was because the east side was not developed until after 1885, when it became clear that commercial activities would do well. Chertsey Road had the few 'multiple stores' as well as Ashby's Bank, built in 1888 and with its head office in Staines, and the Capital & Counties Bank was on the other side of the *Albion Hotel* by the station. Chobham Road had acquired some shops, and was growing in importance, but High Street and Maybury Road (now Broadway) were limited in their potential because the railway-line occupied one side of the street, just as in some American frontier towns. Before 1914 Commercial Road and Church Street had almost no shops and only a few offices and businesses, although their future as residential areas was to be limited.

On the eve of the First World War this pattern had been reinforced, although High Street had grown somewhat in status and quality. More well known names had arrived. W. A. Elton, 'Bookseller; Librarian; Stationer and Printer' had opened at 42 Chertsey Road, Russells the jewellers were in the premises they still occupy, and Hugh Harris, men's outfitter, was on the corner of Chapel Street and High Street. Equally significant, though, was further evidence of the rise of the chain store. The three which had been opened in 1899 were now joined by Timothy White Co. Ltd. at 24 Chertsey Road and Liptons at 1 Chobham Road. Other evidence of change was the appearance of the Woking Autocar Company showrooms in Chertsey Road and its motor works near the canal. Change was coming to the villages, too. The International Tea Co. had opened branches at Knaphill and West Byfleet before the First World War, and the Woking, Horsell & District Co-operative Society was actively expanding its retail business.[25]

The Society was founded by local trade unionists in September 1899, and opened a shop and bakery at the junction of Percy Street and Church Street in 1902, where the RACS Department store is today. The venture was highly successful, and between then and 1920 the original shop was trebled in size and branches opened at Kingfield

(1910), Knaphill (1913), Horsell (1914), Maybury (1919) and Pirbright (1920). Trade turnover rose from £2,316 in 1900 to £175,020 in 1920, and the number of members from 168 to 3,700. In 1930 the Society decided to expand business still further, and in October 1935 it opened the first department store in the town. This was on the opposite side of Percy Street from the older shop, and was built in a very characteristic 1930s' style, with curving facade and flat roof, which Nairn calls 'Dudok Modern'.[26]

In 1939 Woking was still a town of small shops and small traders. The influence of the latter upon the political character of the Council had been strong, and in this way there had been comparatively little enthusiasm for development and expansion. Nevertheless the gradual decline of the small family business had started, as it had throughout the country, and 'national' names were becoming more evident. Sainsbury's had opened their shop at 19 Chertsey Road in 1920, to be followed by MacFisheries at No. 18 and Boots the Chemists at No. 54.

MacFisheries opened a branch in West Byfleet in 1923 and in 1925 John Farmer's shoe shop was added to the attractions of Chertsey Road. Boots were so successful in their competition with the old-style chemists that in 1924 they moved to larger premises at 19–21 Chertsey Road. Similarly Sainsbury's transferred to 20 High Street in 1934 and Timothy White's to 25 Chertsey Road in about 1931. Sainsbury's, too, regarded West Byfleet as an important centre, opening a small shop at Rosemount Parade in 1932. The infallible indicator of change and progress, that quintessence of modernity, Woolworth's 3d. and 6d. store, opened at 55–57 Chertsey Road in 1926 and ten years later was rebuilding and expanding.[27]

The inter-war period thus saw a gradual change in the old order, itself dating only from the 1880s. By 1939 many people regarded the town centre as outdated and inadequate. It was described in 1944 in disparaging terms: 'The shops are mostly small and badly arranged in mean streets'. What was suitable for a small country town of 20,000 people was not so for a fast-growing and increasingly sophisticated community of 40,000. In the early years of the century the shopping centre was small and traditional and the Council, composed in large part of traders and farmers, reflected this character and in turn, by its inactivity, helped to shape it.

The pervasive and universal influences of mass-marketing, car and bus travel, rail-commuting, the media, higher incomes and in-migration from London could not fail to produce change, and from the early 1920s this began to affect Woking. The town was less willing and less prepared to face this challenge than were its neighbours. It had no public car park until 1934, delayed central area improvements, and made no effort to attract nationally known department stores such as Marks & Spencer. Indeed it is popularly supposed that the latter was actively discouraged from opening in Woking in the mid-1930s, with results constantly lamented today. The result of all this is that Woking, although it has a population of more than 80,000, experiences severe competition from neighbouring and smaller towns such as Guildford, Staines and Camberley.

Entertainment

There were few facilities for organised entertainment in the area before the 1870s. Until then the limited hours of leisure were filled by the individual, or by the events which are described in great detail in every issue of the local newspapers: harvest suppers, smoking concerts, annual dinners, church fêtes and Sunday School picnics. Some societies and associations were founded earlier in the century, and from the 1850s at least there were regular parish days, such as the July fruit, vegetable and flower show at Horsell. The Woking Horticultural, Agricultural and Cottage Gardeners Association held an annual exhibition and produce show as early as 1869.[28]

Woking Football Club was founded in 1889, and in the 1890s moved to a permanent ground at Pembroke Road. The present Kingfield Sports Ground was opened in 1923. There was a pack of beagles at Horsell, and the Knaphill and Ripley Harriers were locally celebrated. Prize-fights were a popular entertainment in the area until the mid-19th century. They were held on Maybury Common, and the site of the 'ring' was said to be that of the present Sorting Office in White Rose Lane, whilst a cottage which used to stand in Heathside Park Road was claimed to have been an ale-house, frequented by the spectators and participants. The fights were outlawed in 1853.[29]

The Woking Public Hall Company was incorporated in 1894 and two years later opened a 700-seat building, with stage and meeting rooms, close to the junction of Percy Street and Commercial Road. Previously, private halls had been hired for public meetings and entertainments, as in November 1888 when 'a company of freed slaves rendered a service of sacred song at the Goldsworth Hall'.[30] The Public Hall later became the Grand Theatre.

In 1903 Henry Quartermaine, then a plumber and garage-owner of Chobham Road, opened the first cinema in Woking, at 54 Chertsey Road. He called it the *Central Halls Cinema*, and in 1919 handed over the management to Frederick Charles Iverson, the leading entertainment entrepreneur in the town for over 40 years. Iverson rebuilt the cinema, and in 1927 renamed it *The Plaza*: it later became the *Gaumont*. The *Palace Theatre*, a variety and music hall, had operated at the railway end of Duke Street since 1899, and had diversified into moving pictures in the early years of this century. It was not in a particularly salubrious part of town: Quartermaine recalled that the road was 'a mud track where mud oozed so thick that it covered the tops of boots and after heavy rain ducks swam in a large puddle there'.

In 1925 Iverson took over the *Palace* and sold it three years later to the London & Southern Super Cinemas Ltd., who demolished it and built in its stead the *Astoria*, a shining new cinema with all the facilities of the time. The *Astoria* was itself renamed, as the *Odeon*, when the company was absorbed into the Rank Organization, and in April 1975 it was closed. That left only one cinema in the town, the *ABC*, which as the *Ritz*, had been opened on the corner of Chobham Road and Church Street in 1938.[31]

Industry and Employment

Chapter Nine showed that the area remained almost unindustrialised at the end of the 19th century, and that the only major enterprise then in operation was the printing works of Messrs. Unwins by the river in Woking village. In the 1890s there was some limited industrial development as the central wards of Goldsworth and Chertsey Road were built up.

The Electric Accumulator Supply Co. was a harbinger of the future, for it was electricity which would allow Woking to develop as an important industrial centre after 1914, by providing cheap power in an area distant from traditional fuel sources, and by providing a demand for new products suitable for light industrial concerns. The Accumulator Company opened in a small workshop in North Road in about 1894, not long after the power station of the Electricity Supply Co. began operations nearby. There was a good deal of local opposition initially, because the works produced fumes and noise. In 1904, for example, the company was taken to court by the Urban District Council because it had 'polluted the Rive Ditch with acid and injurious chemicals'.[32]

In about 1910 the company, which had expanded its business substantially, vacated its North Road premises and moved south of the railway to Oriental Road, where it took over some of the land and buildings which until 1899 had been the Oriental Institute. In North Road, too, was the bottling plant and office of the Woking Mineral Water Company. In 1902, when the Council was required to register industrial premises under the terms of the Factories & Workshops Act of 1901, there were only five concerns large enough to come within the scope of the legislation: Unwins; the Accumulator works; the Woking & Maybury Electric Laundry; the gasworks and the electricity power station.[33]

The First World War proved to be a catalyst for industrial development in West Surrey. There had already been some small-scale manufacturing of vehicles, including cycles and motor cars. In 1916, for example, Godwin Bros. had a cycle-making workshop at 85 Chertsey Road, Woking, and S. F. Erskine produced them in Connaught Road, Brookwood. This expertise had been supplemented by the experience of car repair and testing at Brooklands, and by pioneer aviation work at the same place.[34]

It was thus natural that the need for aircraft should be met by this district. In 1910 H. P. Martin and G. H. Handasyde had built the first plane at Brooklands, as a private venture, and in 1914 they formed a company, Martinsyde Aircraft Ltd., which was to produce planes on a commercial basis. The directors urgently needed a weatherproof but spacious building for a factory, so they bought and converted the partially disused Oriental Institute, once the Royal Dramatic College, which had been used in part by Accumulators Ltd. The central hall of the building, broad and lofty, was an excellent makeshift factory, and in December 1914 or January 1915 the first aircraft was produced at the Maybury works.

Throughout the war the company fulfilled Government contracts for warplanes, manufacturing first the SE5 and then a variety of more advanced models. After the war business slumped, and in 1920 Handasyde left the partnership. The firm could not compete with larger enterprises which had modern and spacious premises, and in 1924 went into liquidation, its assets being sold to Aircraft Disposal Ltd. The Woking works were closed, and the old Oriental Institute was once more vacant, since the accumulator works had been closed at the end of the war.

A happier fate awaited the other local aircraft-building concern. The Italia Automobile Company had built a limited number of cars at the Brooklands Race Track until 1913, but since then the premises had lain empty. In 1915, however, Vickers, the armaments group, acquired the site for aircraft production, having been awarded a leading role in this sector of the war effort. The project was a success, and what had been a small plant 'in the idyllic Edwardian springtime of motor racing' was transformed within two years into a major industrial complex.[35]

In 1916 the Government decided to concentrate the production of the SE5a Fighter Scout at Brooklands, and extensions were made to the production line so that by the end of 1917 Weybridge accounted for 10 per cent of all British aircraft production. After the war Vickers chose to continue its interests in the aircraft industry, and to develop Weybridge in preference to the other factory at Crayford. In the 1930s a second phase of growth began, as rearmament ready for the Second World War involved a major expansion of the air force.

Although the aircraft works were, after 1933, in Walton & Weybridge Urban District, until that year they were partly in the parish of Byfleet. They employed many local people, and hence were of great economic significance for the area, bringing income, jobs and money to what had been a largely rural society. Inevitably this sudden industrialisation had dramatic consequences for Byfleet, changing its economy just as the construction of Brooklands had changed its landscape. In the decade to 1921 the population of the parish grew by 40 per cent, most of the increase being explained by the development of the aircraft factories.

In 1926 the Oriental Institute site was bought by James Walker Ltd., a firm founded in 1882 in London. From its original business of supplying ships in the London Docks it had moved into packing materials, helped by the boom in consumer goods which typified South East England in the 1920s. The Woking site was chosen because it offered space and pleasant surroundings, and was well-placed in geographical terms.

The old Institute was greatly altered, and much of it was pulled down over the next 30 years. Today the central hall and tower (minus spire) remain, as do part of the arcade and the chapel. The last now serves as the boardroom of the company, and still has stained glass depicting scenes from the plays of Shakespeare. James Walker Ltd. was the largest industrial employer in Woking by 1939, when it had about 400 workers, and by 1955 had expanded rapidly, to a workforce of 1,700 people or 8 per cent of the total employment in the town. Its importance has been maintained and the factory is still a vital part of Woking's employment structure.[36]

In 1920 the Maybury Laundry at 123–124 Maybury Road closed and the premises became vacant. They were taken over by a small and recently formed concern, the Sorbo Rubber Sponge Products Ltd., which was trying to manufacture a product which it had only just patented, and which seemed to have a great potential. Foam rubber was the name eventually adopted for the new invention, and the Sorbo Company quickly found that its product fulfilled all their expectations. The Company also produced other forms of rubber substitute, and amongst these was a particularly bouncy variety which was made into 'india-rubber' balls; for a time these were known as Sorbo balls.

In 1922, having outgrown its Maybury Road premises, the Company moved to a large new factory at the end of Arnold Road, although it kept the old building for offices. Unfortunately for the finances of Woking Urban District Council the new works were just across the border in Chertsey Urban District, which then included Woodham and Sheerwater. This meant that although the only access to the factory was via Woking roads, and although most of the employees lived in Woking, all the rates paid by the Company went to Chertsey. On several occasions in the 1920s Woking U.D.C. suggested that the boundary should be altered to bring the Sorbo Works into its area, but not until the general reforms of 1933 did this take place.[37]

By 1939, therefore, Woking and Byfleet had acquired several important industries which had helped to diversify their employment structure, and provided jobs for lower- and middle-income groups to complement the exclusive and fashionable residential districts, where commuting to the city was customary. In 1944 it was stated that 'in Woking are manufactured rubber products, wire nails, accumulators, wireless products and aeroplane equipment, and there are packing specialists, printers and timber stores', whilst Byfleet was 'associated with the Brooklands aero-engineering works'.[38]

The area had thus shared in a national phenomenon of the 1920s and 1930s whereby new industries, often connected with the fast-growing electrical and wireless markets or with recently invented or developed consumer products, were located in the South East and Midlands instead of the older, heavy industrial regions of the North and West. The attractions of the South East were many, and Woking had its full share; higher incomes and thus more demand for consumer goods; better communications and access; a pleasant landscape free of the dirt and deterioration associated with the coalfields; plenty of labour, including female workers; and proximity to London with its role as a cultural, social and financial centre.

Railways and Commuting

The London and South Western Railway remained unchallenged in Woking, enjoying a virtual monopoly of traffic from London to West Surrey. In 1903 Woking U.D.C. expressed support for a petition to be presented to Parliament in favour of the Bristol, London & Southern Counties Railway, a scheme to break the monopoly of the L.S.W.R. and the G.W.R., but the plan was rejected. The reign of the L.S.W.R. continued uninterrupted.[39]

In the early 1900s the Company began to experience competition for its suburban traffic from the electric tramways, and so plans were put forward for the conversion to electric traction of some of the intensively used lines out of Waterloo. The first electrification was inaugurated in 1915, and after the war it was continued by the successor of the L.S.W.R., the Southern Railway, formed in 1923. The line to Guildford via Cobham was electrified in 1925, and in 1933 the Brighton line was the first main route in the world to be electrified. The experiments were a great success, and the S.R. decided to extend electrification to embrace most of the routes in Kent, Surrey and Sussex.

At the same time, to increase the potential for rail travel, the Company opened a large number of new stations in rapidly growing suburban and dormitory areas. One of these was at Oyster Lane, Byfleet. A station between Weybridge and Byfleet had often been suggested by local people, particularly after the opening of the Brooklands race-track in 1906. In November 1922 Byfleet Parish Council made a formal request to the Company that it should provide a station or halt, and in August 1926 plans were announced. The new station, which had a simple design and concrete platforms, was opened on 10 July 1927. Its name caused much confusion. Chertsey R.D.C. wanted it to be called either 'Oyster Lane' or 'New Haw', whilst Byfleet P.C. preferred 'Byfleet', with the existing Byfleet station being renamed 'West Byfleet'. For reasons which were completely obscure the Southern Railway preferred West Weybridge, the name which the station was eventually given, despite its geographical absurdity and lack of local support.[40]

In 1933 the S.R. started the preliminary work on electrification to Alton and Portsmouth via Woking. Since this was in the middle of the Great Depression the Government announced, in November 1935, that it would give grants to the Company to finance the work, as a means of reducing unemployment. The Chairman, R. Holland-Martin, told shareholders in February 1936 that the money would be used to speed up the Portsmouth electrification work.

The work was undertaken very quickly, and the first trial runs from Surbiton to Woking were made in November 1936. A few public services from Waterloo to Guildford and Farnham via Woking were electrically operated from 3 January 1937, and to Portsmouth from 11 April. The full public electric services through Woking to Alton and Portsmouth were inaugurated on 4 July 1937. In place of the slow and comparatively infrequent steam trains there was now a fast, frequent and regular service of electric trains, which transformed railway access to Woking. Already good, it became excellent.[41]

The work had involved the complete reconstruction of Woking station, which dated from the widening of the line in the 1880s. The new design was in a very typical 1930s' style, with flat roof and curving walls, and a tiled entrance concourse. It has been described as 'the Southern Railway's best "Odeon" style', although another writer has called the station 'handsome and spacious'. There were four through platforms, each 820 feet long, and bay platforms at each side for local and parcels services.[42]

The station was built of red brick and white concrete. Unfortunately the latter has worn and weathered badly, and is now a most unappealing drab yellow with grey streaks, giving the entire station a dirty and dreary appearance. If, however, it is compared with the unrebuilt Guildford station it can be seen that the older station would now be much worse. There are plans to redevelop Woking station to make use of the valuable airspace above. This would involve a high-level concourse with office tower, and improved parking and access.

The electrification of the line through Woking immediately made the town attractive to commuters. It had always had a small number of workers employed in London, but these tended to be of the 'city-gentleman' type, who did not need to arrive early and could afford the expense of daily train travel. Electrification, and the rapid fall in the real cost of travel during the 1930s, made it possible for others to use the train for regular commuting, and by 1939 it was reported that over 2,300 people commuted from Woking U.D. to London every day, or about 8 per cent of the workforce.[43]

Chapter Thirteen

WOKING SINCE 1939

THIS CHAPTER REVIEWS major changes which have taken place in Woking since the start of the Second World War, a period of more than 40 years during which the population of the town has doubled, and the area has undergone important physical, social and economic alteration. So great are these changes that a full account is impossible: this must await a second volume!

The 1939–45 War

Despite its proximity to London and importance as a railway centre Woking emerged from the war comparatively unscathed. The Council was told in September 1944 that in the preceding four years there had been 58 air raids on the town, in which 434 bombs had been dropped as well as many incendiary devices. 2,844 properties had suffered damage, and of these about two dozen had been destroyed. It was stated that two residents had been killed and 52 injured, but this was erroneous, since in January 1941 seven fatalities resulted from raids on Woking. In addition 13 Woking people were killed in a serious attack on the Vickers aircraft works at Brooklands, in September 1940.[1]

Woking was a reception area for evacuees, and during the autumn of 1939 and the first half of 1940 there were several influxes of people from dangerous areas. In July 1940, for example, children were taken to Woking from south coast towns after heavy bombing. The Council spent much time on the trivia of war administration, and constant efforts were made to adapt to the needs of war. In June 1940 Councillor Derisley of Byfleet asked that 'clippings from the road verges should be made into winter cattle food',[2] and in the next month the town adopted a salvage scheme for the collection of bones, tins, bottles and metal from refuse, 'including the use of scouts to clear scrap iron from the commons'.[3] A Spitfire Fund was started in August, and in September it was resolved that 'Messrs. Spantons, timber merchants, be asked to remove the name "Woking" from their vans'.[4]

Rather belatedly the Air Raid Precautions Committee built public shelters in central places: in October 1940, when the raids were at their height, a total of 200 new places were authorised in five public shelters, to be sited at Plough Corner, Oyster Lane, West Byfleet and Kingfield, and a 100-person shelter on Wheatsheaf Common. Council meetings were themselves affected: 'there is a need to reorganise [them] in view of the frequency of air raids and approach of winter'.[5]

Overspill

After the war ended there was little physical damage to be repaired, and Woking was thus in a position to receive some overspill from the London area, as part of the planned decentralisation of population from the capital. In 1944 the 'Greater London Plan' selected the town for expansion because it had excellent communications and plenty of land for new building. It suggested that about 3,250 people should be housed in the district, about 2,000 of them in Byfleet and Pyrford, to given an eventual size of about 46,000.[6] This compared with the estimated 1941 civilian population of 42,000.

The target figure was already exceeded by 1947, and Woking U.D.C. had by that time expressed a desire to see an ultimate population of 75,000, to be reached in the early 1960s. In 1947 the Minister of Housing & Local Government decided that the growth of the town should cease at about 60,000.[7] The increase in population as a result of overspill would be accompanied by the reception of decentralised London business firms which might use the sites of larger houses then becoming obsolete.[8]

The first, and in the event the last, phase of overspill arrived in 1951–54 as part of the London County Council 'out-county estate' programme, designed to overcome the acute shortage of housing and land within the city itself. In 1948 the L.C.C. chose the Sheerwater Valley as the site for one of these estates, attracted by the excellent rail links with London, the cheapness of the land and the employment potential. After vehement opposition from Surrey and Woking Councils, the latter because it had tentatively earmarked part of the land for its own housing, the Government authorised the L.C.C. to purchase the entire 230-acre site lying between the railway and the canal.

Construction work began in November 1948, but the first house was not ready for occupation until September 1951, because the site preparation was unusually complex and costly. Formidable physical problems were posed, since the area had been a lake until the 1820s and was still waterlogged, and so comprehensive sewerage and flood-water drainage systems, with pumping stations, were needed. The Rive Ditch was diverted and culverted for 2½ miles, and pumping systems were installed.

Sheerwater estate originally had 1,279 dwellings, with 272 flats near the centre and terraced and semi-detached housing comprising most of the remainder. It was intended as a 'neighbourhood unit., with a careful and integrated design which would allow a sense of community to develop; to a considerable extent this aim was realised. The estate was provided with a district shopping centre, churches, public houses and sports and social facilities, together with three schools and a 30-acre industrial complex.[9]

In visual terms, the estate was a considerable success, particularly since it was built at a time of austerity. Although Nairn dismissed it as 'a poor effort, with interminable vistas of cottage units and most of the original trees grubbed up',[10] another writer has noted the 'sylvan setting and scrupulous landscaping, and a worthy architectural effort has resulted in a successful blend of natural and built environments'.[11]

The initial population reached a peak of about 5,500 in the early 1960s, and then began to decline as the first generation of young people moved away. Today it has about 4,300 inhabitants. At first there were many problems in integrating Sheerwater with the existing town, and mistrust and dissatisfaction from both sides. This has gradually diminished, and the old idea of Sheerwater as 'London transplanted' is hardly prevalent now, 30 years on. In April 1980 the management and ownership of the estate were transferred to Woking Council, albeit against the wishes of many residents, as part of the G.L.C. policy of divesting itself of its housing role.

Sheerwater had a profound impact upon the development of Woking, which in the years immediately after the war still had the atmosphere of a sleepy and conservative country town. The influx of 5,000 new residents in just three years helped to end this, and encouraged the replanning and modernisation of the outdated infrastructure of the town. With its strongly Labour politics Sheerwater contributed to the process whereby the composition of the Council altered, producing a small but vocal Labour opposition group, and what might be seen as a 'liberal' Conservative majority, replacing the tradesmen's alliances of the decades before the war.

Physically, too, Sheerwater was important, for it filled one of the few remaining open spaces between the Woking–Horsell and West Byfleet–Pyrford areas, and thus allowed the coalescence of the two parts of the Urban District to become a reality. Its industrial estate provided a model for others in the district, and was a vital part of the diversification of the economic structure of Woking. Lord King, when he drained Sheer Water and planted it with pines in the 1820s, could scarcely have imagined that the eventual consequences of his work would be so significant.

The Green Belt

Before 1939 there had been attempts, only partially successful, to restrain the outward sprawl of London by imposing a 'green belt' where development would be controlled. The 'Greater London Plan' of 1944 placed great emphasis upon the need for such a device, and in 1953 Surrey County Council made it a fundamental principle of the new 'County Development Plan'. This document was given statutory effect by the M.H.L.G. in 1958. Within Woking Urban District it involved the designation as Green Belt of much of the undeveloped land east of Carthouse Lane (Horsell) and the Old Woking Road. The edge of the built-up area was followed closely in the north, along Shores Road and Woodham Lane, but more loosely to the south where land was left for building in Pyrford and Byfleet.[12]

The County Council later submitted plans for the extension of the Green Belt to cover the open land west of this line. Woking and Guildford Councils, which believed that this would create a shortage of housing and would prevent them from acquiring new land for their own building, pressed for the exclusion of their areas. In 1960, after a public inquiry, the County Council conceded the case for a less stringent approach, and the undeveloped land in the western part of Woking was excluded from the statutory Green Belt, although subject to most of the controls applied elsewhere. That meant that in certain circumstances a relaxation of the ban on development would be permitted, so that new building could take place.[13] In 1980 the Secretary of State amended the proposals in the draft Surrey Structure Plan, and brought the outer edge of the Green Belt rather nearer to London than the County Council had wished. Under the decision the line now runs from Windlesham to Tongham, via

Knaphill and Worplesdon. Almost all the undeveloped land in the west of Woking is thus now subject to tight controls, but in the period from 1960 to 1980 building was possible at, for example, Goldsworth Park and Stanley Farm, Knaphill, which would otherwise have been included in the original Green Belt.[14]

The Green Belt has been instrumental in preserving from development the rural and semi-rural parts of the Borough. Had it not been imposed it is safe to say that lower-density housing would have covered the land between Mayford, Westfield and Sutton Green; the fields around Pyrford Green and Church; and large areas between Knaphill, Horsell and Chobham. In consequence the land within the town itself has increased greatly in price, although many other factors have contributed to this process. More recently, as agriculture has continued to decline, and farmland has fallen into dereliction, there has been a growing interest in the Green Belt as an area for new recreational uses.

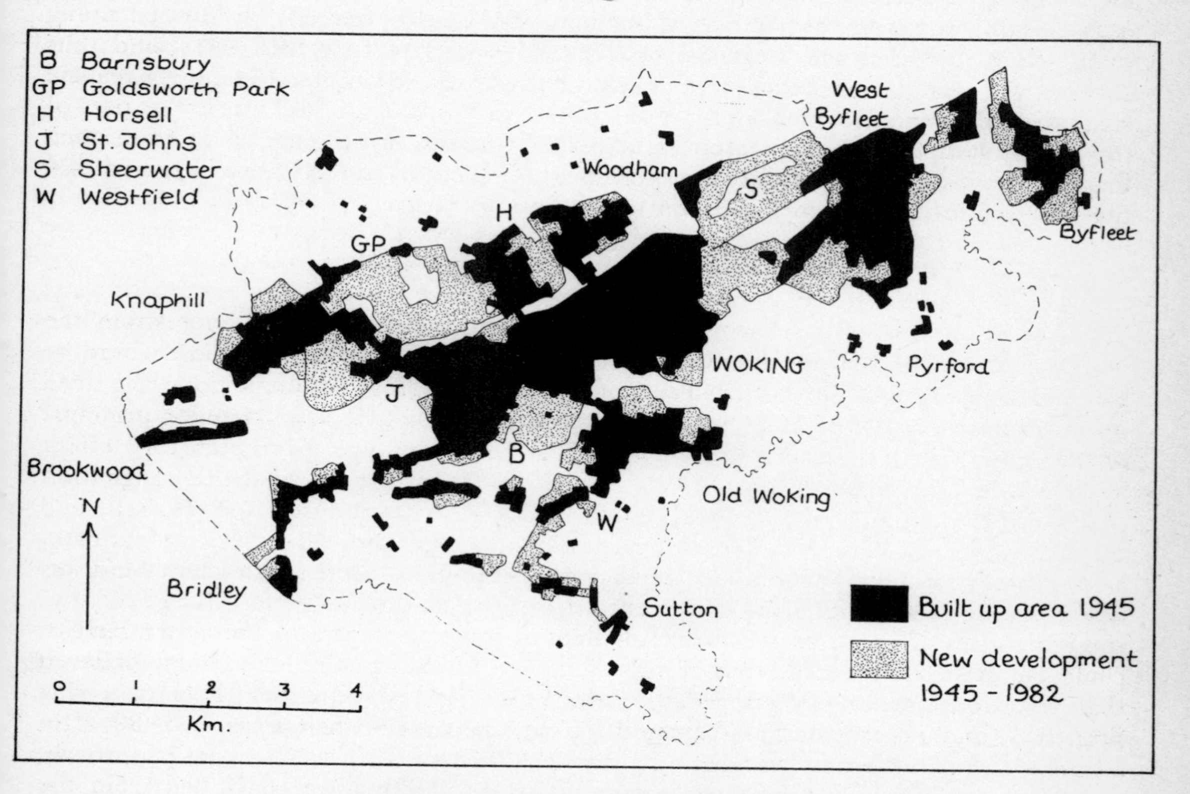

Fig. 27. The Growth of Woking 1945–1982

Council Housing

In marked contrast to its policy before 1939, Woking Council followed a more vigorous house-building policy between 1945 and 1975. In the first decade after the war the rate of completion was over four times the pre-war average, and up to 1956 a total of 1,688 houses were built, as well as 101 prefabs. The next ten years saw a fall in output, with 469 new houses completed, but the development of schemes such as Bullbeggars in the late 1960s led to a revival, and 1,152 dwellings were completed in 1968–76: over the three decades since the war, therefore, 3,309 council homes were built in Woking.

In the first ten years use was made of derelict or deteriorating farmland on the edge of the town, to provide sites for the larger estates at Maybury, Barnsbury, Elmbridge, and St Mary's (Byfleet). They were of a standard design, with curving roads, predominantly semi-detached or terraced houses, and austere landscaping, but they have lasted well and are today the most popular Woking B.C. estates. From 1955–67 there was a frustrating period when land shortages prevented the implementation of housing programmes, and no fewer than 37 sites were considered in just four years. Of them, 19 were rejected and the building on the remainder was almost impossible, because the Government restricted the money available for this purpose. Despite deputations and constant protests, that situation continued until 1961, when the Housing Committee decided to buy enough land in a single site to allow for a large and sustained programme of building.

From 1965, therefore, a second phase of ambitious housing programmes was implemented. The largest project was Bullbeggars (now renamed Lakeview), with 520 dwellings, mostly flats and maisonettes. It was built in 1970–75, and immediately acquired a bad reputation: the renaming was intended to improve its image, but the type of housing is regarded with less favour than the more traditional styles of the other estates, and it remains relatively unpopular. It was followed by the purchase of 24 acres of the disused Inkerman Barracks, St Johns, in 1974: here 275 council homes have been built, as well as 165 by housing trusts. Finally, amongst the larger schemes, the Borough Council has been building about 600 dwellings on the Goldsworth Park development, many of them being low-cost, shared ownership and starter-home projects.[15]

Central Area Redevelopment

A priority of the Council after 1945 was the renewal of the outworn and inadequate centre of Woking. Plans had been put forward at intervals from the 1920s, but the reluctance of the conservative councillors to invest large sums of money on public projects, and their fears of jeopardising their own futures as small traders, had meant that little was accomplished. In the late 1930s limited purchase of town centre properties had taken place, and demolition of some houses in Commercial Road, in advance of road-widening, was carried out in 1937–38.

The Engineer and Surveyor prepared a more detailed plan in 1948, but there was uncertainty as to the likely location of civic offices, and eventually it was decided that the first step was to build a new town hall on the Guildford Road land. The rebuilding of the centre was therefore postponed, although most of the land between the Basingstoke Canal and Commercial Road was zoned for commercial uses, and the Council began to acquire properties in the area. In February 1960 another outline design was approved, establishing three principles which remained at the heart of all subsequent work: the reorganisation of the traffic system; the improvement of the environment and visual quality of the centre; and the major expansion of shopping and office facilities.

In September 1960 the first important part of the redevelopment was approved, and work on this began in the spring of 1962. It involved the construction of a complex of shops, offices and a public house on the site of the *Albion Hotel*, in a prime site opposite the railway station. Shortly after work started, the Council produced a detailed plan for the whole area, and it was about to be approved when the Government instructed local authorities to revise all such schemes in the light of the highly influential report, *Traffic in Towns*, which had recently appeared.

The report confirmed the principle, already espoused by a number of authorities including Woking, that traffic should be segregated as far as possible from pedestrian movement, for safety and environmental reasons as well as for greater efficiency. In December 1965 Woking Council approved a modified scheme incorporating some of these new ideas, and it was this plan which was eventually adopted.[16]

Demolition began in earnest in 1968. About 150 people were displaced, although several hundred others had left in the previous 30 years, either voluntarily or with council assistance and by the late 1960s the only significant areas of residential property still occupied were Clarence Avenue, West Street and parts of Church Street. In 1970 the Council came to an agreement with the Norwich Union Insurance Group for a joint funding and ownership plan, a practice common in this field but not used in Woking before then.

Building work began in the spring of 1971, and has continued for more than a decade, partly because of the vicissitudes of local government finance and partly because many of the associated projects are being undertaken by private concerns. The key to the plan was the dual carriageway relief road, Victoria Way, which takes all through and most local traffic around the north and west perimeter of the town centre. It was opened in 1973, and was the first stretch of four-lane road in the Borough.

The replanned central area is based upon a partly covered and fully pedestrianised eight-acre shopping precinct, linked to Town Square, which has the Central Library, Christ Church and civic buildings and thus forms the focal point which was denied the town on several occasions in the 19th century. Other facilities provided include a new market, several multi-storey car parks, indoor heated swimming-pool, fire station and, in the future, police headquarters and courthouse. Above the precinct are flats and an 18-storey office block, the tallest building in Woking and a landmark visible for many miles in each direction.

Around the core of the new shopping centre and civic area, redevelopment has affected Chertsey Road, Chobham Road and Church Street, and also Goldsworth Road to the west. The town has in recent years become an important office centre because of its excellent rail, road and air links and its pleasant environment, and among the firms moving to Woking have been British American Tobacco, Cornhill and Crown Life Insurance and the British Yachting Association. Office blocks, notably the 18-storey BAT block, the black glass Crown Life House, and the assortment of lower, red brick buildings along Victoria Way and Goldsworth Road, are thus a new but increasingly noticeable feature of the townscape of Woking.

Shopping facilities have been greatly improved and although there are still some deficiencies, the status and catchment area are much increased. It can never hope to equal Guildford, only seven miles away and with several centuries' start, but the town has benefited considerably in recent years from the expansion of the centre. There has been much criticism, some of it justified, of the apparent loss of small shops as a result of renewal, but that is a phenomenon far from unique to Woking. The precinct was built on land which had no existing shops of significance, so its construction was not directly responsible, and it is possible to argue that, by bringing increased trade to the town, it has helped in the revival of Chertsey Road, seen in the late 1970s. More serious is the continuing loss of shops to non-retail uses, and in particular their conversion to banks, building societies and insurance offices and estate agencies. In recent years this process has almost eliminated retailing from the southern side of Commercial Way, and the Council has no means of controlling what seems to be a disturbing change in the land use of the central area.

The shopping facilities are now based upon two large food stores, Sainsbury's and International, with major branches of Boots and Fine Fare; two department stores have also opened, the RACS and British Home Stores. Perhaps the most obvious absence is that of Marks & Spencer, for which the short-sighted Council of the 1930s must bear some of the blame. Pleas for a store have regularly been rejected, although at the time of writing it was rumoured that the idea is being reconsidered. In 1973 the shopping space of central Woking totalled 67,000 ft^2; following the redevelopment and enlargement this had been increased, in 1981, to 125,000 ft^2.

West Byfleet shopping centre is the second in the Borough, serving the Byfleets, Pyrford and some districts beyond the Borough boundary. In the late 1950s it was possibly even more inadequate than that of Woking, and urgently needed revitalising. Clearance of some larger houses on Old Woking and Station Approach began before the war, and in 1959 the Council agreed to extensive redevelopment. Unfortunately it has taken place in a piecemeal fashion, and so although there has been a substantial upgrading of the facilities offered, the centre still has an incoherent plan. A branch library was built in 1963, with an office and shop complex, but although there have been other new shops and a marked influx of more sophisticated smaller businesses, the shopping area continues to be divided in two by an ugly stretch of car parks.

Mount Hermon

As land and property prices increased during the late 1950s, the large and underused grounds of the expensive Victorian and Edwardian houses near Woking and West Byfleet stations became the target for redevelopers. The buildings were falling into disrepair, and had been subject to pressure for conversion to non-residential uses, including doctors' surgeries and offices for small firms.

In 1958 the first serious proposals were made for the complete redevelopment of properties along Guildford Road, Woking, and in January 1959 the Council gave outline approval for a scheme of 68 flats to replace three houses north of Hillview Road. The scheme contravened the density zonings laid down in the 1953 County Development Plan, and so in April 1962 the County Council, after an inquiry, approved the rezoning of the land south of the station. The Mount Hermon High Density Area, as this was known, embraced 70 acres between White Rose Lane, Woking Park, Brooklyn Road and Heathside Road.

In 1966 it was extended by a further amendment to the 1953 Plan, to include the entire area between the railway line, Wych Hill Lane, and Guildford Road. That brought the total area in which redevelopment was actively to be encouraged to 125 acres. Flats, maisonettes and terraced housing were preferred, with a maximum height of ten storeys. Beyond the high-density zone 'more low density areas should be preserved [and] where an area has a special character of quietness and pleasantness, and is away from any centre of activity, the density of redevelopment should be consistent with that of the surrounding area'. A smaller but similar zone was later designated in West Byfleet, to cover the land between Old Woking Road, Sheerwater Road and the railway station. The intention of the policy is thus to protect the adjacent low-density areas, such as The Hockering and Coldharbour, from the pressures of renewal, whilst at the same time making better use of the land near the railway stations and shopping areas.

The high-density zones have been rebuilt in stages since the early 1960s, with all the work being undertaken by private builders or housing associations: the Council has made no attempt to include municipal housing schemes in these areas. There are several types of design: in the first few years the 'Span' concept popularised by Eric Lyons was much favoured, with long low blocks of flats and maisonettes around landscaped courts and lawns. In the latter years there has been a proliferation of short rows of terraced houses, always called 'town houses', with open fronts and enclosed rear spaces. The maximum height reached was in the ten-storey Craigmore Tower, in Constitution Hill, Woking. This is the tallest residential building in the Borough, and since it is a luxury block is far removed from the conventional idea of high-rise living.[17]

Goldsworth Park

The 1953 Plan, intended to operate until the mid-1970s, envisaged an eventual population in Woking U.D. of about 67,000, but the 1961 Census showed that the figure had already been exceeded. When the Plan was revised in 1965, therefore, the target population figure was drastically amended, to an anticipated 97,000 by 1981. The increase, of 30,000 people or 45 per cent in 15 years, was to be achieved in part by natural growth but also by extensive in-movement of population, particularly from London. Three very large new housing schemes were proposed to accommodate the growth: the Mount Hermon and West Byfleet high-density redevelopments, the West Byfleet Golf Course (a scheme first delayed and then abandoned), and what was known then as Slococks. This last was for the building of a 'mini-town' on the 650 acres of low-lying and damp nurserylands between Horsell and Knaphill, owned by the Slocock family.

In February 1967 a Master Plan was produced, and it was decided that the Land Commission should purchase the site, undertake the difficult and costly task of draining and servicing, and then re-sell it to the interested development firms and other agencies. Authorisation was imminently expected when the Commission was abolished by the newly elected Conservative Government in June 1970. New Ideal Homes Ltd., one of the largest housing firms in Britain, then agreed a partnership with Woking Council, so that the huge site could be developed in an orderly and comprehensive manner, avoiding the danger of fragmentation and piecemeal growth. A revised plan was produced and, after a public inquiry, was approved by the Government in June 1973. The project was christened Goldsworth Park, and work began in October 1973.

The development of Goldsworth Park was expected to take at least a decade, and the whole scheme was conceived on a grand scale. It involved about 4,500 homes, the exact figure being determined by detailed applications, and would have a population of about 15,000. This meant that the eventual size would be equivalent to that of a town such as Haslemere or Alton. It was essential, therefore, that the area should be given adequate facilities.

Goldsworth Park is based upon a square of major roads, of which one, Littlewick Road, existed before; the remainder were purpose-built. They form part of a wider scheme of improved road-links to and within the Borough of Woking, and act as primary routes for the development. Within them a series of distributor roads, in loops, takes local traffic around and through the district, and off these lead the estate roads with houses. There is a large and segregated footpath network, to separate pedestrians and vehicles.

In the middle is a 17-acre lake, required as a balancing reservoir for drainage but serving a vital landscape and recreational function. To the north of this 42 acres have been reserved for sports facilities, including a golf course, and open space, whilst to the south is the district centre, with shops, swimming-pool, library and social facilities. In the north-west 25 acres have been developed as an industrial estate and along the Basingstoke Canal, which crosses the southern part, a linear park and recreation area is being laid out.

The housing was intended to be arranged in closes and small groups, with a wide variety of designs, sizes and layouts to avoid the monotony which might otherwise have been a problem. To a considerable extent this has been effective, although it is inevitable that there is some similarity because all the housing is of the same vintage and the landscaping has not yet matured.

Goldsworth Park is claimed by its developers to be the largest single private-enterprise housing project ever undertaken in Britain, and it is by far the largest in the history of Woking. The growth of the town was slow by comparison, for it took 30 years for Woking to reach the size that Goldsworth Park will attain in a decade. In consequence the impact of the new development will be unequalled. Of the 1991 population of the town, perhaps 88,000, some 15 per cent, will live at Goldsworth Park, a major reversal of the trend, noted in recent decades, for the east and centre of the town to be the fastest growing. The traffic congestion, increased rateable value, altered political complexion and environmental changes which are, or will be, the result of the development of Goldsworth Park, cannot fail to have important implications for the future of the entire Borough.[18]

Conservation and Recreation

Until the late 1960s Woking had a philistine attitude towards its historic and landscape heritage, which, although not outstanding, was not without considerable merit and interest. There seemed to be an enthusiasm for the removal of all traces of the past, and a neglect of the rural landscape which surrounds the town. Today there is still neither a museum nor a true civic society.

Many older buildings were demolished in the 1950s and 1960s to make way for road improvements, or new housing schemes. Others were cleared on the grounds that they were unfit for habitation, a claim which was often of very doubtful validity. At one time it seemed that most of Old Woking village would disappear: a large number of timber-framed cottages between Kingfield and the village were demolished before the war, and after it the process continued. In the 1950s the road junction at Send Corner was widened, and the adjacent cottages pulled down, tearing the heart out of the old winding street. As late as 1973 it was being suggested that the High Street should be widened and straightened, despite plans for a bypass: after such a drastic step there would have been no village left to bypass![19]

Horsell village, too, has lost many of its older buildings, although here the post-1930 housing has been rather less intrusive. The greatest losses were in Byfleet, where a succession of unfortunate or inappropriate developments, starting in 1906 with the construction of the race-track, ravaged the old and hitherto unspoiled village, to produce the shattered appearance of which Nairn writes.[20] Only Pyrford, more remote and under less pressure, has been spared the destruction.

Other towns were as culpable as Woking. Guildford, for example, had buildings and a streetscape of the highest quality, but since the 1930s has been damaged repeatedly by new roads, ugly car parks and intrusive modern shopping development. But Woking, which had comparatively few pre-1850 buildings, deserved better treatment than it received. Its old buildings had, and have, great charm and appeal, and whilst the architectural heritage of the town is small if compared to that of Guildford, that is not an excuse for wholesale demolition. Logically the older buildings, simply because they are not common in Woking, should be given particular attention, not forgotten and ill-treated.

By the mid-1960s there was evidence of a changing attitude in the area, and more concern was expressed for the surviving examples of 'old' Woking. The 1968 Town & Country Planning Act allowed local authorities to designate conservation areas, and since 1974 Woking Borough Council has declared three. They are at Old Woking (1975), Pyrford (1976) and Horsell (1978), and all embrace the old church with the surrounding buildings and short sections of street.[21] The earliest has since experienced some improvement. A careful restoration of the derelict cottages which were said to have been the old Market House of 1665 was accompanied by a not unsuccessful infill scheme, with small flats in a building which blends in with the line of the street. The threat of widening and straightening has been lifted from the village street, and Send Corner, although unrecognisable as the delightful spot shown in early views (*see* Plate III), has at least been tidied.

Yet despite this progress, which by the standards of many other towns is scarcely remarkable, the local authority has allowed a housing scheme, Riverside Gardens, opposite the historic Manor House, built to a design of lamentable inappropriateness, and which effectively destroys for ever what was left of the intimate character of this part of High Street. The new estate would be suitable for Goldsworth Park, but is quite out of place in an old village: Conservation Area status should not mean the conservation of old buildings, but the improvement and upgrading of the overall appearance as well. Old Woking shows that the lesson has yet to be learned. There is no point in cherishing what is old, and at the same time ruining its setting with brash, intrusive new development.

Conservation area status should also be considered for some of the more recent parts of the Borough. Although Woking is comparatively poor in buildings dating from before the mid-19th century, it has a wealth of late Victorian and Edwardian architecture in the exclusive low-density suburbs, and of this type of building much is of intrinsic interest, or has connections with important architects or landscape designers. Unfortunately the redevelopment of the large gardens of these houses is increasingly common, and steps should be taken to protect more adequately the very attractive and valuable character of these areas. If this is not done the heritage and history of the town will, in future years, be the poorer.

The rural landscape, too, has suffered from the mistaken belief that, because it is not outstanding, it is not worth protecting. The imposition of the Green Belt helped to avert the threat of complete development of all the open land around the town, but, as Fig. 27 shows, it has by no means stopped the physical expansion. The open land of Woking is of great value, because it separates the town from its neighbours and so avoids a continuous urban sprawl from Chertsey and Weybridge through Woking to beyond Guildford. It is also pleasant countryside, and some parts, such as Horsell Common and the ridge between Old Woking and Pyrford, are attractive and well worth protecting. Surrey County Council have long-term plans to improve and restore the landscape of the Wey valley, damaged by pylons, gravel-workings and loss of tree and hedge cover, and other projects include a linear park along the Hoe valley from Mayford to Old Woking and the creation of open spaces along the Basingstoke Canal. A major problem is the deterioration of farmland around the town, as agriculture is abandoned and the fields are turned over to occasional grazing of horses or are merely left to grow over. One idea that has been put forward is to make use of such land for recreation, and thus in 1980 Woking Council bought 15 acres of under-used farmland north of Saunders Lane, Mayford.[22]

The Basingstoke Canal

In the years after the war the derelict Basingstoke Canal was the subject of a long and tedious dispute between the local authorities along its route (including Woking U.D.C.) and its latest owners, the New Basingstoke Canal Co. The latter wished to see it either culverted or filled in, but from the early 1960s most local opinion favoured a full restoration to navigation, this time for pleasure use. In 1972, after the complete failure of attempts at a compromise, the Surrey and Hampshire County Councils compulsorily purchased the entire length of the waterway, from Greywell near Basingstoke to the Wey Navigation at New Haw.

Restoration work has been in progress ever since, using unpaid labour from volunteers supplemented by job creation schemes. The task is large and complex, involving the dredging and relining of the channel, the replacement of all the locks and rebuilding of the lock chambers, and the provision of all the necessary facilities for mooring and for tourist use. In the Woking area it has meant the opening of the towpath, and the eventual construction of picnic-areas, a quay at Brewery Road in the town centre, and the possibility of a basin being provided here in the future. The reopening of the canal will have a considerable impact upon the town, diversifying and widening its interest and quality: although hopes that Woking will one day be a tourist attraction are perhaps rather over-optimistic!

Communications

The improvement of communications to and within Woking has been a priority of local authorities in the area for over 60 years. Woking Council has repeatedly pressed for more expenditure on new road schemes, and Surrey County Council has, just as often, deferred, postponed or rejected the same projects. Since the early 1920s there has been a series of studies and plans for road improvements, but the result to date has been just three significant new projects. The Byfleet bypass (A245) was opened in 1962, and was the first main road to be built in Woking this century. In 1969 the straightening of the sharp bends on the Guildford road (A320) at Whitmoor Common was a great improvement, although it did have the side-effect of obliterating a good example of enclosure! Finally, in 1973, the town centre relief road, Victoria Way, was completed. The road was the first dual carriageway in the Borough, and although just half a mile long it still retains that distinction.

National road projects have improved access to the area. The M3 was opened in 1973, six miles to the north at Lightwater, and the A3 has been transformed into a semi-motorway. In 1983 or 1984 the M25 London Orbital Motorway, which separates Byfleet from the rest of the Borough, is due to open after more than 60 years of planning. Yet most of the projects which were listed as essential and priorities in the 1920s are still unbuilt. The A324 Goldsworth Relief Road, which is fundamental to traffic circulation in the western part of Woking, and to the Goldsworth Park development, has repeatedly been postponed by the County Council. The eastern and western approach roads, which are to give access to the M25/A3 and M3 junctions respectively, have come no nearer to fruition despite traffic surveys which show appalling overloading of the roads through Byfleet and Knaphill. The dangerous and narrow bends on the A320 at Mayford, which could be bypassed by a short length of new road, are likely to remain for many years to come.

Rail access, on the other hand, has shown continued improvement, despite the frequent complaints of local people. In 1967 the line from Bournemouth to Brookwood was electrified, and the service greatly augmented. In more recent years timetable changes, and the relative downgrading of the Portsmouth line have meant that most of the former through-trains now call at Woking. The local stations have also benefited from revisions in the services, and have attracted new custom from commuters. In 1981 the only trains which passed through Woking without stopping were the hourly expresses from Waterloo to Southampton and Bournemouth: the others gave the station an almost unparalleled service, with seven trains per hour to London in the off-peak period, of which three were non-stop and two stopped only at Surbiton.

Commuting grew very rapidly in the decade after the war, and reached a peak, in terms of the proportion of the workforce who left the town each day, in the early 1960s. The proportion of commuters in the total workforce has since declined steadily, although the absolute numbers show no sign of diminishing. Woking station is by a considerable margin the busiest in the county, and still performs its original role of railhead for a large part of North West Surrey. West Byfleet station is, rather unexpectedly, the sixth busiest in the county, as a result of its greatly improved services since the Bournemouth electrification in particular.

In 1963 the five stations in the Borough had 4,532 season ticket holders to London, and in 1974 this had increased to 5,525, a growth of 21 per cent. The fastest growth of any station was that of Worplesdon, which has seen its patronage increase in recent years as suburban development affected parts of south Woking and the Worplesdon village area.[23] All the commuting has tended to give a false impression of the town as a 'dormitory suburb' of London; thus, Nairn says that the town is 'simply . . . a place to eat and sleep in'.[24] Woking is not primarily a commuter town. It was shown, as part of the survey work for the Surrey Structure Plan (mid-1970s) that approximately 60 per cent of the workforce who live in the Borough also work in the Borough, and that another 15 per cent work in Guildford or Weybridge.

The proportion of those who commute daily to London, about 18 per cent, is lower than in Egham, Reigate or Walton and Weybridge, and less than half that of Esher, Staines or Sunbury. Woking is the second-largest employment centre in the county, after Guildford, and has the second-largest manufacturing and office sectors. With about 35,000 jobs in the Borough, it has a considerable importance as an industrial and commercial centre, and draws labour from other local authority areas: about 70 per cent of the labour force live in the Borough, 23 per cent commute *to* Woking from elsewhere in Surrey, and 7 per cent come from outside the county, including a not insignificant number who come from Greater London.

Population Changes

In 1951 Woking had a population of 47,596, and in 1981 that had risen to 81,358, an increase of 70.9 per cent in three decades. The 1950s, in particular, saw more new inhabitants than any other decade in the history of the town, with the exception of the boom years of the 1890s. The table on the following page shows the population statistics by wards for 1951–71.

Apart from the striking decline in Central ward, analysed in Chapter Twelve, the most obvious feature is the 715 per cent increase in the population of Woodham & Sheerwater ward in 1951–61, as the Sheerwater estate was developed. By 1971 the rise had been reversed, and the population was declining slowly as the children of the first inhabitants moved away from the area. The fastest growth among the more normal wards was experienced in St Johns (145 per cent: 1951–71), followed by

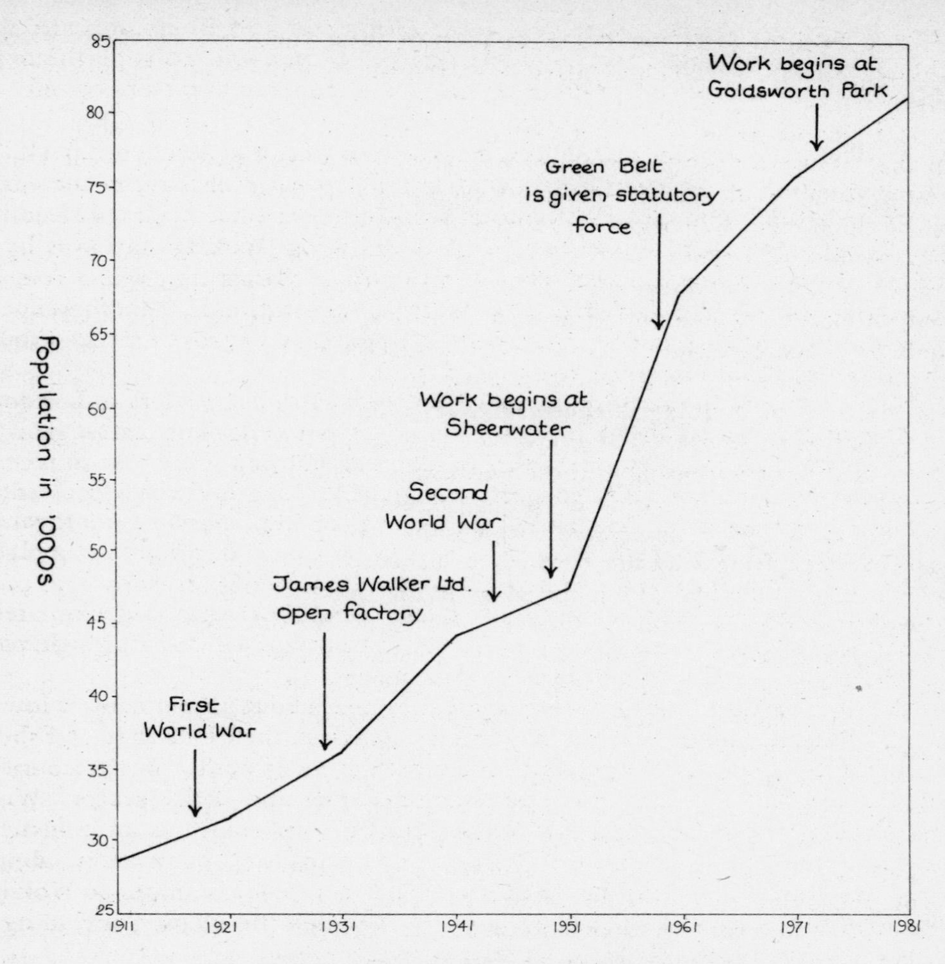

Fig. 28. The Population of Woking 1911–1981

Table 19. Ward Populations 1951–71[25]

Ward	*1951*	*1961*	*1971*
Byfleet	4,605	5,469	7,498
Central	7,353	6,166	5,770
Horsell	5,532	7,062	8,889
Knaphill & Brookwood	8,520	9,261	10,485
Maybury & Mount Hermon	5,171	7,777	9,982
Old Woking, Mayford & Sutton	7,808	9,277	9,480
St Johns	3,627	7,639	8,837
West Byfleet & Pyrford	4,314	8,451	9,542
Woodham & Sheerwater	666	6,417	5,433

West Byfleet & Pyrford (121 per cent). In both of these there was extensive private house-building, with the development of the Hermitage and Pyrford Woods estates respectively.

Byfleet (63 per cent) and Horsell (60 per cent: 1951–71) had Woking U.D.C. housing in the 1950s, but in these wards the greatest part of the growth was accounted for by a large number of smaller infilling schemes, particularly after 1953 when the imposition of the Green Belt began to restrict the supply of larger sites for new building. Maybury & Mount Hermon ward (93 per cent growth in 1951–71) had the largest of the council estates, Maybury, built in the early 1950s; after 1960, too, this ward experienced extensive redevelopment at high densities, when most of Mount Hermon was rezoned for flats. Knaphill & Brookwood and Old Woking, Mayford & Sutton, which grew by 23 per cent and 21 per cent respectively, were the wards most seriously affected by the end of building in the rural areas after 1953. Because they had been more densely built up before 1939 there was less scope for infilling on small sites, and so the amount of new housing in these two wards was limited.

It is possible to visualise a sharply declining population in the central areas, over the period since the early 1950s, associated with comparatively low rates of growth on the southern and western fringes of the town. In contrast, there was a zone of very rapid population increase extending along the axis of the main Waterloo–Woking–Bournemouth railway line from St Johns in the west to West Byfleet in the east. In the 1970s this pattern began to alter, as building land approached exhaustion in many parts of the Borough. The focus of growth switched to the new Goldsworth Park estate, spilling over also into the adjacent areas of Horsell and Knaphill. Elsewhere the rates of increase began to fall sharply.

Over the Borough as a whole the population grew by 7.1 per cent in the decade to 1981, which may be compared to a fall of 0.9 per cent in the population of Surrey. Of the eleven districts in Surrey, only one, Surrey Heath, with a 15.5 per cent increase, grew at a faster rate than Woking.[26] It may be anticipated that this growth will continue for the remainder of the 1980s at least, until the completion of the Goldsworth Park estate and the exhaustion of the high-density redevelopment sites near to Woking and West Byfleet stations. Perhaps that will produce a 1991 figure of around 88,000. After this, stability is likely as the exhaustion of all significant building land is reached: that supposes, of course, that there is no substantial alteration in either the area or the strictness of the Green Belt. By the end of the century Woking will probably have a population of about 92,000. Earlier estimates had put the figure rather higher, at 105,000 or thereabouts, but a falling birth-rate and the severe recession of the past five years have led to the revision of these targets.

Conclusion

It will soon be a century and a half since the first train left London for Woking Common. When its passengers arrived they saw expanses of heathery moorland, dotted with gorse and a few trees. There was scarcely a building to be seen, and the justification for the station must have seened obscure to some. Today the heathland is the heart of a thriving town of more than 82,000 people, covering some 15 square miles including its suburbs, and of increasing significance as an industrial and office centre. Woking is no longer a new town: it is over a century old, enough to have acquired a history and a vanishing past. This book has described that history: let us hope that we do not let the past vanish any further from sight, and that instead of denigrating the Woking that was, we value it and give it protection.

APPENDIX

Populations of the Parishes 1801– 1951

Census of:	*Byfleet*	*Horsell*	*Pyrford*	*Woking*	*'Borough'*
1801	362	493	230	1,340	2,425
1811	392	564	264	1,578	2,798
1821	427	617	294	1,810	3,148
1831	510	673	307	1,975	3,465
1841	672	766	333	2,482	4,253
1851	687	762	365	2,837	4,651
1861	770	788	381	3,819	5,758
1871	915	897	357	6,586	8,755
1881	1,261	900	343	8,544	11,058
1891	1,384	1,021	431	9,776	12,612
1901	1,688	2,105	528	16,244	20,565
1911	2,960	3,026	979	21,782	28,747
1921	4,173	3,385	1,179	23,038	31,775
1931	4,819	4,167	1,401	25,764	36,151
1941*	—	—	—	—	42,000
1951	7,365	6,858	1,760	31,614	47,596

* There was no Census in 1941: the figure given is the Registrar General's estimate of the civilian population.

N.B. After 1951 the district was re-warded, and comparable parish statistics were no longer available: *see* Chapter Twelve.

NOTES AND REFERENCES

Throughout this section, references to local authority sources relate to minute books, unless otherwise stated. For abbreviations see list on page xi.

Chapter One. Background

1. J. E. B. Gover *et al.*, *The Place Names of Surrey* (1934), p. 157.
2. H. G. Dines and F. H. Edmunds, *The Geology of the Country Around Aldershot and Guildford* (1929), chap. VII.
3. *Ibid.*, chap. XI.
4. R. Belsey, 'Prehistory and Archaeology of the Woking District', in *Mayford History Society Newsletter*, no. 22 (Feb. 1973).
5. M. Gelling, *Signposts to the Past* (1978), chap. V.
6. B. Cox, 'Place Names of the Earliest English Records', in *Journal of the English Place Name Society*, vol. 8 (1975–76), pp. 12–66.
7. J. E. B. Gover *et al.*, *The Place Names of Surrey* (1934), p. 104.
8. *Ibid.*, p. 132.
9. *Ibid.*, p. 128.
10. *Victoria County History of Surrey* (hereafter *V.C.H.*) vol. II (1905), p. 8.
11. *Ibid.*
12. *Ibid.*
13. Edward Ryde recorded in his diary for 3 March 1851 that he had attended a meeting called to consider a dispute between Horsell and Chobham over their mutual boundary.
14. *V.C.H.*, vol. I (1902), p. 296.
15. *V.C.H.*, vol. III (1911), pp. 382–83.
16. I. Nairn and N. Pevsner, *The Buildings of England: Surrey*, 2nd edn. (1971), (hereafter *Bldgs. Surrey*), p. 398.
17. *V.C.H.*, vol. III (1911), p. 384.
18. *Ibid.*
19. *Bldgs, Surrey*, pp. 476–79.
20. *Ibid.*
21. *V.C.H.*, vol. III (1911), p. 387.
22. *Ibid.*
23. A. Locke, *A Short History of Woking*, reprinted edn. (1980), (hereafter *Short Hist. Wok.*), pp. 14–15.
24. J. Remnant, *A Survey of the Royal Manour of Woking* (1719).
25. *V.C.H.* vol. III (1911), pp. 400–1.
26. *Bldgs. Surrey*, p. 127.
27. *V.C.H.*, vol. III (1911), pp. 431–33.
28. *Ibid.*, p. 433.
29. *Ibid.*, p. 428.
30. *Ibid.*
31. D. Defoe, *A Tour Through The Whole Island of Great Britain* (hereafter *Tour of Great Britain*), Everyman edn. (1962), p. 147.
32. *V.C.H.*, vol. I (1902), p. 296.

33. *Ibid.*, p. 310.
34. *Ibid.*, pp. 296–325.
35. *Short Hist. Wok.*, pp. 11–20.
36. *V.C.H.*, vol. I (1902), p. 442.
37. *Short Hist. Wok.*, pp. 14–15.
38. From the Loseley mss., quoted in Vine (1965).
39. P. A. L. Vine, *London's Lost Route to the Sea* (1965), chap. 2.
40. *The Kentish Gazette*, 23–26 Aug. 1769.

Chapter Two. The Woking District in 1800

1. D. Defoe, *Tour of Great Britain* (1962 edn.), p. 144.
2. O. Manning and W. Bray, *The History and Antiquities of the County of Surrey* (1804), vol. 1, p. 112.
3. E. W. Brayley, *Topographical History of Surrey* (hereafter *Top. Hist. Surrey*) (1841), vol. 2, p. 11.
4. *Ibid.*, vol. 1, p. 437.
5. L. R. Stevens, *Byfleet; A Village of England* (1953), p. 27.
6. Paterson's *Roads* (1822 edn.), p. 55.
7. Information on ticket in Guildford Museum (LG. 562).
8. D. Defoe, *Tour of Great Britain* (1962 edn.), p. 143.
9. W. Stevenson, *General View of the Agriculture of the County of Surrey* (hereafter *General View II*) (1809), p. 40.
10. *Top. Hist. Surrey*, vol. 2, p. 24.
11. Geological Survey of Great Britain 1:50,000 map, sheet 285 (1976).
12. *Top. Hist. Surrey*, vol. 1, p. 131.
13. *Woking Manor Court Books*, no. 15, 22 Apr. 1813.
14. E. Ryde, *Reminiscences for a Proposed History of Woking* (hereafter *Reminiscences*) (*c.* 1880), pp. 12–13.
15. W. James and J. Malcolm, *General View of the Agriculture of the County of Surrey* (hereafter *General View I*) (1794), p. 23.
16. J. Remnant, *A Survey of the Royal Manour of Woking* (1719).
17. G. Bourne, *Change in the Village* (1912), pp. 9 and 87.
18. Bridley Manor Court: License for Inclosure, 14 January 1652.
19. *Woking Manor Court Books.* no. 14, 22 April 1802.
20. *Ibid.*, no. 16, 7 April 1825.
21. G. Bourne, *Change in the Village (1912), p. 2.*
22. Sources for table: Remnant (1719); Inclosure Awards: Survey of the Parish of Horsell (1834).
23. W. E. Tate, 'Enclosure Acts and Awards relating to lands in the County of Surrey', in *Surrey Archaeological Collections* (hereafter *Sy. A.C.*), vol. 48 (1943), pp. 118–49.
24. H. L. Gray, *The English Field Systems* (1915), p. 364.
25. Byfleet and Weybridge Inclosure Award and Map (1811).
26. Pyrford and Chertsey Inclosure Award and Map (1815).
27. Horsell Tithe Map and Award (1854).
28. Sutton next Wokeing Inclosure Award and Map (1808).
29. Woking Tithe Map and Award (1841).
30. J. Remnant, *A Survey of the Royal Manour of Woking* (1719).
31. This explains the absence of a 'g' in pre-18th century spellings.
32. *General View I*, p. 50.
33. Sources for the table: Remnant (1719); Inclosure Awards: tithe Maps.

34. A. G. Parton, 'The 1801 Crop Returns for the County of Surrey', in *Sy. A.C.*, vol. 64 (1967), pp. 113–23.
35. *General View I*, p. 38.
36. *General View II*, pp. 280 and 288.
37. E. Ryde, *Reminiscences*, p. 14.
38. *General View II*, p. 40.
39. 'Names of those Parties Keeping Sheep in the Parish of Woking and entitled to common or pasture' (1854): Onslow Collection, Woking Commoners Act G.M.R. 97/5/66.
40. *Woking Manor Court Books*, no. 16, 30 March.
41. E. Ryde, *Reminiscences*, pp. 5–6.
42. E. Gardner, 'Weybridge and Byfleet: Traces of Old Ironworks', in *Sy. A.C.*, vol. 34 (1921), pp. 115–16.
43. J. Rocque, *A Map of the County of Surrey* (1762).
44. 'Indenture for the lease of Brookwood Brickkilns' (15 May 1812): Onslow Collection, G.M.R. RB670.
45. *V.C.H.*, vol. III (1911), p. 381.
46. Woking U.D.C. (Sanitary Committee), 30. Jan. 1908.
47. *Woking Manor Court Books*, no. 15, 22 April 1813.
48. *Bldgs. Surrey*, pp. 397–98.
49. *Top. Hist. Surrey*, vol. 2, p. 24.
50. *1801 Census of Great Britain*, vol. 1, Table 2.
51. O. Manning and W. Bray, *The History and Antiquities of the County of Surrey* (1804), vol. 1, p. 162.
52. *Bldgs. Surrey*, p. 418.
53. G. B. Greenwood, *Woking: A Dictionary of Local History* (1970), p. 21.

Chapter Three. The Initial Changes: 1800–1850

1. P. A. L. Vine, *London's Lost Route To Basingstoke* (1968): this is the definitive account of the canal and its history.
2. *Ibid.*, p. 49.
3. *Ibid.*, p. 45.
4. Woking Urban District Council (Basingstoke Canal) Act, 1911.
5. F. Street, *A History of Goldsworth Nursery* (1960), p. 9.
6. *Woking Manor Court Books*, no. 14, 13 Oct. 1802.
7. Notice in *The County Chronicle & Weekly Advertiser* 29 Sept. 1832.
8. *Top. Hist. Surrey*, vol. 2, pp. 27 and 140.
9. E. Ryde, *Diaries*, vol. 24, 8 July 1867.
10. F. Street, *A History of Goldsworth Nursery* (1960), pp. 9–10.
11. Sale plan for Jackman estates: G.M.R. 1216/2/4(1).
12. W. E. Tate, 'Enclosure Acts and Awards relating to land in the County of Surrey', in *Sy. A.C.*, vol. 48 (1943), pp. 118–49.
13. Minutes of the Proceedings of the Commissioners under the Byfleet and Weybridge Inclosure Act (1800–11): S.R.O 2284.
14. Source of all material on enclosure, unless otherwise stated, is the Enclosure Award and Map for each of the three manors affected.
15. The poem is held at Guildford Museum: G8215.
16. Woking Tithe Map and Award (1841).
17. M. Dutt, *The Agricultural Labourers' Revolt of 1830 in Kent, Surrey and Sussex* (1966), pp. 268–69.

18. Woking Vestry Minutes: 6 Jan. 1820.
19. *Ibid.*, Sept. 1818–June 1830.
20. *Ibid.*, 16 Sept. 1818.
21. *Ibid.*, 5 Jan. 1830.
22. *Ibid.*, 20 Mar. 1820.
23. *Ibid.*, 22 Sept. 1820.
24. *Ibid.*, 26 July 1826.
25. *Ibid.*, 22 Oct. 1818.
26. *Ibid.*, 30 May 1819.
27. *Ibid.*, 25 June 1829.
28. *Ibid.*, 22 Sept. 1820.
29. *Ibid.*, 28 Jan. 1822.
30. *Ibid.*, 24 May 1830.
31. *Ibid.*, 24 Oct. 1826.
32. *Ibid.*, Jan.–June 1827.
33. *Ibid.*, Jan. 1822–Jan. 1827.
34. Chertsey Board of Guardians Minutes: 22 Oct. 1839.
35. C. F. Dendy Marshall and R. W. Kidner, *A History of the Southern Railway* (1968), pp. 53–55.
36. J. Francis, *History of the English Railway* (1851), quoted in above, p. 57.
37. Deposited plans of the London and Southampton Railway: S.R.O.
38. E. Ryde, *Reminiscences*, p. 14.
39. C. F. Dendy Marshall and R. W. Kidner, *A History of the Southern Railway* (1968), pp. 60–61.
40. E. Ryde, *Reminiscences*, p. 14.
41. *Ibid.*, pp. 18–19.
42. *Short Hist. Wok.*, p. 54.
43. Deposited plans of the Guildford Railway (1838 and 1840): S.R.O.
44. Deposited plans of the Staines & Woking Railway (1851) and other companies: S.R.O.
45. Deposited plans of the Staines, Chertsey & Woking Railway (1882): S.R.O.
46. 'Proposed St Johns Station': papers in Onslow Collection: G.M.R. RB670.
47. *See also* M. de G. Eedle, *A History of Bagshot and Windlesham* (1977), pp. 179–80.

Chapter Four. The London Necropolis and National Mausoleum Company

1. J. Stevens Curl, *A Celebration of Death* (1980), pp. 288–89.
2. *Hansard* vol. 119 (Third Series), Cols. 926–30.
3. *Hansard* vol. 121 (Third Series), Cols. 891–92.
4. Statement by Onslow family solicitors on the Woking Commoners Act, 1854: contained in papers on the Necropolis Co. etc. In Onslow Collection: 97/5/66(6).
5. Claim of Necropolis Company: in same collection: 97/5/66(4).
6. Solicitors' statement: 97/5/66(6).
7. The Act is never included in published lists of enclosure legislation (e.g. W. E. Tate's article), even though its effect was exactly comparable.
8. Solicitors' statement: 97/5/66(6).
9. Letter from Lord Onslow to the arbitrators, 13 June 1855: 97/5/66(14).
10. The case as to the cottagers' interests: statement by G. W. Cooke on 30 December 1854, contained in the Onslow Collection: 97/5/66(1).
11. Notice of meeting and of certain claims: 97/5/66(5).

12. Deposited plans of the London Necropolis and National Mausoleum Company.
13. *Hansard* vol. 138 (Third Series), cols. 1759–60.
14. London Necropolis Company Amendment Act of 1855.
15. London Necropolis Company Amendment Act of 1864.
16. London Necropolis Company Amendment Act of 1869.
17. *Surrey Advertiser*, 17 July 1880: quoting a speech by Edward Ryde.

Chapter Five. Building a New Town

1. *Bldgs. Surrey*, p. 532.
2. *Surrey Advertiser*, 16 Jan. 1889.
3. *Surrey Advertiser*, 15 Apr. 1905 (Rastrick's obituary).
4. 'Plan of the freehold estate surrounding the Maybury (Woking) station' (1859).
5. *Ibid.*
6. *Surrey Advertiser*, 15 Apr. 1905.
7. *Surrey Advertiser*, 1 Apr. 1899 (Leitner's obituary).
8. Ordnance Survey 6 in. map of 1870.
9. *Surrey Advertiser*, 22 Jan. 1870.
10. *Bldgs. Surrey*, p. 533.
11. Woking Station Estate sale plan: Onslow Collection RB670.
12. The Ordnance Survey 6 in. map of 1870 shows that the laying out of the road pattern was then in progress.
13. Woking Common Estate sale plans: G.M.R. 1295/5.
14. Woking Common Estate sale plans: S.R.O. SP9/53/15.
15. Woking U.D.C. (Sanitary & Lighting), 25 Nov. 1897 and 17 Jan. 1899.
16. Woking U.D.C. (Sanitary), 1 Mar. 1906.
17. *Surrey Advertiser*, 27 Apr. 1867.
18. Cross Lanes Estate sale plan and catalogue: G.M.R. 1192/4.
19. York Estate sale plan and catalogue: S.R.O. SP9/53/13.
20. Cross Lanes Estate sale plan: G.M.R. 1192/14.
21. The Duchess was the widow of Prince Leopold, fourth son of Queen Victoria.
22. Material on the sale of land at Hook Heath: Onslow Collection G.M.R. 1124.
23. *Bldgs. Surrey*, pp. 534 and 600.
24. Sale notice for Jackmans land: G.M.R. 1216/2/4(1).
25. Abbey Farm sale plan and brochure: G.M.R. 1192/12.
26. Horsell Common Estates sale plan and catalogue: G.M.R. 70/51/6.
27. Chertsey R.D.C., 19 Feb. 1901.
28. Woking Co-operative Society, *Pictorial Souvenir of Twenty-One Years' Work* (1920), pp. 12–13.
29. *Bldgs. Surrey*, p. 320.
30. Petersham Place sale plans and catalogue: S.R.O. SP9/10/5.
31. Chertsey R.D.C., 9 June 1903.
32. *Ibid.*, 9 Oct. 1913.
33. Byfleet P.C., 13 Sept. 1913.
34. C. F. Dendy Marshall and R. W. Kidner, *A History of the Southern Railway* (1968), apps. 5 and 6.
35. Byfleet Corner Estate sale plan and catalogue: S.R.O. SP9/2/2.
36. Chertsey R.D.C., Jan. 1906–Feb. 1907.
37. Dartnell Park Estate sale plan and catalogue: S.R.O. SP9/10/1 and 2.
38. Frog Lane Farm sale catalogues: S.R.O. SP9/53/17.

Chapter Six. Local Government and Services 1860-1914

1. Guildford H.D., 1864-80.
2. Guildford R.S.A., 1872-93.
3. Chertsey R.S.A., 1890-95.
4. M. de G. Eedle, 'Street Cleansing and refuse collection from the sixteenth to the nineteenth centuries', in *Sy. A.C.*, vol. 68 (1971), pp. 161-81.
5. Guildford R.S.A., 1875-80.
6. *Ibid.*, 1880-84.
7. *Ibid.*, 1883-93.
8. Chertsey R.S.A., 23 Apr. 1894.
9. *Ibid.*, 8 May 1894.
10. Chertsey R.D.C., 24 Sept. 1895.
11. Woking L.B., Apr.-May 1894.
12. Woking U.D.C., 13 May 1896.
13. Woking U.D.C., 1906-7.
14. Chertsey R.D.C., Aug. 1903.
15. *Ibid.*, Jan. 1904.
16. *Ibid.*, 20 Jan. 1906.
17. *Ibid.*, Oct. 1906-June 1907.
18. *Ibid.*, Feb.-Mar. 1908.
19. Byfleet P.C., Mar.-June 1908.
20. Pyrford P.C., Mar.-May 1908.
21. Chertsey R.D.C., June-Nov. 1908.
22. Guildford H.D., 10 Oct. 1871.
23. *Ibid.*, 7 Oct. 1890.
24. *Ibid.*, 20 June 1871.
25. Guildford H.D., 20 July 1869.
26. *Ibid.*
27. Woking L.B. (Lighting Committee), Aug. 1894.
28. Woking U.D.C. (Lighting and Highways Committee), 1904-6.
29. Guildford H.D., Apr. 1883-Mar. 1892.
30. Chertsey R.D.C., 18 Dec. 1906.
31. P. A. L. Vine, *London's Lost Route to Basingstoke* (1968), pp. 156-66.
32. Guildford R.S.A., 14 Nov. 1874.
33. *Ibid.*, 26 June 1875.
34. *Ibid.*, 27 Nov. 1875.
35. *Ibid.*, Oct. 1877-Dec. 1880.
36. Guildford H.D., 16 Jan. 1883.
37. *Ibid.*, 1890-92 (especially 19 July 1892).
38. Guildford H.D., 10 Dec. 1889.
39. *Ibid.*, 17 Mar. 1885.
40. Chertsey R.S.A., 12 May 1891.
41. Guildford R.S.A., 8 Nov. 1890 *et seq.*
42. Woking L.B. (Sewerage, Drainage & Scavenging Committee), May.-Nov. 1894.
43. Woking U.D.C. (Sanitary and Lighting Committee), Feb.-Dec. 1895.
44. 'Evidence to be presented at Inquiry into Woking U.D.C. Sewage Plan' (1897), Onslow Collection: G.M.R. RB670.
45. Woking U.D.C. (Sanitary Committee), 28 Sept. 1900.
46. Chertsey R.D.C., Nov. 1903-July 1906.
47. Woking U.D.C. (Sanitary Committee), Nov. 1907-June 1908.
48. Chertsey R.D.C., Apr. 1907-Oct. 1908.
49. *Ibid.*, 22 Feb. 1910.
50. Pyrford P.C., 22 Sept. 1910.

51. Chertsey R.D.C., 8 July 1913.
52. Woking L.B. (Sewerage, Drainage & Scavenging Committee). 21 Mar. 1894.
53. Woking U.D.C. (Sanitary Committee), 27 Feb. 1908.
54. Chertsey R.S.A., 28 Aug. 1894.
55. Chertsey R.D.C., June–Aug. 1903.
56. *Ibid.*, 9 Feb. and 20 Apr. 1909.
57. Woking Gas and Water Company Act of 1881.
58. South West Suburban Water Company Act of 1869.
59. E. Ryde, *Diaries*, 7 Sept. 1869.
60. Woking Gas and Water Company Act of 1881.
61. Woking District Gas Company Act of 1891.
62. Woking District Gas Company minutes and accounts, 1891–92 *et seq.*: S.R.O.
63. Woking Electricity Supply Company Order 1890.
64. D. W. Clewley, 'Woking's First Public Electricity Supply', in *SEEBoard Staff Newsletter* (Dec. 1975).
65. Woking (Horsell and Chertsey) Electricity Supply Order of 1892.
66. Woking Electricity Supply (Extensions) Order of 1900.
67. Woking Electricity Supply (Extensions) Order of 1907.
68. Woking L.B. (Lighting Committee), Nov. 1893–July 1894.
69. Woking U.D.C. (Sanitary and Lighting Committee), 28 Jan. 1895.
70. Woking U.D.C. (Lighting and Highways Committee), Nov. 1898–Mar. 1899.
71. *Ibid.*, 3 Aug. 1901.
72. Woking U.D.C. (Lighting Committee), 27 Sept. 1910.
73. Byfleet P.C., 1895–1913.
74. Woking L.B., 8 Aug. 1894.
75. Woking U.D.C., May–Oct. 1895.
76. Woking U.D.C. (Fire Brigade Committee), 6 Sept. 1895.
77. *Woking Mail*, 5 Nov. 1895.
78. Woking U.D.C. (Fire Brigade Committee), 29 Aug.–3 Dec. 1897.
79. *Ibid.*, May 1898–Aug. 1899.
80. *Ibid.*, 27 July 1898.
81. *Ibid.*, 2 May 1900 and 1 May 1901.
82. Chertsey R.S.A., Dec. 1893–1894.
83. Byfleet P.C., July 1906–July 1908.
84. Woking U.D.C. (Fire Brigade Committee), Nov.–Dec. 1902.
85. Pyrford P.C., 7 Nov. 1905, 1 Feb. and 28 Mar. 1906.
86. *Ibid.*, Apr. 1909–1910.

Chapter Seven. The Institutions

1. These engravings (source unknown) may be seen at Woking Library.
2. Deposited plan of the Necropolis Company with hand-drawn amendments: Onslow Collection RB670 (Act of Parliament Box).
3. J. Stevens Curl, *A Celebration of Death* (1890), pp. 288–90.
4. A Plan of Brookwood Cemetery (n.d.).
5. 'Report on burial grounds in the parish of Woking' (1879): Onslow Collection.
6. Brookwood Cemetery Burial Records, vol. 1, no. 1.
7. *Ibid.*, 1854–1939.
8. M. D. Lister, 'Via Necropolis Junction', in *Railway Magazine*, vol. 119 no. 862 (1973), pp. 74–76.

9. *Bldgs. Surrey*, pp. 66 and 120.
10. J. Stevens Curl, *A Celebration of Death* (1980).
11. *The Sanitary Record*, 24 Jan. 1879, pp. 49–51.
12. 'In the matter of the Crematory at Woking': G.M.R. Psh/Wok J/28/1.
13. G. F. Saxby, Paper read to the Westminster Clerical Meeting in 1879.
14. Letter from Rev. F. J. Oliphant to Lord Onslow, 10 Mar. 1884: G.M.R. Psh/Wok J/28/7.
15. *Surrey Advertiser*, 4 Apr. 1885.
16. Kelly's *Post Office Directory of Surrey* (hereafter *Directory*) (1899).
17. *Surrey Advertiser*, 14 Sept. 1867.
18. First Report of the Governor of Woking Prison (1860), pp. 297–335.
19. *Surrey Advertiser*, 31 Aug. 1889.
20. Kelly's *Directory* (1874) and *Surrey Advertiser*, 13 Apr. 1889.
21. *Surrey Advertiser*, 31 Aug. 1889.
22. *Surrey Advertiser*, 23 Mar. 1889.
23. Authorised by the Woking Barracks Act of 1895.
24. *Census of Great Britain* (1911): Surrey County Report, table 9.
25. K. Jones, *A History of the Mental Health Services* (1972), p. 153.
26. Report of the Committee of Visitors of the Brookwood Asylum for Midsummer 1867: S.R.O. 1523/1/9.
27. *Ibid.*, Easter 1868.
28. *Ibid.*, Michaelmas 1867.
29. *Ibid.*, 1867–88.
30. *Ibid.*, Michaelmas 1867.
31. *Ibid.*, Epiphany 1868.
32. *Ibid.*, Midsummer 1868.
33. *Census of Great Britain* (1871), Surrey County Report, B.
34. *Woking News and Mail*, Mar.–Aug. 1981.
35. *The Times*, 22 July 1858.
36. Kelly's *Directory* (1874).
37. *The Times*, 2 June 1860.
38. *The Times*, 6 June 1865.
39. *Surrey Advertiser*, 27 Apr. 1867.
40. *Surrey Advertiser*, 1 June 1867.
41. Kelly's *Directory* (1874) and T. G. Fuller (pers. comm. 1981).
42. Census enumerators' manuscript returns (hereafter Census Returns) (1871) P.R.O.
43. *Surrey Advertiser*, Mar.–Dec. 1877.
44. *Surrey Advertiser*,, 31 July 1880.
45. *Surrey Advertiser*, 1 Apr. 1899 (Leitner's obituary).
46. *Ibid.*
47. *Bldgs. Surrey*, pp. 533–34.
48. *Surrey Advertiser*, 1 Apr. 1899.
49. Kelly's *Directory* (1924).
50. *Ibid.* (1874).
51. Mayford Farm sale plan and catalogue: S.R.O. SP9/53/8.
52. Kelly's *Directory* (1899).
53. *Bldgs. Surrey*, p. 534.
54. Kelly's *Directory* (1924).
55. *Bldgs. Surrey*, p. 419.

Chapter Eight. The Welfare of the Community

1. *V.C.H.*, vol. II (1907), p. 52.
2. *Bldgs. Surrey*, p. 230.

3. A. J. Munby, *Diaries*, 30 Oct. 1868.
4. *Bldgs. Surrey*, p. 534.
5. F. R. Arnos, *The Origins of Christ Church*, Woking (1977).
6. *Bldgs. Surrey*, p. 126.
7. Kelly's *Directory* (1924).
8. *Bldgs. Surrey*, p. 126.
9. *Ibid.*, p. 538.
10. *Woking Year Book and Directory*, 1924-27.
11. W. K. Robinson, *Some notes on the history of Quakerism in Woking and District* (1969).
12. C. C. Colborne, *A Brief History of Horsell Common Baptist Chapel* (1914), pp. 2-18.
13. A. H. Stockwell, *The Baptist Churches of Surrey* (1910?).
14. *A Digest of Parochial Returns Made to the Select Committee Appointed To Inquire into the Education of the Poor* (1818).
15. *Abstract of the Education Returns* (1833).
16. V.C.H., vol. II, (1907), pp. 234–41.
17. Kelly's *Directory* (1874).
18. E. Ryde, *Diaries*, vol. 29, 27 June 1872.
19. *Surrey Advertiser*, 24 Dec. 1870.
20. E. Ryde, *Diaries*, vol. 30, 21 Feb. 1873.
21. *Surrey Advertiser*, 2 Apr. 1880.
22. E. Ryde, *Diaries*, vol. 34, 21 Apr. 1877.
23. *Ibid.*, vol. 35, 1 Aug. 1878.
24. Woking School Board, 1875–78.
25. *Ibid.*, 1874–77.
26. *Ibid.*, 8 May 1879.
27. *Ibid.*, 1880–1901.
28. *Ibid.*, Feb. 1884.
29. *Ibid.*, 29 Dec. 1881.
30. Pyrford School Board, 1891-1901.
31. *Surrey Advertiser*, Oct.–Nov. 1867.
32. Woking School Board, 22 June 1893.
33. Woking L.B., Mar.–May 1894.
34. Woking U.D.C., Nov. 1902-Feb. 1903.
35. *Ibid.*, 11 Oct. 1903.
36. *Ibid.*, 12 Feb. and 11 Mar. 1924.
37. *Ibid.*, Feb.–Mar. 1939.
38. Census returns (1851), P.R.O.
39. *Ibid.*, (1871).
40. Kelly's *Directory* (1899).
41. Woking U.D.C., 11 Nov. 1895.
42. Pyrford Parish Council, 16 Jan. 1896.
43. Woking U.D.C., Aug. 1905-Jan. 1906.
44. Guildford R.S.A., 1881-82.
45. Woking U.D.C. (Sanitary Committee), 30 Nov. 1905.
46. Woking U.D.C. (Sanitary and Lighting Committee), 26 Nov. 1903.
47. Kelly's *Directory* (1899).
48. *Ibid.*, (1924).
49. Woking U.D.C., July-Aug. 1896.
50. *Ibid.*, Oct. 1935.
51. Woking U.D.C. (Town Planning Committee), Jan. 1934–May 1935.

Chapter Nine. The People and Their Work 1850–1914

1. *Census of Great Britain (1801–1911).*
2. *Top. Hist. Surrey*, vol. 2, p. 11.
3. *Census of Great Britain* (1841 and 1851).
4 *Ibid.*, (1881) Surrey County Report.
5. Census returns (1851 and 1871) P.R.O.
6. *Ibid.*
7. D. Hudson, *Munby: Man of Two Worlds* (1972).
8. A. J. Munby, *Diaries*, 4 Aug. 1867.
9. *Ibid.*
10. V. Woolf, *Night and Day* (1919), p. 137-38.
11. Pyrford Common estate plans and sale details: Onslow Collection RB670.
12. Letter from Sir Charles Dilke to Lord Onslow: Onslow Collection RB670.

13. Woking U.D.C., 1917–23.
14. J. Karim, *Rapiers and Battleaxes* (1966), p. 153.
15. V. Brittain, *Testament of Experience* (1957), p. 94.
16. A. Conan Doyle, *The Naval Treaty* (1893).
17. H. G. Wells, *The War of the Worlds* (1898), p. 30.
18. *Ibid.*; p. 36. 19. *Ibid.* 20. *Ibid.*, p. 52
21. *Ibid.*, pp. 47–48. 22. *Ibid.*, p. 60.
23. *Census returns (1851 and 1871) P.R.O.* and *Census of Great Britain* (1911) Surrey County Report, tables 24 and 25.
24. Census returns (1851), P.R.O.
25. A. J. Munby, *Diaries*, 21 May 1864.
26. Census returns (1851), P.R.O.
27. *Ibid.*, and Censuses of 1911 and 1921, Occupation Tables.
28. Woking U.D.C. (Sanitary Committee), 31 Oct. 1907.
29. Knaphill or Goldsworth Brickworks: List of charges (*c.* 1880): G.M.R. 1216/6/1.
30. *Ibid.*, Book of accounts and production statistics (1877–88).
31. *Top. Hist. Surrey*, vol. 2, p. 11.
32. *Census of Great Britain* (1861), Surrey County Report, p. 9.
33. A. J. Munby, *Diaries*, 30 Oct. 1868.
34. *Surrey Advertiser*, 3 Apr. 1870.
35. *Short Hist. Wok.*, p. 55.
36. Billing and Sons, *The Story of Billings* (1962).
37. Census returns (1871) P.R.O.
38. P. Unwin, *The Printing Unwins* (1976), p. 49.
39. *Ibid.* 40. *Ibid.*, p. 53. 41. *Ibid.*, p. 53.
42. *Ibid.*, pp. 54–56.
43. Census returns (1851 and 1871) P.R.O.
44. Kelly's *Directory* (1874 and 1899).
45. *Surrey Advertiser*, 5 Oct. 1888.
46. Kelly's *Directory* (1874).
47. *Ibid.*, and (1887).
48. From regular advertisements in local newspapers during that period.
49. Kelly's *Directory* (1874 and 1899).
50. *Census of Great Britain* (1861), Surrey County Report, p. 9.
51. *Censuses of Great Britain* (1871–1931).
52. Census returns (1871) P.R.O.
53. *Censuses of Great Britain* (1871–1931).

Chapter Ten. Continued Expansion 1914–1939

1. *Census of Great Britain* (1911 and 1921), Surrey County Reports.
2. Chertsey R.D.C. and Byfleet Parish Council, 1914–15.
3. Woking U.D.C., 22 Mar. 1923.
4. Adams, Thompson and Fry, Ltd., *North West Surrey Regional Planning Scheme* (1928), p. 3.
5. *Ibid.*, p. 8. 6. *Ibid.*, accompanying map.
7. Woking U.D.C. (Housing and Town Planning Committee), 2 April 1928.
8. Woking U.D.C. (Town Planning Committee), 16 July 1931.
9. *Ibid.*, 11 Oct. 1938. 10. *Ibid.*, 11 Oct. 1930.

11. Fords Farm still survives, although its setting is altered beyond recognition: it is on the north side of High Street, opposite Hipley Bridge.
12. Plans for the Hoe Bridge Estate (1934): G.M.R. 25/12/1-2.
13. The name seems to have been changed officially in this year.
14. Woking U.D.C. (Town Planning Committee), 1934-39.
15. *Ibid.*, 1934-37. 16. *Ibid.*, June-July 1934 17. *Ibid.*, Nov. 1937.
18. *Ibid.*, 1933-39. 19. *Ibid.*, Apr. 1937.
20. Woking U.D.C. (Town Planning Committee), Mar.-May 1938.
21. Adams, Thompson and Fry Ltd., *North West Surrey Regional Planning Scheme* (1928), accompanying map: Woking U.D.C. (Town Planning Committee).
22. Woking U.D.C. (Town Planning Committee), 1936-39.
23. Woking U.D.C., *Petition for the granting of a Charter of Incorporation* (1955), p. 15 of evidence.
24. Hockering estate sale plans and catalogue: G.M.R. 1311/26.
25. This may be compared with many similar examples described in A. A. Jackson, *Semi-detached London* (1973).
26. Woking U.D.C. (Town Planning Committee), 1936-38.
27. P. Abercrombie, *The Greater London Plan 1944* (1945), para. 386.
28. *Ibid.*, para. 416.
29. For example in 1938-38 Woking U.D.C. debated whether to acquire the 95-acre West Hall estate between Byfleet and West Byfleet.

Chapter Eleven. Local Government and Services 1914-1939

1. Chertsey R.D.C., 20 June 1928.
2. *Ibid.*, 18 Sept. 1928. 3. *Ibid.*, 10 Feb. 1930.
4. Transcript of inquiry into local government reform proposals (Oct. 1931), Day 4.
5. Transcript of discussions between Surrey County Council and local authorities concerning reform proposals (Sept. 1930-Feb. 1931).
6. *Ibid.*, Statement by Mr. E. Nicholls of Byfleet, 4 Feb. 1931.
7. Transcript of inquiry into local government reform proposals (Oct. 1931), Days 5 and 6.
8. *Ibid.*
9. Woking U.D.C., 30 May and 11 Nov. 1930.
10. Woking U.D.C. (Finance & General Purposes Committee), 28 May 1937.
11. Woking L.B. and Woking U.D.C., Oct. 1893-Mar. 1895.
12. Woking U.D.C., 9 Feb. 1898.
13. Woking U.D.C. (Fire Brigade Committee), 12 June 1899.
14. Woking U.D.C., 14 Mar. 1906.
15. Chertsey R.D.C., Jan. 1927-June 1928.
16. Woking U.D.C., 1 Nov. 1935.
17. Chertsey R.D.C., 11 Sept. 1906.
18. *Ibid.*, 9 Oct. 1906. 19. *Ibid.*, 4 May 1921. 20. *Ibid.*, 12 Dec. 1923.
21. Woking U.D.C., 23 May 1933.
22. *Ibid.*, 25 Apr. 1933.
23. *Ibid.*, 26 Jan. and 9 Mar. 1933.
24. *Ibid.*, 17 Apr. 1934.
25. Woking U.D.C. (Fire Brig., Lighting & Rec. Gds. Committee), 6 Jan. 1919.
26. *Ibid.*, 26 Apr. 1920. 27. *Ibid.*, 13 May 1921. 28. *Ibid.*, May-Nov. 1931.
29. Byfleet P.C., Dec. 1923-Mar. 1924.
30. *Ibid.*, 1 July 1924 and 2 Sept. 1925.

31. Woking U.D.C. (Public Health Committee), 2 Nov. 1934.
32. *Ibid.*, 11 Jan. 1937. 33. *Ibid.*, 21 Feb. 1938 34. *Ibid.*, Apr. 1932–July 1938.
35. *Ibid.*, 10 Nov.–11 Dec. 1938.
36. Chertsey R.D.C., Apr. 1925–Nov. 1927.
37. Woking U.D.C. (Public Health Committee), Apr. 1933–June 1937.
38. Deposited plan (with amendments) of London Necropolis Company: Onslow Collection G.M.G. RB670, Act of Parliament Box.
39. Woking U.D.C. (Fire Brig., Lighting & Rec. Gds. Committee), 28 June 1926.
40. Woking U.D.C. (Memorial Committee), 24 June 1901.
41. Woking U.D.C., July 1902–Dec. 1904.
42. Woking U.D.C. (Fire Brig., Lighting & Rec. Gds. Committee), 21 Feb. 1911.
43. *Ibid.*, 30 Mar. 1909 and 1 June 1910. 44. *Ibid.*, 1928–35.
45. Woking U.D.C. (Rec. Gds. & Swimming Pool Committee), 1935–39.
46. Papers relating to Horsell Recreation Ground: Onslow Collection G.M.R. 97/4/22 (1 and 5).
47. *Ibid.* (18 and 19).
48. Woking U.D.C. (Fire Brig., Lighting & Rec. Gds. Committee) Dec. 1920–Oct. 1922.
49. *Ibid.*, 20 Nov. 1924.
50. Byfleet P.C., 22 Nov. 1899 and 20 Mar. 1903.
51. *Ibid.*, 18 Dec. 1912 and 1915–21.
52. Woking U.D.C., 11 July 1911.
53. Woking U.D.C. (Housing Committee), 22 Jan. 1912.
54. *Ibid.*, 26 Jan. 1912. 55. *Ibid.*, Aug. 1917–Aug. 1920 56. *Ibid.*, 3 Jan. 1921.
57. *Ibid.*, 25 July 1921. 58. *Ibid.*, 5 Dec. 1921.
59. Pyrford P.C., 30 Nov. 1918.
60. Chertsey R.D.C., 6 May 1919. 61. *Ibid.*, 20 June 1920.
62. Woking U.D.C. (Housing Committee), 5 Oct. 1923.
62. *Ibid.*, 6 Oct. 1924. 64. *Ibid.*, 5 Jan. 1925. 65. *Ibid.*, 1925–33.
66. *Ibid.*, 3 Oct. 1927. 67. *Ibid.*, 24 June 1935.
68. Chertsey R.D.C. (Med. Off. Health Report), 28 May 1924.
69. Chertsey R.D.C., 15 Oct. 1925.
70. Woking U.D.C. (Housing Committee), 24 Jan. 1938.
71. Ministry of Health, *National Survey of Overcrowding* (1936).
72. Woking U.D.C. (Fire Brig., Lighting & Rec. Gds. Committee), 1 Nov. 1915.
73. *Ibid.*, 6 Nov. 1916 and 5 Nov. 1917.
74. *Ibid.*, June–Sept. 1919. 75. *Ibid.*, 18 May 1925.
76. *Ibid.*, July 1929–May 1930.
77. *Ibid.*, 23 Nov. 1925 and 29 May. 1926.
78. Pyrford P.C., 23 July 1929.
79. Woking U.D.C. (Fire Brig. and A.R.P. Committee), 16 Feb. 1937.
80. *Ibid.* 81. *Ibid.*, 1938–39.
82. *Ibid.*, 27 Oct. and 29 Dec. 1938 and 2 Mar. 1939.

Chapter Twelve. The People and Their Work 1914–1939

1. *Census of Great Britain* (1911–51), Surrey County Reports.
2. This was particularly the case in the Mayford and Sutton area.
3. His diaries are a valuable source of information for 1845–92.
4. Personal communication from Mrs. P. Fosberry of Warminster.
5. Petition to Surrey C.C. to increase the number of councillors: S.R.O. S.C.C. 28/43.
6. Woking & District Chamber of Trade; Charter petition evidence (1955).

7. Woking U.D.C., 1919–31.
8. *Woking News and Mail*, 21 Feb. 1941.
9. Chertsey R.S.A., 1889–92.
10. Byfleet P.C., 5 Nov. 1919.
11. *Ibid.*, Apr. 1922–Apr. 1929.
12. Woking U.D.C., 11 Sept. 1928.
13. *Top. Hist. Surrey*, vol. 2, p. 11.
14. E. Ryde, *Reminiscences* (*c.* 1880), p. 9.
15. E. Ryde, *Diaries*, vol. 25, 22 May 1868.
16. Census returns (1851), P.R.O.
17. *Ibid.*, and (1871).
18. *Surrey Advertiser*, 22 Jan. 1870.
19. Census returns (1871), P.R.O.
20. Kelly's *Directory* (1899).
21. *Ibid.* 22. *Ibid.* 23. *Ibid.*
24. *Surrey Advertiser*, 28 Sept. 1899.
25. *Woking & District Yearbook and Directory* (1916).
26. Woking Co-operative Society, *A Pictorial Souvenir of Twenty One Years Work of the W.C.S.* (1920), p. 12.
27. *Woking & District Yearbook and Directory* (1922–38).
28. E. Ryde, *Diaries*, vol. 25, 3 Sept. 1868.
29. Personal communication from Mr. J. L. Wetton.
30. *Surrey Advertiser*, 3 Nov. 1888.
31. *Woking Review*, 17 Jan. 1981.
32. Woking U.D.C. (Sanitary and Lighting Committee), 1 Sept. 1904.
33. *Ibid.*,, 30 Oct. 1902.
34. *Woking & District Yearbook and Directory* (1916).
35. J. D. Scott, *Vickers: A History* (1962), pp. 118–19.
36. Personal communication from Mr. T. G. Fuller.
37. *Woking & District Yearbook and Directory* (1922–30).
38. P. Abercrombie, *The Greater London Plan 1944* (1945), paras. 386 and 416.
39. Woking U.D.C., 11 Mar. 1903.
40. Chertsey R.D.C. and Byfleet P.C., Nov. 1922–July 1927.
41. G. T. Moody, *Southern Electric* (1968), pp. 56–61.
42. E. A. Course, *The Railways of Southern England: The Main Lines* (1975), p. 245.
43. Personal communication from British Rail, Southern Region.

Chapter Thirteen. Woking since 1939

1. Woking U.D.C., 11 Sept. 1944 and *Woking News and Mail*, 17 Jan. 1941.
2. Woking U.D.C., 11 June 1940.
3. *Ibid.*, 3 July 1940. 4. *Ibid.*, 24 Sept. 1940. 5. *Ibid.*, 2 Oct. 1940.
6. P. Abercrombie, *The Greater London Plan 1944* (1945), appendix 1.
7. Woking U.D.C. (Town Planning Committee), 26 March 1946.
8. P. Abercrombie, *The Greater London Plan 1944* (1945), para. 416.
9. A. G. Crosby, *Housing in Woking since 1945* (1977), pp. 18–21.
10. *Bldgs. Surrey*, p. 538.
11. A. J. Blowers, 'London's Out-County Estates', in *Town Planning Magazine*, vol. 41 (1973), pp. 409–14.

12. Surrey County Council, County Development Plan: *Analysis and Written Statement for Woking and District Town Map* (1953).
13. A. G. Crosby, *Housing in Woking since 1945* (1977), pp. 13–14.
14. Surrey County Council, *Structure Plan Written Statement* (1981).
15. A. G. Crosby, *Housing in Woking since 1945* (1977), pp. 24–34.
16. Woking U.D.C. (Town Planning Committee), 1959–69.
17. A. G. Crosby, *Housing in Woking since 1945* (1977), pp. 35–39.
18. *Ibid.*,, pp. 45–50.
19. In 1945–55 alone, some 11 pre-1850 houses were demolished in Old Woking and Westfield.
20. *Bldgs. Surrey*, p. 125.
21. Woking B.C. (Town Planning Committee), 1975–79.
22. *Woking News and Mail*, May–June 1980.
23. Personal communication from British Rail, Southern Region.
24. *Bldgs. Surrey*, p. 532.
25. *Census of Great Britain* (1951–71), Surrey County Reports.
26. *Census of Great Britain* (1981), Preliminary Report.

BIBLIOGRAPHY AND SOURCES

The location of material is indicated by the following abbreviations:

B.C.O.	Brookwood Cemetery Office
G.B.M.	Guildford Borough Museum
G.M.R.	Guildford Muniment Room
P.R.O.	Public Record Office
S.R.O.	Surrey Record Office
T.C.C.	Trinity College, Cambridge
W.B.C.	Woking Borough Council Offices
W.C.L.	Woking Central Library

1. Unpublished and manuscript sources (general)

Bridley Manor Court: Licences to enclose waste (1652) G.M.R. 166/14/1–2

Woking Manor Court (1800–30) G.M.R. 97/5/45–47.

Inclosure Awards and Maps:
Byfleet and Weybridge (enrolled 1811) S.R.O.
Pyrford and Chertsey (enrolled 1815) S.R.O.
Sutton next Wokeing (enrolled 1808) S.R.O.

Minutes of the Proceedings of the Byfleet and Weybridge Enclosure Commissioners (1801–11) S.R.O. 2284.

Tithe Awards and Maps: Byfleet (1840); Woking (1841); Pyrford (1844); Sutton (1848) and Horsell (1854), all in S.R.O.

Sale plans and catalogues in S.R.O. and G.M.R.

Diaries and Recollections:
Munby, A. J. *Diaries* (1864–80) T.C.C.
Ryde, E. *Diaries* (1851–82) G.M.R. 1244.
Ryde, E. *Reminiscences for a Proposed History of Woking* (*c.* 1880) G.M.R. 1244.

Onslow Collection (G.M.R.): Papers relating to:
Pyrford Court and Hoe Place estates RB670
Woking U.D.C. Sewerage Plan RB670
Burial Grounds in Woking RB670
Proposed St Johns Station RB670
Brookwood Brick-kilns RB670
Horsell Recreation Ground 97/4/22 (1–22)
Woking Commoners Bill and Act 97/5/66
Crematorium at St Johns Psh/Wok J/28/1

Miscellaneous:
Brookwood Cemetery Burial Records (1854–1939) B.C.O.
Charter of Incorporation: Evidence for Privy Council (1956) W.C.L.
A Survey for the Parish of Horsell (1834) S.R.O. 2283/7/1
Knaphill or Goldsworth Brickworks: accounts and notes (1880s) G.M.R.
Woking District Gas Company minutes and proceedings (1891–1914) S.R.O.
Census enumerators' returns: 1841, 1851, 1861, 1871 (P.R.O.).

2. *Local Government Sources*

Minutes and proceedings of the following authorities and their committees:

Byfleet Parish Council	(1895–1933)	W.B.C.
Chertsey Board of Poor Law Guardians	(1836–1839)	S.R.O.
Chertsey Rural District Council	(1895–1933)	S.R.O.
Chertsey Rural Sanitary Authority	(1890–1895)	S,R,O.
Guildford District Highway Board	(1864–1893)	S.R.O.
Guildford Rural Sanitary Authority	(1875–1893)	S.R.O.
Pyrford Parish Council	(1895–1933)	W.B.C.
Woking Borough Council	(1974–1981)	W.C.L.
Woking Local Board	(1893–1894)	W.B.C.
Woking School Board	(1874–1903)	S.R.O.
Woking Urban District Council	(1895–1943)	W.B.C.
	(1944–1974)	W.C.L.
Woking Vestry	(1818–1830)	S.R.O.

Other material: Reports of the Committee of Visitors of the Brookwood Asylum (1867–91) S.R.O. 1523/1/9–10.

Petition to Surrey County Council concerning the number of councillors for Woking Station and Maybury Ward (1899) S.R.O.

Surrey County Council (Local government Reform 1929–36):
Transcript of discussions with local authorities (1930) S.R.O.
Transcript of Inquiry proceedings (1931) S.R.O.

Surrey County Development Plan:
Analysis and Written Statement of Woking and District Town Map (1953).
First Review of Woking Town Map (1965).

Surrey Structure Plan:
Background Paper Volume 6 *Physical Environment* (1974). *Written Statement* (1981).

3. *Parliamentary Acts and Proceedings*

Acts of Parliament:

Byfleet and Weybridge Enclosure Act (1800) 39 & 40 Geo. III, c. 88.
Sutton next Wokeing Enclosure Act (1803) 43 Geo. III, c. 103.
Pyrford and Chertsey Enclosure Act (1805) 45 Geo. III, c. 49.
London and Southampton Railway Act (1834) 4 & 5 Wm. IV, c. lxxxviii.
Guildford Junction Railway Act (1844) 7 & 8 Vict., c. v.
London Necropolis and National Mausoleum Co. Act. (1852) 15 & 16 Vict., c. xlix.
Woking Commoners Act (1854) 17 & 18 Vict., c. 9.
London Necropolis and National Mausoleum Co. Act (1855) 18 & 19 Vict., c. clxiii.
London Necropolis and National Mausoleum Co. Act (1864) 27 & 28 Vict., c. lxii.
London Necropolis and National Mausoleum Co. Act (1869) 32 & 33 Vict., c. iii.
South West Suburban Water Company Act (1869) 32 & 33 Vict., c. cxii.
Woking Gas and Water Company Act (1881) 44 & 45 Vict., c. cxvi.
Woking Electricity Supply Company Order (1890) 53 & 54 Vict., c. cxc.
Woking District Gas Company Act (1891) 54 & 55 Vict., c. clii.
Woking (Horsell and Chertsey) Electricity Supply Order (1892) 55 & 56 Vict., c. xxxviii.
Woking Electricity Supply (Extensions) Order (1900) 63 & 64 Vict., c. cclxvii.
Woking Electricity Supply (Extensions) Order (1907) 5 Edw. VII, c. lxxxviii.
Woking U.D.C. (Basingstoke Canal) Act (1911) 1 & 2 Geo. V., c. cvii.

A Digest of Parochial Returns Made to the Select Committee Appointed to Inquire into the Education of the Poor 1818 (1819), ix.

Abstract of Education Returns 1833 (1835), xli–xlii.

Governor's First Annual Report on Woking Convict Prison (1860) House of Commons State Paper 1860 (35) [2713].

Hansard Volumes 118–122 and 138, Third Series.

4. *Maps and Plans*

Remnant, J., *A Survey of the Royal Manour of Wokeing . . .* (1719) G.M.R.

Rocque, J., *A Map of the County of Surrey* (1762) S.R.O.

Plan of the Freehold Building Estate Surrounding the Maybury (Woking) Station (1859).

Ordnance Survey maps and plans of all scales, 1816–1980.

Deposited plans of statutory undertakings, in the Surrey Record Office.

5. *Other published primary sources*

Directories: Kelly's *Post Office Directory of Surrey* (1874–1924)
Woking and District Yearbook and Directory (1922–1940)

Newspapers: *The Kentish Gazette; The County Chronicle and Weekly Advertiser; Surrey Advertiser; The Times; The Sanitary Record; Woking Mail; Woking News and Mail; Woking Review*

Census of Great Britain: 1801–1981

6. *Secondary sources: Books, pamphlets and theses*

Abercrombie, P., *The Greater London Plan* (1944), H.M.S.O.

Adams, Thompson & Fry Ltd., *The North West Surrey Regional Planning Scheme* (1928).

Arnos, F. R., *The Origins of Christ Church, Woking: A Short History* (1977) priv. pub.

Billing & Sons Ltd., *The Story of Billings* (1962) Billings.

Bourne, G., *Change in the Village* (1912), Duckworth.

Brayley, E. W., *Topographical History of Surrey*, Vol. 2 (1841) R. B. Ede.

Brittain, V., *Testament of Experience* (1957), Virago.

Colborne, C. C., *A Brief History of Horsell Common Baptist Chapel* (1914), C. J. Farncombe & Son.

Conan Doyle, A., *The Naval Treaty* (1894), Murray.

Course, E. A., *The Railways of Southern England: The Main Lines* (1975) Batsford.

Defoe, D., *A Tour Through The Whole Island Of Great Britain* (1724) Everyman edn. 1962.

Dendy Marshall, C. F. and Kidner, R. W., *History of the Southern Railway* (revised edn. 1968) Ian Allan.

Dines, H. G. and Edmunds, F. H., *The Geology of the Country Around Aldershot and Guildford* (1929) Geological Survey.

Eedle, M. de G., *A History of Bagshot and Windlesham* (1977) Phillimore.

Francis, J., *History of the English Railway* (1851).

Gelling, M., *Signposts to the past* (1978), J. M. Dent.

Gover, J. E. B., *et al.*, *The Place Names of Surrey* (1934) Cambridge U.P.

Gray, H. L., *The English Field Systems* (1912) Merlin Press edn. 1962.

Greenwood, G. B., *Woking and District: A Dictionary of Local History* (1972), Martin & Greenwood Publications.

Hudson, D., *Munby: Man of Two Worlds* (1972) Murray.

James, W. and Malcolm, J., *General View of the Agriculture of the County of Surrey* (1794), Board of Agriculture.

Jones, K., *A History of the Mental Health Services* (1972), Routledge & Kegan Paul.

Karim, J., *Rapiers and Battleaxes: The Womens' Movement and its aftermath* (1966), George Allen & Unwin.

Locke, A., *A Short History of Woking* (1924) originally published in the *Woking Review*, reprinted as *Woking Past* by the Nancy Leigh Bookshop (1980).
Manning, O. and Bray, W., *The History and Antiquities of the County of Surrey*, vol. I (1804).
Ministry of Health, *National Survey of Overcrowding* (1936), H.M.S.O.
Moody, G. T., *Southern Electric* (1968) Ian Allen.
Nairn, I. and Pevsner, N., *The Buildings of England: Surrey* (rev. edn. by Bridget Cherry 1971), Penguin.
Pankhurst, E., *The Suffragette Movement (1931), Longmans.*
Paterson's *Roads* (rev. edn. by Edward Mogg 1822).
Robinson, W., K., *Some Notes on the History of Quakerism in Woking and District* (1969), unpub. typescript W.C.L.
Scott, J. D., *Vickers: A History* (1962), Weidenfeld.
Stevens, L. R., *Byfleet: A village of England* (1953), Woking Review Ltd.
Stevens, Curl J., *A Celebration of Death* (1980), Constable.
Stevenson, W., *A General View of the Agriculture of the County of Surrey* (1809), Board of Agriculture.
Stockwell, A. H., *The Baptist Churches of Surrey* (1910?), priv. pub.
Street, F., *A History of Goldsworth Nursery 1760–1960* (1960), Walter Slocock Ltd.
Surrey County Council, *Antiquities and Conservation Areas of Surrey* (1976).
Unwin, P., *The Printing Unwins: A Short History of Unwin Brothers* (1976), George Allen & Unwin.
Victoria County History of Surrey, vols. I (1905): II (1907) and III (1911).
Vine, P. A. L., *London's Lost Route to the Sea* (1963), David and Charles.
Vine, P. A. L., *London's Lost Route to Basingstoke* (1968), David and Charles.
Wells, H. G., *The War of the Worlds* (1898), Heinemann.
Woking and District Co-operative Society, *Pictorial Souvenir of Twenty One Years Work of the W.C.S.* (1920).
Woolf, V., *Night and Day* (1919), Penguin edn. 1969.

Crosby, A. G., *Housing in Woking since 1945* (1977), unpublished B.A. dissertation, University of Oxford: copy in W.C.L.
Dutt, M., *The Agricultural Labourers' Revolt of 1830 in Kent, Surrey and Sussex* (1966), unpublished Ph.D. thesis, University of London.

7. *Articles*

Belsey, R., 'Prehistory and Archaeology of the Woking District', in *Mayford History Society Newsletter*, No. 22 (Feb. 1973).
Blowers, A. J., 'London's Out-County Estates', in *Town Planning Magazine*, vol. 41 (1973), pp. 409–14.
Clewley, D. W., 'Woking's First Public Electricity Supply', in *SEEBoard Staff Newsletter* (Dec. 1975).
Cox, B., 'Place Names of the Earliest English Records', in *Journal of the English Place Name Society*, vol. 5 (1975–76), pp. 12–66.
Eedle, M. de G., 'Street Cleaning and Refuse Collection from the sixteenth to the nineteenth centuries', in *Surrey Archaeological Collections* (hereafter *Sy. A.C.*), vol. 68 (1971), pp. 161–81.
Gardner, E., 'Weybridge and Byfleet: Traces of Old Ironworks', in *Sy. A.C.*, vol. 34 (1921), pp. 115–16.
Lister, M. D., 'Via Necropolis Junction', in *Railway Magazine*, vol. 119, no. 862 (1973), pp. 74–76.
Parton, A. G., 'The 1801 Crop Returns for the County of Surrey', in *Sy. A.C.*, vol. 64 (1967), 113–23.
Tate, W. E., 'Enclosure Acts and Awards relating to lands in the County of Surrey', in *Sy. A.C.*, vol. 48 (1943), pp. 118–49.

INDEX OF SUBJECTS

INDEX OF PEOPLE

INDEX OF PLACES, COMPANIES AND LOCAL AUTHORITIES